# THE PAPER'S
## *Papers*

# THE
# PAPER'S
# PAPERS

A REPORTER'S JOURNEY
THROUGH THE ARCHIVES OF

## Richard F. Shepard

TIMES 𝕿 BOOKS

RANDOM HOUSE

Grateful acknowledgment is made to the General Research Division, The New York Public Library and Astor, Lenox and Tilden Foundations for permission to reprint the cover illustration from *Vanity Fair,* Saturday, August 2, 1862, vol. 6, no. 136, New York: "Henry J. Raymond" (*DX+). Reprinted by permission.

Library of Congress Cataloging-in-Publication Data

Shepard, Richard F.
The paper's papers : a reporter's journey through the archives of the New York times
Richard F. Shepard. —1st ed.
    p.    cm.
  Includes index.
  ISBN 0-8129-2453-3 (acid-free paper)
  1. New York times.   I. Title.
PN4899.N42T5685     1996
071'.471—dc20                                                    95-32709

Designed by Michael Mendelsohn, MM Design 2000, Inc.
Random House website address: http://www.randomhouse.com/
Printed in the United States of America on acid-free paper
98765432
First Edition

# Acknowledgments

THE WORD "dedication" should really be used here instead of "acknowledgments," because the latter is merely a nod of appreciation while the former bespeaks a larger debt. I owe much gratitude to many who helped me fashion this volume:

To Trudy Shepard, librarian and wife, who devotedly and doggedly accompanied me on my explorations of the voluminous archives.

To Susan W. Dryfoos, *Times* historian, who enlisted me in this work, opened all doors, lavished encouragement, and then, with consummate graciousness, stood aside until the work was done.

To Charles St. Vil, *Times* archives manager, and Mary McCaffery, archives analyst, who patiently guided us through their bewildering domain and speedily found what we could not.

To John Rothman, jack of all research at *The New York Times,* including managing the archives in earlier years and a key figure in organizing its files, providing the invaluable indexes to them, and, in retirement, giving me the benefit of time and knowledge.

To eagle-eyed Marvin Siegel, who vetted the manuscript, and to Ruth Fecych, who was burdened with editing the book. Also to Audrey Shepard, who with infinite care read proof to prevent slips that pass in the type. And to Arthur Neuhauser, who as a proofreader of this manuscript lavished on it the same relentless scrutiny he subjected my stories to when he headed the Cultural News copy desk at *The New York Times.*

To Gerald Gold, Herb Mitgang, and Murray Schumach, who read the manuscript and steered me in helpful directions but remain guiltless for those I did not pursue. To Linda Amster and Linda Lake, researchers who found the all-elusive but vital details. To my friend Arthur (Buddy) Weininger, who as outsider went through my account with the educated eye of a *Times* reader.

To Abe Rosenthal and Arthur Gelb, bosses and friends, who encouraged me in this project, as they had with so many other projects during my years on the third floor. To all those *Times* colleagues whose big story never broke, rarely made page 1, but whose diligence and ingenuity gave *The Times* its reputation for honest and thorough reporting and provided the particular flavors that were *Times* specialties.

To the desk editors, news assistants, researchers, secretaries, clerks, copypeople, and others in support jobs who made us look as though we knew what we were talking about. They are rarely mentioned in dispatches but they merit citations for bold dedication and patience with itchy editors and demanding reporters.

To all others who knowingly or unknowingly furnished me with a career that helped me learn something new almost every day.

# Contents

# THE PAPER'S
## *Papers*

# Introduction

THIS is a book about *The New York Times*. It is *not* a history of the newspaper. Nor is it a technical manual for those with ambitions to produce their own *New York Times*. It is a book that tries to explain how *The Times* came to be what it is. This account is a two-legged affair, each leg being antipodally different from the other. One is the official archives of *The Times,* a collection of miscellany left behind by those who have been in charge of it. The other is the archives of my mind—my memories after nearly a half-century as a *Times*man.

Pieces of the archives, a leading character in this venture, appear on almost every page. In 1969 *The New York Times* archives were created to pick up and save whatever the newspaper left of itself in its pursuit of the ephemera of the day. At the time, newspapers, even *The New York Times,* were not in the habit of saving the past except for, as in the case of a morgue with its clippings of older news stories, what might come in handy tomorrow.

The archives have salvaged much of the past of the newspaper, whose own history has become more valued as its importance and age advanced. Publishers and editors wrote letters, notes, memoranda. They made notations on other letters and on newspaper copy that would dictate changes in the look and words of *The New York Times.* They may have had some intimation of history when they put these writings into files that were not thrown out, or they may just have had the feeling that—who knows—someday someone may find this interesting.

Lesser figures, like myself, felt that the world would little note nor long remember what we said here and threw most notes and memos away as soon as these had done their job. I did so when I was cultural news editor in 1969–1972 and I now rather regret it. There are things I'd like to double-check, just as there are some things I'd be happy never to double-check, the embarrassing oversights and the lapses in judgment made by any editors faced with making decisions, although few admit to them.

The publisher, Arthur Ochs Sulzberger, ordered the establishment of the archives from these odd assortments of papers. He also ordered the many departments of the paper to start saving their documents and sending them to the archives. At latest rough count, the archives consist of 421 cubic feet of papers divided into collections of publishers and of executive and managing editors, and including a general file, with financial, circulation, and other business papers, as well as photos, bound volumes, and pamphlets. Also in the collection are "miscellaneous" files of material from the several news desks, Sulzberger, major columnists, business executives, and Mrs. Arthur Hays Sulzberger—Iphigene—whose gentle but firm imprint was to have a far greater influence on *The Times* than is indicated by the fact that she never had any title. To measure all this by cubic feet puts the uninitiated suspiciously in mind of the measurement of trash, but such facile connections are soon dispersed in light of the value set on archival remains of *The Times* by the rest of the world.

After all, Columbia University had applied for *The Times* material to start an archive on its campus, where *The Times,* through its publishers and the School of Journalism, had a long association. The Library of Congress had solicited the private papers of Mr. Sulzberger's father, publisher Arthur Hays Sulzberger. Both requests had been turned down.

In 1972, A. O. Sulzberger replied to the request of the Library of Congress: "Dad passed away in 1968. At that time, the family determined that it would be almost impossible to separate the private papers of Mr. Sulzberger from those that encompassed the history of *The New York Times*."

The family and the newspaper are so tightly intertwined that it is sometimes difficult for an outsider to say where one stops and the other starts, although each member of the family is conscious and observant of the unmarked boundaries between the two. *The Times,* in initiating and overseeing this volume, realized that a centennial would make a fitting milestone, one in which the participants could pause and catch their breath. Adolph S. Ochs purchased the then moribund *New-York Times* in 1896 and proceeded to build it into one of the most powerful instruments of the press ever known, independent of forced governmental proprietorship. He left this legacy to his family, whose fourth generation is now running *The Times*. A hundred-year-old family business in any line is an unusual achievement in an age that has seen solid, Rock of Gibraltar enterprises rooted in American society blown away by radically changed consumer habits and business practices.

Ochs bequeathed that regenerated, influential *Times* to its readership and to those who didn't read it but knew of it and respected its authority, even attributing to it powers that it never sought and had not achieved. I recall when a friend of mine called me frantically, pleading with me to tell the powers that be to prevent the government from testing a nuclear device in the Arctic. It was a time when fears of atomic bombs were widely disseminated and in the context of a cold war were grounded in genuine possibilities.

"The test is scheduled for tomorrow," I answered. "What do you expect *The Times* to do about it?"

"They could do something, tell them in Washington to stop it," she said. "Or stop it themselves."

"What *The Times* could do at best is write an editorial about it, I guess," I said, carefully emphasizing that I did not write editorials. "*The Times* cannot rent a rowboat or a towboat and go to the Arctic to tell the people running the test to go home. Newspapers work with words; they don't do things."

With *The Times*, though, people often believe that somehow the paper is in a position to control events rather than only influence them by virtue of its reputation and that segment of its readers both highly placed and caring to respond to words from its pages. That *The Times* has enormous influence is a characteristic that is valued, maybe even treasured, by those who are responsible for putting its words across. That it would actually have a say in running government or anything beyond itself would be an unwelcome concept for its owners or its workers.

During the forty-five years I worked at *The New York Times*, I often had the impression that there was no one in the world who had not heard of the newspaper. Not that everyone read it, but everyone was aware of *The Times*, either to admire and respect it, or to hate and distrust it, all sight unseen. Recognition, thy name is *The New York Times*. It is not always a comfortable thought, and for an institution that is no more than the product of human brain and observation, it is important for those associated with it never to be afflicted with delusions about themselves and *The Times*. You are always in trouble, an old saying has it, when you start believing your own press releases. But the temptation is always there, virtually inescapable.

I checked into a Shanghai hotel a dozen years ago, when the foreign press was still largely banned from China. The elevator boy grinned at me and asked in stumbling English (which was, however, infinitely better than my hobbled Chinese), "Where you from?"

"New York."

"What work do you do?"

"I work for a newspaper."

"Ah, *New York Times* maybe?"

As it turned out, he knew the name of no other New York, or American, newspaper.

This reputation is not one that just happened. No public relations staff in the world could ever have covered *The Times* with such a patina of perfection that readers rejoice to catch it in error even as they are disappointed to detect signs of human frailty within its pages. Like Tinkerbell, who lives because *Peter Pan* readers believe in her, *The Times* gains influence because its readers believe in the paper. Even *The New York Times,* which commands respect, perhaps, cannot demand respect from its public. It is the readership that confers influence on *The Times*. That respect derives from the qualities we will touch upon in these pages.

Our rummaging through the archives was planned to throw some light on the thinking of those who contributed to changing *The Times,* because change is what *The Times* has done during these many decades. Archives do not tell all and what they tell may not be gospel truth, but they do tell what an executive was driving at when some action had to be taken. In this review, the records speak for themselves, but a sharp note—or a loving one—does not necessarily indicate enmity or affection, although it may evidence spleen or admiration.

The archives provide source material for historians. There have been four major histories of *The Times* written, each by a man who had been a *Times* reporter. Two were commissioned by *The Times* for an anniversary celebration and two were written as independent projects. This book is, emphatically, not a history of *The Times,* although it is constructed from historical data. This volume is not intended to be a thoroughgoing analysis of the million or more pieces of paper in the archives. This task would not only be impossible, it would be stultifying. I prefer to call my sifting of the archives a browse rather than a study, more the approach of a window shopper than of a doctoral candidate.

I glanced through many of the early financial documents, through scads of reports on press runs, through scores of corporate statements. All are valuable to the student of this aspect or that but numbing to the sightseer in search of attractions linked more directly to what he or she reads in the paper itself. One of the most useful browsing tools, incidentally, is the archival compilation "Facts About *The New York Times:* A Guide," a loose-leaf volume of photocopies of catalog cards. It is studded with dates and specifics of aspects of the paper that we have sprinkled liberally throughout this work as seasoning minutiae added according to taste.

The cry goes up: Value judgment! It is the watchword of an egalitarian era in which all things, not merely humans, are given equal consideration. But editorial diktat is based on value judgment. The more extensive the experience, the more curious the editor or reporter, the more value that judgment has.

The ways of indulging curiosity have changed in this computer age. Now investigation is a game of Twenty Questions. You know what it is you don't know and set about asking Plexus, or whatever program you are imbibing, to go and get it. B.C., Before Computers, this was only part of the game. A reporter went to the morgue, that repository of "clips"—clippings from newspapers past—and embarked on a rambling hunt through these scraps of newsprint. Often the major find was in something that caught the eye, an item that the eye never set out to look upon. There was an element of discovery, of chance, in this sort of thumbing-through research. And so it was, in doing this book. Serendipity was the watchword. I and my partner in looking backward, Trudy Shepard, waded through whatever was alluring and followed files that led us either up the garden path or else at least to a half-sentence in the chapters that lie ahead. There are major *Times* players that are underplayed here and minor *Times* players that are overplayed. This is not an equal-time production.

In that case, what, then, to select? The short answer, not meant in the slightest to be flip, is whatever subjects caught my fancy. I have not touched on, or merely hinted at, vital areas important to the paper—science, sports, financial, business news, and that most valuable ingredient, advertising. They are scanted here not because they are less interesting than the subjects I do write about, but because I was not as involved in those subjects as I was in those I do mention.

I have been part of *The Times* for fifty years (I have maintained a presence there in the years since I retired), half the period that this centennial celebration of the Ochs acquisition celebrates. I did not realize that I was meeting *The Times* on its fiftieth Ochs Dynasty year when I walked into the newsroom as copyboy in 1946. It has only been since my retirement in 1991, when I started writing only intermittently for the paper, that I became aware that I, too, had been there during AN ERA. Eras are usually not clearly marked by start and stop signs and, for those who live through them, it is hard to regard one's own career as an era, sliced off in history like a piece of salami.

The third-floor newsroom, when I saw it for the first time in May 1946, looked like the newsrooms that appeared in movies. There was the three-segment horseshoe-shaped copy desk. Editors, some with eyeshades, most down to vests (rather than jackets) in the balmy weather, pored over the pages that the reporters had filled on their typewriters. The copy desk ran from Foreign News at the south or 43rd Street end, through Financial (only two or three copy editors in those days) and the City News, to the National News Desk at the northern rim. Off to one side was the Society News Desk, which handled birth, wedding, and obituary news (breezily summed up as hatch, match, and snatch, and also as womb to tomb) as well as reviews and news of art, theater, movies, books, music, and radio-television.

It was a different world and I smile when I see such expressions as "cut" and "paste" on the menus of high-speed computers. In those days, youngster, cut and paste meant that the copy desks were equipped with scissors and with paste pots whose sticky white contents were replenished by copyboys (no, there were no copygirls then on the third floor). Editors snipped and pasted and slashed copy with decisive No. 2 black pencils. Air-conditioning was by way of windows and fans. In very hot weather, salt tablets were available to the faint at the water fountain. A haze of smoke hung over this chamber, and spittoons were deployed like memorial markers of the days when chewing tobacco fueled fast-working editors.

Reporters wrote their stories, which were called "copy." When they finished writing a page, on a "book," a flimsy ten-part sheaf, they hollered, *"Copy!"* We ran to their desks and carried the copy to the City Desk, or whatever other desk was in order. The book was filleted, with flimsies going to copy editors, senior editors, and the desk that produced newscasts for the radio station of *The Times,* WQXR.

The newsroom on the third floor in the late 1940s. In suit, at right, night city editor Robert E. Garst is seated next to assistant editor Will Weng, later the popular editor of *The Times* crossword puzzle. At rear, copy editors are at the center of a long horseshoe desk over which all stories passed.

The desks began to get busy about 6:00 P.M. The reporters were generally back from their assignments then and were letting the editors know how their stories had worked out—whether they matched the aspirations indicated in the early schedule or whether they had washed out. The reporter reported to the city editor, who listened, asked a question or two, and then said, "Give me a short spread," which meant about 500 words, or merely held up his hand, thumb and index finger only inches apart, and said, "Maybe a D head," which meant a short, short item, fewer than 100 words. The reporters went back to their desks and played cards, some in an ongoing round of bridge and others with quick-action poker. These were games interrupted by deadlines and other exigencies, tourneys that did not really settle down to unrelieved concentration until the frenzy of putting out the paper eased off, after midnight.

The managing editor was Edwin L. James, once a famous foreign correspondent and, amid that slovenly assemblage of off-the-rack press, a dapper fashion plate, down to his very spats. Mr. James smoked a cigar and played the horses. His bespoke bookie was the clerk in charge of directing the flood of wire copy that flowed in from overseas, from Washington, from points outside the city. It was a challenging job, choreographing all this copy for the three hours or so that it poured into 43rd Street, but the clerk channeled it without missing a bet from Mr. James or from any other horse fancier on the floor. When irate wives, bereft of paychecks that never made it home, made complaints to the police about gambling at *The Times,* the scene was out of *Casablanca,* with Claude Rains expressing shock to learn that there was gambling on the premises. The police arrived after the clerks had been given early leave and were entertained in Mr. James's office before they left, stumped for clues and witnesses.

There was drinking. Another copyboy and I were once rushed over to help a rewrite man back to his seat after he had fallen off it. Drinker he may have been, but alcohol did not interfere with rewriting that night, once he was reinstalled in his chair of journalism. Alcoholism caused all sorts of family problems and it slopped over into work, but not as frequently as it did at other papers. *The Times* seemed to have a sobering effect even on the most bibulous. Of course, there was the memorable case of the Telegraph Desk editor (that was the old name of the National News Desk, just as Cable Desk indicated the desk that received news from abroad). He was a serious man, a pipe smoker and an assiduous head of the copy desk. During the night, bottles of ale sprouted in front of him. By evening's end, they looked like ninepins in a bowling alley. One night, after carrying out his duties with his usual exactitude, he fogged up on his way out of the building and ended up sliding down a chute into a newspaper delivery truck. What a way to go, out with the city edition!

These are newspaper anecdotes that could be told in any newsroom across the country. However, for all of these diversions, there was an esprit there that became particularly evident when crisis erupted. The afternoon that President John F. Kennedy was killed was one of those occasions that showed *The Times* at its best. There was none of the usual nitpicking that is part and parcel of putting out the daily paper. The standards were met. The printers, one flight up on the fourth floor, worked with a precision and a speed that belied the laid-back, often exasperating languor that delayed corrections and held up pages on ordinary days (although they, too, never missed deadlines; they just waited until the last minute to get to things, just like the people on the third floor).

The paper that *The Times* put out the next day was extraordinary, with a wealth of detail on what had happened in Texas, what it meant, and how it compared with similar atrocities in history. I know about that, because, when I ran back to the office from lunch, I was immediately assigned to do a column on Lincoln's assassination, just as others were doing pieces on the killings of Garfield and McKinley and the failed attempt on Franklin D. Roosevelt's life in Miami in 1932. I found myself in the ridiculous position of having no one to telephone for the details and sparse material in the files. The library came to my rescue. It was the job of a spear-carrier in the human opera that was being covered, but it is a typical instance of how *The Times* tries not to miss any angle.

This sort of memorabilia is the stuff of oral history, but going through the files starts the train of recollection. Every big event was composed of many small pieces. There was a pride, at least retroactively, in having been part of a project that no other daily publication could match in terms of time and volume and thoroughness. That is what has made our journey through the archives especially fascinating.

The trip has been fun. We have touched on matters ponderous and trivial, although there is nothing about *The Times* that may be dismissed as trivial. Someone is always out there, candling every word and ready to pounce on the one that rankles. The page 1 story is, of course, momentous. The editorial, whether on the Middle East or on the azalea-blossom season, is controversial. There are stacks of files on the weather, strong opinions about how it should be represented. No, there is nothing trivial about *The Times,* although there are things that I feel are less ponderous, even light and eventually not earthshaking. Our luggage includes, inevitably, some dirty laundry, soiled either at the time it was used or in terms of latter-day morality. But this is not an account riddled with scandal. The sins uncovered tend to emphasize how otherwise clean the operation as a whole has been. They also remind us of how human this journalistic nonpareil is, how it is the product of thinkers and doers, of drinkers and drys, of prophets and profits. The miracle is that *The Times* has done as magnificently as it has, considering that it is a creature of human brain and behavior.

This all ties in with that business of press notices. I always advised young reporters at *The Times* that they should not be carried away by the deference accorded them when they were on assignment from the paper. Remember, I preached, people look at you but they see *The New York Times* emblazoned on your forehead. Such advice keeps a reporter from having to buy larger-size hats. It is also advice that warns against immolating oneself at *The Times*, that recommends a healthy outside life to supplement a career easily confused with taking priestly vows.

Adolph Ochs, naturally, did dedicate himself to *The Times*, but he enjoyed it as much as he molded it and devoted himself to it. Letters in the archives express the pride of creative ownership not in poetic terms of self-satisfaction, but in numbers, the increased circulation, the rise in advertising, and, yes, the elevation of respect by the world for his newspaper. If the family owned *The Times, The Times* owned the family, claimed the pride of all members, whether legal proprietors or not. Here is a letter from Adolph Shelby Ochs, a family member in Chattanooga, written to publisher Arthur Hays Sulzberger on April 19, 1942. He told of a local appearance by Britain's ambassador at large:

Dear Arthur:
    I have just returned from a luncheon at which Sir Eric Gordon Underwood addressed an audience of several hundred Chattanoogans. He said that after visiting all 48 of the United States he had prepared a list of "the seven wonders of America." No. 4 on his list was "The New York Times on Sunday."
                                   Cordially,

Talk about influence! Here's a note, an archival document marked "Confidential," sent by a secretary to publisher-designate Orvil E. Dryfoos in October 1960, at a time when the United Nations General Assembly was in session and potentates from the world over were gathering in Manhattan.

Mr. D:
    Mr. [John B.] Oakes [editorial page editor] called while you were down waiting for Nkrumah [president of Ghana] to say two of the officials of the Israeli delegation had been in to

see him—on the Q.T.—to suggest that The Times invite King
Hussein to lunch. It was thought that Hussein was lonely here
and had the feeling he hadn't been treated with enough attention, etc. as some of the others had been. The Israelis
thought it would be a good thing if some of the editors were
to meet him.

The person to talk to about any invitation would be a Mr.
Wasfitel, Minister of "Something" as Mr. Oakes put it, and he
is reachable at The Waldorf Towers.

This was in keeping with a plaintive comment from a press agent
friend of mine: "I get 'em a whole column in Earl Wilson," he said,
referring to his show biz clients and to the erstwhile popular columnist in the *New York Post.* "What do they say? Nothing. You give me a
sentence at the bottom of the radio-TV column on Saturday that nobody's supposed to read and I come in Monday and I'm a hero!"

Does the world need yet another book about *The New York Times*?
As long as the readers keep believing in it, there is always room for
one more. And that goes for the nonreaders, too. What may be the
tersest summing up of what *The Times* means to the world at large is
contained in a message sent to Arthur Hays Sulzberger by Arthur
Krock, doyen of the Washington Bureau, on the Washington wire to
43rd Street:

ADD TO COMMENTS ABOUT THE TIMES THIS ONE—NEW TO ME—BY
E. A. BACON, DEPUTY ASSISTANT SECRETARY OF THE ARMY: "TOO BIG
TO READ, TOO IMPORTANT NOT TO."

# IN THE
# BEGINNING

OR WANT of mythological heroes, the roles of the Romulus and Remus of *The New York Times* fall to a working newspaperman, Henry J. Raymond, and a banker, George Jones. In 1850 they both worked at the *New York Tribune*, the pioneer news-gathering journal established by Horace Greeley and incubator for some of the brightest journalistic talent that would write its way through the late nineteenth century. Raymond reported and edited and Jones studied profit and loss in the business office.

During the winter of 1850–1851, Raymond was a Whig member of the New York state legislature, recently elected as speaker of the state assembly. He and Jones were walking across the frozen Hudson River in Albany to the railway station on the other side. A deal they had been offered to take over another newspaper had fallen through, and Raymond suggested that if Greeley could turn a handsome profit with his strident paper, why could they not do as well with a journal of their own?

Seven men put up the capital, $100,000, and, with Raymond, held the eighty-nine shares of that first subscription. The first issue of *The New-York Daily Times,* published in an old brownstone in the newspaper district on Nassau Street, hit the sidewalks of New York on September 18, 1851.

That was the story of the birth of *The New York Times.* The temptation to be a publisher occasionally infects any reporter who has been handed an unreasonable assignment, a sort of if-I-were-king fantasizing. A. J. Liebling, the curmudgeonly press critic of *The New Yorker* magazine and a onetime newspaperman himself, postulated that freedom of the press is guaranteed only to those who own one. For those who work for one, the publisher takes on the dimensions of the Almighty who hands down a ten-point editorial to His managing editor, Moses, and insists that it run in full with no copydesk meddling.

The first copies of *The New York Times*, initially *The New-York Daily Times*, were published here on September 18, 1851, at 113 Nassau Street, on Newspaper Row, near City Hall.

In 1846, While he was still in his twenties, Raymond wrote to Jones an extraordinarily detailed proposal for a newspaper, an idea that would not be fleshed out for another five years. It is such a basic summing up of what goes into the making of a newspaper, its blood and bones, if not its spirit, that it is worth examining.*

* The letter is with other Raymond material in the New York Public Library archives but is available in transcript in *The Times* archives, which contains microfilm or other reproduction of documents that have in the past been given to other institutions.

The costs are piddling by current standards, but they were steep in those days. The investment needs involved still ring alarm bells in the front office: paper, ink, advertising, circulation, presses, and personnel—and a point of view. Unions had not the strength they were later to assume (and have more recently lost). There were no competing television and radio media. Printers still set type by hand. Reporters did their work on foot without benefit of telephone, and they wrote their stories in pencil, not on typewriter, by light of gas or oil lamp.

In that first proposal, Raymond described a newspaper that would print 10,000 copies a week. The total weekly expenses, he wrote, would be $350, a cost that would include "an assistant editor, two editorial contributors, city reporters, money market, etc., ship news, Washington Correspondence, Paris & other Foreign, Domestic correspondence" as well as fifteen compositors and clerical help. The price of twenty-one reams of paper, at $3.50 each, would be $431 a week. Income from 5,000 papers a day, at 1½ cents a copy, would bring $75 daily.

Raymond proposed a Paris correspondent to send a "full summary of continental news—which always centers there." English news, he wrote, could be had from English papers to better advantage. A "good" Paris correspondent would be worth $10 a week.

The editor should see & examine *everything* that goes into the paper—in every department, & should besides write such editorials upon matters of news as might be needed. This would serve to *fill up* and give life to the editorial department. The editor should also take care that nothing immoral should get into any part of the paper & would of course see that all em-

---

### The New York Dash

The hyphen in the newspaper's name linked "New" and "York" until December 1896, when it was dropped. It was not a peculiarity of the newspaper but a mark that was often used in the name of the city. It survives today in the New-York Historical Society.

ployed as writers, reporters or correspondents worked in such a way as to promote the interest & built up the character of the paper.

He emphasized coverage of the courts, which should be "carefully accurately & more fully reported than is usual—as they relate to the business, and thus enlist the attention & interest, of a very large class of the people." Great pains, he wrote, should be taken to publish "city intelligence," matters that happen all over the city, including sermons and other meetings and dinners. Ship News, a staple of nineteenth-century reporting, was also important, as were "the doings in stocks, markets etc."

This was a working treatise and the morals would be outlined later in an editorial, one that fittingly announced the paper's arrival in that first edition. It was rather cozily entitled "A Word about Ourselves." The piece spoke of the difficulties of establishing a new daily paper in the city and the principles it announced were in many respects, but not all, cut from the same moral cloth as that tailored to the Ochs persona a half-century later:

"But we know also, that within the last five years the reading population of this city has nearly doubled, while the number of daily newspapers is no greater now than it was then;—that many of those now published are really *class* journals, made up for particular classes of readers;—that others are objectionable upon grounds of morality;—and that no newspaper, which was really *fit* to live, ever yet expired for lack of readers."

In explaining its penny-a-paper policy (a half-penny cheaper than what Raymond had proposed five years earlier), the editorial said, "We have chosen this price, however, deliberately, and for the sake of obtaining for the paper a large circulation and corresponding influence. That influence shall always be upon the side of Morality, of Industry, of Education and Religion."

Its professions of objectivity were stated:

Upon all topics,—Political, Social, Moral, and Religious,—we intend that the paper shall speak for itself; and we only ask that it may be judged accordingly. We shall be *Conservative*, in all cases where we think Conservatism essential to the public good; and we shall be *Radical* in everything which may seem to us to require radical treatment, and radical reform.

We do not believe that everything in society is either exactly right, or exactly wrong; what is good we desire to preserve and improve; what is evil, to exterminate, or reform. . . . We do not mean to write as if we were in a passion, unless that shall really be the case; and we shall make it a point to get into a passion as rarely as possible.

In a way that was to become a *Times* tradition, often enough honored in the breach, the paper promised not to become a crusading publication, observing that "there are very few things in this world which it is worth while to get angry about." The new voice in town vowed to engage in controversy only when it considered that the public interest was involved and "even then, we shall endeavor to rely more upon fair argument than upon misrepresentation or abusive language." The editorial concluded by assuring the public: "We shall seldom trouble our readers with our personal affairs; but these few words, at the outset seemed to be required."

Page 1 illustrated what would be the hallmark of *Times* make-up, its compartmentalization of contents. The first three columns on the left (the big news of the day would eventually travel to prominence on the right-hand side of the page) dealt with foreign news, followed by a column of national news—namely, a story about a fugitive-slave incident in Pennsylvania. The fifth and sixth columns on the right were filled with city news, mostly brief items, followed by a short dispatch from Brooklyn (even then, as now, *The Times* had to take note of its suburban readers). The chatty little tidbits of local news probably shed as much light on social change as any of the longer pieces.

New York City in those days consisted of Manhattan Island, and most of its half-million burghers lived and worked south of 14th Street. The newcomers, the working classes, were mostly Irish fleeing famine and Germans fleeing repression, greenhorns arriving in a floodtide of immigration that old-comers viewed as inundation. The old-line gentry, Anglo-Dutch aristocracy or Protestant merchants and lawyers and other professionals, set the tone for what was called good citizenship and proper conduct. These people were a substantial element in the Whig Party, which had been established in the 1830s as reaction to the egalitarianism of Jacksonian democracy; it lasted until the mid-1850s. Raymond, a Whig when he launched *The Times,* became a founder of the new Republican Party, and it was as an impor-

> ☞ A Bloomer Costume made its appearance in Sixth-avenue day before yesterday.. A crowd of "Conservatives" manifested their hostility to this pro-gressive movement by derision. "New ideas" are com-pelled to wage fierce battle in this world before they ob-tain recognition and favor. Two Bloomers appeared in Broadway, and two in Washington square yesterday.
>
> ☞ It has been stated that Senator Douglass was too ill to fulfil his engagement, to deliver the oration at the State Fair. We understand that he has so far recovered from his indisposition, that he left for Rochester last evening.

Page 1 was not altogether sobersided, as indicated by this item in column six of the first edition, describing excitement on Sixth Avenue caused by the appearance of a woman wearing bloomers.

tant Republican rather than as a journalist that he established close links with the Lincoln administration in Washington.

By its ninth issue, the paper claimed a paid circulation of 10,000 copies. A year later the price went to two cents because, the publisher wrote, "We have been compelled to keep our advertising down by fixing so high a price upon it, that we could reserve a reasonable portion of room for reading matter." Circulation that had zoomed to 26,000 dropped by 8,000 with the doubling of price, but made it back and more in five years.

The relatively few documents from those beginning years are scarcely Dead Sea Scrolls, but they do give some indications of where *The New-York Times* was headed and what would become part of its fabric in future generations. They also show where the political correctness of that day has been politically corrected in today's *Times*: the open affiliation of a publisher with a political party that his newspaper professes to be covering with the neutral (and unobtainable) objectivity of the honest journalist.

The documents reveal something else, too; a condition that reminded me of my early newsroom education. It was a remark made by a clerk on the City Desk, a man whose years of sifting grains of

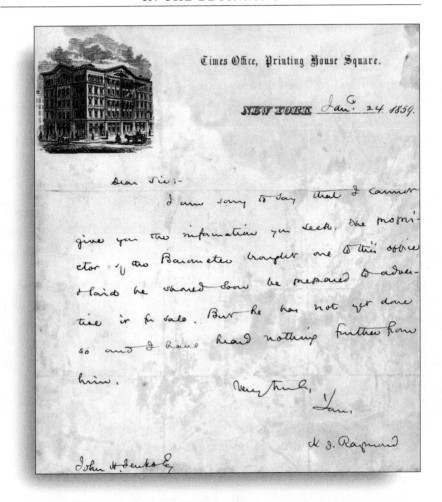

The new, specially built home of *The New-York Times* on Printing House Square, opposite City Hall, can be seen in this 1859 letterhead.

news from the chaff of publicity blowing across the desk had left him in a state best described as jaded. He had just crashed the phone down angrily, as though beheading the unfortunate pleader, and he turned wearily to me and said, "It's all the same stories, just different names, different datelines." He had not made that up all by himself, he said, but had received it as a hand-me-down from generations who had preceded him.

Contrary to popular fiction, the best newspapermen are not jaded. They have a passion to appear so because this somehow bolsters an image of impartiality, an attitude that says, "I'm only interested in the story, no difference to me who comes out on top as long as the story is right." Yet the most seasoned reporters hustled into work anticipating an assignment, something juicy, something novel, something that would warrant space in the paper.

Jaded they were not, yet it is true that the general run of stories was analogous to those that had been filling the pages for a hundred years: corrupt governments, political investigations, outstanding crimes, poor boys making good, mighty men who had fallen. The manner in which these events were treated in *The New York Times* spills out of the archival grab bag.

Cultural coverage has always been highlighted in *The Times*. Early in 1860, Raymond was looking for talent in that area. "Do you suppose it would be possible for me now and then to get a literary, critical or other article from Dr. Williams," he wrote to the Rev. D. Anderson. "I mean to add a stronger and fuller literary department in *The Times,* and should prize his occasional aid in it very highly." The query followed an acknowledgment of an encouraging letter from Mr. Anderson and it contains as much of a *Times* credo as will be found in any document.

> The great mass of men belong to one or other of the political parties,—and each is more or less incredulous as to the existence of evils in its own ranks. I have learned, however, not to look for absolute & unmixed good—or evil,—in any one organization and I believe it to be a good & patriotic service to criticise both and all parties, in the light of common sense and exclusive regard for the public good. Such a cause I find *offends* all by turns, & secures the warm attachment of none. While this does not in the least diminish my conviction of the necessity & utility of precisely such service, I confess it does sometimes dishearten & depress me in its performance.

A working publisher, especially one who is also editor, can devote only a small part of his time to Lofty Thoughts. At the same time that he was weighing national policy just before the Civil War, Raymond was confronting the nagging matters that harry deskmen in war and peace.

"Please write only on *one side* of the sheet," he began brusquely in a letter written in 1858 to a correspondent addressed here only as "Dear Sir": "Your letters hitherto have been upon both sides and it has been impossible to get them ready for the press until a day after they are received. They require also considerable correction, which is of comparatively little importance however.

"In your report of the proceedings during the laying of the cable, be as minute & detailed as possible as a good deal of the interest of such accounts depend upon the fulness with which incidents are *printed*."

From its inception *The Times* was presented as a gentleman's paper (women were sideliners at that time). It had vowed to be temperate in language, moderate in temperament. Its inaugural message had declared that there was little reason to get angry at things, because the only things worth anger were those that could not be remedied in any case. Barely five years later, in 1858, as it was moving into its handsome and spacious new home on a prominent corner up the street from its old quarters, *The Times* received a summons from a lawyer for James Gordon Bennett, feisty editor of the *Herald,* a penny paper famed for its popular newsy and scrappy formula.

In his lengthy complaint, Bennett, speaking through his lawyer, charged that *The Times* had published "false and defamatory" statements about him and his *Herald.*

The summons, on its first page, cited a passage:

The *Herald* (the said *New York Herald* meaning) was in its earlier existence a quasi obscene publication edited by a Scotchman (the plaintiff meaning) as hideous in mind as ill shapen in body and who ere long earned for himself the surname of Mephistopheles of the Press. Transforming his printing press into an engine of torture he used it to extort infamous black mail from the unfortunates about whom he had discovered some unfortunate secret.

The Civil War soon trivialized the war between the publishers, although that conflict continued, with Raymond training his guns again on Bennett, who had questioned *The Times*'s circulation figures. But Raymond also kept in touch with the White House. A letter in which he begged permission "just once" to intrude upon the president's time, went from *The Times* office to the White House on November 25, 1862. Raymond advised the president to go easy on implementing the Emancipation Proclamation.

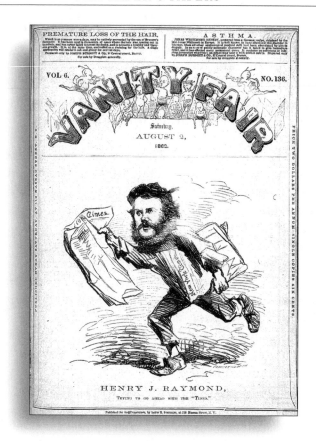

This cartoon in *Vanity Fair* on August 2, 1862, lampooned the frenzy publisher Henry J. Raymond generated in promoting *The Times.*

"I think it clear that any attempt to make this war subservient to the sweeping abolition of slavery, will revolt the Border States, divide the North and West, invigorate and make triumphant the opposition party, and thus defeat *itself* as well as destroy the Union," he wrote. Emancipation, he said, should be used against rebels as a military weapon.

The archives do not reveal an answer from the president, but it does offer a letter on War Department stationery, written in 1864 and sent to Raymond by Charles A. Dana, a great name in newspaperdom, who, like the publisher of *The New-York Times,* had worked for Greeley. Dana had become managing editor of the *New York Tribune* but was fired in 1862 because of a political disagreement with Gree-

Henry Raymond, a founder of the Republican Party, often communicated with President Lincoln. This envelope, mailed in 1862, shows the hyphenated *New-York Times* masthead across the top, along with a large picture of *The Times*'s building on Printing House Square.

ley. He then was appointed to a War Department post by Lincoln. He went on to become the brilliant editor of the *New York Sun*.

In his letter to "My Dear Raymond," Dana replied to Raymond's position on the Emancipation Proclamation.

> It is still pretty clear to my mind that if the President had left slavery out of his letter he would have done himself and his party a great injury hopelessly alienating the great part of the Radicals. As you are very well aware, he is more or less under suspicion of a want of earnestness upon this supreme question and if on such a communication he had omitted all reference to it people would have taken for granted that he was willing to sacrifice his emancipation proclamation and let the Southern States come back with their old power.

The year 1864 was not only a year of war, during which Raymond the editor had covered battles on the field, but it was also a year of elections, and Raymond the Republican Party influential was immersed in the politics of it. A curious brief message to Lincoln, without any amplification, pops up in the archives.

Election Day was at hand and perhaps this plea, not for mercy but for an extension, might have had something to do with putting off an execution until the votes were in. The archives, eloquent on so much, are mum on this question.

The assassination of Lincoln in 1865 was, of course, well covered by *The Times,* but there is a memento of the funeral rituals locked in the safe. It is a black badge sent to Raymond because he was then a congressman. The House's sergeant at arms also sent Raymond, as a memento, a pass that admitted him to the funeral at the White House. Accompanying the objects was a letter from the official that indicated the exchange of favors prevalent in the field.

The much-sought funeral badge to gain admission to the services for President Lincoln was sent to Raymond by an official who in the same letter asked *Times* support for his own political ends.

After explaining the badge and the pass that commemorated the national tragedy, the letter got right down to politics as usual: "As the first of December will soon be around, allow me (at this time) to remind you that I am the only officer in the organization of the House from New England and that I have served but one term. I also desire to say to you that I shall be a candidate for reelection and would be happy to receive your support."

Was he soliciting Raymond's support as a congressman, which was politically correct, or as a publisher, which was ethically questionable (in return for a gift)? Like a rich but plain woman, the thought always nags at a publisher who has a dual role: Do they love me for myself or for what I have?

Raymond died in 1869 at the age of forty-nine, and his partner, George Jones, succeeded him as publisher. Any thought that *The Times* would be less scrappy with a banker running things was abruptly disposed of when the paper, less than a year after Raymond died, turned its editorial guns on William Marcy Tweed, the boss of Tammany Hall, the blue chip of power groups in city politics. Tammany in general, and Tweed in particular, were living beyond any means that showed on their books, and Jones and *The Times* kept wondering why. Along with *Harper's Weekly,* where Thomas Nast's cartoons relentlessly assailed "The Boss," *The Times* found itself leading a crusade opposed by most other papers and a good part of the public.

The disaffection within Tweed's ranks led to the passing to *The New-York Times* of proof of corruption, extensive and irrefutable. In July 1871, the paper began printing its revelations of the misdeeds of the Tweed-driven municipal administration. The newspaper thwarted an attempt by the machine to buy *The Times*; Jones turned down a $5 million bribe to quash the stories.

The reports culminated in the publication of "The Secret Accounts," an item-by-item exposé of the ludicrously inflated prices charged to the city for the construction of the new courthouse being built just north of City Hall. It was a story that led to outrage by the voters and the imprisonment of Tweed and brought national attention to the newspaper that had initiated it. So intense was the interest in the story that *The Times* printed this scandal in a supplement that included a section in German to meet the needs of what was then New York's largest foreign-language element.

In 1884, Jones made a fateful decision. The longtime Republican newspaper switched its support to the Democratic candidate for president, Grover Cleveland. Cleveland won, but *The Times* lost. Republican supporters—advertisers and readers—defected and income plummeted. When Jones died in 1891, his heirs proved not to have the intuitive genius that infuses the successful publisher. In 1883, the paper, on the brink of extinction, lowered its price from three cents to two cents (the Sunday edition went from five cents to three). To draw attention to this reduction, the newspaper, for the first and

# Connolly's geheime Conto's.

## Riesige Betrügereien des Rings an's Tageslicht gezogen!

### Millionen von Dollars ausbezahlt auf betrügerische Warrants hin!

### Staunenerregende Rechnungen eines Möbelhändlers, eines Bauschreiners, Gypsers und Plumbers!

### Rechnungen, welche vom Mayor als "möglicherweise übertrieben" bezeichnet wurden.

## $9,789,482.16 ohne Anstand genehmigt und ausbezahlt!

### Sind die Führer der Tammany=Partei ehrliche Männer oder Diebe?

Wir bringen nachstehend ein vollständiges Verzeichniß von Conto's, welche wir bereits theilweise veröffentlicht haben und sind daraus die Beträge zu ersehen, welche hauptsächlich in den Jahren 1868 und 1869 unter verschiedenen Daten an vier Firmen für in den County Gebäuden und Waffensälen berechnete Arbeiten bezahlt wurden. Indem wir diese Rechnungen noch einmal zusammengestellt bringen, ersuchen wir, den folgenden Punkten spezielle Aufmerksamkeit zu schenken:

1) Es sind wörtliche Abschriften aus den Büchern des Controllers Connolly. Dieses Factum steht nunmehr außer Frage, da Mayor Hall und Comptroller Connolly bis jetzt noch nicht einen einzigen Beweis des Gegentheils gebracht haben. Wir haben dieselben in unzweideutiger Weise dazu herausgefordert, und in einer Sache, bei welcher ihr Ruf so sehr in Gefahr steht, daß kein vernünftiger Mann annehmen kann, sie würden nur einen einzigen Augenblick zögern, unsere Aufstellungen als falsch zu widerlegen, wenn auch nur ein Anschein zum Gelingen vorhanden wäre.

2) Die von uns publicirten Conto's sind lediglich solche für das County. Wir wiederholen die Behauptung, welche wir stets aufgestellt haben, daß die Untersuchung der Conto's für die Stadt Betrügereien von noch größerem Umfange an's Tageslicht bringen wird.

3) Die einzige von Hall und seinen Genossen vorgebrachte Vertheidigung, geht da hinaus, daß die von uns aufgedeckten Betrügereien unter dem „alten Regime" verübt worden seien. Laßt uns ein für allemal feststellen, daß diese Art und Weise der Vertheilung bloß auf eine Ausflucht des Schuldbewußten hinausläuft. Hall, Tweed, Connolly und Sweeny waren die wahren Leiter der alten Verwaltung, nur besteht der Unterschied, daß sie unter „dieser" gezwungen waren, die Gewalt einigermaßen mit verschiedenen andern Leuten zu theilen, während diese 4 Männer jetzt unter der neuen Verwaltung die ganze absolute Gewalt allein in den Händen haben. Zudem sind jetzt noch ganz dieselben Contraktoren angestellt, wie früher, und sie haben genau die nämlichen Gelegenheiten, „übertriebene" Forderungen aufzustellen, welche sie unter dem alten Bureau der Supervisoren hatten — denn die letzteren hatten nur die nominelle Gewalt. Wenn das alte Bureau corrumpirt war, so hat der Mayor seine Kenntniß hinsichtlich dieser Thatsache auf ganz eigenthümliche Weise verrathen. Das wichtigste Amt unter der „neuen Verwaltung" wurde Tweed zu Theil, der doch gerade die leitende Persönlichkeit des alten Bureau's der Supervisoren, und also auch Mitwisser eines jeden in dieser Körperschaft ersonnenen betrügerischen Streiches war.

Der Repräsentant des republikanischen Theiles der Supervisoren war „Hank" Smith und ihn ernannte der Mayor zum Polizei-Commissär! Konnte denn der Mayor in auffallenderer Weise die Verantwortlichkeit für alle die Spitzbübereien der alten Verwaltung auf sich nehmen, als gerade dadurch, daß er diejenigen Männer, auf welche, nach des Mayors eigener Beweisführung, diese Rechnungen eine so große Schmach werfen, unter der „neuen Verwaltung" auf die höchste Vertrauensposten stellte?? Der Mayor weiß sehr wohl, daß er die unten veröffentlichten Rechnungen bloß vor den Gerichten streitig zu machen braucht, um dieselben auf ein einigermaßen billiges Verhältniß reduciren zu sehen. Nicht ein Einziger der Anspruch Erhebenden würde gewagt haben, es angesichts einer so offenbar betrügerischen Anschwellung ihrer Rechnungen auf eine gerichtliche Untersuchung ankommen zu lassen. Und der Mayor mußte dieses auch sehr gut! Von der Summe von $9,789,482.16, welche an A. J. Garvey, Ingersoll & Co., Keyser & Co. und J. W. Smith bezahlt wurden, hätte Mayor Hall der Stadt allermindestens Sieben und drei viertel Millionen Dollars sparen können.

Wir überlassen es unsern Lesern, sich ein Urtheil über den kolossalen Umfang der Unterschleife, welche durch unsere gegenwärtigen Machthaber verübt wurden, zu bilden, wenn bei gesetzlich anerkannten Anweisungen für bloß vier Rechnungen und in einem Department der Controllers-Office solche ungeheuerlichen Resultate erzielt werden. Man beachte wohl, daß noch andere Geschäftsleute, als Stuckateure, Plumbers und Möbel-Händler beim Baue des neuen Gerichtsgebäudes, sowie bei den Arbeiten in den übrigen County-Gebäuden beschäftigt waren! Man bedenke außerdem, daß schon lange zuvor, ehe eine der von uns angeführten Anweisungen ausgestellt wurde, großartige Bewilligungen zum Baue des Gerichtsgebäudes gemacht waren.

**1869.**          **Ingersoll & Co.**          **1869.**

The disclosure by *The Times* of the "secret accounts" of Boss Tweed was so much in demand that the paper published a special edition in German for the large immigrant population that was intensely interested in the story.

until now the only time, printed in color on page 1; it printed a stripe that ran the length of the right-hand side of the page in either red, blue, or green, depending on which part of the press run the copy was in.

As the 1890s started to unreel, the Joneses sold their shares in the paper for less than a million dollars to a group of *Times*men whose leaders were Edward Cary and Charles Ransom Miller. Miller was the editor in chief and would be an important link in taking *The Times* from the nineteenth into the twentieth century and from management by its founding fathers to a new life, never before imagined, under the leadership of a thirty-something publisher from somewhere out West. The stage was set for Adolph Ochs to make what would be one of the most dramatic entrances in the history of journalism.

# ENTER OCHS

Today, a bronze Adolph Ochs in the lobby of the 43rd Street building stares benignly at the motley traffic traipsing past the security desk. For the observant and the sensitive, his visage may induce a twinge of guilt in the *Times*person leaving work even legitimately after an early good night from the editor.

The real Ochs emerges in the archives. They do not tell all but they tell much about this man and how he fashioned *The New-York Times* into the journalistic scripture it soon became. There is no better way to sum him up than with an excerpt from a letter his wife, Effie Miriam Wise, wrote to him from Atlantic City on August 13, 1896, the day that her husband became owner of the newspaper.

> Dearest boy:
> This is a great day for the little boy who tramped the streets of Knoxville selling papers, or delivering them rather, and for those who are fortunate enough to be related to him by blood and "otherwise." . . . I only hope that now you are in possession you will keep your health and make a grand success of the paper so that in a few years you will be rid of your incubus of debt.

Others at that time indicated that they knew all along that Ochs had the right stuff: "God was with you and you won. You have achieved a splendid victory, and I mean no flattery when I say there is no other man in this whole broad country who could have accomplished what you have, with no money." Those are the opening words in the spidery hand of Harry C. Adler, Ochs's brother-in-law, then in the management of the *Chattanooga Times,* written on that same day as word flashed back from New York with the electrifying news that a leading citizen of Chattanooga had all at once become a leading citizen of the country's largest city.

Adler's letter, whether flattery or mere statement of fact, also testified to the status of Adolph Ochs as patriarch.

Ochs never claimed to be a patriarch, but he was helmsman of his family before he started to shave. In the best Horatio Alger tradition, he came of a family that was poor. Maybe "broke" more aptly describes it, because "poor" implies an acceptance of bottom-classmanship. Ochs's father, a German-Jewish immigrant and Union officer in the Civil War, was a failed businessman, a dreamer in his own right, but one whose commercial ventures did not materialize. Ochs's mother was a Jewish woman whose family sided with the Confederacy. Adolph was born in Cincinnati on March 12, 1858, but the family moved to Knoxville, Tennessee, when he was seven years old and it was there, in that middle state, divided between North and South, that he grew up, the oldest of six children.

By all accounts, it was a caring family. It was as deep in poverty as it was in the work ethic; everyone worked, yet, at first, little came of it. Apparently being Jewish in a small Tennessee city did not impose the hang-ups that outsiders might have anticipated. The family wore its Jewishness openly but not ostentatiously. Adolph occasionally used Jewish (Yiddish or Hebrew) expressions in his family correspondence and was proud of being a Jew who had ascended to the first rank of what was then a largely Gentile profession, still selling papers but on the level of publisher.

In a way, succeeding as a Jew was no less an achievement than was success as a small-town publisher arriving to take a seat in the cultural and financial capital of the United States. The road from Tennessee to New York was laid out on a straight, if bumpy, upgrade.

The early years, usually the longest and slowest-moving for an individual, can be telescoped in this nonhistory of *The New York Times*. Here is a run-through: Adolph at eleven, trudging door to door delivering the *Knoxville Courier*. Adolph at twelve, off to Rhode Island and working in an uncle's grocery. Adolph at thirteen, back in Knoxville, sorting out pills for a drugstore. Adolph at fifteen, finally in the newspaper business: "chore boy and printer's devil" at the *Knoxville Chronicle*. Adolph at seventeen, off to the *Louisville Courier-Journal* as printer and part-time reporter.

It would be reasonable to say that Ochs matured more quickly than most teenagers do. Because of his being away from home so long and so often, there is correspondence from those years.

Although there are not too many instances of Ochs as memo writer, he was prolific as a correspondent. In 1970, shortly after *The New York Times* archives were organized, Chester M. Lewis, its first director, wrote to Mrs. Arthur Hays Sulzberger: "Recently I have gone through 7,000 of your father's letters which I found in one of Mr. Frank Cox's storerooms. They were all in locked tin boxes."

The letters from his youth show how he and his young relatives, particularly his brother George Washington Ochs and his cousin Ben Franck, looked to the present and to the future. The letters are not hortatory or inspirational but they are mostly sobersided reports, with only an occasional lapse into boyish confessions of mischievousness, missives with little of the frivolity one might expect from kids.

One example of impishness is cited, charmingly, in a letter seventeen-year-old Adolph wrote to Ben in August 1875 to tell of the betrothal of his sister Nannie.

"Well, Nannie is engaged. Hurra! Bravo! Hurra! Ti-ger!" is the lead on what turns out to be a play-by-play account, detailed in the way he would later insist his reporters cover news events, except for the keyhole kibitzing that was generally eschewed at *The Times*. Even then, Ochs was no great writer, but to judge from his recounting of the major Ochs family development, he had the makings of a fine reporter.

"So I divested myself of my boots, coat and vest, and everything in my pockets that would rattle, and silently crept downstairs," he wrote to Ben. "Looking through the keyhole I saw Simon and Nannie sitting very near each other and talking very low—so low that I could hear but few words. But after 5 minutes I heard enough to convince me that he had proposed. So I immediately crept upstairs again, and woke up my father and mother with 'Masseltoff.' My father asked me how I knew, I confessed to having eavesdropped, but he was so pleased that he only lectured me a little and told me not to do it again."

A few sentences later, exulting over his scoop, young Adolph bragged, "I, me, Adolph, was the first to know she was engaged and the first to congratulate her. Wouldn't take a dollar for the honor." That letter was a comic interlude from the procession of desperate letters seeking emergency help from the young patriarch.

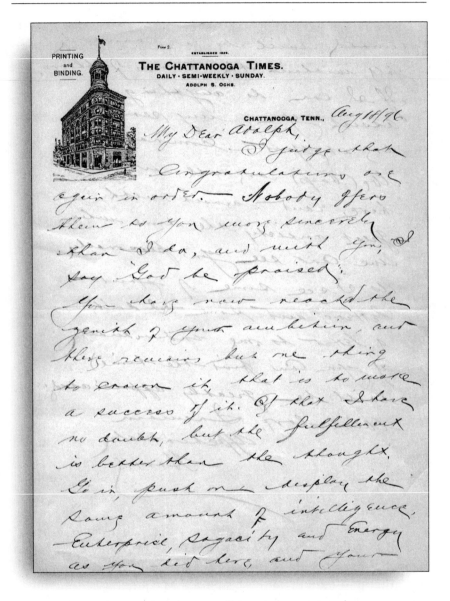

A letter from brother-in-law Harry C. Adler, congratulating Ochs on August 18, 1896, five days after purchase of the *Times*. Adler, an executive at Ochs's *Chattanooga Times,* had also sent felicitations on the day of the sale.

"Dear Brother," wrote George from Knoxville in May of 1877, "Mama is in a veary precarious position. She is almost out of money, with no hope of getting any next week unless she borrows it from Blaufelt or Schleier. She says that you should send her some up, if possible. We received a letter from papa yesterday, from Louisville. He says prospects are good."

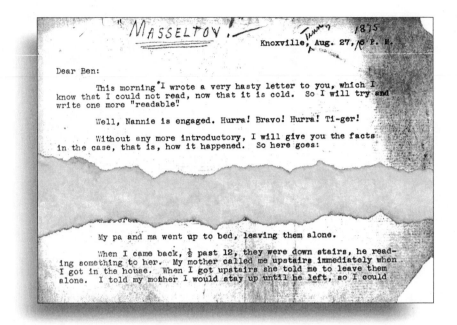

In 1875, young Adolph played reporter at home, eavesdropping on the proposal of marriage to his sister Nannie by Simon Burger and then writing a detailed account of the excitement to his cousin, Ben Franck.

In examining the life of any person who has made the leap from obscurity to renown, the moment when that life left the springboard is vital to the story. The decisive instant may well have arrived in 1878, when Ochs acquired a half-interest and the title of publisher of the *Chattanooga Times*. This came about when he persuaded a backer to extend a $300 bank loan for the purchase of the paper. He was nineteen years old and, as a minor, had to have his father sign the transfer papers. The deal was an early instance of Ochs's talent for persuading older, responsible men to help him, although he had little collateral aside from his own ability and ambitions.

The name of Adolph S. Ochs as publisher first appeared on the masthead of the *Chattanooga Times* on July 2, 1878, and it was as though he had purchased a sinking ship. Debts, an outbreak of yellow fever, no cash: all these plagues threatened the newspaper's life. But Ochs was diligent and stubborn—and imaginative. He set about establishing the *Times* as an independent daily with an objective news approach that contrasted starkly with the standards of Tennessee journalism at that time.

- 2 -

close the house, and so she went to bed. In a little time I heard the door
closed down stairs, and I immediately thought there was something up. Thinking that he was proposing to her, I thought it would do me no harm to listen
and see how he did it, that thereby I would learn how to do it myself when
the time arrives for me to chose a wife.

So I divested myself of my boots, coat and vest, and everything
in my pockets that would rattle, and silently crept downstairs. Looking
through the keyhole I saw Simon and Nannie sitting very near each other and
talking very low - so low that I could hear but few words. But after 5
minutes I heard enough to convince me that he had proposed. So I immediately crept upstairs again, and woke up my father and mother with "Masseltoff".
My father asked me how I knew, I confessed to having eavesdropped, but he
was so pleased that he only lectured me a little and told me not to do it
again. The temptation was, however, too great, so I slipped down again, but
in a short time they began moving, and I only had time to get up the stairs
before they came out - an engaged couple. They stopped at the front door
and talked there about an hour. During that time I was lying flat on my
belly at the top of the stairs listening, but not a darned word could I hear
on account on account of the roar of the mill race near our house. At 2
o'clock he left - with a kiss, I think, and "Now, don't get excited".

My ma called Nan in as she came up and I made out as if I had
just been awakened by the slam of the door. Ma and I pumped it out of her -
it didn't take much pumping - and I immediately congratulated her and gave
her a "bully" kiss - I, me, Adolph, was the first to know she was engaged
and the first to congratulate her. Wouldn't take a dollar for the honor.
I turned on the gas and asked Nan to let me see her face, but she wouldn't.
She confessed to me afterwards that she was so excited that she could not
sleep, and sleep she did not.

In 1883, young Ochs made what was probably the most important
merger of his life: he got married. His bride was Effie M. Wise, the vi-
vacious daughter of Rabbi Dr. Isaac Mayer Wise, president of the Hebrew Union College in Cincinnati, where the *Commercial Gazette*
described him in the account of the wedding as one of the most widely
known and brilliant orators among American Hebrews, as well as one
of the most scientific Talmudists in the country. Effie was obviously
taken by Adolph, although he seemed somewhat awkward. Her amuse-
ment was expressed, not long after their first meeting, in a deft caricature of the young man with the mustache that seemed designed to
add years to what was otherwise an uneradicable impression of youth.

The wedding was a magnificent affair in Cincinnati's Plum Street
Synagogue. The *Commercial Gazette* tagged the groom "one of the
youngest and brightest newspaper men in the South, [who] has built
up, in the last five years, by his own exertions, a most prosperous
business. He is, besides, a man of excellent presence, and that he can
woo as successfully as he can work is proven by being able to carry off
from several competitors one of our reigning belles."

Ochs's uncanny talent for choosing correctly, in business as well
as in marriage, had served him well. The *Chattanooga Times* and other
publishing ventures prospered. Ochs never shrank from debt and

Effie M. Wise was impressed by her suitor but was not overcome by his demonstrable virtues. In 1882, the year before their wedding, she drew this caricature of A. Smarty Ochs.

made his reputation by always paying off what he owed. When real estate deals in Tennessee went bad, he traveled to New York City in search of loans. Ochs always enjoyed New York and went there often with his family. He came to know the city and the financiers and journalists who were among its brightest names.

A deal to buy one New York newspaper fell through, but an even better prospect attracted the young publisher from the west. Harry Alloway, a financial reporter for *The New-York Times,* telegraphed Ochs to tell him that his paper, fallen on hard times, was on the brink of realizing its own obituary and that someone like Ochs might revive it. Alloway persuaded moneymen in New York that Ochs was a master resuscitator who could breathe new life into the respectable journal, moribund for want of readers.

The thirty-nine-year-old publisher of the *Chattanooga Times* who came to New York in 1896 was anything but stuffy. He was an adventurer, perhaps even a gambler, with a rare talent for business dealing. A series of letters by him and by others communicates both the caution of the sellers and the éclat of the buyer in that first half-year of 1896.

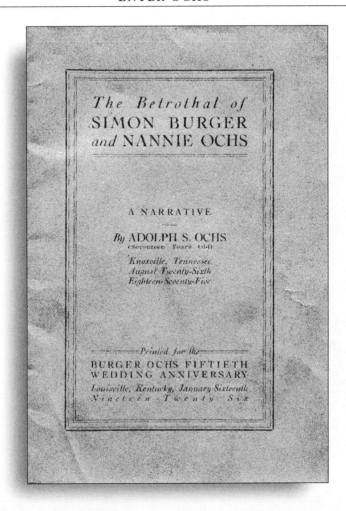

On the occasion of Nannie's fiftieth wedding anniversary, Ochs brought out the letter that he had written at that time and, as a cover to the typescript, had an introductory page that subtitled it "A Narrative" with his byline on it and a notation that he was seventeen years old when he wrote it.

In April, Jacob H. Schiff, the financier who would later enjoy a cordial relationship with the publisher, sized Ochs up in a letter to Charles R. Flint, owner of a controlling interest in the stock of *The Times*: "From what I learn I am strongly impressed that he is a man of exceptional energy, experience and talent in the journalistic line, and, so far as I can judge from the information I have received about Mr. Ochs, he appears to be the very man who might be able to resurrect the paper."

KUHN, LOEB & CO.

*27 & 29 Pine Street,*

*New York,* April 6th *189* 6.

Dear Mr. Flint:-

I have your letter of the 4th inst., enclosing receipt for my stock in the New York Times.

Mr. Trask has inquired of me as to Mr. Adolph S. Ochs, of the Chattanooga Times, and I have taken special pains to make careful inquiries as to the latter's standing and capabilities for the position which he seeks in connection with the New York Times. From what I learn I am strongly impressed that he is a man of exceptional energy, experience and talent in the journalistic line, and, so far as I can judge from the information I have received about Mr. Ochs, he appears to be the very man who might be able to resurrect the paper.

I much hope your Committee will be able to make an arrangement with Mr. Ochs mutually satisfactory, and I am,

Yours truly,

Charles R. Flint Esq.,

66 Broad Street, City.

Ochs drew the respect of the owners but they were reluctant to give control of *The Times* to the rustic from Tennessee. But his powers of persuasion, and his ability to win support from influential persons, eventually swayed the New Yorkers. He had turned down their offer of a high-level position because he wanted more than a job; he was aiming at full control.

"I am succeeding beyond my wildest flights of imagination," he wrote to his cousin Ben Franck. "Did you ever know a man to say as much? The fact is, my dear fellow, I have in the past two weeks had

Adolph Ochs was in his vigorous late thirties when he bought *The Times* in 1896.

such experience that the stories of the Arabian Nights sink into in-
significance in comparison. What has already taken place would be
considered a fairy tale if all the conditions and facts could be told."

Ochs descended from cloud nine to detail the dollars and cents
of the deal but soon rose up to buoyant elevations once again:

If I can maintain myself properly and achieve results I will furnish a text from which to preach application, integrity and earnestness to young men. This whole thing is so remarkable that I can scarce believe but what I am dreaming.

The New York Times has been the acme of my ambition as it is the ideal newspaper of every publisher in America. It was as far out of my reach a short time ago as the throne of Great Britain.

The practical dreamer talked of money and then reverted to reflection: "It's curious, isn't it? Just twenty years ago I was working as an apprentice in Louisville; and now to be the responsible head of one of the greatest newspapers in the world—and a Jew!"

He knew that he had won, even though the deal was not yet sewn up, as a letter to Spencer Trask, chairman of the New-York Times Publishing Company, written on May 9, a month after his euphoric correspondence with his cousin. "I begin with the hypothesis that it is generally conceded that the New York Times, as now circumstanced, is bankrupt," he wrote. "I hope to be able to so manage the property while conducting it as a decent, dignified and independent newspaper that this deficit will be extinguished." Ochs summed up his financial goals and wrote:

> I contend that a man capable of accomplishing such results as outlined in the foregoing paragraph, is entitled to fully one-half the earnings in excess of so large a sum as a fixed annual charge.
>
> Let me say at this point that at a fixed salary, I would not undertake the task, even if the salary were made three times what I hereafter mention. I have no need to seek employment. I say this for I do not wish the salary hereafter mentioned to be considered as full compensation for my services, but rather a provision for my necessary living expenses.
>
> I am impelled by only one desire in these negotiations, and that is to secure permanent control of the New York Times which I believe I can make a successful and very profitable business enterprise, and at the same time make it the model American newspaper; a model, high standard daily journal, a model for fairness, cleanliness, independence and

enterprise, a welcome, daily visitor in the homes of intelligent and respectable people.

The battle was over when the old owners surrendered to the new on August 13, 1896. On August 19, the famous declaration of principles appeared on the editorial page. Ochs, still at the Madison Ave-

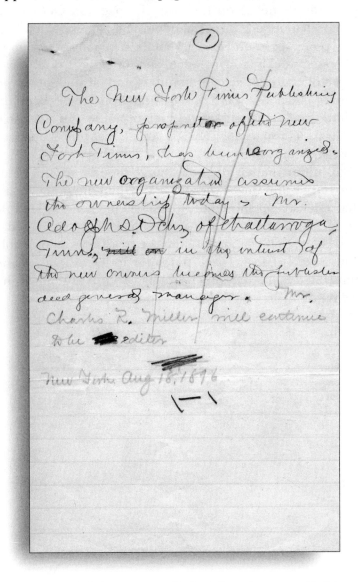

Excerpt from Ochs's statement of principles as it appeared in his drafts.

nue Hotel, labored over it, using the hotel stationery, rewriting it by hand in at least three versions until he was satisfied that it said what he wanted it to say. It was a statement that promised to cover every-thing "in language that is parliamentary in good society," to get the news out fast, and to present it "impartially, without fear or favor. . . ."

The overweening but popular slogan "All the News That's Fit to Print" made its debut on the editorial page on October 25 and moved to what became its permanent roost, the upper left-hand box at the top of page 1, on February 10, 1897. In any other newspaper, a Tennessee weekly, for instance, such a claim would have been shrugged off as forgettable, pretentious, and meaningless hype. Like everything else about *The Times,* this catchphrase has been debated for a hundred years, in-house and out-of-house. For a newspaper as exacting in its usages as *The New York Times,* this is a slogan that promises the impossible.

Ochs unfortunately did not change the face of American jour-nalism, but he and those who succeeded him did set new standards of what a newspaper should be, what it should aim for. They demon-strably elevated the standards to a level never before attained. It may never be able, in the affairs of humans, to achieve absolute objectiv-ity, but *The New York Times,* pursuing its Ochsonian principles, demonstrated that it was imperative that failure to attain such objec-tivity did not mean a publisher should not even try.

# TAKING OVER AT
# *THE NEW YORK TIMES*

*3*

I T SAYS a lot about Ochs that he did not buy *The New York Times* as the ultimate flourish of success, as the crown jewel of a fortunate business empire. This was frequently the style of other potentates of industry who had capped their careers in Manhattan marble. He came to New York as hundreds of others were doing. He needed the money. A bad hunch (or was it his perpetual optimism?) on investments in Chattanooga real estate had put him in a tight corner. Ochs did not approve of bankruptcy or paying a few cents on the dollar: that offended his sense of responsibility. So he looked for a way to make new money to supplement the bare-survival income from the *Chattanooga Times.*

"I think he had a bit of genius and a bit of insanity in him, since he concluded that the solution lay in buying another newspaper," his daughter Iphigene recalled years later to her granddaughter Susan W. Dryfoos who wrote the memoir *Iphigene,* published in 1979. She recalled that her father told her he needed $100,000 and that the only way he believed he could raise it was by expanding his business.

That was when word came that *The New-York Times* was on its uppers and up for sale. Alloway arranged for Ochs to meet the controllers of the paper in New York. The negotiations resulted in acceptance of the Chattanooga man's proposal for the reorganization of the paper, a plan that gave him ownership of 5,001 of the 10,000 shares. To do that without sufficient money, which was after all the reason he entered into the deal at all, he put up $75,000, an ante raised by scraping the bottom of his own barrel and by borrowing, to buy the bonds that entitled him to the stock.

The exhilaration that had Ochs pinching himself during negotiations now turned to jubilation as he waded into the business of turning a profit from a paper that had not been able to pay its bills. This self-confidence was evident in the first letter the new publisher wrote on his newspaper's letterhead.

Ochs, as philanthropic and generous a man as ever published a newspaper, believed in financial responsibility not only for himself but also for his closest associates. Even as negotiations for the purchase of *The Times* were in progress, he was turning down a request for a small loan from Alloway, who had befriended him. As this letter indicates, it was not a hard-hearted spurning of a friend in need but the practice of a principle he stood by in later years when some of his top staff also needed money. A debt might be written off later on, but in no case was such money ever presented as a gift to the needy.

"You no doubt were surprised to receive my telegram in answer to yours wherein I stated I could not accept your draft for $400 to be returned in thirty days," Ochs wrote on May 26, 1896, adding that he was sure his candor would not risk their friendship. "As I have time and again stated to you, I feel under great obligations for the part you have taken in making it possible for me to secure the N. Y. Times, and should I succeed in getting that property it will be my most earnest desire to give you an opportunity to occupy one of the best positions in connection with the paper that will be within my power to give to anyone, and if you do not largely profit by reason of the fact that I am put in control of the New York Times, I am quite sure you will have only yourself to blame."

Ochs explained, "I do not think it best to have financial transaction with you. If I were to begin something of that kind, later on I am sure it would be much more embarrassing for me to decline to continue to accommodate you in the way you suggest." He told Alloway that in his experience such transactions always marred the relationship between the parties.

Ochs was never one to beat about the bush. Even at the expense of amiability, although rarely lacking courtesy, he was forthright in expressing his beliefs. He was also jealous of his achievements. A long letter, more of a full documentary thesis, written in 1932 by Ochs to his longtime business manager, Louis Wiley, illuminates his insistence on giving credit where credit was due, particularly where it was due to him. I have not seen any other writing by the publisher that so well exemplifies his manner, forthright, explicit, and, in his view, balanced with only the merest trace of choler.

The double-spaced, seven-page typewritten exegesis was a restatement of his achievements, written in response to *A Giant of the Press*, a volume of tribute written by Benjamin Fine for the retirement in 1932 of Carr Van Anda, legendary managing editor of *The Times*. The publisher objected that many of the author's observations and conclusions were

> exaggerated statements of Mr. Van Anda's contribution to the success of The Times, and I fear may create a false impression of what made The Times the great newspaper it is

today, and was during Mr. Van Anda's editorship, and was before Mr. Van Anda came to The Times. . . .

But the high journalistic principles of The Times, the integrity of its news reports, the honest and fair expression of
its opinions and the standard of ethics maintained in all departments were not of Mr. Van Anda's creation, but were the
cardinal principles that were announced with my first issue of
The Times, and they were firmly and successfully established
by struggle and sacrifice for eight years before Mr. Van Anda
appeared on the scene, joined our forces and added his talents and genius to our organization.

Ochs elaborated on the "free hand" that Fine said Van Anda was
given. It was, he wrote, "quite true, but within the established principles and policies of The New York Times aiming to uphold and practice the highest ethics of journalism, and moreover, he was assured of
a free and independent institution that had no embarrassment, in
any shape or form, arising from any one's political, financial or social
affiliation or ambition and no friends to favor. A free atmosphere
and environment made possible an honest and capable free hand."

To make his position unarguably clear, Ochs asserted, "He was an
important cog in the machine, but not the whole machine, as one
would be lead [*sic*] to believe from Mr. Fine's thesis."

It is a remarkable letter, its intentions etched clearer than any
*Times* editorial even though they are expressed in longish sentences . . . but what editor is going to cut a publisher? In each paragraph, the acknowledgment of Van Anda's extraordinary talents is
emphasized—usually just before the next shot is fired.

Nevertheless it should not be overlooked that he was supplied
with able assistance, financial backing and every encouragement. He never undertook a large operation without my
knowledge and approval. As you well know he concentrated
his activity to the general news of the day, and took little interest in the routine news confined to the back pages of The
Times, and which was one of the most important factors in establishing The Times on a firm foundation. . . . He was free of
responsibility for the Feature Sections of the Sunday Times,
The Times business management, and its financial operations.

The New York Times
Times Square

*This letter was read by Mr. Wiley at my request put in his files*  A.S.O.

"Abenia"
Lake George, New York
October 17th, 1932

Mr. Louis Wiley
The New York Times
Times Square
New York City

Dear Mr. Wiley:-

I have hastily read Mr. Fine's eulogy of
Mr. Van Anda, and shall later read it more carefully. There
is no gainsaying that Mr. Fine has done a skilful job, and
written a very interesting and enthralling tale, but many of
his observations and conclusions are exaggerated statements
of Mr. Van Anda's contribution to the success of The Times,
and I fear may create a false impression of what made The
Times the great newspaper it is to-day, and was during Mr.
Van Anda's editorship, and was before Mr. Van Anda came to
The Times.  The Times had about 125,000 circulation when
Mr. Van Anda joined us, and this was twelve times its circulation of 1896.  The Times had already arrived and was firmly
established.

I do not wish to deprive Mr. Van Anda of an iota
of the credit that is his due, for his uncanny nose for news,
his masterful presentation of it, and his strict watchfulness
as to its trustworthiness and accuracy, fairness and impartiality, was the best newspaper work that ever came under my observation, and I took pains (as is quoted in the book) to pub-
licly pay tribute to Mr. Van Anda as an important factor in
The Times' upbuilding, but, the high journalistic principles

The start of a long letter from Ochs to his business executive Louis Wiley complaining about a tribute to his widely hailed editor Carr Van Anda, which the
publisher felt did not sufficiently credit Ochs and the newspaper.

Ochs was relentless: On page 100, "Mr. Fine begrudgingly says" that *The Times* might have become great, or not, because it had a "publisher of the brilliance, foresight and ability of Mr. Ochs." The publisher was not appeased by these acknowledged attributions. "Of course, that's speculative, but I might observe that 'possibly' Mr. Van Anda with another publisher or other environment might not have had an opportunity to develop his abilities and bring into play and success his genius."

The letter's lengthy conclusion reaffirms the esteem Ochs has for Van Anda. The fact that "we have the most amiable personal relations," he writes, would have prompted the editor to ask for changes, if he had read the manuscript, so that it would not appear, "as the Editor and Publisher said editorially, that Mr. Van Anda was virtually the architect of The Times."

Ochs signed off on a note of whimsy: "You may regard this as a book review for your private and personal information."

Less than two years later, a note on a piece of paper pasted in an inside cover of the copy of the book preserved at the archives notes, "After consultation with Mr. Carl [*sic*] Van Anda," all copies of the volume, *A Giant of the Press,* were withdrawn and destroyed. In 1968, the book was reprinted by Acme Books.

Benjamin Fine survived to become education editor of *The Times* and winner of a Pulitzer Prize. This incident also illustrates the unusual combination of sensitivity and directness that typified Ochs.

A handwritten letter to editor in chief Charles R. Miller, sent in mid-June 1896, as negotiations were still going on, illustrates the Ochs approach to his key employees.

"As I have often said to you, and to others, it is my earnest wish to have you continue as editor-in-chief of the N.Y. Times," he wrote. "I have been encouraged to undertake the management of The Times by the expectation that I will have your hearty and active cooperation, and advice and counsel in all matters that may have a tendency to again make The Times one of the most influential and prosperous newspapers in the country. Your distinguished ability, high and honorable purposes and popularity as an editorial writer and your wide knowledge of public affairs, men and measures all combine to make you the man I most desire as editor-in-chief of such a newspaper as it is my ambition to make of The New York Times.

"I shall certainly endeavor to make you feel at all times that you are not a 'mere employee' but an important and integral part of The New York Times sharing in renown and profiting by its success."

Money? *The Times* was not making income sufficient to cover the salaries earned, Ochs wrote to Miller, but he promised him salary commensurate with his work, and, the neophyte publisher concluded, "I shall endeavor not only to be just but liberal."

He had installed close family at the *Chattanooga Times* and would do the same at *The New York Times,* as in the case of Ben C. Franck, who came up from Tennessee to join cousin Adolph and served as an executive officer and secretary of *The New York Times* until he died thirty-six years later. His secretary, Kate Stone, who had also come to New York from the Chattanooga office, was for many years his principal pipeline when he was out of the office. Her letters are a blend of vital statistics, gossip, and chitchat.

"I telegraphed you yesterday that Mr. Love had taken in $9400 on the 21st," she wrote the boss on February 23, 1898, in what is a typical missive. "The circulation figures showed a falling off to 23067, but they show 22913 this morning, which I know will gratify you. They also have 27 columns of advertising today compared to 19 last year, and Mr. Love reports some $800 taken in yesterday, which you know was a holiday."

Three days later, she updated him, in a few paragraphs that encompassed observation, figures, and roguishness: "Everyone in the publication office looks serene unless it is Mr. Wiley and Mr. Pacirelly. They may be overcome by the responsibility they feel tho' I know of nothing to make them pull long faces; in fact Mr. P. is quite beaming when the circulation is mentioned. What do you think of Wiley for Sunday 33311 and for Monday 24534? This is an increase of 330 for Sunday and 358 Monday week ago. We don't do as well as that when you are here at home, do we?"

The best archival source for what Ochs was aiming for, and what he was finding, was a series of upbeat letters he sent to Effie and his little daughter, Iphigene, in Tennessee. Ochs wrote a letter almost every day, at least several times a week, and his missives not only tell of his own work at *The Times* but constitute a New York diary, describing the social and business life of the period. He went to dinners, met the socially prominent people in New York life, entered into both the general life and the upper-crust Jewish life of the city.

Most of all, his letters are a fever chart of development of *The New-York Times* in those crucial months after the takeover.

In that start-up August, Ochs wrote to Effie, still summering in Atlantic City, about a dinner at the University Club:

> It was quite a swell affair. There were twelve plates about a round table, and in the center of the table a bank of roses and chrysanthemums six feet in circumference. It was a splendid banquet. I was the guest of honor. We sat down at 8 o'clock and got up at 12. I made quite a little speech and was rewarded with generous applause. I shall not accept any more such invitations however as the loss of last night at the office has thrown me behind with my work, and I shall not leave the office hereafter until I get matters so arranged that I leave nothing undone.

The letter continued with gossipy social notes and contained a paragraph that illustrated Ochs's deep sensitivity to his Jewishness and his ongoing interest in matters that affected Jewish people:

> I herewith enclose a curiosity,—a Hebrew paper containing, I suppose, a complimentary sketch of your humble. You had better preserve it. You may possibly find somebody in Atlantic City who can read it. I was asked to-day to join the Hardware Club, which is the swell down-town merchants club, and a very convenient place for me to dine. I am, however, withholding my decision until I can consult with Oscar Strauss. I do not believe Jews are admitted in that club, and I am not going to join any club where Jews are prohibited even though I myself can be admitted.

A few days later, he wrote Effie more about his work and his letter is in the ethical tone he would maintain.

> I am receiving compliments from all directions on account of this morning's Times. I have not yet commenced my campaign. I am going to make things hum here. We are already beginning to receive business on account of the improvements of The Times. . . . The N.Y. Times does not accept rail-

road passes. I paid today for tickets for three men to Indianapolis. None of the leading newspapers accept passes.

In early September, he spoke of his arrival at the office about
noontime:

> I found a splendid Rosh Hashanah present in an order from
> the city for an advertisement to appear seven times in the
> New-York Times beginning on Friday morning for which we
> will charge $7,000. It was a surprise to the whole office. The
> Times is favored by the Corporation Counsel with the order.
> This is no part of the $15,000 election advertising. We had a
> very profitable paper this morning and the outlook is cer-
> tainly encouraging. Our supplement Sunday I think will be
> a very decided improvement on last Sunday. Everybody in the
> office is beginning to feel interested and impressed with its
> prospects.

Two days later, he is telling Effie about "slashing" his way through
the payroll and cutting as much as $400 a week out of it, although
things are "mighty rocky yet." On the other hand, he writes, everyone
is pleased with the paper's Sunday supplement, with its feature articles pegged to current events, such as an opera opening or a horse
show, and the newsstands are reporting increased demand for *The
Times.*

"The New-York Times this morning had by far more advertising
than any paper in the city of New-York," he wrote. "If it will only keep
up that kind of a gait I will be very much pleased."

A week later, his bulletin to "My darling wife and baby" reports:
"We had a fairly good paper today and an increased demand. The
supplement is in no wise up to my standards but I hope soon to get
it there."

Three days later, his dispatch to Atlantic City is, as always, optimistic: "I have every reason to be very much encouraged by the splendid reports I am getting from newsstands in the city . . . 'sold out first
time in years' . . . 'People stopping Tribune and taking Times.' . . . If
business will only revive and our advertising show up a little better I
think I will soon be all right. I am cutting down expenses in every
direction."

Another progress report on October 10: "I think you will acknowledge that I am quite an artist when I tell you that last evening I discharged the advertising manager, who was receiving the modest sum of $90 a week, and I did it so nicely that he accepted an invitation from me to dine and went over to the Hardware Club and took dinner with me. Don't you think that is doing things in fine shape? Ben Franck says it was the refinement of cruelty."

At the end of October, he crowed over one special triumph that was to signal *The Times*'s specialty in journalism down to the present day.

"You will be delighted to learn that the New-York Times broke the October record for four years past in the number of books advertised in its columns," he wrote. "In view of the fact that The Times has been especially noted for carrying the largest amount of this kind of advertising, you will see some encouragement in this direction."

Ochs had, indeed, from the very start, set his cap for the literary reader. Two weeks after his takeover, he had already begun to refurbish the way the paper covered books. He was considering a comprehensive list of suggestions for an extensive overhaul. The proposals, probably by Francis Whiting Halsey, the literary editor he had inherited from the old owners, are dated September 4, 1896, and established goals that are mostly still applicable today.

The first item described the general picture: "Important books of general interest, such as forthcoming Tennyson Biography and Gibbon Letters, to be treated in extended articles independent of book reviews proper, and when particularly good, to be signed."

The list suggested that literary notes be "freshened up" and should contain "gossip and comment as well as bare announcements." It asked that current literature be more "timely." Reviews on Monday, a bad day, should be transferred to Saturday, "the chief advertising day." (Sunday, it noted, was not a good day from a business point of view.)

It continued: "Old time formal book reviews need to be brightened up and given greater news value, and freshness of interest." Also, books and art matter should be separated from the regular news pages; book advertisements might more eagerly be placed in such a section.

It is less than coincidental that the coverage of culture went hand in hand with enhanced business news. The Arrivals of Buyers feature, listing out-of-town buyers come to shop for their stores in season, in

SEPTEMBER 4th, 1896.

Suggestions for Improvement of Literary Dept. of The Times.

1. Important books of general interest, such as forthcoming Tennyson Biography and Gibbon Letters, to be treated in extended articles independent of book reviews proper, and when particularly good, to be signed.

2. Literary Notes to be freshened up and to contain gossip and comment as well as bare announcements.

3. Current Literature to be more timely. Might be converted into a department resembling that of "The Review of Reviews",--the real beginning of the success of that magazine.

4. Reviews on Monday to be done away with: Monday a bad day: Saturday far better: Saturday the chief advertising day of the week. Sunday not a good day from a business point of view.

5. Much matter available from magazines and English papers, not used at all now, but could be worked over and constant features, interesting, newsy and exclusive, could be provided.

6. Old time formal book reviews need to be brightened up and given greater news value, and freshness of interest.

7. Books and Art matter should have a place by themselves apart from the regular news pages. In this part of the paper book advertisements ought to go and I believe they would steadily go there, publishers forsaking their present place---the fifth page.

Ochs and his staff set about revamping the look and content of *The Times* almost immediately upon his takeover. This memo, written in September 1896, was probably written by the literary editor who had survived the managerial changeover. The proposals are mostly still in general use.

New York's garment center, first appeared on September 29 (and continued until April 1, 1970). The Saturday *Review of Books and Art* first appeared on October 10, less than two months after he had assumed ownership of the paper, and book readership and advertising immediately increased. Barely a week later, Ochs was replying to an inquiry from J. B. Lippincott Company, the Philadelphia publishers, who were interested in the new section:

The announcements of new publications to which you refer were published without charge, as news matter, and we take pleasure in publishing your list in our next Saturday's edition. We would have written to you for it as soon as we had completed the publication of this we have on hand. We are pleased to inform you that this feature of The Times has met with great favor. We are sending out thousands of copies to book buyers throughout the country and you will no doubt find it a very palatable advertising medium. Our rates are 30 cents a line for outside pages and 25 cents a line for inside pages.

Toward the end of that election-year October, he informed Effie, "I don't believe I ever had as much interest in the result of an election as I have in the election next Tuesday. If all the promises that have been made me conditioned upon the election of McKinley are realized, I think I shall be somewhere near the end of my difficulties."

Ochs was referring to his stance as a "sound money" supporter of the Republican candidate. He had led a *Times* contingent in a McKinley parade on Broadway in which, he told Effie, no advertising devices, no extraordinary display would be permitted: "It is simply an outpouring of the business men in dark clothes and derby hats, and every man is to carry a flag."

McKinley's victory over William Jennings Bryan heartened Ochs and evoked from him a singular effusion of self-analysis in his letter to Effie of November 4, 1896:

Hurrah for Weuns'es!!!

I never myself felt any concern about the result of the election, though I doubt very much whether there were many men in the United States whose future was so largely dependent upon the result as mine. I could not help thinking last night, as I went up town to see our display on 23rd St., how deeply I was interested in the result and how it would affect a great many of my plans. But I must be peculiarly constituted for the closer quarters I get into the calmer and cooler I become. I do not think that is usually the case with men of large affairs. It may be a lack of understanding of the seriousness of the situation; it is certainly not indifference. Be that as it may, by my prophetic soul I see much in the future of encourage-

George has tickets to all theatres and is taking them in, Latinjur Brian Boru; tonight Geisha; tomorrow night - Bijou; Friday (I promised to go) Koster & Bial's,

41 Park Row.
New York.

Nov. 11/96

My darling wife & baby,

Last night I attended the Minfield wedding. The ceremony took place at the Marlborough Hotel in the presence of about thirty-five people nearly all relatives. It was a very simple affair. Belle looked quite nice. Her husband is a nice looking fellow who will always manage to get along. I made a little speech which was well received. I left them about 10 o'clock when the wedding party broke up. Rabbi Davidson formerly of Montgomery officiated.

I am asked to respond to the toast "The Press" at the Delmonico dinner Saturday night to Joseph Jacobs. I will do so with some misgivings, but I do not want to let the opportunity pass to get acquainted.

George, who is here, will probably remain for the dinner. George says he finds it difficult to realize it is not a

In a chatty letter to Iphigene on November 11, 1896, Ochs described the social life he was enjoying in New York and then revealed that *The Times* would the next day publish an expose of a bribery effort to secure the paper's acquiescence to shady municipal machinations.

ment. I am not now seeking the bauble of fame or honor, distinction, notoriety, power, glory, or anything of that kind; I have one great fixed purpose and that is to be freed from the thraldom of my friends—my creditors. If I did not owe anything I believe I could get about as much satisfaction out of life in my situation as is accorded to any mortal being, but that feeling of supreme satisfaction is not the lot of any man.

In November, he tipped Effie off to a scoop that would appear next morning in the November 12 edition. It was a man-bites-dog story in which the publisher rejected more than $30,000 in advertising by the city, *The Times*'s share of $200,000 the Board of Aldermen wanted to divide up among six papers for printing the complete New York voting returns. The Ochs scrawl seemed to radiate the joy of a boy about to shock his elders as he described it to his wife.

The tumultuous year 1896 drew to a close with good reviews from the new publisher:

"We beat the Tribune this morning in advertising, the first time. I hope not the last time," he wrote to Effie at Thanksgiving time. "The Times is being much talked about and it is the right kind of talk."

# THE FAMILY'S FIRST PUBLISHERS

I T SMACKS of sour grapes, but I have never envied *Times* publishers. During the working day, maybe, particularly when I was being second-guessed and being misdirected by my betters, I may have felt a twinge of jealousy toward the man who could never be, as I then believed, overruled. But in the evening, when I emerged from 43rd Street with relief and fatigue, I could feel *The Times* falling off my shoulders. Not always. Leaving behind a story that the editors were still nattering about, which meant getting home and being informed, in sepulchral tones, by wife and kids, "Call the office," could be unsettling. Sometimes the telephone rang at 11:00 P.M., when the fresh-ink early edition *Herald Tribune*s were carried up to the third floor and editors could see in its stories what I might have missed in my own. But that was routine nervousness, not worry.

One night on the subway home to Queens, I was chatting with a fellow *Times* straphanger, who also lived where *Times* brass did not, and I was telling him my problems in getting through to the White House and Lady Bird Johnson's press secretary. I was dropping names in the course of detailing a routine journalistic frustration, but I did not realize it. At Roosevelt Avenue, where many passengers detrained, my friend said, "Did you see that guy next to you give you a look while you were talking? He must be going home and telling the wife, 'I stood next to the biggest liars in Queens on the subway. Here they are, talking White House, Johnson, and they're riding home on the subway.'"

Of course that was as good a definition of reporter as I ever heard: a person who deals with the mighty all day and goes home on the subway. Publishers do not enjoy such bolt-holes from the business that is their life, their inheritance, and their legacy. A *Times* publisher cannot amputate himself from his job. He does not take it home with him, because it is already in his home.

Although they did not realize it, I have always gotten along splendidly with the four men who published *The New York Times* during the years I worked there. The first of this quartet of publishers, Arthur Hays Sulzberger (publisher from 1935 to 1961), probably never knew I was there. The second, Orvil E. Dryfoos (1961 to 1963), who passed away much too soon, was a democratic, cordial person who went out of his way to meet the people in his employ, including me. The third, Arthur Ochs (Punch) Sulzberger (1963 to 1992, when he relinquished that title but remained board chairman of The New York Times Company), was the publisher I knew best, and vice versa; a genial man about my age, and an enthusiast of circuses, which I was regularly assigned to cover for many years. The fourth, Arthur Ochs Sulzberger, Jr., the present publisher, is the newest broom to sweep through *The Times*; he took the publisher's cloth at a time when revenues were in short order and he has presided over ambitious plans to emphasize the "new" in *The New York Times,* a period that saw new faces arrive and old faces, among them mine, depart.

Ochs left many letters, AHS left many memos and poems and philosophical observations, Orvil Dryfoos displayed an inquiring mind and talent for detail, Punch left very keen down-to-business judgments on content and technical progress at a critical period in *Times* fortunes. As for Arthur Ochs Sulzberger, Jr., his legacy in paper, if not in *the* paper, is still just beginning.

Each of these publishers made a different mark on *The Times,* according to individual temperament and talent. What they had in common was family. They were all descendants of Adolph Ochs, two of them through marriage and two of them by birth. Each of them, like disciples of a religious-order founder, measured his stances by the Ochs newspaper creed of independence and honesty. Whatever has happened to *The New York Times* in the hundred years since 1896 has been influenced by the compass directions issued by the dynasty's founder. Even when conflicting courses have been taken (the reticence about giving full play to the Bay of Pigs Cuban invasion plans in 1961 and, ten years later, the triumphantly defiant publication of the Pentagon Papers), the publishers of the moment acted according to what they believed to be the loftiest ethics in the tradition of Ochs, who never believed that standards should be obliterated in the name of expediency. Exactly how those standards apply has generated debate worthy of Holy Writ wrangles.

With the arrival of Adolph S. Ochs as publisher, *The New York Times* joined the trend that was establishing the publisher as a completely separate entity from the news side, from the editor. With the suddenness that molten metal jells into cold type, newspapers were out for earnings, in contrast with earlier owner-editors, like Raymond and Greeley, political creatures whose treatment of news was influenced by ideology and party connections rather than by instant lucre at the bookkeeping office.

"The problem began in the offices of the publishers and their business managers," writes Paul Lancaster in *Gentlemen of the Press,* a thoroughly absorbing account of newspapers in that period. "Newspaper business offices frequently shaped news with little attempt at subtlety. As newspapers came to depend increasingly on advertising income in the 1880s and 1890s, solicitude for the sensibilities of advertisers grew and some editors kept handy in a desk drawer a list of businessmen and firms to be treated respectfully."

Ochs, with the assiduity of a founding father's arranging a constitutional balance of power, immediately set about estranging the News Department, the Business and Advertising departments, and the editorial page of *The Times* from one another. It was a separation of authority that, with rare exceptions—and there were some—became the keystone of *Times* responsibility. The surest way for an insistent caller to be rebuffed on a plea for space in the news columns was to tell a reporter or an editor that he was an advertiser in the paper and therefore deserved coverage. This was the Ochs legacy and I applied it many times, with the ineffable courtesy demanded by management in dealing with even the most intractable of beseechers, to space-seekers who staked their claim on their ads or even on their acquaintance with the publisher himself.

That this separation of powers did not lapse into uncoordinated anarchy at press time was the responsibility of the publisher, theoretically the one link among the various departments and the one to point the direction of the paper.

Not that temptation was not always there, as we have seen in the case of Boss Tweed and his offers for suppression of scandal. In 1898, Ochs wrote of one enticement dangled by the lawyer Samuel Untermyer, who would become a close friend. The offer was on behalf of Richard Croker, head of Tammany Hall.

Ochs was a business-minded publisher. If one were guided by the archives alone, the memoranda and letters of his early years as *Times*

A letter from Ochs to Iphigene, written in the summer of 1898 and describing a bribe offer from Tammany Hall, which he rejected.

publisher would give the impression that circulation and advertising were his overriding concerns. When he was away from the office, his associates forwarded the numbers and dollar amounts that defined the health of the paper with the frequency of temperature readings taken of a critically ill child. Comparatively little was remarked about the editorial content of the paper. Yet the Ochs imprint, as we shall see, was strongly impressed upon the news side of *The Times* and it was this constant improvement of content that resulted in the glowing reports from the bookkeepers.

Ochs's jealous protectiveness of the impartiality of *The Times* appears in a vigorous letter to Spencer Trask, a year after Ochs had assumed ownership. Trask was chairman of the committee to reorganize the paper and was a principal in the negotiations that made Ochs the publisher. Trask was apparently one of those people who become "constant correspondents," *Times* readers who are impelled to write letters to the paper and often establish relationships, adversarial or friendly, with writers and editors. He wrote to the publisher to complain of stories, to remind Ochs to caution reporters, to recommend a certain writer. He was someone Ochs answered with courtesy that barely masked his annoyance at what was an intolerable intrusion.

Ochs wrote that he was grateful to Trask for the efforts that had been made in his behalf for the purchase of *The Times*, but he objected to a demand by Trask that he should have the final say on a story dealing with two universities. This letter of September, 14, 1897, is one of the most eloquent by Ochs to be found in the archives. The words get to the heart of *The Times* legend and are the sentiments that each Ochs successor has had to interpret in the light of new changes in new worlds:

> I do not recognize that you have any right to expect me to comply with any such request. I do not understand that you have any control whatsoever of the editorial conduct of The New-York Times. I cannot agree that any publication which is to appear in The New-York Times or that is proposed for pub- lication should be submitted for your approval other than when it may be entirely voluntary with me.
>
> As I believe I stated to you on a previous occasion, you will every once in a while be subjected to some embarrassment if you permit your friends to consider you responsible for the editorial conduct of The Times. However friendly everyone in the office may be toward you, it would be impossible to avoid publications that do not meet with your approval. Notwith- standing the strict supervision I exercise, it is not an uncom- mon occurrence that publications are made which if my attention had been called to them before they appeared, would either have been omitted or materially changed.
>
> . . . I wish to add that if my recollection serves me correctly, you have on frequent occasions coincided with me in the opin- ion that the New-York Times will only be a success when it is conducted strictly as a newspaper, free from the control and the influence of anyone except those who are wholly occupied in its publication. In the conduct of a newspaper along the lines on which The Times is now gaining favor, it will be next to impossible to avoid mistakes, and no doubt it will happen at times that some of my best friends will be led to believe that in the appearance of some publications I am careless or indif- ferent to their interests (if they do not go further and even consider me antagonistic) when in truth I may be innocent and the purpose of the publication likewise, but such occur- rences are simply incidents of a business that is frequently as embarrassed by its friends as it is annoyed by its enemies.
>
> I feel quite proud of the progress The Times has made in the past year and of the reputation it is earning among the thoughtful people of New York, and am more convinced than ever that there is a field here for an honestly conducted

newspaper; free as possible of political bias; a newspaper for cultured and refined people. To have the respect of such readers the editorial page must be independent of outside influences, the writers must not only be competent but free to express their honest views so long as they do not conflict with the fixed policy of the paper, and at the same time there must be more or less aggressiveness shown.

There were other pressures less boldly resisted. Publishers do not exist in a vacuum. They have friends and relatives, and friends and relatives have other friends and relatives. From this "clan bank" come supplicants, if not for oneself, then for someone who knows someone. On newspapers, it is not a problem that is restricted to publishers; it affects all hands, down to the lowliest copykid. But where lesser ranks can always plead that his betters won't do anything about the request, the publisher can only blame himself.

Here is Ochs with his new property, busy establishing himself as a pillar of probity, a disciple of disinterest in reporting, and here, in the archives, is a sheaf of letters from his distinguished father-in-law, the great Rabbi Dr. Isaac Mayer Wise, an indisputably brilliant theologian, historian, and editor (*The American Israelite*), and a very kind man, to judge from his correspondence, who did not mind sending people to his daughter's illustrious husband.

The new publisher had barely settled in New York when Rabbi Wise was recommending likely contacts. In a letter of October 4, 1896, he was introducing to Ochs, Michael Rodkinson, "the English translator of the Talmud, for the first time in existence, two volumes of which appeared in New York."

He concluded, "If you can do him a favor do it for the sake of the cause he represents and the rare literary work he does, contributing a unique part to American literature."

Running a newspaper in the way Ochs chose to run *The Times* had the publisher occasionally writing letters denying any malice toward friends who had been receiving bad notices in the news columns. Many of these friends, like Trask, had been enthusiastic about Ochs's professions of evenhandedness in the news, of his intentions to publish news of what was happening, without regard to the effect it might have on prominent friends and acquaintances. In 1904, Jacob Schiff, the financier at Kuhn, Loeb, wrote a frosty "Dear Sir" to Ochs, with whom he had had a cordial correspondence.

**The New York Times**

"All the News That's Fit to Print."

New York, ......September...14th,... 1897

Dear Mr. Trask:

I am in receipt of your letter of Sept. 12th.

I am very sorry that you believe you can write such a letter to me, but on the other hand it may be as well, for as there seems to be some misunderstanding as to our relationship in connection with The New-York Times, it is best that the matter be discussed now so as to avoid more serious misunderstandings later.

I wish to say before going any further that I exceedingly regret that anything should appear in the columns of The New-York Times to cause you annoyance or that appears to disregard our very pleasant and friendly relations and your valuable, untiring and unselfish efforts to successfully establish The Times Company. I wish to assure you that The Times at no time, while under my management, shall lose an opportunity to do you a friendly turn when it can be done without too serious a departure from its fixed policy. You have been of great aid to me, and your friendship I highly appreciate and very much desire, and it would cause me much regret if you should consider me unmindful of what an important factor you were in the reorganization of The Times Company and in placing me in the position of its responsible head.

With these preliminary references, which I hope you will understand are no idle terms but honest and just, I want to enter my emphatic protest against receiving from you such communications as the one I have before me. I cannot enter an order such as you

In many thousands of the best homes in New York City and Brooklyn THE NEW YORK TIMES is the only morning newspaper admitted

The letterhead and the promotional slogan at its bottom, on a letter written by Ochs in 1897, were typical of the commercial stationery of the period. The letter was sent to Spencer Trask, who had played a prominent role in Ochs's acquisition of the paper the year before.

"I cannot prevent you from insulting me," it began and went on to accuse *The Times* of "making false and malicious statements for which its publisher declines to take responsibility upon the plea that The Times must have been victimized."

This represented a frigid interlude in their relationship. However, in 1917, Schiff wrote a warm, appreciative letter to Ochs thanking him for praise written by the publisher in *The American Hebrew* on the occasion of his seventieth birthday. It was typical that the tribute, a rare bit of Ochs's writing for publication, should have appeared elsewhere than in the pages of *The Times,* where he rarely, if ever, intruded his own prose.

In 1908, Ochs's friend Sam Untermyer wrote a friendly letter telling the publisher about the hostility expressed by August Belmont, another New York moneyman. Belmont took personally coverage of his business by *The Times.* Untermyer had, he wrote, defended Ochs's position in discussions with Belmont in London, "knowing as I do your views on the subject and that you have no personal feeling whatever and that even if you had, you would be incapable of permitting it to be reflected in your paper."

Belmont had, Untermyer wrote, sent him a letter and clippings, which "seem rather petty to me and read like so much Greek. . . . I tried to explain to Mr. Belmont how impossible it would be to attempt to hold the proprietor of a great newspaper responsible for the many items and clauses of items that appear in its paper every day."

Right to the end, Ochs continued to nail down the principles he had brought to *The Times* in 1896. In 1931, he addressed a vigorous personal letter to a man who had cut off his *Times* subscription because he had read allegations about the paper in a book.

> It is also true that The New York Times is not a crusading newspaper. It is impressed with the responsibility of what it prints. It is conservative and independent, and so far as possible—consistent with honest journalism—attempts to aid and support those who are charged with the responsibility of government. There are many newspapers conducted along different lines, some of them vicious, ill-natured and destructive of character and reputation, and for mere purposes of sensation they frequently terrorize well qualified and well meaning men to the point where they are discouraged from

302                    THE AMERICAN HEBREW                    January 5, 1917

# The American Hebrew
### and Jewish Messenger

Issued Every Friday at 44 East Twenty-third Street, New York,
by The American Hebrew Publishing Co.
AMERICAN HEBREW, Established 1879
JEWISH MESSENGER, Established 1859

Herman Bernstein, President and Treasurer; Adolph Lewisohn,
Vice-President; Bernard Edelhertz, Secretary.—Address, 44 East
Twenty-third Street, New York.

*Entered January 9, 1903, at New York, N. Y., as second-class
matter under Act of Congress, March 3, 1879.*

**Herman Bernstein, Editor**

Friday, January 5, 1917                    Tebet 11, 5677

## EDITORIALS

### Mr. Schiff at Seventy

When the friends of Jacob H. Schiff discovered that his seventieth birthday was approaching they wished to mark it by a celebration befitting such an occasion. Some of his admirers planned banquets, receptions, meetings in his honor on that day. Organizations were eager to express their appreciation of the achievements of the great American Jew whose name and work are esteemed throughout the world.

But Mr. Schiff declined all honors. To the writer of these lines he said:

"I cannot accept any demonstrations on the occasion of my seventieth birthday. I do not feel that I have done anything for which I should be honored. I am one of the fortunate men of our race. With the aid of God I have acquired the means which enables me to be of service to those of my fellowmen who are less fortunate than I am, and what is more, I am happy that I derive pleasure from such service. Indeed, I am grateful to the Jewish people for the opportunity I have had to be of service."

This beautiful spirit is characteristic of Mr. Schiff, in whom the finest traditions of Judaism and the noblest ideals of Americanism are so happily blended. Jacob H. Schiff has impressed himself upon the world by his big-heartedness, by his deep sympathies for the Jewish people, whose cause he has championed unceasingly and courageously, by his many-sided interests in the promotion of education and the betterment of human conditions, by his genius as a financier which has lent glory to the Jewish name because of the idealism and public-spiritedness that are back of his actions, by his courageous denunciations of Russian loans sought here at a time when millions of our brethren are hounded, persecuted and humiliated by the Russian government.

The hearty tributes published in this issue of THE AMERICAN HEBREW, representing practically all elements of the Jewish people and the foremost American public men and educators, reveal the astounding multiplicity of Mr. Schiff's benefactions, the human side of a truly great man who is beloved of all classes as but few men are beloved.

A great tower of strength and inspiration, even though his views on Jewish aspirations are not shared by a large number of the Jewish people, Jacob H. Schiff has served the Jewish people for upward of a half a century with boundless love and devotion and energy.

May his energy be undiminished for many years to come. We know that his devotion to the best traditions of Judaism, his zeal for the loftiest ideals of Americanism, and his work for the emancipation of the Jewish people, will not diminish in his service as Jew, as American, as humanitarian, as philanthropist, as patron of education and culture, as courageous champion of righteousness, justice and peace.

### Jacob H. Schiff: Ideal American

Dear Mr. Bernstein:

You say Mr. Jacob H. Schiff will be seventy years of age on January 10 next. This cannot be!

Jacob H. Schiff seventy years old? Never! "Seventy years young," you mean, though this would be the wrong way to measure Jacob H. Schiff.

Years play no part in his make-up because as his friends know him he defies Father Time and grows like the oak—stronger and more vigorous, more majestic and far-reaching—with increasing years.

If one wishes to think of Jacob H. Schiff in years it should be said: He is twenty in romance and sentiment, thirty in daring and enterprise, forty in courage and determination, fifty in activities and leadership, sixty in prudence and conservatism; and to express in years his wisdom, his experience, his broad sympathies and benevolence, he is as old as Methusalah.

I have had the great privilege to enjoy Mr. Schiff's friendship and in no small measure his confidence, and from that intimate relationship I have learned to know his personal characteristics, his unselfishness, his intellectual equipment, his sentiments, his wide sympathy and his deepest convictions; the more I have learned of the man, the more profoundly grow my respect and admiration for his broad vision, his sound reasoning, his high aims and noble purposes.

All my life since I reached manhood—and I am not a young man—I have been brought in contact with men of light and leading in this country, and have had, perhaps, unusual opportunities for forming judgment as to their mental equipment, their moral standards, their heart-throbs and their usefulness as citizens. Thus classifying the men I know and know of, I place Jacob H. Schiff among those heading the list of the most eminent and best citizens of the United States.

I stand in wonder and admiration at his knowledge of world affairs in their multitudinous ramifications; his deep interest and activities in the humanities and his indefatigable efforts to advance, with generous financial aid and with his time and rare talents, innumerable and colossal undertakings to succor the distressed, to relieve the unfortunate, to stimulate and promote the work of patriotism, education and religion.

A seer, a patriarch, philanthropist *par excellence;* an ideal American, a model husband and father, a loyal friend; such is Jacob H. Schiff. I rejoice that he is in good health and full strength at three score and ten, and join with the host who know him and love him in hoping he may be spared to enjoy many more years of useful life.

ADOLPH S. OCHS.

### A Tribute to Mr. Schiff

We have received the following striking tribute to Mr. Schiff from a friend, who is himself a humanitarian and philanthropist of wide renown, devoted to the best traditions of American Israel:

Gentle of manner, guided by tact,
Forceful and useful in every act—
"Man in God's image"—in Word and Deed!
"All men are brothers" is Israel's creed.

An article written by Ochs, who rarely wrote in his own newspaper, in tribute to Jacob Schiff in *The American Hebrew.*

accepting invitations to give their ability, genius and experience to the administration of public affairs.

It was an expression that is as fresh today as tomorrow morning's *New York Times*.

As the years rolled by, Ochs delegated more authority to Arthur Hays Sulzberger (AHS), and to Julius Ochs Adler, his nephew, whose father, Harry Adler, the *Chattanooga Times* executive, was married to Ochs's sister Ada. Sulzberger had met the Ochses' daughter, Iphigene, briefly at Columbia University but came to know her better after World War I through the offices of Julius Adler, whom he had met during Army wartime service. Ochs wrote to Harry Adler, while aboard the liner *Leviathan* in 1931, that he was passing a substantial part of the publisher's job load on to the two younger men.

"I am quite determined to do more traveling—not rapidly but leisurely," he wrote. "I believe it is a good thing for Julius and Arthur to be charged with responsibilities, and not to have to be at hand to relieve them of making decisions."

The division of labor between son-in-law and nephew worked well, cementing the family authority over the paper and, perhaps not coincidentally, taking advantage of the strengths of each. Sulzberger was active in the editorial and newsgathering sphere while Adler became the mainspring of the Business, Circulation, Promotion, Production, and Mechanical departments. Each maintained a lively contact with the other and both familiarized themselves with all facets of the business. With the death of Ochs in 1935, AHS became the president and publisher, and Adler held the title of vice president and manager. It was a fortuitous combination, strengthened by family and friendship.

The planning of Ochs prevented the discontinuity that so often attends the passing of a strong leader. His death did inspire a singular outpouring of grief and mourning that rarely is afforded any figure in journalism, much less a publisher. The archives are crammed with volumes bulging with press accounts and obituaries, letters from notables, and expressions of condolence from lesser-known mortals.

His legacy, the publisher's chair, was a hard seat to fill, because the new publisher, as seen in the archives, had difficulty chasing Ochs's ghost from it. Sulzberger lived for decades in the shadow of his father-in-law's fame, although he himself proved to be an accomplished and creative executive who navigated *The Times* through the Depression, World War II, and technological change.

Yet, a thread of exasperation runs through his archives, a sense that he was constantly being needled as a lightweight fumbling with

In 1943, during the Battle of the Atlantic, the Liberty ship *Adolph S. Ochs,* one of the fleet of freighters on the lifeline to Britain, was launched in Baltimore. She was operated by the British, who were going to name her for their "Sam" Class Liberty ships (Americans named theirs for illustrious citizens, like Ochs, and like his father-in-law, Isaac Mayer Wise). AHS prevailed on the British to retain the Ochs name, citing the publisher's strong admiration of the British. And so the *Adolph S. Ochs* was the only one of its kind under the British Red Duster not to be called Sam-something-or-other. When the ship called at New York, *The Times* feted the crew, which gave *The Times* ashtrays made from shells that had been fired on the Murmansk run. The ship was scrapped in 1968, but her nameplate was given to *The Times* in 1973. Mrs. Sulzberger recalled lunching aboard the ship and remarking to the captain that a picture of her father hung in the messroom. "Oh, that's who you are! I wondered why we had to invite you to lunch," the captain said, following up with toasts to all hands.

* Daniel W. Pfaff, *Joseph Pulitzer II and the Post-Dispatch* (State College: Pennsylvania State University Press, 1991).

the gloves. An executive of Joseph Pulitzer's *World,* assessing what he took to be the weaknesses of other New York newspapers at the time of his own paper's distress in the 1920s, remarked that Ochs was nearly seventy: "The Times, in my opinion will not be as ably conducted when Ochs goes."* Such attitudes could and did hurt.

Sulzberger was a sophisticated, well-educated New Yorker, a modern in every sense of his times. He was a literary man whose papers are filled with poetry and humor and, when needed, adroitly expressed outrage. His verse appeared from time to time on the editorial page, whimsically signed "A. Aitchess." He did not have an inferiority complex and, in some writings, seemed to resent others who, he felt, were saddling him with one. This AHS poem, of May 7, 1957, illustrates the sensitivity of a man who has had a tough act to follow but feels he has performed, on the whole, rather well.

> Our error most egregious
> Was made some time ago
> When I became the Publisher
> As all the records show.
> Just one score and but two years more
> (That's twenty-two to you)
> On May the seventh, thirty-five,
> They tested what I'd do.
> They knew The Times would go to hell
> Just as your Father did
> But keep it in the family
> Hold it at least to few.
> Well, now the day has come and gone
> The Times somehow survived
> And though the rhyme's imperfect,
> I'm sure you're all surprised.
> I had a hunch you'd pass the day
> So I had Uncle Ben
> Recall it to you in a note
> But who and what and when,
> Was, is and ought to be that guy?
> At any rate, the day
> Is passed; The Times still flourishes,
> And I have had my say.

The strains of melancholia in this poem may have been occasioned by a change in the life of *The Times*. Sulzberger, still publisher, had relinquished the title of president and taken up, in that year, the newly minted title of chairman of the board. Not much of a change except perhaps to a publisher with a poet's heart.

If Sulzberger were to be judged on the basis of his own comments on his place on the fourteenth floor—where publishers and other high executives hung their hats—his semicomic, rueful ruminations would make him seem a much more ineffectual officer than he actually was. In 1965, a friend commiserated with him for being downplayed in a lengthy piece about *The Times* that ran in the *Saturday Evening Post*. In reply, AHS thanked the friend but observed that the piece had been titled "The House of Ochs" and was about the "Ochs clan": "Therefore, the in-laws—both Orv and myself—came in for scant attention. It took me a little while to realize that, and I felt very much out of things. Your letter put me back in the sun a bit and warmed the cockles of my heart."

**DECEMBER SEVENTH**

He worked very hard and he never watched the clock
And he polished up the handle of the big front door
By dint of hard labor he rose to the top
And in thirty-five years The Times was no more.

The Japs tried this day with their bombs at Pearl Harbor
But they never got past the Pacific
It was A.H.S. in his diligent way
Who finally found the specific.

He spent millions of dough to achieve some good will
Which he spread like thick butter on bread
A policy welcomed by everyone here
Till it blew up and fell on his head.

Oh, he worked very hard and he never watched the clock
And he polished up the handle of the big front door
By dint of hard labor he rose to the top
And in thirty-five years The Times was no more!

                              A.H.S.

December 7, 1953

There was a gloomy verse that poured out of his soul during the photoengravers' strike of December 1953, the first shutdown of *The Times* in a generation.

While he may have chafed at constant comparison with his self-made father-in-law, AHS admired the man and his principles. In a letter to Nancy Green, daughter of a *Times* executive, who wanted a comment for a school theme on the freedom of the press, he wrote about his own views, consistent with those of Ochs:

> After Adolph S. Ochs took over The Times in 1896, he published one of what I believe to be the only two statements that ever appeared in this paper over his name in which he dedicated this property "to give all the news impartially, without fear or favor." That continues to be the role of The Times in the community.
>
> We know that all men have their prejudices, their predilections, their special interests or biases and, accordingly, we would not put the writing and editing of the news into the hands of any single group—political, economic, religious or social.
>
> We would not knowingly employ any so-called Communist or any other kind of totalitarian in our news or editorial departments, for we have a deep-seated faith in our capacity to develop under a system of law.
>
> On the other hand, we believe that trained and skilled newspaper men and women, who have no common denominator other than their Americanism, have the ability to write and evaluate a news story that will be acceptable to most of our readers as an accurate report of what transpired. I stress that this is for our readers—not for all; for every newspaper must decide upon the clientele it wishes to cultivate.
>
> For our part, we solicit that patronage of intelligent Americans, who desire information rather than entertainment, who want the facts unadorned and who place first their country and the freedoms which it guarantees.
>
> We do not crusade in our news columns.
>
> We are anxious to see wrongs corrected, and we attempt to make our position very clear in such matters on our editorial page. But we believe that no matter how we view the

world, our responsibility lies in reporting accurately that which happens.

Even before he became publisher, AHS was displaying an independence of thought that seemed unlikely for someone who, as he often wryly remarked in later years, got his job by being the boss's son-in-law. An archives exchange in 1933 demonstrates this. Ochs sent AHS a clipping from the *New York Herald Tribune*. It was an across-the-page splash headed "Expressions of Confidence from Business and Professional Men and Women," in which dozens of executives paid tribute to the new Franklin D. Roosevelt administration in terms so effusive that a reader might well have thought they were obsequies rather than comments.

"The attached revives memories of a thought I had when I first came to New York," Ochs wrote in his memo. "Someone asked me what I would do to attract attention to The Times. I said I would put a group of reporters to work to get a thousand interviews on general conditions and the outlook for the future, all to be printed in one issue of The Times. This was thirty-seven years ago, and the idea still seems to have life. I never did it, but it occurred to me as a good scheme to attract a thousand people and their friends to The Times."

AHS's terse comment: "This is paid advertising, despite the fact that it is not so indicated."

All *Times* publishers have been hands-on owners but each extended his hand in different directions and with different emphases. Ochs, for instance, avidly followed the daily financial readings from the Circulation and Advertising departments. He, in common with his successors, rode herd on the major editorial views. In the newsroom, however, he relied more on his chosen editors, although it was his vision, his concept of what a paper should offer its readers, that converted *The Times* into the mighty instrument it became. Of course he read it thoroughly almost every evening, when he returned to the office to pick up a copy hot off the press.

A. H. Sulzberger did not by any indication ignore the business side of *The New York Times,* but he had Julius Ochs Adler as his alter ego in charge of those things and of technical considerations. He admired good writing and loathed sloppy reporting. For all that, he also sought to maintain the News Department as an independent organism.

"Mother told me last night that she had asked you to 'get people together' and tell them about local news or in effect how to run the paper. Please note that I do not want that. As long as I am Publisher, The New York Times is not to be directed personally that way," he wrote to heir apparent Orvil Dryfoos in 1959, adding that there was no need to "worry about this between Mother [Iphigene] and me. I'm sending her a copy of this note."

Though he was proud of his work at the office, AHS was in the mold of *The Times* when it came to keeping a modest profile, as shown by a note whose message he felt required to reissue several times during his career:

"I meant to tell you yesterday but it slipped my mind: In the story about the White House dinner for President [of Germany, Theodor] Heuss, my name was listed but it was among only a selected few," he told managing editor Turner Catledge in 1958. "That runs contrary to a policy that I attempted to establish a good many years ago, that is, that I am only to be listed when the list is complete; when it is a selected list I should *not* be among those mentioned."

A year later, he was again informing an editor: "I'm getting a little embarrassed to see 'Sulzberger Gets Honor at Columbia' as a standing head in The Times. Last Saturday, for example, I should have thought the main head could have been on the graduating class and the bank, not on the honor to me."

Although AHS was never self-effacing to the point where he did not make his views known forcefully on 43rd Street, he was obsessive about the responsibility of a publisher to allow his staff to report the news as it occurred. He also worried about family ownership and participation in activities other than *The New York Times.*

"I guess you've heard me say it often enough, but it won't hurt to repeat it just once more: I am definitely opposed to joint newspaper ownership or any kind of responsibility for more than one newspaper's editorial page," he wrote in 1959 to a friend, Lewis Strauss, then secretary of commerce. "All of which counts for nothing, however, in view of the way Mr. Ochs left his property to his trustees. I am the responsible officer for The Chattanooga Times as well as for The New York Times."

The letter was addressing a dilemma that such dual ownership posed. The *Chattanooga Times* had run an editorial on Strauss's nomination and AHS noted that "I wrote to the Editor calling his attention to the difference between his expression and that of The New York Times. For some reason or other, he misinterpreted that and, as a result, ran another editorial. . . . That was not my intention when I

wrote him, but I'm sure this second one will be more to your liking."
As AHS explained the policy, "The Chattanooga Times is under the
restriction that in national matters it should follow the policy established by The New York Times. Locally it is on its own."

At about the same time, AHS confided his thoughts to James B.
(Scotty) Reston, the Washington columnist and bureau chief: "I have
left a letter for my children saying that it is my judgment that on their
mother's death (I expect to die first), Ruth and Ben should divest
themselves of part of their New York Times stock and secure from the
other three the control of the Chattanooga Times. Duplicate responsibilities in different parts of the country are very onerous for a
man who takes his work seriously. You don't have to look beyond the
question of segregation to find that out."

As he prepared to retire and turn the publisher's office over to
Orvil Dryfoos, he sent his son-in-law some advice in December 1960
that again summed up what he felt was the role of a publisher:

> I think you should have a definite understanding with your
> new editor (when he is appointed) that in the event of dis-
> agreement on policy between the two of you, there must be
> no flamboyant resignation. Ownership, which you represent,
> must have the final voice, and disagreements are not to be
> publicized.
>
> If, for example, you should differ on politics (and I ex-
> pect to take part as long as I am around), it will be up to him
> to designate someone else to write the article and he merely
> edits the page but does not make any public statement as to
> the difference. We are not going to have The New York Times
> changed into a New York Post.

# THE INHERITORS

I DON'T know whether my office told you or not, but I think I would rather see those memorandums that you address 'For the File' or, 'For Diary' addressed either to me or, 'For the Publisher,'" AHS wrote in a 1957 note to his heir apparent, Orvil E. Dryfoos. "I am trying to let go of a lot of responsibility and put it on the shoulders of you and your associates. But, I would like it plainly indicated on the record that the former is made to me." That was the aging publisher's lesson in how to be a publisher, to make it clear that ultimate responsibility landed on his desk alone.

Upon his retirement, AHS wrote an article for *Times Talk*, the lively house organ of the newspaper. This vintage "A. Aitchess" essay speculated on what qualities a good publisher should possess and how Orv measured up. Expressed in his own writing style, a sophisticated perspective that blended wry observation with wit and modesty (by no means self-deprecation), he ticked off the dos and don'ts.

"First of all, like the Elephant's Child, he should have '[in]satiable curiosity' and he should be sufficiently educated to know the wide range of things in the universe about which he would like to know more. Second in importance I would put his ability to read, to comprehend what he reads, and to appreciate the style in which it is written."

Other elements included having a heart (understanding the other fellow's point of view), background (he must know that Rome was not built in a day), an open mind, and convictions as to right and wrong that "have been formed in a humane cultured environment." The ideal publisher must be courageous, "even to the extent of being somewhat of a gambler, which implies that he must be optimistic in his outlook." In addition to an acute sense of indignation, a publisher needs "no interests other than The Times, except eleemosynary, should not ask favors because he can give no favors in return.

Integrity, sound judgment, no shame in admitting ignorance of a subject, a determination to learn what he doesn't know and the ability to pick able associates who are not 'yes men.'"

After this stringent shopping list, AHS observes, with typical frankness, "To the best of my knowledge and that covers three publishers, The Times has never had such a paragon in command, and yet we have managed to get along. Orvil has some of these traits but I'm glad to say he hasn't all. . . . At any rate, he is much too nice a fellow to have too many of the traits I've outlined because he's a real human being."

AHS was not a buttering-up type and those last thoughts about Orvil Dryfoos in that *Times Talk* piece were not only generous but accurate and shared by those who came in contact with the new publisher. He died tragically young of a heart attack at the age of fifty-one, following a bitter strike that lasted four wintry months. His incumbency had lasted only two years. In a business where remarks about new bosses are rarely anything but snide, Dryfoos seemed immune from nastiness.

Dryfoos was a caring man who was intent on getting to know his employees, abnegating the office of sun god that, intended or not, is accorded publishers by lesser mortals. Only from his archives did I come to know AHS as a man with humor and sensitivity; as copyboy and news assistant, I felt that he was a remote personality when I saw him walk through the newsroom. But Orvil Dryfoos actually sought me out. At that time, monthly awards were given for good writing or ingenious editing. I had won one for writing a "short," as smaller articles too brief for bylines or featured play on the page were called.

I received a note to pick up my $25 prize money in person on the fourteenth floor from Mr. Dryfoos. I put on my suit jacket and straightened my tie, as I had seen my betters do when headed northward. Mr. Dryfoos was waiting for me, so relaxed that I relaxed. He handed me the envelope, which I did not tear open on the spot, and asked me about myself. He was trying to meet and learn about the people he worked with, he said. A small thing, perhaps, but enough to make me feel that I had formally been initiated into what was then called "*The Times* family."

In a memo in 1959 to his boss, publisher Sulzberger, he testifies to the range of duties high office at *The Times* involved. Even then,

Dryfoos appears to have been in tactical control at the paper as a de facto publisher, reporting to AHS, who had sent him a brief, characteristically ironic note: "I was flabbergasted today for I received a beautifully printed copy of The New York Times on excellent newsprint. How did this happen to get out?"

A few days later, Dryfoos wrapped up, in an eighteen-item memo, replies to all the memos AHS had been piling on. It is a rare summary of what goes into publishing a newspaper.

Yes, he wanted to speak about the international edition. A technical matter concerning Chattanooga had been worked out. Yes, he had spoken to Catledge about the Paris office situation, which seemed to be a "problem." About the *Herald Tribune*'s RCA section, we (*The Times*) didn't get it because we didn't solicit it and the *Trib* did and, Mr. S., you must have noticed that there was editorial matter praising the job done by RCA, which we could not do. I will discuss with you any inside information I have on Canadian pulp and paper companies being accused of conspiring to fix prices on pulpwood. I

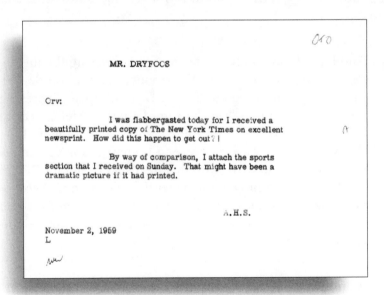

The closer his associates were to him, the more ironic, even sarcasting, could A. H. Sulzberger be in his messages. Obviously, they were intended to stimulate rather than to embitter, but they could always jolt an underling. This one to Orvil Dryfoos, who had in point of fact taken over many of the publisher's duties, is an example of pointed wit.

will be happy to talk about that "Rockefeller Pocantico Hills" story. I am attaching a memo on the Sports Section.

Also, the foreman in the Moulding Room has been asked to check each mat personally before sending it to the Mail Room. The Mechanical Department has been told about those poorly printed pages you complained about. About the picture of Dr. von Braun and the Saturn model that you didn't like, Catledge and I agree to disagree with you. That other picture about the boat accident, on page one, that you didn't like: "I'm afraid I must disagree with you on this." Here is the explanation why our story on the WQXR Network did not mention our news bulletins. About that plastic wrap business, I thought we had that settled, "now, frankly, I am at a loss to know what you are suggesting on Nov. 2nd." Here is a "conglomeration" of several memos you sent about the opening of the Eastern Airlines Building at Idlewild (later Kennedy) and questions you believed should be answered in the story. Here's an ad about our paperback book section that starts next month. We are actively working into teletype setter operations for setting of our stock market tables.

> And last—I have a blue note from you covering the memorandum you wrote to Ivan Veit about a circulation department publication called "Route Dealer." In the covering memo to me you say "Don't forget I am the chief executive officer. Or am I?" Certainly these memoranda would indicate that you definitely are. However, I hope you don't mind my saying that I do have the wish that the Chief Executive Officer would find something in the paper that pleases him. Because all these young fellows that he has been training for some years now would like to get a blue note without a black border around it.

John B. Oakes, in charge of the editorial page, recalled later how Dryfoos approved publication of an editorial that sharply attacked a project just before it was to be widely advertised in *The Times*. The advertiser, a friend of the publisher's, was outraged, Oakes recalled in an "As We Knew Him" piece in *Times Talk*. As we shall see in other chapters, in matters of firmly establishing journalistic ethics at the risk of alienating friends and advertisers and of enforcing a ban on gift-giving, the Dryfoos tenure may have been brief but its influence outlived it for decades.

The arrival of thirty-seven-year-old Punch—Arthur Ochs Sulzberger, nicknamed in capricious contrast to his sister, Judy—on the fourteenth floor in 1963 was accompanied by the usual unease among the staff of an institution like *The New York Times,* which was loath to plunge headlong into change. I remember the water-fountain talk: he was a lightweight, not a patch on AHS, too interested in the business end to care about the editorial. Looking back, I realize that this was typical changing-of-the-guard worry, the sort of thing that accompanied the accession of anyone who was put in charge of anything, from copykids to janitorial services. Naturally, things would be different with a new publisher; how could they not be? Punch, whatever the differences, did not fulfill any of those early premonitions.

In his thirty years as publisher, Punch presided over perhaps the most radical changes undergone by the "gray lady" of 43rd Street. It was a period when the very nature, the look of the paper changed in everything except its guiding principles of thoroughness and accuracy. News columns shrank from eight to six per page (a cosmetic enhancement, easy on the eyes), the four-part daily paper was born, existing sections were revamped and new ones were added, and the new cold-type computer technology was installed. All that and the turnaround of Ochs's *New York Times* from purely noncontroversial news coverage to investigative reportage and publication of the Pentagon Papers.

In throwing away the old-established-rule books without diluting the principles that had made *The Times* well respected, Punch assembled a team of executives who had strong beliefs in what should be done. Among them was Abe Rosenthal, who wrestled with the problem of revolutionizing the paper without traducing traditional ethics.

Abe was a tense, hard-driving man who oversaw most of the changes that readers noticed in *The Times* during his tenure. He was utterly devoted to his job at *The New York Times,* the only place he had ever worked, starting as a college correspondent from City College. He was an extraordinary foreign correspondent, infusing his stories with the feel of life in India, in Japan, in Poland—wherever he was assigned.

Turner Catledge was so impressed with the Rosenthal talent that he brought Abe back from Japan and installed him as metropolitan editor. Abe chose as his number two Arthur Gelb, who had covered the hospital beat before being inducted into the Drama Department, where he flowered as feature writer, news reporter, and critic. The two were equally brilliant and intense, although with different styles—Abe projected a tight personality, contemplating problems, often to the point of ignoring others within his ken; Arthur was warm, passionate about his work, and deeply interested in the lives and motivations of his staff. Seymour Topping, managing editor while Abe was executive editor and Gelb was assistant managing editor, served as a gentle buffer between the whirlwind duo and the staff.

Rosenthal's fanatical insistence on maintaining journalistic values, as evidenced in the archives, bordered on monomania. He chastised reporters, copy editors, senior editors, production executives, and even the publisher when he scented a breach in the code he had adopted as the purest way to put out a newspaper. In terms of news, the Rosenthal philosophy, which was often debated and criticized, was best exemplified and almost universally acclaimed by journalists, with the publication of the Pentagon Papers.

The papers in the Punch archives emphasize the generational differences in the writings of the publishers. The Ochs documents, many of them in longhand, reflect a fin-de-siècle affinity for long sentences and polite circumlocutions when it comes to telling someone off. Ochs was a direct person, even in his writings, but he couched his directness in terms that were more wordy than those used by his successors.

AHS, who flourished from the 1920s through the 1940s, would have been a credit to the Algonquin Round Table. His papers represent a love of wordplay, a blunt testiness (when required), and a constant humor that ranges from withering to benign.

The papers in the Punch Sulzberger archives bespeak a memo age that wasted little time on literary ornamentation. Sometimes the wit seeps through, but mostly it is subordinate to the business at hand. Even before Punch formally became publisher on June 20, 1963, he was showing signs of authority, an assurance in asking questions and making suggestions in a way that only a publisher could. The archival note sent to executive editor Turner Catledge in early June 1963 is not a manifesto, but it is a weather vane pointing to the arrival of a sure-minded administration. It concerned two stories in the paper.

> The first concerns the Cezanne Exhibition. I am curious to know how we decide where to put the little black dots [the single dots inserted in stories both to break up long texts and to separate topics]. It would seem to me that the first dot should conclude the discussion on Cezanne and divide it from the second discussion on contemporary sculpture.

The publisher also suggested that it might have been better to start the article with the story on contemporary sculpture because that was what the photograph depicted.

About the other story, "Elite of Racing," Punch reminded Catledge, "You and I talked some time ago about this business of running a lot of names of people who attend these parties. Have you had any further thought on cutting them out?"

Catledge responded that the little black dots (known as "bullets") were intended to mark different aspects of a story, but often, because of layout, they were inserted at awkward points.

Catledge's reply to the question of the names in the racing story suggested a thorough review of "our entire society news policy because society news consists of practically nothing but names. Take away the names and what have you got?"

And Punch Sulzberger, like his brother-in-law, like his father, like his grandfather, did read the paper. As the Ultimate Reader, he may not have been an ombudsman speaking for the general public but he was enough of an outsider to spot questions that were unanswered and enough of an insider to make someone do something about it.

For instance, in that first October as publisher, he wrote his executive editor about reading an "interesting story this morning about the new yacht that sailed into the harbor." The story, he noted, rightly called the vessel a throwback to days when "one had to be as rich as Croesus to afford this luxury."

He continued, "We then indicate that Mr. Kenneth G. McCart of Stamford and Palm Beach was this rich. Don't you think we should at least have said he had inherited his money or was the president of Alcoa or whatever he was?"

If it was attention to detail that brought glory to *The Times,* even greater glory came from its stance on public issues. On March 10,

1964, a memo to Catledge pointed to a caution for fairness that was later to be put to larger tests in reporting of events and policies: "I think it might be a very wise idea if, in the light of the Supreme Court's decision on libel, you were to issue a memorandum to your staff pointing out that this decision does not in any way affect the standards of The Times and is not license to recklessly criticize public officials."

An assiduous publisher was constantly balancing the books between what was patently expected of *The Times* by its faithful readers and what *The Times* could do to sharpen its personality for newer publics. In one illustrative memo, dated May 13, 1965, Punch commented on the space-eating question of printing full texts of documents and speeches:

> Having no particular examples in mind, I wish you would give a fresh, new look at our policy on the printing of texts.
>
> I realize that it is terribly difficult to have your cake and eat it, too, and I know that I have been impressing upon you the necessity of reducing our overall news hole. I do not think, however, that we should do this at the cost of leaving out something that for years has been considered the bread and butter and sometimes boring grist of The Times. If our problem of printing important texts is one of space, I will be happy to either reconsider enlarging the news hole or suggest something else that can be left out.

Iphigene Sulzberger was one of the great presences at *The New York Times,* a gracious and thoughtful woman who endowed the paper with an on-site dignity that others could not. Reportedly, such was her reputation that during a printers' strike, the printers actually opened their picket lines to escort her through and into the office. She also had ideas, not only for the running of the paper but also for possible stories. She approached such matters gently but they were usually translated into actuality by others more forceful.

"Mother has suggested having an article on parades in New York," Punch wrote to Catledge in 1966. "There seems to have been an increase in them over the years. I think it might be interesting to get a piece on their effect on business—adverse, because you cannot get into the stores; and positive, because many organizations only come to New York if they get the o.k. for a parade. Also, let's not leave out in the story the organized littering of our streets by what used to be known as spontaneous ticker tape parades."

And, as ever, there was the push and pull of friends and acquaintances, that constant indefinable pressure from those in a position to make a personal pitch. This was the sort of thing that nipped at Punch Sulzberger as it did at Adolph S. Ochs.

One such letter came in January 1970, from a friend, a stockbroker, who wrote that he had read that *The Times* was thinking about discontinuing, the coming winter, the traditional listing of gifts to the Neediest Cases Fund. The friend had contributed for nearly forty years in memory of his grandmother and his mother.

> While I do not in any way question that the printing of names is expensive and that in many instances people give perhaps with a thought of seeing their own name in print as a donor, I suspect that the group to which your decision will cause the greatest disenchantment is the anonymous group which includes people like myself who derive some minor comfort from seeing the name or initials of a loved one coupled with a deed in his or her memory—often on a particular commemorative date. In my own case, in all honesty, I doubt very much whether the newly announced policy of The Times would encourage me to continue my giving to the Neediest Cases Fund as heretofore.

In an amicably couched response, Punch spoke about the steadily increasing demand for news space in *The Times*.

> I guess what we are doing in giving up the listing of names is balancing this against the broader interest of providing more news to our readers. There has been a virtual explosion of news in various fields such as education, religion, environment, etc. in the past few years and we have been searching out every possible way to provide the News Department with space in which to report all the worthwhile developments. To me, this is a far more important reason for the decision than the saving of the expense involved for The Times in printing the names. As you know, the costs of administering the Fund are absorbed completely by The Times and every cent of

every dollar contributed is given to the charitable organizations involved.

Dealing with outsiders on one hand and with insiders on the other, Punch was after his third-floor editors to do "something about the way the City Room works" in 1970:

> It's impossible for Artie [Gelb], or anyone else, to be able to have reasonable contact with the huge number of people for whom he is responsible and all this while worrying about assignments, stories, editing, etc. Shouldn't we therefore be thinking of somehow creating a number of smaller units which would allow Artie to reflect, to talk with the staff and to think of some longer-range ideas?

He was right, of course, in attributing the impossibility to "anyone else," but he obviously at that time was not that familiar with the working process of "Artie," or Arthur Gelb, the volatile metropolitan editor. It was Arthur Gelb who brought to the routine of covering the city and its various "urbs" brilliant flashes of intuition that were followed immediately by the thunder of troops of reporters clumping out to stories that had been conceived on the spur of the moment. The Gelb administration was a potpourri of liveliness, imagination, and doggedness in pursuit of a story that left even some of his most severe critics mourning his departure when he moved up to become managing editor, the first onetime *Times* copyboy to gain that title.

Yet this publisher could read *The Times* not only as its chief but as someone who had just bought a copy at the newsstand. And he could be as acid as any outsider. Punch as critic's critic: "I think there should be a standing rule at The New York Times, that what goes into the paper should at least be comprehensible to some segment of our reading public. I would guess that about 90 percent of Buckminster Fuller's stuff this morning was not. Indeed, I would appreciate your translation of the attached."

And, finally, the House Story, that hallowed article that deals with *The Times* itself. A House Story is meticulously vetted, foolproofed from release to print, and admits of no small mistakes. By definition, any error or misjudgment is a large one. I don't know of anyone's getting fired for transgressions on a House Story, but I don't know of any promotions or bonuses being given for them, either. Here is an example of one, an instance of myopia rather than error, but it must have shaken somebody's morning after.

The one-column headline in the Financial News Section read: TIMES CO. SHOWS DROP IN PROFITS. The subhead: Special Tax Cuts Quarter's Results—Year Has Gain. The story itself noted at the top that profits for the year had gone up.

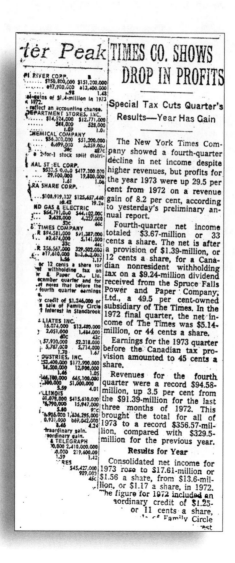

The publisher's reaction:

MR. ROSENTHAL

Abe,

What a strange headline?   It seems to me that
the interesting fact is that profits for the year were up 29. 5%.
Are we trying to prove that we're not an oil company, or what?

As the head of Exxon said, "I am not embarrassed. "

A. O. S.

February 5, 1974
Enc.

The thrust of this selection is not to emphasize the authority of
the publisher, which is a nondebatable fact of life. It is rather to explore the limits to which publishers restricted themselves in relation
to the coverage of news in their paper. Publishers made important,
vital decisions on the overall business of putting out a paper, a fragile
bit of consumer goods subject to the economy of the nation, the
whim of the public, and the survival of literacy.

# THE EDITORS

6

THE EDITOR strides through the newsroom, a few shreds of copy in hand, stalking quivering clumps of reporters. Bold men and strong women who have won Polk Awards and Pulitzers for braving gunfire and bloodthirsty mobs look for cover. Some flee to the washroom, others seek asylum at the telephone. Look busy. But there is no refuge. Nemesis, known as the editor, has a short item of no lasting merit to be written, and a body must be found to write it.

The editor is the engine that makes the paper produce. The publisher may establish the voice, but the editor bestows the vocabulary. At *The Times* there are all sorts of editors, all levels, all functions. They are the commissioned officers, but they range in authority from second lieutenant to four-star general, from copy editor to executive editor. I was an editor of cultural news for two years and hated it; others have been editors all their working lives and love it. (I missed getting out, I missed writing stories, I missed getting bylines, I detested crises bigger than those I could control. That is not the stuff that good editors are made of.) Editing is a question not only of ability but of temperament. The best editors confine their egos to shaping what comes in, acting as surrogate for the reader; among the worst are the born reporters who cannot look at someone else's story without feeling, I would have written it differently. As one editor phrased it, "If the reporters are the actors, the editors are the directors."

Where publishers have the ultimate power of ownership, the editor, particularly the executive or managing editor at the top of the heap, has ephemeral influence. The day after the editor steps down, he is once again a mere mortal. The people who were solicitous when I, as editor, sniffled, barely paid heed when I, back on civvy street as a reporter, had a real cold. The pods of reporters who would be laughing happily together and fell nervously silent when the editor approached did not pause for breath when the restored writer nudged into the frivolous circle. Were I a philosopher, I would reflect that all life is situational behavior that depends on status: editor or reporter.

The day starts with frowns. Caustic memos from above and below. The publisher was led astray by a wrong television listing. A star reporter is beefing about a vital adjective that those dunderheads on the desk amputated. The main figure in a big story this morning is objecting to its phrasing—he wasn't caught with his hand in the till, as intimated, but was illegally trapped by the Feds. The weather ear proclaimed a beautiful day coming up, and the editor has just gotten drenched on his way in. The day ends in crisis: stories that overrun the length they should be in order to fit in the paper, stories that do not fulfill the expectations that accompanied their assignment, stories that are arriving late to the editor's desk, too many stories to fit the space, bickering reporters who have to be placated at the editor's desk. The editor leaves the office brooding that his day has been spent in hysterical compromise rather than in clear-cut decision.

Despite this gloomy portrait, prejudicially tailored to my own outlook, men and women enjoy editing, do not feel harassed, and, as they insist, find it better to give ulcers than to get them. It is an opportunity to put into effect one's own idea of how news should be treated, how a newspaper should look. It is a challenge to take a few hundred talented men and women, each with strongly individual attitudes, and get them to produce a newspaper that will be the envy of the literate world. Edwin L. James, Turner Catledge, E. Clifton Daniel, James Reston, A. M. Rosenthal, Max Frankel, and Joseph Lelyveld were the editors who ran the newsroom during my residence, and each one had been a first-class reporter before going to the other side, the side most of them had jousted with when they were still writing.

Some, like Catledge and Rosenthal, presided over the news at particularly trying times, when money was short and the very nature of newsgathering was in dramatic transformation. They enjoyed their tenure, relished their authority, and changed the look of *The Times*. Others also faced the pressures of time and *The Times* and—always— the urgency of the clock. In some ways, that sweeping second hand of the wall clock was helpful. I dreaded it, but it prodded me into making up my mind one way or the other on a story. "Might as well run it and see if the building will fall down," an assistant managing editor muttered to me late one night when I, then a copyboy, handed him a late-breaking, insubstantial, but apparently accurate, bulletin. That served as my guideline when I became editor. Sometimes the building fell down, leaving a rubble of nasty morning-after recriminations, but more often it did not.

There is, for the editor, more to the story than just the story. The editor is a big-picture executive, and the higher the editor, the bigger the picture. In 1968 managing editor Clifton Daniel wrote a note to Joan Whitman, the family/style editor, saying that he would have hesitated to run a story by Craig Claiborne about an embarrassing dinner at La Caravelle. Although interesting, perceptive, well written, and completely accurate, "in my view, it is entirely too personalized," he said, and gave the impression that the writer was at odds with the restaurant management.

"As a general rule, I think it is better to avoid the appearance of conducting feuds in the columns of The New York Times or giving vent to personal animadversions," he continued. Daniel went on to describe how music critic Harold Schonberg had written so vehemently against the management of the Metropolitan Opera that, for fear of appearing to be in a vendetta mode, he sent someone else to cover the season's opening production, one that Schonberg had already reviewed and panned in an earlier season. In another example, he questioned the wisdom of "a piece about Richard Nixon's somewhat erratic behavior during recent days because Mr. Nixon had just attacked The New York Times, and we felt that our readers would interpret an article that seemed to be critical of him as an attempt on our part to fight back."

The principal editors were given important territories to govern, each independent of the others and subject only to the will of the publisher. There were the editor of the editorial page, the Sunday editor, and the managing editor who commanded the newsroom. In 1964, the new post of executive editor was created, with Turner Catledge as incumbent. This organizational change was designed to coordinate the often rival Sunday and News departments. In 1976, the position of Sunday editor was abolished and that department was unified—which meant more than coordinated—with the News Department; Abe Rosenthal was executive editor, and Arthur Gelb, the deputy managing editor who supervised the news sections and the cultural news, was placed in charge of the Sunday Department.

This plethora of editorships meant territorial wars in all directions, Sunday with the daily, editorial with the news. Despite their renown in the journalistic halls of ale and academe, the only thing editors shared was anonymity before the public. They may have made their names in byline print but now they were making other names. Some, of course, like Reston, Rosenthal, and Frankel returned to writing, as columnists, after their executive sojourn, and one, Frederick Birchall, whose title was "acting"* between 1929 and 1932, went on to become a foreign correspondent covering the rise of Hitlerism. Edwin L. James, who had distinguished himself earlier as correspondent in London and Paris, wrote a column in the Week in Review section while he was managing editor (1932–1951), but I have not met anyone who remembers what it was about. Charles R. Miller, who was editor in chief of the editorial page for almost forty years (1883–1922), wrote a six-column summary of President Grover Cleveland's accomplishments in 1896 and had his initials under it, "the only signed editorial, except those dealing with the paper's own affairs, that has ever appeared in The Times," Miller's obituary declared.

Miller had been an important figure, the principal stockholder in a syndicate formed to keep the weakened paper afloat in the early 1890s. When Ochs entered the scene, Miller, the second-largest shareholder in The New York Times Company, stayed on his job. He was much esteemed and in concord with most of Ochs's own views. But even as lofty a man as editor in chief of *The Times* was subject to the publisher's command. In 1897, Ochs cut Miller's pay to $150 a week.

If ever there was a journalistic Leonardo da Vinci, it was certainly Carr Van Anda, who came to *The Times* as managing editor in 1904 and, during more than twenty years, piled one investigative achievement upon another, one scoop-producing hunch after another, to produce a reputation of *Times* omniscience that has made the world particularly intolerant of slip-ups in *The New York Times*. When he retired from active duty as managing editor in 1925 (he retained the title until 1932, a profile in *The New Yorker* magazine described him as "the most illustrious unknown man in America."

We have seen that Ochs had mixed feelings about Van Anda. He both admired and envied the man whom he had chosen and who had done so much for the paper. This clash of perceptions is evi-

---

*Birchall was a Canadian citizen, which deterred the publisher from naming him permanent managing editor.

Ochs's note informing Charles R. Miller, the editor in chief, that his salary was being cut to $150. It turned out to be a temporary reduction.

denced by a note written by Ochs in 1922. It offered a pay raise and, in almost the same breath, asked the editor to spend more time on being an editor in charge of things rather than a newsman nosing around in things others were paid to do.

In the 1920s, archaeologists opened the Egyptian tomb of Tut-Ankh-Amen. Van Anda jumped on the story, secured exclusivity in New York for the account, and set to work studying the material himself. Russell Owen, a star reporter on *The Times,* was assigned to uncover the King Tut story, which unfolded over the course of several years. His managing editor was not only going over his reporter's copy but was also poring over the "copy" engraved on the stele itself.

He found that, although the stele was signed by a military chief, that name had been substituted for King Tut's, who had written it and was then, according to Van Anda, probably killed by the officer. It was a discovery of a forgery that made news.

Although a scholar had previously suspected a forgery, it was not until Van Anda's analysis that the deed was nailed down as fact. In a letter to Owen, who had queried Princeton about Van Anda's find, Christian Gauss, a Princeton dean, replied with an extraordinary wrap-up of the Van Anda genius:

"It occurred in connection with Professor Einstein's first lecture here at the time when relativity was only understood by Mr. Einstein and the Deity," the dean wrote. Einstein's lectures were translated and abstracted for the press, he recalled, "by which time he had already lost even the professional mathematicians who were here to hear him."

He continued, "The Times called me up before going to press and asked me whether there was not a mistake." Dean Gauss questioned the translator, who said that he had put into English what Einstein had said in German, but he queried the eminent scientist anyhow. Einstein reviewed the matter and said, "Yes, Mr. Van Anda is right. I made a slip in transcribing the equation on the board."

One of the most curious editor-publisher relationships was the one between Lester Markel and the fourteenth-floor incumbent over the course of more than four decades. Markel, who had joined *The Times* in 1923, had fashioned the Sunday sections into a formidable weekly attraction. He was a stern editor, a forceful man who was jealous and zealous about his prerogatives and fought a running battle with the daily paper, the editorial section, and even the publisher.

Markel's intense sense of primacy was nowhere more vividly illustrated than in the Marilyn Monroe caper of 1958. Arthur Gelb, who was a reporter-critic in the Drama Department, tells the story, one bursting with Shakespearean complexity.

Gelb had reviewed a play by Alice Childress, a black playwright who had been accused during the Communist-hunting 1950s of being a Communist. Arthur wrote a rave review of the work, and this prompted a call for his investigation by a publication called *Red Channels,* which was devoted to ferreting out "Communists" in those McCarthyite days.

According to Arthur, Lester Markel, who had been taking the heat in the Sunday Department from "Red-hunters" during those days, was almost relieved to see a charge leveled at the newsroom and suggested to Turner Catledge that it might be a good idea to check out Gelb.

Catledge went to Brooks Atkinson, the drama critic, and asked him about investigating Gelb. "Brooks blew up, gave an emphatic no and wrote an enraged note to Markel," Gelb recalled.

Not long after, Paula Strasberg, with her husband, Lee, of the Actors Studio, told Gelb that Broadway wanted to do the unprecedented, to honor a theater critic, Brooks Atkinson. Oriana, Atkinson's wife, welcomed the idea and wanted everyone invited, except . . . Lester Markel. It was a memorable bash, with the biggest names in the business toasting the modest critic. *The Times* carried the story, with photo, the next morning.

Gelb recalled that Markel was furious at having been left out. Never again, he ordered (Gelb said) should a Strasberg, including their daughter, Susan, be mentioned in the columns he controlled. Susan was starring on Broadway in *The Diary of Anne Frank* and had been scheduled to be highlighted in a big Sunday section piece. What to do?

The Strasberg seniors arranged a dinner at which Lee's disciple, Marilyn Monroe, then probably the most glamorous property in Hollywood, perhaps in the world, sat next to Markel. The editor, having immediately forgiven the Strasbergs for the unforgivable Atkinson affair, invited the actress to visit *The Times* the next day.

Markel's revenge was a pinnacle of *Times* upmanship. He paraded the star through the newsroom, which he rarely visited from his eighth-floor aerie, with the air of triumph of a Roman conqueror returning to the Forum with a display of golden loot. She stopped traffic and the news on the third floor more than any labor dispute ever did. Men rushed, goggle-eyed, from their desks to see the screen goddess step pertly through the detritus of lesser events of the day. (It was a scene in which strong men proved to be weak, and it was not to be duplicated until a visit by Robert Redford a few years later sent hardened women reporters and outspoken feminists into a frenzy of semicomic shrieking and flutter.)

For all his surefootedness in dealing with the world, Markel seemed to be less than certain of himself when it came to gauging his own standing at *The Times*. In memos to Arthur Hays Sulzberger, he several times complained that he felt unwanted. In an otherwise cordial note congratulating AHS on his birthday, Markel somewhat plaintively wrote, "And, while I am writing you as friend to friend, I wonder whether I have done anything to offend you. Maybe I am cock-eyed about it but somehow I get the impression that you are avoiding me these days. If I am cock-eyed about this, please forget it—and remember only the good wishes."

In answer, "Arthur" reassured "Lester": "If I may be a trifle face-tious and make my reply, it is that I have avoided you by being at the of-fice each day for luncheon instead of having been invited out with you. If I should say 'mea culpa' for that I'll say it, for I have had no desire to avoid you and quite the contrary have missed you and thought you might have looked me up on those days when we didn't meet."

In 1950, the "Arthur–Lester" axis was again out of synch, this time about a piece Markel had written about Israel that AHS did not care for. Markel rebutted the criticism and concluded: "Sometime I wish you would give me your definition of news. I see in the daily paper half a dozen pieces every day which I would not print in the Sunday on the ground that there is no news peg. You may recall my debate with [Edwin L.] James [the managing editor] once on that position. I said to him: If you think of it, it's news; if I think of it, it's a feature." Markel said he was sad, not mad, that the publisher did not want him to write and would not give him the same leeway he granted other editors.

In 1951, Turner Catledge, the genial man from Mississippi who had gained renown as a Washington correspondent, succeeded Edwin L. James as managing editor of *The Times*. There was a venerable and probably unwritten rule in those days that people who left *The Times* were not readily readmitted into the temple of journalism on West 43rd Street. Catledge was one of the illustrious few for whom the rule was made to be broken. In 1943, amid the lamentations of Arthur Krock, Washington Bureau chief, and of the brass in New York, Catledge left *The Times* to go to the new *Chicago Sun,* where he be-came editor in chief. Two years later he was back with *The Times,* this time as assistant managing editor in New York.

Catledge was the most affable of men, a gentlemanly editor with the gift of golden gab and the ability to mediate the many messes that confront editors. I never minded that he always called me "Bob," obviously never nailing down my true identity, a situation that had al-most no effect on my career, so great was the gulf between us. In-deed, I felt somewhat more secure for not being singled out, something like the laundry officer in *Mr. Roberts* who was always a stranger to the captain.

Under Catledge, *The Times* became more than ever attracted to "wrap-up" stories, the sort that put together situations reported piecemeal elsewhere as they developed. They had become a most readable feature on the first page of the *Wall Street Journal*. Frequently, a billet doux with a clipping from that other paper asking why we hadn't covered it arrived from the front office, usually over the signature of Clifton Daniel, who was then Catledge's assistant editor.

No use explaining that, yes, we did have it because we were covering it every day, in smaller pieces—daily bits and pieces that were handy references for other news organs to put together as a packaged whole.

In 1962, Daniel had outlined his thoughts on competing with or matching the *Journal's* "roundups or takeouts, a field in which The Journal excels and which is responsible in great measure for its popularity among general readers." *The Times,* he said, could easily outrun the *Journal* in that respect. He was shrewdly aware of the fatalistic attitude among lesser editors.

> I almost never circulate The Wall Street Journal's special pieces among our editors without getting back the word that we carried the same thing or something like it days or weeks earlier. In other words, what The Wall Street Journal is doing is using The New York Times as a source for ideas. If we should set out to develop these ideas ahead of The Wall Street Journal I think we would have very little trouble outrunning them. . . . Our problem at the moment is relatively simple. We don't have any regular space for daily takeouts, and we don't have anybody specifically deputed to see that the space is filled and well filled.

In retrospect, the idea, a nuisance to the just-facts school at that time, proved to be a valid approach to the new ideas on presenting the news. In 1963, Catledge, one of Punch Sulzberger's closest associates on the paper, sent the young publisher a note that indicated his own indecision about going afield from the news itself. It had to do with an investigation of the link between organized crime and narcotics and the possibility of a *Times* story on the topic.

Catledge's response to Punch's inquiry about whether there was a story in this for *The Times* said, "However, I think we should stick to the news formula and not get into anything that smacks of crusading. This is a subject on which you can crusade the rest of your life and never make an appreciable dent. The main thing is for us to cover the news and keep the subject in proper focus with the rest of the news."

In 1964, with the retirement of Lester Markel, Catledge became the first executive editor, in charge of both the daily and the Sunday paper (but not the editorial page). There are those who are no more sure of what an executive or managing editor at *The Times* does than they are of how a Broadway producer functions. Daniel conscientiously kept Catledge abreast of what was happening at *The Times* when the latter was out of town. He wrote meticulously detailed reports that better than anything else delineate what an editor worries about. They were insightful and analytical. Here are some bits culled from a thirty-five-item letter in 1964:

Joe Herzberg [cultural news editor] raises again the question of whether we shouldn't be covering theater previews. He points out that one incoming show will be here for a month before it has its formal opening. I told him you were interested in the subject and we should wait for your return to discuss it.

You always want to know about new bylines. Abe Rosenthal tells me that a foreign desk copyreader named Alan Oser writes quite a few nice features and he wants to give Oser a byline from time to time. I told him he might do so with discretion. I trust Abe's discretion because he has been the chief one interested in restricting bylines.

Attached you will find a story about a motion by Roy Cohn to have the charges against him dismissed on the grounds that the Justice Department has been intercepting mail sent by him to his lawyer, who is also a member of his own firm. There was some feeling inside the office and out that we were taken in by this story and overplayed it. . . . I think the story is perfectly defensible and will give the details if you want them.

We are being sued for $50,000 by the fellow on Long Island who we stated killed a dog. He is also suing other papers.

You may not recall, but while you were away we ran one of those women's page personality pieces about a Mrs. Kempner. As might have been expected, the various Sulzberger ladies didn't like it. A.H.S. relayed their complaints, but he didn't seem to be too upset.

There is one more bit of reading attached—a delightful column by John Canaday about which I have been expecting all day to get a blast from Bob Moses. I am ready to take him on, but I haven't heard from him.

Daniel was a leading exponent of moving ahead with innovation in news coverage. In 1964, he replied to a complaint from Sydney Gruson by defining his own brand of new journalism.

It seems to me that our correspondents make a mistake in dividing news into two rigid categories—hard news, on the one hand, and feature stories, on the other. We really ought to forget words like "featurous" [sic] and "color." There is too much of a tendency to think of features and hard news as separate kinds of journalism. What we should be doing, in my opinion, is getting more good stuff into the main body of all stories. And by "good stuff" I mean illuminating flashes of color, description and background that can be obtained only by first-hand original reporting and skillful writing.

The best hand I ever saw at this was Abe Rosenthal. Abe never wrote a story from abroad that he didn't include some piece of personal observation. And he never complained about lack of space because he seemed to be able to tell any story in 600 words. And he didn't have much reason to complain about queries from New York because he was usually ahead of them. He brought these qualities of skill and alertness to his job as metropolitan editor and I think he has done remarkably well.

In translating his reportorial excellence to the editor's desk, Abe Rosenthal proved to be a prolific and dynamic executive, one who faced creating bold new alternatives at a time when *The New York Times* was threatened by deadly financial doldrums. Rosenthal dedicated himself, as a flood of memos testify, to ensuring that the new features in *The Times* did not become mere filler for the advertisements they were designed to attract. He sternly reviewed them and insisted that they be written to the same standards that applied to the older news sections.

For Abe, the job was the big picture—the struggle to get the Pentagon Papers into print—and the tiniest possible picture—the decision on the size of type that would affect how many words a reporter could fit into a column.

Each editor brought his own particular, even peculiar, talents to bear on the look and content of the paper. If there has been one common factor, at least in my time, it is the "meeting." *The Times* breeds meetings in the same measure that famine breeds discontent. Reporters in every generation of editors have always complained that they could not get the boss's ear when they wanted to because the editor was at a meeting. There were intradepartmental meetings, when the metropolitan or national or foreign or other editor would meet with his staff. Then there were page 1 meetings later in the day, and editors' conferences in the late afternoon.

It was all very easy to sneer at, but *The Times* is a large institution and the meetings provide the most direct channels for avoiding conflicts and for charting paths that make the paper more accessible to its readers. In 1968, Clifton Daniel notified the plethora of editors that the afternoon news conference that had been originated by Turner Catledge would be drastically modified. Instead of a mass turnout by all leading editors, only the foreign, national, metropolitan, and picture editors would attend, with the assistant managing and managing editors. Instead of reeling off the interminable list of all their stories, the editors would report only the top stories and others that required special attention. Business and financial, sports and women's news editors would come only when they had special news to impart. "I hope these changes will reduce the amount of time that the editors give to preparing for the conference—time which cannot easily be spared at the busiest hour of the day," Daniel's memo declared. "We should continue to limit the conference to 30 minutes or less."

It all seemed centuries away from earlier days when a top editor would walk over to the desk of a lower editor, deliver his message, learn what he wanted to know, and get on with putting out the paper. But a bigger, more complex paper meant that there was more to know about and that it was more important for all editors to know what the others were up to. We could laugh at memos and conferences, but they were the last human contacts in the increasingly electronic newsroom.

# "WE"—THE EDITORIAL BOARD

I T WAS on a weekend in January 1964 that Herbert Mitgang was assigned to write an editorial for *The New York Times* about a historic report of the surgeon general's special committee that linked cigarette smoking to lung cancer. Mitgang, a member of the editorial board whose "beat" included following the activities of federal regulatory agencies, wrote his piece in the office on that Saturday or Sunday and called the editor of the editorial page, John B. Oakes, and read his piece to him over the telephone. Oakes approved of it but asked Mitgang to check it out with Punch Sulzberger because the question of cigarette advertising would have a visible impact on *The Times*'s pocketbook.

Mitgang telephoned the publisher at home and read the editorial to him. "It was the first time in more than ten years on the board that I, or anyone else as far as I knew, had to check anything with Punch," Mitgang recalled when we spoke about it. "He got copies of editorial galleys and spoke with John Oakes, but not with us. At any rate, I read and he listened. When I finished, he just asked, in his humorous way, 'Must you also include pipes and cigars?' I said, 'I'm afraid so, it's in the surgeon general's report.' Punch said only, 'Too bad, I'm sitting here smoking my pipe,' and that was all there was to it. The editorial ran."

The point of this story is not to praise the publisher for standing back from an editorial, nor is it to criticize him for insisting on knowing what the paper is saying in his name. It is to illustrate the balance that a publisher of *The Times* strives to establish before rushing into print with a mere proclamation of position. In 1923, Ochs wrote to a Washington correspondent of the *Buffalo Evening News* that "the editorial council does not determine the policies any more than the President's cabinet determines the policies of the President."

He explained how the council, which later was named the editorial board, functioned: "At our council meetings there is free discussion and a very frank interchange of opinion, and those who may be present, who determine the policy of The Times, are frequently influenced by the opinions expressed. . . . There is an inviolable rule that no editorial writer shall write an article expressing an opinion that he does not honestly and conscientiously entertain."

Even before he became publisher, Ochs's son-in-law, AHS, was taking a lively interest in *Times* editorials. In letters to Ochs, in 1932, when the newly elected administration of Franklin D. Roosevelt was about to take office, AHS feared "that an opportunist is in the White House." A week later, however, he asked Ochs to "call off" two editorial writers who, he felt, kept going after the administration like a "pair of hounds." He was not suggesting that *The Times* commend what was being done in Washington but was "merely urging a little more tolerance and effort to understand."

In his reply, Ochs chided his heir apparent for his own strong language in describing the editorialists. "I also do not find myself in agreement with the thought that in taking a critical attitude it means 'sitting in a corner and crying, when it might be up and doing.' I have never been much given to being up and doing—in other words, assuming an air of authority. Our vocation should be more to inform and interpret. . . . It has been the policy of The Times to be conservative and cautious and not involve itself in all public clamor for a change, etc. This is a big subject. I would like sometime at an early day to give you a better understanding of my views of the conduct of the editorial page of a newspaper, such as is The New York Times."

He said that lowering the temper of an editorial might make criticism more helpful, but doubted it. Calvin Coolidge had once told him how a president had to make progress slowly but "he thought it extremely fortunate there was a great and influential newspaper like The New York Times that was presenting and advocating the ideals."

But right from his start at *The Times,* Ochs wanted the points of view to be buttressed by a reportorial assessment of the facts. In August 1896 the new publisher wrote to Charles R. Miller, who was covering a convention in Indianapolis, asking for an editorial of 1,000 to 2,000 words every convention day.

"I believe it would be an innovation that would be a hit to have an editorial reviewing the proceedings of the convention by the editor-

## Tobacco Road

The editorial page, which represented *Times* ideals, and the Advertising Department, which represented *Times* income, were in rare conflict when the propriety of accepting cigarette advertising was raised as an issue. In 1967, the editorial-page editor advised the publisher that "My thought on *cigarette advertising* is that we really shouldn't refuse it, but should fully comply with the FCC [Federal Communications Commission] ruling. To refuse the advertising would, I think, open up a whole new aspect of the censorship question and I think the precedent might prove to be very unwise." Oakes said he did not see anything wrong with running a cautionary note in cigarette ads in *The Times.*

Ivan Veit, head of *The Times* Advertising Department, presented Punch with the various options in 1969. He wrote that although the paper had rejected unacceptable advertising because of questions of taste, obscenity, libel, fraud, and the like, it had not been rejected because "we thought that the product or service would not be good for the reader." *The Times* should continue its present policy, he said, unless the government took action on cigarette advertising in broadcasting. "That would be to accept the small amount of cigarette advertising that is being offered to us, not to make active solicitation for this advertising and of course to continue our vigorous editorial policy and the comprehensive reporting of scientific and medical developments in the cigarette smoking field."

Should cigarette commercials be banned on television, Veit wrote, "a new yardstick of acceptability" would have been enunciated by the government and, also, tobacco companies "might flood into print media," which would be undesirable. "We would hear from lots of readers, which would not help us in schools, and, I think our institutional standing would be somewhat tarnished." In this situation, Veit said, he would favor rejecting all cigarette advertising.

A business-office executive reminded the publisher's office that should cigarette advertising be banned from *The Times,* "it is extremely important that we bear in mind and be prepared to accept financial repercussions, above and beyond the direct loss of cigarette advertising revenue per se (1968 volume: 115,753 lines; approximately $240,000)." Diversified cigarette companies would likely boycott *The Times* for other advertising, he said. Alcoholic-beverage manufacturers, fearing that *The Times* would then "go after them," would also withdraw advertising. Advertising agencies and broadcasters would also blame *The Times* for using its influence to bear on matters that could hurt them financially.

Finally, *The Times* announced that as of January 1, 1970, it would accept cigarette advertising only if it clearly carried the statutorily mandated declaration of the dangers of smoking and disclosed the tar and nicotine content in the cigarette smoke. The announcement took note that *The Times* had long warned about cigarettes on its editorial pages but that the paper did not "play the role of censor."

in-chief [editorial-page editor], who was present and participated, and whose opportunities for observation naturally would be far superior to those who were viewing the proceedings from a distance."

Nearly thirty years later, AHS was explaining to a later generation how editorials developed under his own regime. A letter to a friend outlined it eloquently.

When I first became responsible after Mr. Ochs' death, Rollo Ogden was the editor in charge of the editorial page. He was a man a great deal my senior, extremely able and astute, and I could no more talk to him than fly on my own. . . . When he died and Dr. [John H.] Finley took over, it was different. By that time Charlie [Charles] Merz was on the editorial page and he and I in effect ran it. Finley was a lovely man but he just didn't know very much about the world, or at least the nasty part of it. And when Finley retired and Merz became editor, things started to change. Up to that time I had read every editorial in proof before it appeared in the paper. After I'd worked with Charlie and realized how much he and I thought alike, I knew that was no longer necessary, I also knew that if he wished to take a different position from what had already been established, Charlie would tell me about it and consult with me. The result was that I left things very largely to him but as to who was responsible, the answer is that I was and I alone.

Ochs made one dramatic switch in editorial policy that was to get *The Times* "reclassified" as a Democratic paper, more or less, instead of a staunch Republican journal, which it had been from its founding. The $2 \times 3$ cards in the archives list all of the presidential candidates backed by *The Times* from 1852, when Raymond, later a founder of the Republican Party, and Jones supported Winfield Scott on the Whig ticket. In the three elections before Ochs came aboard in 1896, the paper backed a Democrat for the first time, Grover Cleveland. Ochs strongly plumped for McKinley in 1900, but the paper was to be in the Democratic ranks for most of the twentieth century, lapsing into Republicanism only to endorse Wendell L. Willkie in 1940 (against Franklin D. Roosevelt, whom it favored for his three other candidacies), Thomas E. Dewey in 1948, and Dwight D. Eisenhower in 1952 and 1956.

The hands-on interest of the publishers in having their views correctly pronounced is evidenced in the archives where several editorials directly acted upon by Ochs are found, with his cross-outs and comments on the galley proofs. Of the four samples preserved, three are on editorials dealing with World War I matters in 1915–1916. The fourth, in 1932, about Roosevelt's try for the Democratic Party nomination, bears his notation at the top, "Killed by A.S.O. because the implication that Gov. Roosevelt was not sure of NY State."

AHS put his trust in Charles H. Merz, whom he had chosen to head the editorial page, and was relieved of the chore of reading the galleys, but he also had ideas and put them into the form of editorials. More than two dozen of those written are listed in the archives. They cover many different topics—labor, press freedom, the Palestine situation, Soviet-American relations, among others. Many are short, several are humorous, others were submitted in handwriting, but the biggest surprise is to learn that some of AHS's offerings were not used and some were even rejected by the page's editor!

How do you say no to the man who owns the paper? Bluntly. AHS's editorial, submitted on January 9, 1961, was attached to a note gently requesting its publication. Merz's response was almost brutally frank, probably more direct than those he sent to unfamiliar applicants. The editorial did not run.

This relationship endured even with differences of opinion that were more literary and strategic than questions of outlook. There is even a plaintive note from AHS to Charlie, in 1950: "I have got a bone to pick with you. I sent you a little two paragraph editorial before you left which you apparently didn't care to use, but don't you think I ought to at least have gotten a rejection slip?"

At the level of the publishing family, there was no lack of debate on editorial policy. The ranks of older generations, vacated by seniors, were filled by aging juniors who went through the same process of putting their juniors in their place. In 1959, AHS, in a note, told Orvil E. Dryfoos, his son-in-law: "Yesterday you were complaining about our editorial page. Please read today's with care and tell me what's wrong." Dryfoos replied in a confidential message: "What is our position on the steel strike other than it should be settled?"

"As you'll note, I have written on the attached, 'What is yours?' But I'd like to add, do you expect us to take a position on everything? Gosh, that's an awful thought," AHS responded.

Dryfoos came back with his ideas and another question about the Pacific Fleet on the coast of China and concluded, "Sorry to be so lengthy, but I think you have stirred me up."

In the final word, AHS told Dryfoos:

Personally, I don't know enough about the manufacturing of steel to take a position between the two sides. My inclination is to side with the employer because of some of the sad union experiences we've had here. . . . I feel that we are being very tolerant in not taking the industry's side as our own.

As to China and the Seventh Fleet, I disagree with you one hundred per cent. . . . And I wouldn't admit China to the U.N. until they have purged themselves or at least until Chiang Kai-shek is dead.

So maybe you're just as happy that we don't take such strong positions!

A year later, with Dryfoos being groomed to become publisher, AHS observed in a note about an editorial that the young man felt deserved better:

But cheer up—a little more than twenty-five years ago I used to come home to Mother sick at heart about The Times's editorial position, and then I'd suddenly perk up and say, "Well, I don't suppose I really ought to complain because when your Father dies, he's going to leave such a magnificent newspaper that it will be quite impossible for me to show any improvement except perhaps in the editorial page and I can make that more positive." Now, you're going to have the same chance when I'm no longer here so, as I said, cheer up!

Among my first published writings in *The Times* were editorials I composed while still a copyboy. A copyboy writing editorials for the most powerful expression of opinion on the paper? The editorials I and others of my caste submitted did not tackle seminal issues of the world. During the Christmas season, an editorial was mandated daily to draw attention to the Neediest Cases campaign.

Perhaps it was too much to ask one member of the board to wring the last drop of emotion out of a typewriter every day. But the Neediest Cases proved to be a helpful vehicle for strivers. Editorials were not signed and I do not recall any inquiries about the author of my brilliantly short appeals to the pockets of the readers, but the department did pay $15 when they were accepted. In the off-season, there was always the possibility of selling another short on the changing season and the joys of birds/flowers/sunshine/snow.

Like the rest of the paper, the editorial page of *The New York Times* has changed radically since the newspaper was founded, but it still has a look that distinguishes it from any other section. The editorials now are arrayed in two wide columns, far less forbidding-looking than they used to be in narrower precincts, to the left of three thinner columns devoted to Letters to the Editor. Until this profile emerged in 1970, the page had for a dozen years also featured a Topics column and a columnist's regular contribution.

The Facts collation in the archives has a summary of "unusual" editorials in *The Times* from the outset of the Ochs era. Among them are marathon editorials, like the six-column summation on President Cleveland's record, March 2, 1897, the ten-part editorial commenting on the State of the Union, on January 7, 1955, and the editorial written in Latin on June 1, 1962, that was commentary in its very wordage when the classical language was dropped as a public-school course.

The Topics column made its debut in *The Times* on March 16, 1867, a day-brightener that relied on good writing or philosophical outlook to lighten the burden of the day's news for readers. "The column was inspired by the first publisher, winked on and off thereafter, and revived by Adolph S. Ochs almost as soon as he became publisher in 1896," Herbert Mitgang wrote in the introduction of *America at Random,*\* a volume of columns that appeared in Topics, which Mitgang describes as the oldest editorial feature of the paper. First appearing under the rubric "Minor Topics," it was among Ochs's first interests. In 1926, Simeon Strunsky emerged as its principal contributor and eventually was its only one from 1932 to 1947. Strunsky was an incredibly versatile writer, described in a letter from Brooks Atkinson to Mitgang (upon publication of the book) as "an intellectual with a sense of humor—an almost impossible combination."

After that, it was written by various people, among them myself. Like editorials, it was a golden, if unsigned, opportunity to write on a much-read page. Topics was longer than an editorial and could be on any sort of theme that lent itself to well-phrased, probably whimsical musing. The articles were fun to write and they were, at least for me, inspired by any random thought or any aspect of New York living that invaded the imagination. And they paid $25 a column for Topics, or more than a week's pay for copyboys at that time. Later, when it was nestled in a prime position at the top right corner of the page, above the letters column, the rate was more than tripled, the column was signed, and the attention received by the writer was much more satisfactory.

In the early 1960s, the column, now formally called Topics, was relegated to a once-a-week frequency and today survives, marginally, as a title over an occasional short editorial.

## "YOU"—THE OP-ED PAGE

As John Oakes recalls it, the idea for the Op-Ed page in *The New York Times* came from an article that couldn't be used. Oakes, a nephew of Ochs, had not yet been made editor of the editorial page, which he became in 1961, but he was on the board. A friend sent him a piece that he liked very much but "it was too long for a letter, too short for

---

\* *America at Random*, edited, with an Introduction on the Journalistic Essay, by Herbert Mitgang (Coward-McCann, 1969). Mitgang, who had left *The Times*, where he had been an editor and writer in the Sunday Department, and went to CBS News, where he was deputy executive editor and assistant to the president, was brought to the editorial board by Oakes. He also edited Topics and was continued on the board as deputy editor of the Op-Ed page.

a magazine piece." He advised the friend to try it somewhere else, and "to my distress, I saw it in place in the *Herald Tribune*, where they could publish an article of that length."

He was outraged that *The Times* had no room for such things. When he assumed editorship of the page, he recalled in a conversation, he spoke to Orvil E. Dryfoos. Dryfoos had become publisher and, on the same day that he assumed office, Oakes had started in on his new job heading the page of opinion. He suggested to Dryfoos that an Op-Ed page be located opposite the editorial page, on a page which until then had carried the obituary news. The name Op-Ed, he said, was possibly in his memory because it was the name of a page in the old New York *World*. Herbert Bayard Swope, the *World*'s editor, filled the page with articles by columnists, not outsiders, so the Oakes concept was original even if the name might not have been.

Oakes's idea was to open the space to all sorts of ideas expressed by people outside *The Times*. It was not Op in the sense that they would be replying to editorials, although that, too, would be part of it. Dryfoos liked the idea, but said to "put it on ice" because AHS would not stand to see the obits shunted off elsewhere. Punch Sulzberger, after he became publisher and AHS was no longer on the scene, liked Oakes's concept but it still did not fly at once. There were some meetings and Punch appointed a study group of editors and executives. Oakes remembers that the idea was warmly received, except by the News Department. The third floor, he later learned from the publisher, felt that the new page would be under the Editorial Department's control (which is what happened) and was not enthusiastic about giving up the space. Oakes was so intent on making the Op-Ed page live, he offered to relinquish control should that be necessary.

In addition to making room for outside observations, Oakes wanted to get the *Times* columnists onto the new page from the editorial page, where they had long been a fixture. He wanted more room for the popular letters column and also he felt that being on another page would prevent the comments of columnists from being confused by readers with the opinion of *The Times* itself. He himself had always regarded the columnists as such independent entities that he never read the copy they turned in.*

---

* His only demurrer was that ads did not belong there any more than they did on the editorial page. But economics dictated that he comply with the wishes of the publisher for the small ad that appears on the page's lower right-hand corner.

The Op-Ed page made its debut on September 21, 1970, nearly a decade after it had been proposed. That first page carried an institutional ad by U.S. Steel. On the facing page was an editorial flaying the steel company for what it was doing.

"That delighted me," Oakes recalled.

The page's first editor, under Oakes, was Harrison E. Salisbury, up from the third floor to the editorial tenth, a crack correspondent who had represented the cautiousness of the newsroom in the talks leading to the Op-Ed (it was a question of space, fear in the News Department that a new feature would take a page away from the daily news coverage). With Mitgang as deputy, Salisbury set about opening the page to the widest diversity of opinion, soliciting pieces from leading figures in every area of American life which supplemented those from lesser-knowns whose humor, anger, analyses, and indignation turned Op-Ed 180 degrees from the style and position of *Times* editorials.

### POETRY

*The Times,* truth to tell, has always gone heavy on prose. But it had always leavened its declarative sentences with verse. Newspapers printed poems throughout the 1800s, but it was only in 1905 that poetry found a home regularly on the *Times*'s editorial page, where it flourished until 1973. Frederick Craig Mortimer, who had done the same for the Topics column in 1896, originated the custom of a daily poem on the page on January 1, 1905. Among the poets whose work he chose for the page were Rudyard Kipling, Alice Duer Miller, and Henry Van Dyke.

In 1932, newspapers, like everything else, were being told in mournful numbers that the Great Depression was at center stage. A *Times* executive, Rollo Ogden, told Ochs that it would be a mistake to cut down on poetry.

"No feature of the editorial page brings more letters," he wrote. "It is a kind of traditional obeisance to literature which The Times has long made and which would be wondered at if it were discontinued."

Ochs replied that it was the cost of staffing, not the price of poetry, that bothered him. "I presume the poetry on the editorial page serves some purpose," he wrote. "Certainly it is useful in its flexibility so far as make-up is concerned. I confess, however, that my educational equipment leaves me far short of a proper appreciation of most of that which we publish under this heading."

There is poetic justice that poetry's last flare-up in the pages of *The Times,* where it would be evicted from the editorial page on March 16, 1973, was inspired by the man in the moon. "Men Walk on the Moon" said the headline, July 27, 1969. At the lower left of page 1 was "Voyage to the Moon," a poem by Archibald MacLeish specially commissioned by *The Times.*

# CROSSWORDS, BRIDGE, CHESS, AND . . . CARTOONS?

### CROSSWORDS

There are those who reckon the revolutions in publishing by the invention of the printing press, the introduction of the Linotype, and the eradication of pen, pencil, and typewriter by the computer. As for me, I date the revolution in publishing at *The New York Times* from February 15, 1942, with the publication of its first crossword puzzle.

It was an otherwise dismal moment in world history. The Axis powers dominated Europe, were entrenched in North Africa, and were flooding over East Asia. It seemed perhaps eccentric, to say the least, that this period found *The Times* fretting over its own historic break with tradition. A crossword puzzle? It is typical of *The Times* that it putters over small features with the same dead earnestness it bestows on major issues. In this case, the emergence of the Sunday puzzle into the pages of the *Sunday Magazine* section was directly related to the war that was raging on page 1.

The crossword, which several influential *Times* editors had opposed—a dilution of *The Times*'s news brew, neat with no chasers—is today the most prominent crossword in America. It has become, like its container, an institution, much beloved by those it most vexes, the puzzlers, but an institution that, again like *The Times* itself, must constantly struggle against institutional fossilization.

I have never been a drinker, and so was never to be found across 43rd Street in a bar during working hours. But I am a puzzler, and over the years, where others might play cards on company time, I did crosswords. The Joycean flow of disconnected vocabulary sweeping across or down brought a certain peace to my mind, which was making its living by tying words together in meaningful union.

*The Times* had little patience with this novelty, the crossword, when it burst upon the world, appropriately enough in the *World,* in 1913, the brainchild of Arthur Wynne. His simple word whimsy was a pushover, answers like "are" ("the plural of is") and "face" ("part of your head"), yet the contraption caught on immediately and spread to the remotest corners of the globe, wherever newspapers were published.

In 1923, young Julius Ochs Adler, managing the store with AHS during Ochs's absence, wrote to his uncle: "The idea of a crossword puzzle has met with hearty approval on all sides with the exception of Mr. Markel who thinks that The Times would be trading with the other newspapers in instituting such a department and secondly that it would be a departure from 'strictly news.' Of course these arguments are good but do not overcome the balance in favor of such a department. However, that is of course something for you to decide on your return."

The thumbs-down decision was buttressed in an editorial a year later, in which the prevalence of crosswords was deplored as "a primitive form of mental exercise." *The Times* predicted the attraction would soon disappear. Eighteen years later, *The Times* became one of the last newspapers to surrender to the crossword.

It says something about the nature of influence that *The Times,* completely uninfluential in extirpating the crossword, turned around and made its puzzle the most influential in the land. It was a diversion in this sobersided journal of record, but its readers, like the paper, treated it with the same attention they focused on an Arthur Krock analysis of what was wrong with Washington.

The origins of the crossword in *The Times* have rarely been investigated. It's not, after all, the Pentagon Papers. But as an instance of how *The Times* gets to be what it is, the story is instructive, particularly because it illustrates how individuals have always made a difference at *The Times.*

The individual who paved the way for the crossword was almost certainly AHS, who was reported to have been long chagrined at the need to buy the *Herald Tribune* to do a crossword. But the first relevant document in *The Times* archives is a memo dated December 18, 1941, less than two weeks after the bombing of Pearl Harbor. It was addressed to AHS and was written by no less a former adamantly anti-puzzle figure than Lester Markel, whose fascination with solutions for the cosmos did not seem to extend to this type of puzzle. Now, in this note, he conceded that, considering what was going on in the world, the crossword merited space. He referred to a number of meetings with Margaret Farrar, one of the pioneers of across-and-down, and reported on his conclusions.

December 18, 1941

Mr. Sulzberger:

We have had a number of meetings with Mrs. Farrar on the cross word puzzle thing, and she has prepared several samples, one of which was worked out by Mr. Merz. After this exploration, I am convinced of these things:

1. That we ought to proceed with the puzzle, especially in view of the fact that it is possible that there will now be bleak black-out hours--or if not that, then certainly a need for relaxation of some kind or other. (That, in turn, raises the question of whether we ought not to have a cross word puzzle in the daily also--but that's a different story.)

2. That we ought not to try to do anything essentially different from what is now being done--except to do it better.

I attach a memorandum from Mrs. Farrar which sums up her conclusions.

Shall we proceed?

L. Markel

Attached was a memo from Farrar:

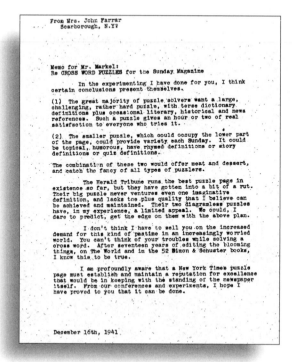

The next day, AHS took a vote on it from an electorate of two, Charles Merz, editor of the editorial page, and Edwin L. James, the managing editor. He sent them Markel's memo and Farrar's note and asked:

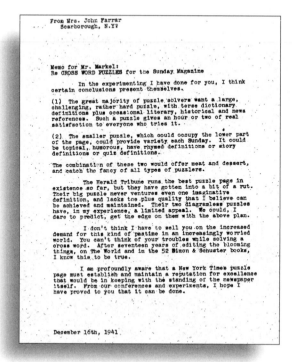

The publisher did not include himself in the balloting but there is every indication that his own vote outweighed whatever votes the other two cast. For on February 15, 1942, the crossword puzzle took its place in the pages of *The New York Times* and soon became as indispensable an element as the weather, market reports, and columns reporting the arrival of steamships. Although it remained as a Sunday-only feature until 1950, when it went daily and makeup editors had to learn something new: never place it on a page where it would be split inconveniently in two by readers who had learned to fold *The Times* in the approved mass-transit way—in half, lengthwise.

Readers were subjected to no suspense at all in waiting to see how *The Times* would go about preserving its austere news-only profile while giving it a face-lift of entertainment in the form of a puzzle. As though to reassure readers who might be shocked, the puzzle, by Charles Erlenkotter, was the first of hundreds supervised by Farrar, who had wisely been selected as the first puzzle editor at the paper. It was titled "Headlines and Footnotes." There was a war going on and that first crossword picked its teasers from the headlines. Definition: "Famous one-eyed general." Answer (in six letters): "Wavell," the British general of Western Desert fame. Diversion, perhaps, but not far enough off course to let one forget the news for a few blank squares across or down.

The puzzle's establishment was an instant success, not least with AHS and Charles Merz. They competed with each other in solving speed and they even constructed puzzles. By that June, they themselves made news, modestly, but worthy of mention, as puzzle constructors in their own right.

There have been four puzzle editors at *The Times,* and each has placed a very personal stamp on the crossword. Margaret Farrar, who launched the puzzle, had been something of a midwife at the very birth of crosswords, and she set standards that still guide *Times* puzzlemakers today.

She was succeeded by Will Weng, a congenial, soft-spoken midwesterner who had been head of the paper's metropolitan copy desk and who injected a broad streak of humor and unorthodox orthography during his incumbency, from 1969 to 1977. When I was a copyboy clerking at the City Desk, I sat opposite Will Weng. He was usually engrossed in either solving or creating a crossword and seemed genuinely put out when news interfered with his preoccupation. I was mildly surprised when I learned that the man whose

This is the first crossword puzzle published in *The New York Times*, on Sunday, February 15, 1942.

*Times* life had been dedicated to clarifying the paper by carrying out the commandments on *Times* style had been appointed to a job whose purpose was to confuse readers.

Weng was succeeded by Eugene T. Maleska, poet, former superintendent of schools in the East Bronx, and a leading authority on the crossword-puzzle art. It was Maleska who devised the famous (or infamous, depending on your taste) thread of connected words known as the stepquote, a quotation that cascades through the puzzle, usually from upper left to lower right.

To fashion the orthographic jungle gym that is a crossword puzzle, one must have the talents of a poet and punster—limited only by the bounds of a good standard dictionary—and a willingness to keep it clean and tactful. Will Weng said that he never used "tan" as the response to a clue that mentioned the result of sunbathing because he felt that the answer would be meaningless to darker-skinned solvers. Among the many precedents established by Margaret Farrar was the avoidance of the mention of diseases; the closest it gets is the perennial puzzle placebo, "acne."

The trick of a puzzle, of course, is not so much in the word that is the answer as it is in the definition. It matters little that the answer is "ira" if you can't pin down the definition, "name from Hebrew for 'watchful,'" "retirement account," "insular insurgency faction." Addicted solvers absorb the style of a puzzle, sense the response of its queries after an apprenticeship with it. They then either revel in their ability to tear through a puzzle in record time or lament that it is much too easy. When the new puzzle editor takes over, the solvers have to adjust to new channels of thought and for many it is a disruption of a comfortable pattern. When Will Weng took over, some readers found his style too frivolous. By the time he had—justly—become beloved by thousands of solvers, he retired. The new editor, Gene Maleska, was criticized for being too academic, but readers also eventually fell into a Maleska mode. When Gene Maleska died in 1993, Will Shortz became crossword editor and fostered his own revolutionary brand of puzzle, an even more radical break with the past in the acceptance of brand names as answers.

All of *The New York Times* Sunday puzzles have themes, sometimes a season or an event or a word-trick that will eliminate a letter of an alphabet or substitute a symbol such as a heart in certain boxes. *The Times* is generally and sourly anti-pun in its other wordage but puns flourish merrily and outrageously in the puzzle. If there is any stricture at all, it is, don't be stodgy.

The puzzle can also be a thriving arena for culture clash. One summer weekend, I was doing the Saturday puzzle when a downword, seven letters, ineluctably emerged as "schmuck," as response to the definition, "oaf." I almost reeled at the appearance of a Yiddish vulgarism, meaning the male sex organ, in the pages of *The New York Times,* when the most liberal editor would not allow it in a column of the Jewish *Daily Forward.* At the office, I mentioned it to Abe Rosenthal, who suggested sensibly that rather than make a federal case of it, I speak to Will Weng, who had not been the incumbent puzzle editor long. I did, rather embarrassedly. . . . Yes, he replied in evident confusion, he was surprised at the reaction. He had had several telephone calls from solvers. But, said Weng, in the best *Times* tradition he had checked it out and he showed me a standard dictionary in which the word was defined as an oaf or foolish person. A good definition in American English where TV comics had planted it, perhaps, but not printable in New York, where Yiddish terms were part of the city's lingua franca.

AHS, having established the crossword, was one of its most diligent followers and one of its keenest and most persistent critics. As much as anything in the paper, the puzzle page—crossword and other brain-bashers—reacted to the publisher's billets-doux.

AHS to Turner Catledge, 1956: "I am told that our daily crossword puzzles are too hard and I'm wondering if there is any record on the third floor from readers to this effect. I got into the habit of doing them when my eyes got bad and I wasn't able to read consistently and I am perfectly willing to admit that they're toughies. On the other hand, what's the purpose of the puzzle?"

Catledge's response: "There is no record down here that our readers think our crossword puzzles are too difficult. We receive an occasional complaint that our definitions are sometimes vague, but nothing that would indicate a consensus of opinion."

AHS to Mrs. Farrar, 1957: "I hate to tell you this again but I think some of the definitions on the daily puzzles are pretty hard to take. I've been away for four weeks and have been doing them quite religiously. Faithfully yours . . ."

Farrar's reply: "Your note hits home. I had already issued a warning to myself that the definitions were taking on a Charles Van Doren aura—this is insidious and I promise to guard against it." (Charles Van Doren was a star contestant on the television quiz show *Twenty-One,* just before he and it were revealed as having inside knowledge of the answers.)

AHS to Mrs. Farrar, 1958: "In the puzzle today you had the definition 'jungle rover' and it turned out to be 'lion.' But the lion does not live in the jungle—it lives in the veldt. I looked it up and found 'It (the lion) is not the inhabitant of deep forests but rather of the open plains.' "

Robert E. Garst, an assistant managing editor, to Catledge, 1958: "On this crossword-puzzle business, I have done these for a week and reached the conclusion that very few of the definitions are extreme, and only occasionally is one so bad as to be annoying. I am sure this is what the Publisher has run into, such as the one he cited yester-

```
                              Nov. 23, 1977
Memo for Ed Klein:

    A scrutiny of the puzzles over the last two weeks
leaves me wondering why there should any serious exception
taken to them.  The puzzles themselves, daily and Sunday,
are of excellent quality, so the only issue could be some
of the definitions.  It was mentioned that the puzzles were
generally found too easy.  My personal appraisals are these:

        Daily puzzles:  Fairly hard to hard    5
                        Medium                 4
                        Easy                   1

        Sunday puzzles:
                    Risteen        Fairly difficult
                    Micci          Tricky and challenging
                    Canning        Difficult

    On the daily puzzles I find the mixture of difficulty
about right.  And the Sunday puzzles all passed muster.
    The chief thing I note that might cause annoyance
to solvers is the liberal use of literary references to
define simple words, thus "Your bonny ⊢—⊣ was brent:
Burns."  Answer:  Brow.  I don't think Times solvers
want or need to be enlightened on unfamiliar literature,
and might even feel they were being talked down to by a
professorial editor.  In this case the editor could easily
                                               though,
be asked to cut down on such references.  In many cases, they
are needed in defining word combinations.
    As for asking that the puzzle definitions be made
harder, I would suggest standing pat for the time being
and see if the storm subsides.  I have found that frustrated
solvers tend to brand the puzzles as too hard or too easy
rather than pinpoint certain specifics that bug them.
    If harder puzzles are asked for, either daily or
Sunday, there is the danger that they will be made too hard,
with a resulting dropout of many people in the solving ranks.
For the present I think a de-emphasis of the literary
aspect might go a long way toward clearing things up.

                                        Will Weng
```

A note from Will Weng to Ed Klein, then editor of the *Sunday Magazine,* clarifies the constant debate over what is hard and what is easy.

## CROSSWORD SPECIFICATIONS — THE NEW YORK TIMES

The New York Times looks for intelligent, literate, entertaining and well-crafted crosswords that appeal to the broad range of Times solvers.

Themes should be fresh, interesting, narrowly defined and consistently applied throughout the puzzle. If the theme includes a particular kind of pun, for example, then all the puns should be of that kind. Themes and theme entries should be accessible to everyone. (Themeless daily puzzles using wide-open patterns are also welcome.)

Constructions should emphasize lively words and names and fresh phrases. We especially encourage the use of phrases from everyday writing and speech, whether or not they're in the dictionary. For variety, try to include some of the lesser-used letters of the alphabet—J, Q, X, Z, K, W, etc. Brand names are acceptable if they're well-known nationally and you use them in moderation.

The clues in an ideal puzzle provide a well-balanced test of vocabulary and knowledge, ranging from classical subjects like literature, art, classical music, mythology, history, geography, etc., to modern subjects like movies, TV, popular music, sports and names in the news. Try to conjure up mental images with your clues as often as possible. Puns and humor are welcome.

Avoid at all costs: long partial phrases (OF LA MANCHA, A STITCH IN, etc.), uncommon abbreviations, little-known foreign words and uncommon prefixes and suffixes. Keep crosswordese and uninteresting obscurity to a minimum. Difficult words are fine—especially for the harder daily puzzles that get printed late in the week—if the words are inter-esting bits of knowledge or useful additions to the vocabulary. However, never let two obscure words cross.

Maximum word counts: 78 words for a 15x15 (72 for an unthemed 15); 140 for a 21x21; 170 for a 23x23. Maximums may be exceeded slightly, at the editor's discretion, if the theme warrants.

DIAGRAMLESS, CRYPTICS, ETC.

For diagramlesses, follow the style as shown on the Sunday puzzle page. Puns 'n' anagrams and cryptics are done by assignment only.

FORMAT

Use regular typing paper ($8\frac{1}{2}$" x 11"). Type the clues double-spaced on the left (no periods after the numbers), answer words in a corresponding column on the far right. Give a source for any hard-to-verify word or information. Down clues need not begin on a new page. Include a filled-in answer grid with numbers *and* a blank grid with numbers (for the editor's test-solving). Put your name, address and social security number on the two grid pages, and your name on all other pages. Send to:

Will Shortz, Crossword Editor
The New York Times
229 West 43d St.
New York, NY 10036
Please include a stamped return envelope for reply.

PAYMENT

$60 for a daily; $225 for a Sunday; $100 for a novelty puzzle

Each editor of the puzzles in *The Times* has issued a list of minimum specifications and rules for puzzle constructors. This one was created by Will Shortz in 1994.

day in which the word 'where' meant 'in what respect?' That is far fetched but you can twist your mind enough to make it fit the definition. As I say, these are only occasional, and we could go through the motions of suggesting to Mrs. Farrar that more care be taken to avoid extreme definitions. I note that the Publisher says he has been having correspondence with her. I dare say he has made these suggestions, too."

Garst to Francis A. Cox (in 1960, treasurer of *The Times*), in reply to a complaint about the daily puzzle's placement: "The only answer we can give to complaints of this sort is that wherever we place the crossword puzzle in the papers, or any other feature of the kind, it backs up on material that some other reader would like to clip and send to a friend. For many years the puzzle has been put on the book page and the book page has always backed up on the editorial page, and we feel this is proper classification. The one effort we do make is to put the puzzle at the bottom of the first two columns so that it backs up on Letters to the Editor, sometimes the poem and on the list of our offices. This seems to us to be as harmless as we can achieve. Just privately, I am surprised anyone would want to clip one of those poems and send it anywhere."

From E. Roland Harriman, president of the American Red Cross, to his friend, "Dear Arthur," 1953: "Imagine my chagrin when doing the Times crossword puzzle a couple of weeks ago when I came across a three-letter definition 'The G.I.'s favorite organization.' Of course I immediately filled it in with 'ARC' only to find when I did the verticals that 'USO' were the correct initials. This of course, is written in a facetious vain [*sic*] but I thought then that even the great New York Times makes a slip once in awhile [*sic*]."

AHS's reply to Harriman: "Even crossword puzzles can be editorial and this particular one takes a wrong point of view! The editor has had his wrist slapped."

For veteran puzzlers, those who reject any reference help as well as those who plod through mounds of dictionaries and atlases, the institution of a 900 number for puzzle help seemed a sad surrender to the new age of no-sweat computer solutions. If you don't have to work at it, why do it at all, the line ran. But there was another line, the bottom one. A high executive casually remarked that in a period of diminished revenue, the dial-a-puzzle was one of the few *Times* ventures producing a profit at the moment.

## BRIDGE

Bridge, the most cerebral of card games, naturally was the chosen pastime of many *Times* readers. It was also one of the longer-running pastimes in the third-floor newsroom, but it did not draw kibitzers, as the larger, noisier poker sessions did. The players were reporters, obviously deeper thinkers than the hunch-playing poker crowd. The reporters took the game as seriously as they did their assignments, sometimes, it appeared, even more so. One front-desk reporter was in the habit of writing a page, calling for a copyboy, then returning to complete the silent foursome for another rubber before writing the next page. Deadlines were later in those days, the late 1940s.

According to the invaluable *Times* Facts book in the archives, "In the early 1900s, Florence Irwin was *The Times*'s auction-bridge editor. A regular bridge column started in 1935 in the Sunday Drama Section, and on July 6, 1959, in the daily issues." Albert H. Morehead presided over the bridge column from its start through 1963, when he resigned and handed it over to Alan Truscott.

The idea of a daily bridge column, proposed by Morehead in May 1946, is an example of the dual nature of *The Times*. It can move like lightning to cover the news and like molasses to modify its format and contents.

"I think that the apparent interest in the recent reports of bridge tournaments may make this a proper time for us to discuss a daily bridge story, to start, perhaps, around September 1," he wrote to Edwin L. James, then managing editor.

A few days later, AHS asked Lester Markel if he favored running a daily crossword in the paper. Markel answered, "I should say that the day we put in daily cross-word puzzles, we should also include a bridge column. They belong, in my mind, to the same category." But the daily bridge column did not make the paper until nine years after the daily crossword made its successful debut.

In 1958, assistant managing editor Garst sent a series of memos to city editor Frank S. Adams about a note favoring bridge space (Adams as reporter had been one of the bridge regulars) and one memo summed up managing editor Catledge's attitude: "His view at the moment is that there is enough going on now in the way of current matches to supply our needs. I think he wants bridge in the paper more frequently, so we might keep a close eye on the better tournaments. His ultimate aim is, I think, a daily bridge column, but that may be hard to sell and I think he will be satisfied with more frequent stories rather than a daily column."

That assessment was not altogether on the mark. Pressures mounted for *The Times* to span the daily bridge gap. In 1959, a steel company executive wrote to AHS: "*The New York Times* is the greatest and most complete newspaper in the world—by an incredible margin—yet in one department it is inadequate. Although a very large percentage of your readers are Bridge players you have no daily Bridge column like most other New York papers. I know some people who buy the TRIB [*sic*] and even the NEWS in preference to the TIMES for that reason. My friends and I think the introduction of a GOOD daily Bridge column, like Gorens [*sic*] for instance, would be a much appreciated additional service and would gain you more readers."

One month later, Catledge reported to AHS: "We have made arrangements to begin our daily bridge column with the issue of Monday, July 6. It is to be done by Mr. Albert Morehead, who is regarded by the bridge experts on The Times as perhaps the best man in the bridge-writing business. He has been writing our Sunday column for a number of years and is highly regarded by Mr. Markel and his associates."

The mechanics of the column were spelled out in a memo by Frank Adams. Morehead would write six contract-bridge columns a week, every week, for $180, on a contractual basis—which meant that he was not a *Times* employee, but with subsidiary benefits: he would get expenses paid for three national tournaments a year and for the international tournament in every other year. Copy would be filed at least twenty-four hours before publication, except when he was covering a "current tournament." Stories, including headline, would run two-thirds of a column each. Turner Catledge suggested that in Morehead's coverage of a major tournament "the illustrative hand and comment should appear in the column, but the progress of the tournament, including the names of the winners, etc., should be covered in a separate sidebar, which Mr. Morehead will provide."

It would all run under a two-column headline, "Contract Bridge," with a bank beneath the head "describing some point of interest in the current column."

The feeling that serious bridge players were also serious *Times* readers seemed to be justified. In 1962, Morehead, in his twenty-eighth year as bridge columnist, reported that the response was "steadily enthusiastic." He received thirty to forty letters each week, a number that had doubled once the column started to appear in both the Sunday and the daily paper.

## CHESS

The time and thought that go into a move in chess were mirrored somewhat in the consideration of a chess column by *The Times*. The game was moderately popular among those who worked there, at least those on the third floor, where work went in spurts, like the routine at a firehouse or a lunch counter, and there were intervals of idleness in between. Some rewritemen and clerks, either too lofty or too impecunious to sit in on poker, also genteelly maneuvered on the board. In later years, the advent of computers to the newsroom prompted the inauguration of electronic chess among many staffers.

Still, in the early 1950s, *The Times*, corporately, was not particularly interested in the game. A letter from Lessing J. Rosenwald, the philanthropist, to his friend, "Dear Arthur," brought a reply from AHS:

> Dear Lessing,
> I am sorry to report that after checking both the Sunday and the daily departments of The New York Times, we have come to the conclusion that we would not wish to have a man reporting on chess exclusively.
> By the same token, we do not wish to purchase a syndicated column. So I am afraid your suggestion is out.

AHS really *did* respond to outside requests and suggestions and he *had* canvassed his people. Sunday editor Lester Markel had advised him, on March 24, 1953:

> I do not think we ought to add any departments to the Sunday paper at this time.
> If we are going to add any space to the Drama section, we ought to add a general hobby department which would have much more circulation. That also involves adding space, of which I am informed we are very leery these days.
> P.S. As a matter of fact, chess for some unknown reason has always been covered on the sports page.

Markel held to his position even two years later, in a note to Orvil Dryfoos, in which he said he had had "the chess business analysed" and did not feel there was enough interest to justify a weekly column.

Even so—other times, other *Times*. On April 16, 1962, a chess column began its long run as a feature in the Sunday paper and irregularly in the daily, under the signature of Al Horowitz, who presided over it until the 1970s, when he was succeeded by Robert Byrne. In anticipation of all of this, the paper set about retiring the man who, as Markel had noted, had been covering chess in the Sports Department.

Clifton Daniel, assistant managing editor, sent a memo to Catledge:

> Confirming my verbal outline to you, Jimmy Roach [sports editor] recommends that The New York Times terminate the part-time employment of Hermann Helms as our chess correspondent and put him on a retainer of $50 a week to supply us with soccer results and certain other minor sports information. Mr. Helms, as you know, is now 92 years old and has been a contributor to this newspaper on a part-time basis for the last 52 years. We are in the process of retaining a replacement for him as chess correspondent. Mr. Helms is delighted with the arrangement we propose to make with him.

The next day, Adams wrote to I. A. (Al) Horowitz, of the *Chess Review*, that *The Times* would like him to start writing about chess, with two columns a week for the daily, each two-thirds of column long, and a two-column Sunday article, plus daily coverage of important international tournaments. *The Times* would have exclusive rights. The Sunday column would appear in the Drama Section, bidding farewell to its old home in Sports.

Almost immediately after taking over, Horowitz reported that he had checkmated the market for chess readers. He had, within two months of starting, received more than 200 letters and 95 percent of them favored the column. He was thinking about running one puzzler that would not offer a solution and would invite readers to send in their solutions. This would indicate the volume of readership. Of course, he was new at the job and didn't yet realize that the surefire way of gauging who's reading is to make an error in an article. But that's another story.

## CARTOONS, CARICATURES, AND COMICS

I like cartoons, caricatures, and comics, but like everyone else, I rarely went to *The Times* to find them. Nowadays, art illustration has infiltrated many sections of the newspaper, including full-page drawings in the style sections and symbolic sprawls keyed to Op-Ed essays, and funny little drawings accompany some letters to the editor. Political cartoons from other papers are a staple of the Week in Review. Generations of theatergoers have grown old in pursuit of "Nina"s embedded, as a tribute to his daughter,* in the caricatures of Al Hirschfeld.

The role of such artwork in *The New York Times* has not always been clearly defined or happily accepted by all of its authorities. Despite this, it has a long history in the paper's pages. On December 11, 1861, two of what may have been the first cartoons ever to appear in its pages harpooned James Gordon Bennett of the *The Herald,* the "enemy" in a circulation war. A page of political cartoons by Hy Mayer started in 1904 and appeared every week for ten years. On November 10, 1918, the day before the armistice ending World War I, a Mayer cartoon on page 3 depicting the abdication of the German emperor, Kaiser Wilhelm, may have been the first cartoon to accompany a news story in the daily paper.

Edwin Marcus, who first put pen to paper for *The Times* in January 1908, for many years did caricatures for the Sunday Drama Section. He later was editorial cartoonist until 1958, when he retired. As often (but with lamentable and notable exceptions) happened at *The Times,* age remained a bulwark against change; wait until attrition sets in and then we can do what we have wanted to do for a long time. A statement prepared by a Sunday section editor explained to the world what Marcus's withdrawal meant:

> The Times has decided not to try to replace Mr. Marcus as editorial cartoonist. When Mr. Marcus began drawing his

* This innovation set in after Nina's birth in 1943. By the time she was seven, in 1950, her hidden name was an institutionalized *Times* feature (in *Times* tradition), and the artist indicated in the space next to his signature how many Ninas were to be found in the caricature.

cartoon for The Times it was the illustration for a page of letters that appeared opposite the editorial every Sunday. In redesigning the sections of the Sunday paper some years ago, the letters were consolidated on the editorial page itself and the science and school departments were given the

**DECEMBER 11, 1861.**

Brother Bennett ( Profanely Styled " the Satanic,") Inflating his Well-Known First-Class, A No. 1 Wind-Bag, Herald.

*From the Herald, Nov. 2.*

Whether the *Tribune* or the TIMES has the larger circulation, we are unable to decide. According to recent accounts, they *both of them distribute somewhere between* TWENTY-FIVE AND THIRTY THOUSAND *daily.*

Of this we are not certain. but concerning the *Herald.* THERE CAN BE NO DOUBT. *Its daily*

For a paper not generally associated with cartoons or caricatures, *The Times* has often shown illustrations on its pages. In 1861, a cartoon lampooned the *Herald*'s James Gordon Bennett.

THE NEW YORK TIMES, SUNDAY, NOVEMBE

Citizen Hohenzollern---"Where Do We Go from Here?"

Hy Mayer's cartoon of the abdication of Kaiser Wilhelm on November 10, 1918, may have been the first to accompany a story in the daily news report.

opposite editorial page. Mr. Marcus, who was a valued member of the staff, was continued and his cartoon appeared on the education-science page.

The Times always felt that space should have been used to illustrate one of the departments but in deference to Mr.

Marcus' long and useful service, his cartoon continued to appear. With his retirement, The Times is doing what it has believed for many years was the logical thing to do, that is, it is illustrating the departments that appear on the page.

For all of its reluctance to create its own political cartoons, *The Times* continued to sift through the press of the world in search of its cartoon observations, several of which appeared Sundays in the Week in Review. In a long memo to AHS in 1964, Lester Markel suggested a reply to a reader who had apparently inquired about *Times* policy.

"The reason why The Times does not employ editorial cartoonists is this: We have always believed that our editorial position should be set out in a calm, reasoned, but always positive way," he wrote. "We do not believe that most issues can be dealt with in black or white terms. An editorial cartoon, on the other hand, if it is to be worth anything, must be simple and utterly definite. It is necessarily emotional rather than logical."

Markel went on to say that *The Times*'s philosophical statements must be expressed in words and added, "We do print cartoons from other newspapers in the belief that they represent various points of view in the country and should be put before our readers just as the editorial opinion of other newspapers is republished in The Times."

Those "other cartoonists" were not altogether happy about the reprint they were given in *The Times* and papers other than those they were created for. At a meeting of the National Cartoonists Society in 1959, Herbert L. Block, famous as Herblock, complained that some papers picked up such work free and "mutilated" them by such editorial croppings as those that made horizontals out of vertical cartoons. This report ignited a memo from Markel, who asked whether *The Times* was one of the newspapers guilty of such tinkering. A response from an editor said that out of the last dozen Herblock cartoons in the Sunday edition, four were changed "to a large degree," four were "slightly" altered, and four "remained pretty much the same."

What do you propose to do about it? Markel queried the editor in charge. The editor proposed to avoid changing the shape of cartoons, a policy that might prompt some changes in makeup of a page, but would be "preferable to opening ourselves to complaint."

When it comes to venerability, Al Hirschfeld is surely in the running for a record. Al started his acclaimed series of more than 3,000 theater caricatures in 1925 in *The New York Times,* with a drawing of Sir Harry Lauder, the British music-hall star. They still appear as of this writing, seventy years later, although, since the 1970s, not weekly on the front page of the Drama Section as they had for almost fifty years. (Later, for many years, his work was a staple of the Theater News column in the Weekend Section.) He made his preliminary sketches at performances, drawing on paper in his pocket.

His work was almost universally hailed, but publisher AHS was not a confirmed believer in the caricature medium. In a memo, written in 1954, he noted a conversation about the use of "cartoons" in the Sunday Drama Section. He thought he had worked out, he said, a system by which a photograph would always accompany a cartoon.

"The Herald Tribune yesterday had three photographs of The Caine Mutiny. If we had had two and the cartoon, or one and the cartoon, we would at least know what the people who play the roles are supposed to look like. I think a cartoon alone is meaningless."

For the next few years, the archives show, AHS complained about the way "cartoons" were used in the Drama Section. "What can I do to get rid of some of those cartoons which appear constantly?" he asked Markel plaintively in 1955. It is a credit to *The Times,* in a way, that even the publisher had difficulty in getting cut down, immediately, what everybody else considered an asset.

As for Al Hirschfeld, he has always retained his humor, even when he had a problem. Witness the letter to Markel on the opposite page.

(P.S. He got it.)

And now to comic strips. The only real comic strip ever to appear in *The Times* was "The Roosevelt Bears," heralded in the promotion reproduced here as "Wholesome Fun for Old and Young." It ran from January 7 to July 22, 1906, in the Sunday rotogravure section, and was the handiwork of Paul Piper. The strip chronicled the travels of two bears from Colorado to back East. The name "Roosevelt Bears" is not explained, but an educated guess might associate it with Teddy Roosevelt, the bear hunter, whose name lives on in teddy bears.

That was the first and last attempt to run a comic strip as a comic strip. Basically, Adolph Ochs was not enthusiastic about such frip-

Lester Markel Esq.,
New York Times
West 43rd Street
New York New York


Dear Lester;

    I should like more money for my drawings. The realization that I am not a member of a Union, I have no agent, no boodle from a loving relative awaits me, Foundations ask ME for gifts, in short..gevalt! It also occured to me that perhaps the Times management may never offer me a raise and so I make this belated request for myself.

    I was thrown into this mercenary mood by a check I received from the Times for my expenses to Philadelphia and return on a drama assignment. My bill for the day in Philly was $20.35. The accounting department in its infinite wisdom deducted .50 cents for 'meal disallowance' and forwarded to me the balance of $19.85. Needless to say, I have returned the offending draft with commendable restraint...offering no suggestion of ultimate disposal by shoving the promissory note up their alimentary canals.
It would be the height of folly to point out to these humorless drones that it was not my intention to rook the Times out of.50 cents. This knowledge gives me small comfort. I find it difficult to explain my sudden need for brooding darkly in corners, frustrated and furious..unhappy and sorry for myself...pride in my work no longer enough to satisfy my ego ..I take refuge in wife screaming and child yelling..even thought of shaving off my beard.

    To get back on the rational trolley would it not be possible for the Times to put up the extra fare.....
                        Your friend and mine,

May 30th 1962

## Wholesome Fun for Old and Young.

"Well, I guess that's going some."

### "THE ROOSEVELT BEARS"

I am told at THE NEW YORK TIMES office that unless the orders from newsdealers reach them to-day they cannot increase the supply of THE SUNDAY NEW YORK TIMES sent to any particular point. People everywhere are already talking about this newspaper feature; not simply in New York, but in every large city in the United States. A children's story as jolly and as clean and as stimulating as this should be *welcomed by every parent* in the country. "The Roosevelt Bears" are two fine fellows. They start from the mountains of Colorado and make a tour of the East. They ride on Pullman trains, eat in dining cars, stop at the best hotels and

have all kinds of good, wholesome fun. There is "something doing" every minute. The story is told in rollicking rhyme; just the kind of jingle that youngsters enjoy. Those who know something of newspaper printing know that extra editions of a Sunday paper cannot be gotten out till Saturday night orders. If you want to be sure of getting a copy place your order with the newsdealer or carrier **to-day**. Simply tell your newsdealer to-day to be sure to keep a copy for you or to deliver it at your home Sunday morning. Every copy will sell.

*Paul Piper.*

NOTE TO PARENTS: Children need pictures and stories. It is just as necessary to feed their imaginations with good food as it is to feed their bodies with good food. Here is a story full to the brim with adventure and fun, and crowded to the page limit with comical and entertaining picture, and at the same time clean and wholesome and elevating. It has been written for all the boys and girls of the United States. If you want to be very sure of getting the first installment (Jan. 7) place your order to-day for THE SUNDAY NEW YORK TIMES. If you need extra copies to send to distant points, order them in advance.

peries in a serious publication (although he sanctioned comics in the *Chattanooga Times*). Yet there erupted every once in a long while an urge to try something along a comic-strip line. In the first issues of the Living Section in 1976, a comic artwork on food made its appearance. In 1981, the use of a splashy mod comic strip to illustrate and explain information drew one bad review. It came from the publisher, Punch Sulzberger.

"Also, if somebody downstairs thinks that those 'comics' are funny, they must have something loose in their head. Sydney [Gruson, at that time a vice president] disagrees with me, but I think they're tacky," he wrote in a brief note that had the veto effect on fur-

ther moves in this direction—for a while. Fewer than ten years later, a cartoon strip by Garry Trudeau had become a regular visitor to the Op-Ed page.

Artwork has now carved a permanent niche in the shape of *The Times,* but as ever, it is still a question of balance.

# FOOD NEWS

U NTIL THE 1990s, Fernando's cart was a regular 4:30 P.M. visitor to the third floor. Fernando Rivera, with his stock of coffee, sandwiches, and not particularly tasty pastries, was as welcome in the newsroom as a Saint Bernard with a keg of brandy would be in the Alps. Drinking was a problem in the newspaper business, but snacking ran a close second, maybe even a first. Fernando's cart paved over the restlessness that afflicted those who had much to do and those who had little to do but were expecting something to drop any minute.

There was one other nibble-venue on the third floor that those in the know managed to pass by on the pretext of getting clips from the morgue. This was the patch of floor governed by Food News, the section in the jurisdiction of Family/Style News. On the counter alongside the corridor, the leftovers of delicacies sent to the department by supplicants for coverage were put out for the passersby. It could be a gourmet cheese, a new dietetic pretzel, pizza slabs from the Upper East Side, even ice cream. This was one of the most rewarding departments to walk past, and it was believed that serious dieting by the general staff set in after Food News and its cohorts moved to the fourth floor.

*The Times* covers food in all of its guises. It presents recipes. It runs stories about products, about the people who prepare food, and even about those who eat it. It reports on the politics of food and of its antithesis, famine and malnourishment. Its correspondents in the oddest corners of the globe write stories about unusual dining habits, strange foods, and diverse cookery.

As early as 1938, *The Times* had inaugurated a Food News of the Week as a Friday feature but it was not until pre–Pearl Harbor 1941 that it launched the regular Food News column, with news and recipes. The reception in the office was apparently one of mild dismay, that perennial old-hand nagging fear that *Times* standards were being sapped. It was not unlike the greeting, a little more than a year later, accorded the inauguration of the crossword puzzle. Both have now been enshrined in the structure of respectability in which *The Times* lives. A reminder of this is in the form of a telegram sent, jokingly, he said later, by Julius Ochs Adler, nephew of Adolph Ochs and the *Times*'s general manager, to publisher Arthur Hays Sulzberger.

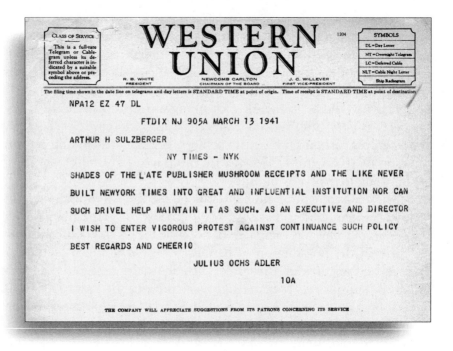

The best of friends have differences. In 1941, Julius Ochs Adler sent a telegram that kidded the new Food News coverage by *The Times*. AHS bristled and wrote a strong reply (shown opposite), but never sent it when he was assured that Adler's intentions were purely humorous.

There are good clues and straightforward statements that explain the evolution of the department. Robert E. Garst, an assistant managing editor, shed a little background on it in a memo, with reference to an expense account question, sent in 1953 to managing editor Turner Catledge, in which Garst referred to its start under the previous managing editor, Edwin L. James:

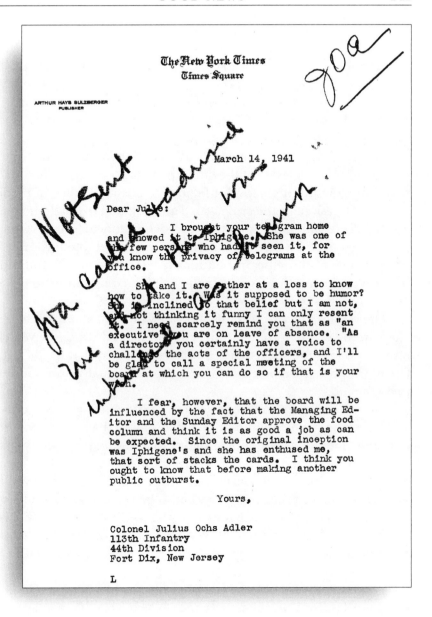

The New York Times
Times Square

ARTHUR HAYS SULZBERGER
PUBLISHER

March 14, 1941

Dear Julie:

I brought your telegram home
and showed it to Iphigene. She was one of
the few persons who had seen it, for
you know the privacy of telegrams at the
office.

She and I are rather at a loss to know
how to take it. Was it supposed to be humor?
She is inclined to that belief but I am not,
and not thinking it funny I can only resent
it. I need scarcely remind you that as "an
executive" you are on leave of absence. "As
a director" you certainly have a voice to
challenge the acts of the officers, and I'll
be glad to call a special meeting of the
board at which you can do so if that is your
wish.

I fear, however, that the board will be
influenced by the fact that the Managing Editor and the Sunday Editor approve the food
column and think it is as good a job as can
be expected. Since the original inception
was Iphigene's and she has enthused me,
that sort of stacks the cards. I think you
ought to know that before making another
public outburst.

Yours,

Colonel Julius Ochs Adler
113th Infantry
44th Division
Fort Dix, New Jersey

L

I think this business of covering restaurants in certain circumstances by Jane Nickerson started under Mr. James'
regime because, as you know, he was very much interested in
food, particularly in restaurants. I raised the question some
years ago, not on the basic idea of whether we should cover,

but on the basis of some of the unusual expense accounts turned in by Miss Nickerson. Mr. James said that was okay. I am inclined to agree that Mrs. French [then in charge of women's news] has a good point since many New Yorkers do eat in restaurants and food is food whether we eat it out or in the home.

The glamour job, the most-talked-about job in the Food Department, and often in terms of the entire paper, belonged to the restaurant critic, the point person for legions of gossipy diners, in media and out. Occasionally the critic issued an invitation to lunch. It made for a most elegant break from the sandwich routine. Here was an opportunity to test the best at no cost to yourself and to tell your dear one at home with the peanut butter that you were merely fulfilling your duty because the critic actually needed companions to check out the broadest possible menu offerings.

The restaurant critic was the only one who went about a beat regularly in the company of a group. The drama critic might have tickets for two and the sportswriter might have a pass that would get a friend into the press box, but the food critic actually *needed* others to do the job.

I broke bread, or croissants, with five different *Times* food critics and I never met a meal I didn't like; that's more than the critics did, but their standards were much higher than mine. It was a fascinating procedure. The reservation was never made in the critic's name because the critic was in constant identity crisis. To be recognized in print as a leading taster was good, but to be recognized at table was courting disaster. Craig Claiborne's picture, it was rumored, was posted in the kitchen of one of New York's most posh restaurants, a placement about as popular with him as the hanging of a picture in the post office is to a criminal.

There were rules of behavior at a critic's table. Never call Mimi [Sheraton] or Bryan [Miller] by name while at table. If possible, keep shop talk, about *The Times,* at a low buzz. The formation of judgment, it was believed, depended on the anonymity that would let the critic be served as a member of the general public rather than as an important person from *The New York Times.*

Each had different strategies, but the assignment was about the same in every case—to assay the widest variety of food on the menu. The guests were encouraged to order whatever they wanted, but no two people should order the same dish. During the meal, there was a sharing of dishes, as at a Chinese repast. (The job was easier in a Chinese restaurant, where all dishes were laid out for all to pick at.) For the accompanying group, all this was a treat. For the critic, it was a job that might require several visits to any one establishment before a fair appraisal could be made. It was a beat that had many advantages over others—it was certainly more comfortable than covering the homeless—but, like anything that must be done, it was work that required thought and energy and a strong stomach that rarely had a chance for a home-cooked meal.

Mimi Sheraton on the job could transform herself at first bite from gracious, laughing hostess to a seriously clinical analyst. She cherished her anonymity and wore disguises to protect it. I once wrote a lighthearted column in the Long Island Section in which I said I never liked to recommend restaurants to friends who were gourmets. They would say that the lettuce was limp or that the roast potatoes had not been sedulously pared. I showed it to this caring critic, and she said that she was very much like that. She invited me often enough and I always enjoyed it, but I never invited her.

Bryan Miller took notes, sometimes asked the maître d' about a dish, but managed to appear more like a food-minded tourist than like a critic from *The Times.* He did not usually wear a disguise, but on at least one occasion he grew facial hair and applied stage makeup to gain access to a hostile restaurant that resented critics, at least Mimi. Craig Claiborne dealt imperturbably with the handicap of familiarity, He was known to many of the great chefs from his earlier days as a student of cooking or as food reporter, an assignment where the object was to make yourself known.

By the end of the 1940s, food news was an important segment of the section then known as Women's News. *The Times* had its own modern kitchen, which it used for testing the edibles it was about to put before the eyes and appetites of its readers. When Gerald Gold, mostly a formidable editor on the foreign, cultural, and Sunday Arts and Leisure sections, was taking time out as a reporter writing the paper's first consumer column, he used the kitchen often to test "drained weight," to determine whether a can that was labeled six ounces really contained only four ounces after the liquid preservative was poured out. It was as one of his test targets that I first became acquainted with the kitchen. He was checking out hamburger meat for some reason neither he nor I recall, and invited a gaggle of reporters upstairs to compare the various meats and the several cooking intensities, rare, medium, or well done. We all gorged on hamburger, no potatoes, no ketchup, no onions, no buns—merely bare, cooked meat. I don't recall that I could tell the difference, one patty from another, but I do recall that it took a long time for me to buy another hamburger and that I have ever since had respect for the force-fed staff of Food News.

This was an intensely read section, not least of all by the ever-vigilant publisher, A. H. Sulzberger, who read it closely and often made his views known. He had an aversion to anything that appeared to be free advertising taking up news space. In this instance, he objected to a photograph caption, and perhaps the photo itself, for a story on the Jewish New Year, Rosh Hashanah:

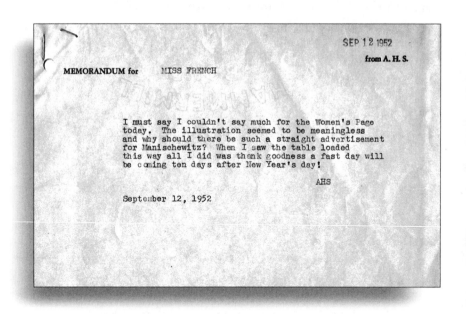

SEP 12 1952

from A. H. S.

MEMORANDUM for        MISS FRENCH

I must say I couldn't say much for the Women's Page today. The illustration seemed to be meaningless and why should there be such a straight advertisement for Manischewitz? When I saw the table loaded this way all I did was thank goodness a fast day will be coming ten days after New Year's day!

AHS

September 12, 1952

The publisher's overview seemed eternal. On August 30, 1956, an acerbic note questioned "the propriety" of a food picture in that morning's paper.

"Even to my bad eyes there is evident a bowl containing cans of Rheingold beer. I see no reason why the labels should have been displayed," he wrote, with a witheringly sarcastic parting shot that asked "how much" the photographer had received from Rheingold. Catledge evidently tried to explain but Sulzberger turned a deaf ear. He replied:

MR. CATLEDGE

    No, I don't quite agree with the attached. Those beer cans could have been rotated just a trifle and the name would not have been legible. They would still have looked like cans. I don't recall the brandy bottles but I'm perfectly certain that they also could have been angled a bit so that the name would not have shown.

    I don't think that it's the same as the question of the Miller Golf Tournament. If we were publishing a picture of Rheingold or the Rheingold beauties, why of course the name "Rheingold" would appear, but not in just a straight food picture where any beer -- begging Mr. Rheingold's pardon -- would have done as well.

                  A. H. S.

September 6, 1956
L

A major change at *The Times* was heralded by the appointment of Craig Claiborne as editor of Food News in 1957. His writing and his tastes, geared to the gourmet dining that American affluence was digesting in those prosperous years, set the pace for the smother of food writers that covers print and television today. The note from Turner Catledge that introduced Claiborne's name to the publisher is certainly one piece of paper that brought quick changes to *The New York Times,* and its worry about a man replacing a woman in the food department is its own comment. Along with the penciled OK from

Sulzberger, it can be interpreted variously as (a) an indication of the liberality of *The Times* in accepting a change of sex in what had been a type-cast role or (b) a comment on the general belief of where a woman's place really was, at *The Times* or elsewhere.

The letters from readers of Food News probably had more influence on the contents of the section than did the mail to other sections. *The Times* was not browbeaten by its mail generally, and more often than not, stood up to its viewpoint despite letters. But letters to Food News often hit home.

In a polite but anguished letter to the editor in 1959, a woman who lived in Nutley, New Jersey, complained that although she was a cosmopolitan cook, the recipes in *The Times,* under its new culinary leadership, were becoming too much for her taste. "I find the recipes given and the dishes presented either too fattening, too expensive, or too, too exotic. . . . For example, there is a tremendous overemphasis on pastries and no encouragement of creative use of fruit. . . . If they don't call for fantastic concoctions popular in the South Seas, they present items wrapped in dough, deep-fat fried, etc."

The letter found its way to Garst's desk, where it apparently stung him. He passed it along to the department head, Elizabeth Howkins, with his own view that "we are moving a little too much to the

from R. E. GARST

MEMORANDUM for: ~~Mrs. Howkins~~ *Mr. Claiborne, Let's discuss — with a month's file of daily copies & Sunday. — before us.*

It seems to me that this letter from a reader is a very thoughtful one and brings up a rather fundamental point of view about our food columns and therefore deserves thoughtful consideration and a reply. I must say that I have felt at times that we are moving a little too much to the gourmet point of view and that perhaps we should give some thought to getting back to bread and butter recipes.

R. E. G.

June 11, 1959

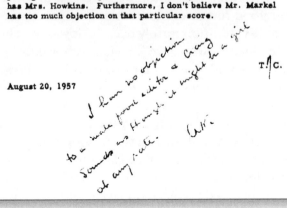

from **TURNER CATLEDGE**

U's news

MEMORANDUM for: MR. SULZBERGER:

The problem of obtaining another food-cooking editor has come up because of the pending resignation of Miss Jane Nickerson; she is leaving us about the first of October because she is moving away from the city. We would like to get someone else as soon as possible. This would allow her replacement the opportunity to spend sometime with Miss Nickerson before she left.

The best candidate in Mrs. Howkins' view is a young man by the name of Craig Clayborne. There were other candidates for the opening, but Mrs. Howkins has centered on him as the best choice. In fact, she is quite impressed with him, as is Mr. Burritt, who screened him. I have had a talk with the young man and find him to be most capable. He writes beautifully, and he certainly seems to know his subject. He has trained himself for food journalism.

As you know, the selection of people of this type are handled as joint projects by Mr. Markel and myself. While he has some misgivings about Mr. Clayborne's general approach to food news, I don't think that he would interpose any serious objection to Mrs. Howkins' taking the responsibility. I do not doubt that she would select the young man.

The primary reason I am bothering you with this is to see whether you have any objections or qualms about putting a man in that position. Personally, I do not. Neither has Mrs. Howkins. Furthermore, I don't believe Mr. Markel has too much objection on that particular score.

August 20, 1957

T.C.

*I have no objection to a male food editor & Craig sounds as though it might be a girl at any rate. (AHS)*

Turner Catledge's suggestion for a new "food-cooking editor" elicited from the publisher a laconic, pencilled approval: "I have no objection to a male food editor and Craig sounds as though it might be a girl at any rate."

gourmet point of view and that perhaps we should give some thought to getting back to bread and butter recipes."

Clifton Daniel was one of the keen managing editors who treated food news with the seriousness he had brought to news from wartime London or Stalinist Moscow. Foreign correspondents do a lot of eating out and, as a correspondent, Daniel had been attracted to gracious, polite society and was knowledgeable about cuisine, haute and otherwise. He was a prolific memo writer on the subject, and his notes indicated familiarity with food and the proper way to eat it.

At the other end of the food spectrum, Daniel demonstrated that, in terms of coverage, he had the breadth of tolerance and curiosity that separates genuine reporters from ideologues. In 1968, he was suggesting a topic that Claiborne might want to sample. "We hear that Army chow is becoming more sophisticated and varied," he informed Claiborne's editor. "He might want to sample it some day—if he can stand it."

Daniel's memos were constructive and sympathetic to the Claiborne palate. They shared a delight in the artistry of great chefs and in the elegant service of food that had been prepared with infinite care. Claiborne covered a multitude of repasts at *The Times*, including a rather good review of a restaurant on Queens Boulevard that had come to his attention purely because it was the chosen trysting place of gang leaders who gave it instant renown by being arrested there in a police raid. But as many of the food critics I know have said, the work is not all bouillabaisse and babka. Inevitably, eating out includes meals that are served cold, food that is badly, if at all, cooked, service that is slovenly. And the pressure to find new words for familiar dishes. After fourteen years as food editor, Claiborne decided to go at a slower pace in East Hampton.

"My principal motivation is an increasingly active dislike of New York City," he memoed the head office late in 1970. His plans were to write books on cooking and food. However, three years later, *The Times* announced that he would return as editor, writing for the daily paper and the *Sunday Magazine*. John Canaday, who had been art critic, would review restaurants.

In 1975, Claiborne set what must certainly have been a record for *Times* staff dining out. He dined at a costly Parisian restaurant, Chez Denis, a meal paid for by American Express, which had donated a dinner for two, money no object, to the high bid in a public television fund-raising auction. Claiborne won the meal ticket by bidding

*Food*

Mr. Claiborne

I can't make out from reding The New York
Times whether I am a gourmet or not.

In the piece yesterday about Alexander Schneider,
it says that, like all connoisseurs, Mr. Schneider likes
unsalted caviar. Yet, not so long ago, you were telling
me that true connoisseurs preferred pressed caviar,
which is most certainly salted.

You also say that unsalted caviar is unavailable
through commercial channels in New York. Yet, I would
swear I had some from Fraser-Morris on Christmas Eve.
Maybe it was what is called malossol--that is, with
little salt.

I am under the impression that all caviar has
some salt, and that it wouldn't otherwise keep.

Please straighten me out some day.

E.C.D.

January 20, 1967

Clifton Daniel, then assistant managing editor, was as assiduous in attention to back-of-the-paper affairs, such as food news, as he was to page 1 stories. And he was particularly knowledgeable about dining, which led to these comments about caviar.

$300 and ran up a $4,000 tab for two. It made lip-smacking reading and doubtless encouraged the sale of lottery tickets, but virtually all of the 250 readers who wrote letters found it scandalous that so much could be spent on one dinner in a world where hunger and famine set the table for millions of earthlings. Alfred A. Knopf, the publisher, wrote a "Dear Punch" letter to *Times* publisher Arthur Ochs Sulzberger. He was a friend and admirer of Craig Claiborne, he said, and had even enjoyed in his home a meal cooked by the critic and his colleague, Pierre Franey, but . . . "Fun's fun, but every person I have spoken to or has spoken to me about this four-thousand-dollar dinner for two has reacted in the same way—that to most people the

---

### Side Order

Among Claiborne's many achievements was one that put *The Times* into book publishing. He had years earlier found a publisher for *The New York Times Cook Book,* which turned out to be a perennial best-seller. This was not lost on *Times* management, who saw the profits from what had been its talent and material leave the office for alien pockets. The *Times* bought a publishing company, Quadrangle, and proceeded to oversee its own books. Quadrangle became Times Books, which was later sold to Random House.

---

whole business smelled of the utmost in vulgarity and that it was inappropriate if not indeed socially irresponsible for The Times to feature the story on page one. I am afraid I feel the same way."

Sulzberger, in a response of the sort one could write only to a friend, because usually publishers will back reporters in public (even though they may chastise them in private), ruefully admitted to "Dear Alfred":

> I am not going to argue with you because I can't. All of our mail ran against the Craig Claiborne piece.
>
> Frankly, I do not think it was the end of the world as some of our readers would have me believe.
>
> They must throw away ten times that amount of edible food from the plates of customers every night at 21, and no one has suggested bagging it and sending it to Bangladesh. However, $4,000 for two, even without a tip, is going a bit too far.

The maintenance of standards in what many graybeards in the newsroom referred to, with noticeable condescension, as "soft" news sections, remained an urgent concern in the front office and upstairs in the executive suite, where that sensitive balance between detachment and profit was constantly being weighed. Along about that time, a publisher of a frozen-food magazine wrote a letter that is a classic example of what we know as situational ethics. Frozen-food producers had placed ads in thirty newspapers, including *The New York Times,* as part of a consumer promotion.

"Some of the newspapers including the New York News and the New York Post gave frozen foods editorial support either in the form of tie-in articles or complete supplements," the letter to Sulzberger, written in March 1977, observed. "The Times saw fit not to provide this type of support. I assume that you feel it would reflect unfavorably on your editorial integrity and, if that is your position, it is thoroughly understandable.

"What beats me is this," the letter continued. "Your Living Section for the date I have referred to features as its lead story on page 1 and continuing for a full page on page 8 an article on fresh asparagus. Page 3 carries a smaller feature on fresh shrimp.

"What kind of integrity has you soliciting business from frozen food advertisers on the one hand and them knocking their brains out with editorial material in the same section devoted exclusively to the products they are competing with?"

Executive editor Abe Rosenthal, who was assigned to reply by the publisher, answered in an explanation of *Times* policies on advertising that might have flowed from the pen of Adolph Ochs.

"We do not run news stories about specific products or groups of products simply because they are advertised in The Times," he wrote. Nor do we exclude stories about products or groups of products that are advertised in The Times. . . . We have covered and will cover stories about frozen foods—when editors and reporters think there is a story involved. We do not cover stories as 'editorial support.'

"We ran the story about asparagus and fresh shrimp because we considered them newsworthy. We often write stories about fresh foods when they are in season, and we will continue to do so, of course.

"We are not interested in 'knocking your brains out,' but if we run our Living section on the basis of the needs of any particular advertiser, it would quickly cease to be the kind of section we are interested in producing."

Punch Sulzberger relished fine cooking, but he was also able to distinguish what readers might find appetizing from what more rarefied tastes might savor. His memos in all fields could be flavored with exasperated wit. The following note, written in 1976 to Rosenthal, evinced a thorough reading of his paper as well as an awareness that in *The Times* an overworked eye at the top sometimes was blind to an overlapping coverage that could leave a reader disoriented. It was a small occasional thing, but publishers, who do not confront the minutiae that cover the editor's desk, often managed to have their strongest effect by being good and faithful readers. They can ask those simple questions that seasoned hands in the business might hesitate to put because they are so obvious. Here's an example:

> If anyone were to tell me that we were not an integrated paper, I would tell him he was a liar.
>
> Not only do we use page after page on Wednesday telling readers how to cook eels, on Sunday we again tell them how to catch and prepare eels, and how to cook them. Is Nelson Bryant's [the field and stream columnist] recipe better than Craig's?
>
> Seriously, what is it with eels? Do you know anyone who eats them? Why can't our food pages have something on them that most people like?

By 1976, *The Times* was working out plans to make news of food a centerpiece of the sections it was devising as supplements to the traditional main sections of the daily paper. The topic had already been stabilized in the Wednesday paper under the "Best Food Day" rubric. It was a department that offered recipes and news and many advertisements. A memo in May 1976 from A. M. Rosenthal to Joan Whitman, editor of Family/Style, represents one of those pivotal moments when *The Times* was taking a historic turn. He advised her that *The Times* might be going to a four-section paper three times a week that fall.

"It would open up the possibility of a whole family/style section, with its own front on Wednesdays," he wrote. "The emphasis would be on food, but as at present, we would not make it entirely a food section, but include the best of our coverage in other fields. If we are to do it, it should be done magnificently, obviously and in high style."

He asked her to keep the project "as confidential as possible." There was an additional possibility, he said, that there might be a four-section paper five days a week and, if this should happen, a second family/style section might be inaugurated. He requested her to make suggestions on the content of these new sections and, in considering them, to drop all other work.

That November the Living Section made its debut and was an instant success.

With a whole section of their own, the Food News staff, as well as knowledgeable outsiders, were able to roam widely, presenting attractive, profusely illustrated articles that ranged from interviews with great chefs to reports on trendy and traditional cooking, reviews of restaurants, feature pieces, and columns. Food News spilled over into the Thursday Home Section and occupied a weekly niche in the *Sunday Magazine*.

The active mind of an active editor concentrated on comparatively small matters in Food News with the assiduity applied to larger issues, such as the Pentagon Papers. Rosenthal kept a close watch on the food pages. One memo objected to a list of Danish pastry bakers that named those considered to be of "no merit."

"I really object to this kind of blacklisting without critical comment," he wrote, expressing confidence that the reporter's judgment was valid. "But I think it is very destructive and unfair simply to list a lot of businesses and products and denounce them, particularly when we don't even say why we are denouncing them. This is not criticism, but a kind of God-playing which I think is a misuse of the power of the press."

Covering food was often no less controversial than covering politics, and the recipients of notices that were less than raves often struck back, either by letters to the publisher, letters to the editor, or advertisements condemning *The Times*'s reporting. Zabar's bought an ad to rebut a story that reflected on the caviar being sold over the store's busy counters. The writer promptly complained to her bosses that the ad was "not only insulting but categorically false."

The proprietor of Le Périgord, one of New York's most elegant restaurants, complained about the vigor of a review and asked for space to reply. Sulzberger suggested that Rosenthal allow the restaurant owner to have his say. Rosenthal quickly defended his space and his critic, Mimi Sheraton. He reflected upon the significance of such permission.

"It would mean that every time a critic writes an unfavorable criticism, we would have to provide space for a reply," he said. "That would mean that every time Mimi criticizes a restaurant, we would have to print a reply from the restauranteur [*sic*] because, believe me, if we print one, everybody else would demand the same privilege. We would have to do the same thing whenever we had an unfavorable book review, music review, dance review or whatever. We really would not be able to accommodate it. The function of a critic is to have opinions, based on expertise, and that is exactly what Mimi has."

Rosenthal added that, in any event, the owner's letter could not be printed as it stood. "It seems to me we can hardly print a letter accusing our critic of a personal prejudice."

The executive editor, who could be on occasion dismayingly blunt in his memos to the world he oversaw as well as to the world outside, also did not stint in bestowing praise when he thought it bestowable. For instance, he wrote to Mimi Sheraton in appreciation for her review of one of the nation's priciest and most highly regarded establishments.

*Mimi Sheraton*

1977

**Miss Sheraton**

    I've often said to you that it is the critic's job to be critical when necessary but not to be unduly wounding--not to draw blood for the sake of blood.

    If you would like to read a fine example of how this can be achieved, read Mimi Sheraton on Lutece. I thought that was a first-rate job. You explained exactly why it deserved three stars and made it clear that it was an excellent place. You also explained lucidly, but not cruelly at all, why you could not give it four. And then you put the whole thing in perspective.

    I think you achieved exactly the proper critical tone--which, for a paper like the Times, is almost as important as the critical expertise itself. What we need is both the proper tone and the right expertise and, I repeat, I think you achieved them in the Lutece review.

                  A.M.R.

cc:  Mr. Greenfield
      Miss Grant

That started him musing about four-star ratings, which he realized Sheraton would certainly not give this particular restaurant. "It must have the quality of greatness," he observed in a philosophical vein. "Greatness means that not only are certain things present—such as superb food—but certain things are absent. A place must be at least pleasant to dine in. There must be no slovenliness about it, cleanliness must be unquestionable, and so on. . . . I do feel that up to and including three stars, a critic really speaks for herself or himself. When you give something four stars, you speak not only for yourself, but in an almost mystical way, you represent the paper itself. Who would ever have thought that a vegetable curry could be mystical?"

Small wonder that some of these adversarial situations ended up being chewed over by *The Times*'s Legal Department. In one case, it informed the critic that the other three people at her table supported a recollection that the shrimp was served in cocktail sauce. "Therefore, no correction will be made concerning the sauce" was the conclusion.

In yet another case, an angry advertisement by a restaurant that had been critically scorned sent the critic to the lawyers, with proof that, contrary to the restaurant's stipulations, visits had been paid to the place under contention and that the items criticized in the review had indeed been tasted. This strong refutation of the advertisement was brought to public attention in an Editor's Note that replied to the ad.

Food News has become one of the best-read sections of *The New York Times,* according to circulation surveys. There was a time when the Wednesday supermarket ads featured in other papers were passed over by *The Times.* However, new pressures—the move of a downtown readership to the suburbs, the move of big-store advertisers in the same direction, and the competition of television, among others—dictated more inclusive coverage in a section that catered to a wider range of tastes than had existed earlier. The solution was not to cheapen the coverage by doing what others had been doing in one way or the other, but to elevate the subject. As with crime ("When *The Times* reports on it, it's sociology"), so it is with food—when *The Times* writes about it, it's not cooking but gastronomy.

# DINING AT
# *THE TIMES*

*10*

INING at *The New York Times* has always been arranged as
though it were a three-class transatlantic-liner ritual.

There is the cafeteria, a large, pleasant room on the
eleventh floor and certainly a great asset in horrible
weather or when writing on deadline without any time for lollygag-
ging in restaurants or bars or, as it happens, when there is one of
those sudden slack periods when no one is dying or speaking and the
call for copy is muted. It is an assembly hall for gossips and I have
learned much about what was never explicitly told to me by joining
reporters, editors, clerks, secretaries, printers, editorial writers, and
even executives at table in the cafeteria.

The several dining rooms at the end of the hall are set for executives and their guests. Third-floor editors often brought their staffs
to the dining room for lunch and shop talk. Sometimes, these groups
were fed a prominent politician, artist, writer—anyone whose name
was making headlines at the moment—and lunch became an interview covered by one of the invited staffers, who in that event did not
have time to down much food.

When I was a member of the Cultural News Department, the no-
free-lunch truism almost always applied to me during such meals.
The critics would discuss learnedly the state of the arts with our
leader, Arthur Gelb, the ever-alert and stimulating chief of cultural
goings-on. Arthur extracted from the generalities and the profundi-
ties the germ of a strong story that we ought to be covering. Who
could do it? The critics were all tied up, and they often thoughtfully
suggested topics outside their own disciplines, which meant that neither they nor their reporters should handle it. The eyes ranged up

and down the long table and Arthur would spot me, a general reporter in a gaggle of specialists, and say, "Dick, can you do this?" Of
course I could, but it did take the edge off of lunch to return to the
third floor heavy with caloric assignments.

Finally, there is the publisher's dining room. It is a room with a
long table, and some of the most eminent diners in the world have
visited it in hopes of force-feeding *The New York Times* their own particular menu. Heads of state, governors, presidents, kings, and prime
ministers have all been guests of honor at the publisher's lunches.
The publisher's lunch is a distinction, a sort of public relations medal
of honor for the invited and an information booth for the host.
Sometimes lunch at *The Times* can be a trial for either one or both
of the parties. And the crush of foreign dignitaries in town for the
opening sessions of the United Nations each fall can create a waiting list for *The Times* lunch.

"Thank you for writing about the forthcoming visit of President
Nardone to New York between September 20 and 25," Orvil Dryfoos
wrote to a Uruguayan go-between in 1961. "I regret very much that
our lunches here at The Times are completely booked during that
period. As you know, the United Nations General Assembly will be
in session then, with a number of state visitors here whom we have invited. Therefore it will be impossible to issue an invitation to President Nardone."

Thirty years later, Joseph Papp, the feisty director-founder of the
New York Shakespeare Festival, thanked Punch Sulzberger for *The
Times* power lunch: "Even though I didn't eat anything, there was a
lot of food for thought," he wrote. "Not to mention that great Ha-
vana! All in all, you were exceedingly gracious and supportive of the
work of the New York Shakespeare Festival in the city."

There was one item on the menu in the Ochs days that has disappeared from today's bill of fare in the publisher's dining room. It
was a prayer, "Grace Before Meat" (yes, that's meat, not meal), which
had been written by John H. Finley, the scholar who was in charge
of the editorial page, and it was read at Ochs's insistence.

"My father-in-law used to insist on its being read but at times that
was highly inappropriate so we had it printed and now place it on the
table before the guest," Arthur Hays Sulzberger wrote in a letter in
1965. Here is how it went:

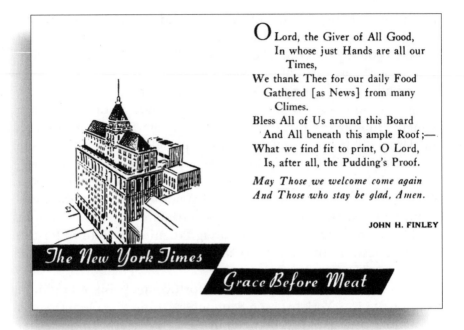

O Lord, the Giver of All Good,
   In whose just Hands are all our
      Times,
We thank Thee for our daily Food
   Gathered [as News] from many
      Climes.
Bless All of Us around this Board
   And All beneath this ample Roof;—
What we find fit to print, O Lord,
   Is, after all, the Pudding's Proof.

*May Those we welcome come again
And Those who stay be glad, Amen.*

**JOHN H. FINLEY**

*The New York Times*

*Grace Before Meat*

These meals were working meals, but *The Times* also had more formal dinners that celebrated explorations, anniversaries, special achievements. Whereas dinners were hearty affairs in the robust old days, they have slimmed down considerably in recent years. The round of cigars that capped every meal in the dining rooms has, of course, gone the way of the Linotype and the green eyeshade. For those who prefer to review history in terms of the infinite appetites of humans, the menus displayed here are interesting not only for the ingredients they list but for their variety of designs, whether *Times* motifs or explorers' likenesses.

In January 1912, Ochs wrote a letter to his relatives about a lunch he served William Howard Taft—an event that he described "as the capstone of my career and that is entertaining the President of the United States in my home. The whole affair was a glorious success and I am as proud as Lucifer."

The presidential lunch at the Ochs home on West 75th Street was an elaborately staged affair, befitting the most exalted American presence that one could possibly host. Here are the menu and the crucial seating plan, which, as glaringly evident, provided no table space for the women of the house, in keeping perhaps with the custom of the time if not of *The Times*.

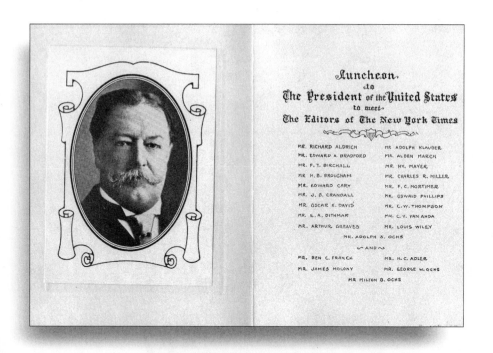

Luncheon
to
The President of the United States
to meet
The Editors of The New York Times

| | |
|---|---|
| MR. RICHARD ALDRICH | MR ADOLPH KLAUBER |
| MR. EDWARD A. BRADFORD | MR. ALDEN MARCH |
| MR. F. T. BIRCHALL | MR. HY. MAYER |
| MR H. B. BROUGHAM | MR. CHARLES R. MILLER |
| MR. EDWARD CARY | MR. F. C. MORTIMER |
| MR. J. B. CRANDALL | MR. OSWALD PHILLIPS |
| MR. OSCAR K. DAVIS | MR. C. W. THOMPSON |
| MR. E. A. DITHMAR | MR. C. V. VAN ANDA |
| MR. ARTHUR GREAVES | MR. LOUIS WILEY |

MR. ADOLPH S. OCHS

AND

| | |
|---|---|
| MR. BEN C. FRANCK | MR. H. C. ADLER |
| MR. JAMES MOLONY | MR. GEORGE W. OCHS |

MR MILTON B. OCHS

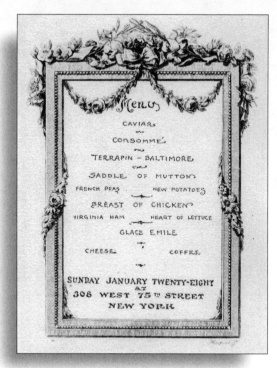

Menu

CAVIAR

CONSOMMÉ

TERRAPIN — BALTIMORE

SADDLE OF MUTTON

FRENCH PEAS     NEW POTATOES

BREAST OF CHICKEN

VIRGINIA HAM     HEART OF LETTUCE

GLACE EMILE

CHEESE     COFFEE

SUNDAY JANUARY TWENTY-EIGHT
AT
308 WEST 75TH STREET
NEW YORK

The menu for Ochs's luncheon for President Taft and, above, a portrait of the
chief executive on the all-male seating list.

The banquet in honor of Commander Robert E. Peary's historic journey to the North Pole in 1909 was held in the Times Tower, the triangular home of the newspaper that gave Times Square its name. The menu was an autographed eighteen-page booklet with a picture of the explorer's parka-enclosed face on the cover. The dishes for the dinner (facing page) were appropriately titled for Arctic triumphs.

MENU

✣

Blue Point Oysters

Petite Bouchee Walrus

Veloute Ptarmigan aux Croutons

Supreme de Narwhal, Veronique

Mignon de Musk Ox, Victoria
Pommes Parisiennes

Mousse de Pemmican, Kossuth
Epinards aux Fleurons

Sorbet "North Pole"

Perdreau Roti, barde aux Feuilles de Vigne
Coeur de Romaine en Salade

Biscuit Glace Knickerbocker
Corbeille de Mignardises

Cafe

## THE
## CONQUEST OF THE NORTH POLE

### BY ROBERT E. PEARY

*Copyright, 1909, by The New York Times Company*

BATTLE HARBOR, LABRADOR (via Marconi Wireless, Cape Ray, N. F., Sept. 9).—The steamer *Roosevelt*, bearing the North Polar expedition of the Peary Arctic Club, parted company with the *Erik* and steamed out of Etah Ford late in the afternoon of August 18, 1908, setting the usual course for Cape Sabine. The weather was dirty, with fresh southerly winds. We had on board 22 Eskimo men, 17 women and 10 children, 226 dogs and some forty odd walrus.

We encountered the ice a short distance from the mouth of the harbor but it was not closely packed and was negotiated by the *Roosevelt* without serious difficulty. As we neared Cape Sabine the weather cleared somewhat and we passed close by Bree-vort Island and Cape Sabine, easily making out with the naked eye the house at Hayes Harbor occupied by me in the winter of 1901-02.

From Cape Sabine north there was so much water that we thought of setting the lug sail before the southerly wind, but a little later appearance of ice to the northward stopped this. There was clean open water to Cape Albert, and from there scattered ice to a point about abreast of Victoria Head, thick weather and dense ice bringing us some ten or fifteen miles away.

From here we drifted south somewhat, and then got a slant to the northward out of the current. We worked a little farther north and stopped again for some hours. Then we again worked westward and northward till we reached a series of lakes, coming to a stop a few miles south of the *Windward's* winter quarters at Cape d'urville. From here, after some delay, we slowly worked a way northeastward through fog and broken ice of medium thickness through one night, and the forenoon of the next day, only emerging into open water and clear weather off Cape Fraser.

From this point we had a clear run through the middle of Robeson Channel, uninterrupted by either ice or fog, to Lady Franklin Bay. Here we encountered both ice and fog, and while working along in search of a practicable opening were forced across to the Greenland coast at Thank God Harbor.

The fog lifted there and enabled us to make out our whereabouts, and we steamed north through a series of leads northward toward Cape Union. A few miles off that cape we were stopped by impracticable ice, and we drifted back south to Cape Union, where we stopped again.

#### TWICE FORCED AGROUND

We lay for some time in a lake of water, and then, to prevent being drifted south again, took refuge under the north shore of Lincoln Bay, in nearly the identical place where we had our unpleasant experiences three years before. Here we remained for several days during a period of constant and at times violent northeasterly winds.

5

The culinary tributes for successful adventurers continued well into the 1900s, while there were still new worlds to be found. In 1926, the U.S. Navy's famous explorer Richard E. Byrd and the aviator Floyd Bennett accomplished a "first," a flight over the North Pole. Surely that called for a luncheon to honor the intrepid airmen, whose signed photographs topped the printed menu, along with a drawing of a plane flying over an Arctic scene.

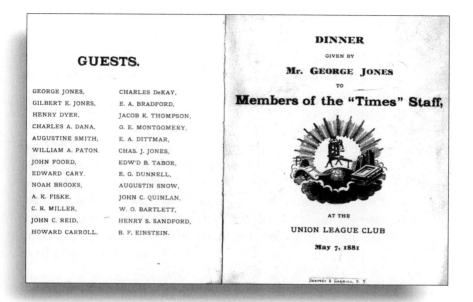

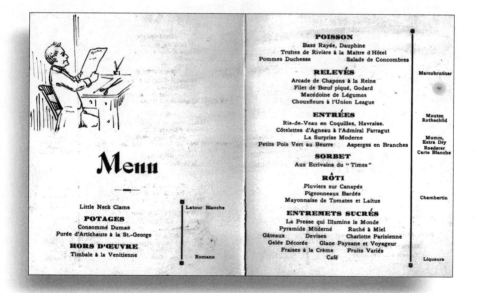

One of the earliest menus in the archives is this one for a dinner given at the Union League Club in 1881 by publisher George Jones for his staff. Note the sorbet "Aux Écrivains du 'Times,'" and the entrémets sucrés that stars "La Presse qui Illumine le Monde."

If there was one thing that explorers seemed to need more than anything else when they returned from groundbreaking journeys, it was a good meal. According to accounts of victory receptions, the explorers were as stuffed as the specimens they brought back with them. *The Times*, with its avid interest in scientific exploration and its contribution to journeys, either by advancing funds or by buying exclusive rights to stories, entertained many explorers.

One of the most distinguished guests to grace a table at *The Times* was Winston Churchill, as the man who came to dinner on the evening of March 28, 1949. As his father-in-law had done for the president of the United States, but on a much less elaborate scale, Arthur Hays Sulzberger made detailed arrangements for seating the eminent wartime prime minister of Britain whose monumental memoirs were appearing in the pages of *The New York Times*. All twenty-eight of

---

THE NEW YORK TIMES
Monday, March 28, 1949
7:15 p.m.

Guest List

The Right Honorable Winston S. Churchill
Mr. Bernard M. Baruch
Gen. Walter Bedell Smith
Mr. Henry Luce
Mr. Randolph Churchill
Capt. Christopher Soames

| | |
|---|---|
| Julius Ochs Adler | Louis M. Loeb |
| Hanson Baldwin | Raymond McCaw |
| Theodore M. Bernstein | Anne O'Hare McCormick |
| Amory H. Bradford | Neil MacNeil |
| Turner Catledge | Lester Markel |
| Edward H. Collins | Charles Merz |
| Orvil E. Dryfoos | Godfrey N. Nelson |
| Robert L. Duffus | William D. Ogdon |
| Foster Hailey | James B. Reston |
| Edwin L. James | Howard A. Rusk |
| Waldemar Kaempffert | Otto D. Tolischus |

Arthur Hays Sulzberger

the other diners were *Times* executives and editors. Unlike the womanless repast for President Taft, the Churchill dinner guest list provided for one woman, Anne O'Hare McCormick, the first woman to join the paper's editorial board.

The occasion was social and the speeches were informal. But the morning after, AHS made it clear to his *Times* colleagues that he was still heading a newsgathering organization. He asked the diners from the news and editorial staff who were there to report on what Churchill had said. The reports, considering that no notes are known to have been made, jibed one with the other with remarkable consistency, although there were the usual variations in emphasis.

"This confounds me a bit, and I think it is but a fair criticism to say that you should have tipped us off beforehand. I was sitting a long way from Mr. Churchill and next to General Bedell-Smith, who didn't stop talking all during the dinner," commented managing editor Edwin L. James in his report.

With all the temptations to gather around the table to taste the thoughts of leading minds, it was not always easy even for the publisher to gather a clutch of editors and executives at the board. Orvil Dryfoos in 1962 put it to his high command in a plaintive memo.

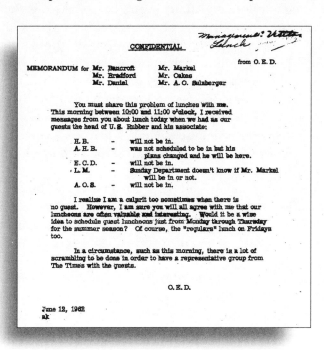

# FOREIGN NEWS

CIVILIZATION as we knew it, or at least as we had been reporting it in the foreign news pages of *The New York Times*, had been, if not collapsing, at least changing radically by November 1992, when Bernard Gwertzman, the foreign editor, summed it up in an unusually long—six-page, single-spaced—memo to his staff. The Soviet Union was gone and it was time to think about what this meant for the Foreign Desk, which, with the National News Desk, was the most prestigious *Times* neighborhood, the area in which suspicions of *Times* influence and power were most apt to be aroused around the world.

"Coverage of Foreign Affairs in the Post–Cold War Period"\* was not, the editor stressed, a diktat, but was designed to stimulate discussion. It was almost more of a philosophical rumination on what had happened, a document that might have made a Sunday piece in itself. It also serves as a rare and direct window into the thinking that goes into creating policies and strategies at *The Times.*

"When one looks back, it is remarkable but not astonishing, how much of newspaper coverage since World War Two was devoted to foreign affairs, and how much hinged on the cold war and East–West rivalries," Gwertzman wrote.

This competition affected newspaper coverage not only in terms of major crises but of "lesser developments that received heavy attention" because events in the most minor regions assumed importance in light of their role in the overriding clash of the two big blocs.

Thus otherwise abstruse debates in Soviet literary journals like Novy Mir became dramatized in the pages of The Times as struggles between liberals and conservatives over the

---

\* Not in the archives. Courtesy of Mr. Gwertzman, former foreign news editor.

mind and heart of Russia, suggesting somehow that over time such struggles might decide if there were war or peace in the future. In a way that emphasis on coverage of internal developments paid off because The Times was particularly well-placed to report on the collapse of Communism throughout Europe when it happened.

The first question is obviously this: Is foreign coverage still important to The Times. The answer is an unambiguous "yes." In many ways, we are asking more and not less of our correspondents, even though the proportion of front page hard news stories from overseas may have dropped in the past year. We still have as large a foreign staff overseas as before the end of the cold war. . . . What is new is not that we are covering foreign news less, but that we have to cover it differently. We have to be as flexible and multi-flexible and multi-talented a corps of editors and correspondents as ever existed.

Reporters, Gwertzman said, now had to follow ecology, histories of ethnic friction, and those economic developments that had once been routinely shrugged off to the Financial-Business Section. *The Times*, he wrote, was "still a NEWSpaper," and still aimed to be first with the news. "Scoops will be rewarded."

"We are interested in what makes societies different, what is on the minds of people in various regions. Imagine you are being asked to write a letter home every week to describe a different aspect of life in the area you are assigned."

Actually, it had been many years since the starchy stories emanating from "Whitehall," "The Quai d'Orsay," or "The Wilhelmstrasse" dully confined themselves to news from the upper levels of government, those precincts in which *The Times* had always had an inside track. The reporting was often devoid of the flavor of the turbulent pre–World War II years, although, when exposed to actual events of upheaval, correspondents could file stories that matched others for conveying a sense of history, as Herbert L. Matthews had done during the Spanish Civil War.

Readers were less often exposed to a sense of what life was like in foreign climes on a day-to-day basis. In the 1950s and 1960s, a new type of reporting supplemented the "highest circles" clichés that dominated the news in *The Times*. Reporters like A. M. Rosenthal wrote of what they saw in the street life of Calcutta, in the empty markets of Warsaw, in the rebirth of Japan. They reported events, as their predecessors did, but they also invoked personal perspectives that emphasized the effects of those events on the lives of the people in those countries.

Reporters abroad in earlier times were no less aware of these things, but New York was not that interested in what it seemed to regard as trivial, if not frivolous, detail, worthy perhaps of space in the back of the magazine or in some less imposing backwater section of the paper. The correspondents, instead, wrote of these things in long, chatty, sometimes charmingly discursive letters full of incident and rumor, which went to the publishers, mainly Ochs and AHS. As Charles St. Vil, *Times* archives manager, explained it, "Correspondents used to write memos and letters about how they covered a story. Now, with things like 'reporter's notebooks,' writing is more personalized and they get into the paper. They are no longer part of the archives."

For those of us whose working world was pretty much bounded by the city line, the particular panache of the foreign correspondent was deeply felt.

Bill Farrell, for instance, was a foreign correspondent who had once covered Albany legislatures, a beat that rarely produced drama approaching Shakespearean dimensions, although often matching it in chicanery. As we watched the antics in the Israeli Knesset, or parliament, where he was correspondent and I was tourist visiting the parliament, Bill nudged me and said, "See that guy over there, and that one there? They're not speaking English, but there's a deal being made. It's the state legislature all over again." The particular electricity sparked by human interaction was detected everywhere by Francis X. Clines, the peerless reporter who had written so many sparkling About New York columns. During his later years abroad, he told me, "It's all About New York, the same thing."

I have never, except for one month awarded me at the London Bureau, worked as a foreign correspondent, and I always relished the anecdotes the overseas reporters brought home with them. There was Homer Bigart, back from a double-play in 1956—the Hungarian revolution and the Suez war. Homer was a formidable reporter, two-time winner of the Pulitzer Prize, and his boast was "I never wrote a book." Homer could bound out of the office at the drop of a bombshell in any latitude and write the most graphic, revealing, and insightful accounts. Yet when we asked him what it was like, Homer, with his most jaded-reporter growl, answered, "There wasn't a decent restaurant anywhere."

There are more than 140 boxes in the archive's Foreign Desk papers collection. They are a grab bag of trivial and seminal, of personal and professional.

Since communications more often tell of problems than of smooth going, the archives are records not only of policies and strictures but also of squabbles and the usual adversarial relationships that are the hallmark of free journalism. Because distance dictated more lengthy communication on paper, the Foreign Desk archives perhaps more than others reflect what nagged at people. The correspondents squabbled with a desk they felt was glacially impervious to their Flaubertian writing. The Foreign Desk competed for page 1 space with all the other desks every day. The correspondent, if a probing type, wrangled with foreign offices much less susceptible to pressures for openness than offices back home (and the correspondents, like their colleagues back home, had to deal with foreign offices that were eager to use *The Times* as a convenient window on the world for their own ends). Finally, there was the constant competition with the competition, the daily battle to beat the other correspondents at getting the news out. These were problems similar to those encountered at any desk at *The Times,* but overseas, they somehow became magnified.

The archives indicate an almost ritual constancy in what foreign news was expected to be at *The New York Times.* On closer inspection, they tell us of changes that made this sort of correspondence radically different, especially within the last fifty years. During that period, *The Times* moved away from its traditional official-level relaying of governmental pronouncements, which it did, almost always garnishing them with the insights its reporters had gained by virtue of their influential access to the "highest sources." When I was new at *The Times,* a clerk on the Foreign Desk assured me, straight-faced, that C. L. Sulzberger, an influential and eminent foreign affairs columnist for many years, never spoke to anyone below the rank of prime minister unless it was to tell them where to put his luggage. That was probably gross exaggeration, but it indicated a state of mind.

In later years, correspondents, less anchored to capitals, roamed their territories and wrote about the forces that were shaping the way people lived. Hard news was backed up by well-written pieces that exuded the flavor of foreign parts.

There was a core of correspondents who managed to stay away from HQ for years. Turner Catledge, then assistant managing editor, mentioned this in a letter from Paris to Arthur Hays Sulzberger, in 1948:

> I think we should do something to indoctrinate the people who have never worked in The New York Times home office. Cy [Cyrus L. Sulzberger], incidentally, is one of them. But there are also [Drew] Middleton, [Sydney] Gruson, [Sam Pope] Brewer, [M. S.] Handler, [Camille M.] Cianfarra and others. It would be a great thing for the people and the paper if we could bring each of them home over a period of a few years to work an actual stint of three months or more on the Foreign News Desk, so they might see how their stuff is handled and, more importantly, get to know the people who handle it. As it is, all sorts of little hurts have occurred and little antagonisms have arisen between correspondents and desk men.

Some did return to become deskmen and more themselves; others managed to keep their distance.

In September 1867, publisher Raymond wrote to a new man in Paris, John J. Ryan, spelling out what *The Times* expected in the way of a foreign correspondent.

Raymond, who signed Ryan up during his visit to Paris, explained that he was to be a utility man for *The Times,* keeping an eye on advertising and business matters as well as the news. Yet news obviously was the cornerstone of the job. The formula he dictated has not basically changed, although it has been expanded since then.

> In regard to correspondence we shall expect from you twice a week, by the steamers likely to arrive earliest, summaries of Paris, French general news in all departments—such as your general knowledge of the wants and interests on which a paper as the Times may suggest. . . . I need not say that everything relating to Americans and American topics and interest in Europe is always especially desirable.

especially desirable.

I shall be glad to have you keep a lookout for events of special importance that are likely to happen in other parts of Europe and to make suggestions to our other correspondents, by telegraph or letter, in regard to their going to write specially about them. Mr. A. J. Jones, Care of Maquand & Co. Florence is an Italian correspondent and will go at any time whenever his services may be desired. Col. O. Corvin Frankfort on the Main, will do the same in Germany, but I am sorry to

Paris, Sept. 3, 1867.

My dear Sir:—

I believe we arrived in our conversation yesterday at a pretty full understanding of everything relating to your activity as agent and correspondent for the N.Y. Times in Paris. One of the first things to be done will be the preparation of a circular for general distribution, stating the terms of help in [subscription] and advertising. Messrs. Bowles, Drevet & Co. will receive all money on account of either, & will send us statements thereof. If you find an

inquiry that it will be worth while to employ an agent to canvas for subs. and advertisements, you may pay from whatever sums may be thus collected & paid in a commission not to exceed 20 per cent.

In regard to correspondence we shall expect from you twice a week, by the steamers likely to arrive earliest, summaries of Paris, French & general news in all departments,—such as your general knowledge of the wants and interests of such a paper as the Times may

suggest. Dr. Johnston (10 Boul. Malesherbes,) who has been our correspondent for many years will continue to write,—but will discuss special topics rather than attempt a summary of general news. Your letters may be prepared without any reference to him: but you will find him at all times ready to consult with you on matters of interest to the paper. He knows Paris very thoroughly and is on good terms at the U.S. Embassy. I need not say that every thing relating to Americans and American topics & interest in Europe is always

Publisher Raymond, for all his involvement with Republican Party politics and the momentous events in American life, was always intent on securing foreign coverage. In this letter of September 3, 1867, he writes in detail what would be expected of a new man in Europe, John J. Ryan. Raymond told Ryan what sort of coverage he wanted, what his relationships to other *Times* correspondents would be, and finally, how Ryan should also function in business capacities, including advertising.

say I have lost his address & must send it [Dyar] from N.Y. as also that of an English correspondent.

As a general thing we do not wish at present to receive special Cable despatches: but if you hear anything of special importance, write a despatch in your judgment, you have authority to send it — direct from here to our office: and to draw

Very truly
Yours

H. J. Raymond

John J. Ryan Esq

I shall be glad to have you keep a lookout on events of special importance that are likely to happen in other parts of Europe and to make suggestions to other correspondents, by telegraph or letter, in regard to their going to write specially about them. . . .

As a general thing, we do not wish at present to receive special cable dispatches; but if you hear anything of special importance, worth a dispatch in your judgment, you have authority to send it—direct from here to our office.

That business of communications and costs has always been a consideration. Here, nearly a century later, managing editor Turner Catledge is cautioning Drew Middleton, London Bureau chief: "There is just one thing I want to caution you to watch, and that is unnecessary cable messages. Our cable bill is biting us hard and that is why I am suggesting that every time you think of sending a long cable to the home office or anywhere, you think twice and see if you can't arrange to handle the same matter by airmail."

There was always a suspicion in New York that *Times* foreign correspondents were not innocents abroad, at least not when it came to expense accounts. A polite exchange of letters in 1929 between Edwin L. James, then the stellar foreign correspondent in London, and the top executives on 43rd Street illustrates some of the problems. James wrote to *Times* vice president Julius Ochs Adler, "I have just bought a car for $2000, which with insurance and taxes calls for a payment of $2,100, which I have made. I wrote you last week that it stood me $2,900 to move over here, and the car brings it up to $5000, which it has cost me to get fixed up about as I was in Paris. . . . I do not write this to make any claim on you, but merely to show you how things stand."

"We wish to do anything that would make you happy and contented, but in my opinion it would establish a bad precedent to supply an executive with a car" came the response from Adolph Ochs in New York. "You would probably have no more need for a car than has Mr. Oulahan, for instance, in Washington; to say nothing of the many officials of The Times in New York who have their own cars of which they make frequent use in connection with the affairs of The Times. . . . As the amount involved is not of any great consequence to you, I should prefer to say 'no' on a joint expenditure for a private car."

Ochs concluded by saying he hoped to visit Europe that fall and that "Mr. Krock gives an enthusiastic report on your attractive home—says it is fit for a prince."

This diplomatic tiptoe, with Ochs insinuating that James was well enough off without further emolument, continued. James replied at length, explaining that the only reason he had mentioned the car was that, when transferring from Paris to "more expensive" London, he had "the impression that I would be reimbursed the difference in rent, the difference in taxes and would be given a car in London, as well as a differential for living expenses of other kinds. Please do not think I write this in a complaining spirit."

As for that fit-for-a-prince business, well, "I appreciate what Mr. Krock said about my home, although in a way it is scarcely mine. It is the house of Rear Admiral Evans, who I happened to know. . . . I am paying $625 a year, including the 42 per cent tax on rents. It seemed to me a better bargain than than paying $2100 a year for a flat."

For all that it casts a cautionary eye on the price of performance, *The Times* has always prided itself on sparing no expense when it comes to getting the news first. It has always been eager to try the newest innovations in rapid communication. On January 9, 1927, the inauguration of radiotelephone service across the Atlantic brought an unusual three-column headline to page 1, trumpeting the "first private call to New York." The bottommost subhead announced that "Two Advertisements Also Cross Ocean to The Times."

Even with the advent of faster communications, there was always the human element, the need to think things over, elements that held up the swift delivery of the news—particularly when policies involved factors other than getting the news out quickly.

Take the case of the Kaiser Conversation. This was a *Times* exclusive that even the interviewer believed was too hot to handle. So did everyone else, except maybe the Kaiser, and it took thirty-one years to get into print, at a time when it no longer made news and nobody cared. In 1908, William C. Reick, general manager of *The Times*, assigned William B. Hale to interview Kaiser Wilhelm II. The Kaiser agreed to a session while he was aboard his yacht cruising off Bergen, Norway. As Meyer Berger tells it in *The Story of the New York Times*, Hale took no notes during the two-hour interview, for fear of inhibiting the Kaiser, but he wrote it down from memory immediately after the meeting.

"Three cheers for Hale!" Reick wrote jubilantly to Ochs on July 19, 1908. "Last night, with the thermometer about ninety, and nothing to do but chase mosquitoes and flies I received the following cable:

" 'Just had two hours audience with the Emperor. Result so startling that I hesitate to report it without censorship of Berlin.'

"I was very much disturbed because I did not want to instruct Hale to ignore the censorship. At the same time I wanted him to see that in our judgment it was unnecessary. I therefore sent him the following cable:

" 'Impossible advise except anxious avoid even appearance betrayed confidence. Consult Lowenfelt [Lowenfeld was in the German Foreign Office (spelled with *d*, not a *t*)] or Hill [United States ambassador to Germany].' "

The Kaiser had been as outspoken and intemperate in his remarks as any scoop-inspired newsman could wish. In his letter to Reick, Hale summarized the interview. The emperor was "exceedingly bitter against England and full of the yellow peril." The Kaiser, he wrote, said England, "traitor to the White man's cause," will lose her colonies to Japan. The solution to the Eastern Question, Wilhelm said, was about to be made by Germany and the United States, policy devised by himself and President Theodore Roosevelt to become recognized friends of China and so "divide the East against itself." He was bitter against the Catholics.

"He is keeping friends with the Mohammedan world—yes, he is supplying them with rifles—because they are devils in a fight and stand there between the East and the West where they can break first force of attack," Hale wrote to Reick. "Japan and America will fight within ten years. And so on."

The correspondent told Reick that all this was "unquestionably of first importance. . . . I realize it, so much so that I am leaving for Berlin to let the German Foreign Office object, if they want to (and I fear they will) *before* publication. No restrictions of any kind were laid on me, except that Baron von der Bussche, of the Foreign Office said that I could not be received as a newspaper man. Everybody concerned knows that I am. . . . At the same time, I believe the Emperor was eager to talk for publication, and to be talked to. He hears little, except through a court circle."

Hill and Lowenfeld were predictably horrified when Hale showed them the interview in Berlin and they asked for its suppression. When the reporter returned to New York, Ochs and his editors sent Hale to Washington to show it to Theodore Roosevelt, with whom Hale had established an acquaintanceship by way of earlier stories. The president said he could have no say in whether the interview should be published, but he said he felt that its suppression could benefit mankind, implying that the interview might start a war—six years earlier than the one that began in 1914.

Ochs put the interview in his safe in scrapbook form, with the correspondence that went along with it, where it remained until 1939, on the eve of World War II, when Arthur H. Sulzberger, going over Ochs's files, found the cache and allowed its publication in the *Sunday Magazine.*

The correspondence between Drew Middleton, the London correspondent of *The Times* and Emanuel R. Freedman, the longest-reigning foreign news editor (1948–1965), as well as his messages to others back on 43rd Street, are a sort of running script of what concerned foreign correspondents. Middleton, dapper and pipe-smoking, was dubbed "the colonel" by his staff and he appeared the very model of a military man as he toddled off to his club. His suavity may have been British, but his feistiness and even his journalistic talent were honed in New York, where the Brooklyn-bred Middleton established himself as a good reporter and many years later became military editor of *The Times.* Freedman, a former foreign correspondent himself, was no less urbane and the two conducted a long-distance pas de deux that combined aggressiveness with civility.

"Very interesting to watch the variations in editing between New York and Paris these days," Middleton notified Freedman (November 17, 1960), commenting on changes to his copy as it ran in the Paris edition of *The New York Times* and in the main edition in New York. "I notice that in my last Q-head [an article that bore a special headline and represented an analysis short of an editorial] Paris used the word 'savvy' which I would have thought was intelligible to most bright children of 12, while New York used 'knowledge.' In other words a long word for a short one. This is the way, I suppose, copy editors think the paper's writing can be made more attractive to the average reader. I also note that the phrase 'Mr. Kennedy is in the big leagues now' was run in Paris but deleted in New York.

"All very mystifying to the innocent bystander who gets stabbed by the blue pencil," Middleton continued.

Unfazed, Freeman replied, "I, too, have noticed with interest some variations in editing between New York and Paris, but Paris light-handedness in some cases is worse than New York heavy-handedness."

Middleton was not one to minimize trivia, particularly when it came to his own writing. In 1957, Middleton sent off a note to the assistant Sunday editor in which he commented about the treatment of a weekender piece he had filed.

"I sent, 'They [Khrushchev and Bulganin] do not repeat do not have tuxedos but they will travel.' This was meant to be a joke—a poor thing but mine own. You are familiar with the old Vaudevillian's appeal, 'Have Tux, will travel.' But, apparently the Desk is not; where do they get these guys—out of Convents?

"Anyway, it came out, 'They do not have dinner jackets but they will travel.' That's no joke."

Appeasingly, the editor wrote back: "Your complaint is well taken. . . . I recommend a straitjacket instead of a dinner jacket for the copy reader who unquestionably already has a chastity belt."

In 1960, the Middleton–Freedman exchanges were still in full flow. At one point, Middleton had complained about a copy editor's changing his copy from "Whitehall" to "Foreign Office," which in this case appeared to be wrong. "Whitehall" was a venerable journalistic cliché to describe the center of British governmental authority ("Downing Street," of course, always referred to the prime minister), as the Quai d'Orsay did for the French and Unter den Linden for the Germans, or, across the Atlantic, Foggy Bottom meant the U.S. State Department.

"It is a fact, of course, that the term Whitehall does not ring a clear bell among American readers, except for a minority," Freedman replied to Middleton. "Although Whitehall is not a synonym for the Foreign Office, it is, figuratively, the British Government, and for that reason, the copyreader or the writer might have done better to use a phrase such as 'governmental sources.'

"This just shows some of the pitfalls we face in writing and editing to make everything comprehensible for most of our readers."

Middleton worked hard at covering his stories, getting dirty during wars and gritty in remote locales, but as London Bureau chief, especially, he plunged into a life that sometimes seemed to have been packaged by central casting for a film starring David Niven. He concluded an otherwise businesslike note to Clifton

1851  HUNDREDTH ANNIVERSARY  1951

# The New York Times

TIMES SQUARE  NEW YORK 18  N Y
LAckawanna 4-1000

HOTEL METROPOLE
MOSCOW, U.S.S.R.

October 14th 1951.

Dear Manny:

I would like you to take a look at the censorship on my copy of the last few days because it has been unusually severe and it has rigorously eliminated a very important point which I have tried to make regarding Soviet atomic development.

It has been a long time since my copy has been so thoroughly chewed up and I doubt if you found much of it useable. Censorship on the Stalin statement, at the start, followed the usual pattern. All copy filed on Saturday, day of the statement, cleared rapidly and virtually without cuts. But twenty-four hours later the lid came down with a bang.

The point I have been trying to make is that on the basis of what we know about Soviet military doctrine, particularly air doctrine, it is reasonable to suppose that they have concentrated on tactical atomic weapons and that they will continue to do so. Nothing but a bare hint of that has gone through the censorship as you can see.

The second point which I tried to make in my dispatch of the 12th was that there is little or no serious talk here about negotiating about atomic control or any other international issue. It is notable that Stalin in his last two Pravda statements has made not a hint of such an approach. The censors effectively killed that one, also.

Prior to this atom thing I had noticed a gradual general tightening up of censorship in sharp contrast to the free and easy treatment of the summer months when the "News" campaign for understanding with Anglo-Saxon countries was going strong. In that period as the desk must have noticed there was almost full freedom to speculate about Soviet action and what was most unusual we were allowed to discuss matters which hadn't appeared in the local press and suggest why they hadn't been published.

As of the moment censorship is back to normal with unusual stringency on atomic topics.

Best regards,

*Harrison*

Mr. Emanuel Freedman
The New York Times
New York City .

cc CLS Paris.

"ALL THE NEWS THAT'S FIT TO PRINT"

While correspondents haggled and fretted over the copy desk in New York, there were other copy meddlers with whom it was even more difficult to cope. This letter to the foreign news editor in New York tells of the tribulations of Harrison E. Salisbury, the *Times* man in Moscow, when the Soviet censors were especially overbearing.

Daniel, his colleague now in New York, with this social note: "Went to Mike Todd's giant party to celebrate the opening of 'Round the World in 80 days' [*sic*] last night. Finished up at the Guards Club with Tom Butler and Jock Whitney, all drunk as goats playing snooker—it's a great life!"

Clifton Daniel had been a foreign correspondent himself and had strong ideas about how those beats should be covered, from reporting on the local aristocracy to meeting the people at the grass roots. It was the latter that bothered him when he became managing editor and in 1962 he wrote to Sydney Gruson, then a leading *Times* correspondent on his way to take over the London office:

> As I told you the other day, we used to sit around in the London office, reading the papers and the PA ticker and grousing because we couldn't get anything in the paper in New York. Ray [Raymond] Daniell [longtime foreign correspondent, former head of the London Bureau] never went anywhere because he hated contact with the British people. Herb Matthews went out quite a lot, but he never encouraged anyone to go out. I am sorry to say that this condition still prevails somewhat. . . . I have the feeling that the London bureau, in spite of all the hullabaloo about *Oswald Mosley [head of the British Fascist movement], has never sent anyone farther than Trafalgar Square to see what he was up to. If they have sent anybody, none of the feeling of being present has¹ ever crept into The New York Times.
>
> What puzzles me is that they did not have curiosity enough to go and seek out the facts. . . . I don't say this to criticize the London bureau in particular because it is one of our best foreign bureaus, if not the best.

In the archives is an extraordinary instance in which the publisher did not print the news as much as he was instrumental in making it. It illustrates the changes in morality that have affected the thinking of the owners and the staff of *The New York Times*. In our own tell-all era, the role of a publisher as go-between for governments is a questionable one. The deed is compounded by the fact that *The Times* did not disclose the incident as news. Yet in those days early in the twentieth century, such participation was viewed by the publisher, and by many others, as an act of simple patriotism.

The story is told in two typescript memoirs written in 1932. They recall a moment of history in 1921 when the world was poised on the brink of an economically and socially disastrous armaments race, particularly in regard to naval strengths. One memoir was written by Lord Lee, who had been appointed First Lord of the Admiralty in hopes that he could reach an agreement with the Americans and thereby avoid competition between the two English-speaking nations he felt were dominant factors in world affairs.

Warren G. Harding had just hinted in his inaugural address that he would favor an agreement. Lee, in a speech in England, responded favorably, but the speech was not picked up and nothing came of it.

"Then Mr. Ochs came on the scene," Lee recalled. "Owing to American psychology the American people would accept nothing that wasn't settled on American soil and at the suggestion of America. . . . Could the American Government be pressed to make the first move? . . . It was then that I suggested to Mr. Ochs that he was in a position of great power and influence. 'The New York Times' held in America a position like 'The Times' in England. I told him that he was persona grata at the White House and asked him if he could, in fact, act as informal envoy in the matter and assure President Harding that the offer made in my speech was not just talk, but real business."

Ochs's memoir takes up the story from there. The meeting was almost fortuitous. The publisher was sailing home from a stay in France in that April of 1921, when the ship developed propeller problems and put back to Southampton. While waiting for another ship, Ochs was invited to breakfast with Prime Minister Lloyd George. A note arrived from Lord Lee, an old friend, requesting a meeting.

"[Lord Lee said] he was encouraged to speak frankly and confidentially to me because of the well known attitude of The New York Times toward the cause of friendly relations between the United States and Great Britain; that the attitude of The New York Times had pleased all Englishmen greatly and was regarded as most helpful," Ochs recalled.

"I had always felt that the peace and welfare of the world rested with the English speaking nations . . . and that I regarded it my patriotic duty to promote that as far as lay in my power; that The New York Times was dedicated to that policy."

The peer asked the publisher to serve as bearer of an unofficial communication from Britain to the United States, a message outlining the United Kingdom's position and its willingness to give America equality in naval armaments.

"At the time, I did not appreciate the significance of an unofficial communication, which I afterwards understood was the only step that could be taken without arousing suspicions in other directions, more particularly from Japan," Ochs wrote. "I left this conference in a high state of elation, feeling very much complimented to be entrusted with so important and epoch making a message. I became almost emotional about it."

A few days later Ochs sailed for home, accompanied by Ernest Marshall, the *Times*'s London correspondent, and also by some serious second thoughts. Ochs realized that it might be "unwise" to be personally identified with the proposal, "in view of the fact that malevolent critics of The New York Times had assumed some relationships between The Times and the English government, and particularly with the Northcliffe press, in view of our very outstanding policy of cultivating and advocating friendly relations between England and the United States."

His solution was to eliminate himself from the equation but to involve the London correspondent. Marshall was filled in and sent to Washington to meet the secretary of the navy, Edwin Denby. The cabinet member apparently welcomed the Lee proposals and asked Marshall to return in a few days. At that point, Ochs wrote, he did not know what happened in the negotiations, but the secretary of the navy put some questions to Marshall for delivery back to Lord Lee. Shortly afterward, Harding convened a disarmament conference in Washington. Parity was achieved.

This was not the first or last time that *The Times* kept secrets, not because of journalistic judgments, but because of its sense of responsibility to the national interest. It was a policy that was not to be changed for many years, until it was realized that the national interest might be better served by disclosure of the facts.

By way of proving that the Ochs position of selective confidences was a generally accepted stance, there is a report sent to Ochs in October 1921 and labeled STRICTLY NOT FOR PUBLICATION. A handwritten note attached to it explains, "It is a talk the President gave 40 correspondents last night—*strictly confidential,* it is unnecessary to say they have kept faith—I did not receive the included from Mr. Oulahan [Washington correspondent of *The Times*] or any member of

The Times staff. . . . It is a valuable guide as to probable proceedings of the Conference and one of the most encouraging signs—only wish it could go to the country."

The report, directly quoting President Harding on his approach to the naval conference, certainly contained news of stop-press dimensions. Japan must be acknowledged to have the right to expand. Britain cannot do without "conspicuous sea power."

"I want the League of Nations to abide. I was against entering it except under very important reservations." It is mainly useful for Europe.

"The Administration frankly is embarrassed, now that the Conference is assured, by the well-meaning but misguided propaganda of pacifists, super-optimists and enthusiastic women. Thousands of these have got it into their heads that the United States has moved in the direction of 'disarmament.' We are not dreaming of even approximate 'disarmament.' "

Obviously, with so many juicy news tidbits left on the plate, it is clear that yesteryear's judicious restraints barely qualify as today's judicial restraints.

*The New York Times* is at its best when big news breaks. No matter that television brings the live footage, that other papers make do with a box, *The Times* does its inimitable in-depth act. In 1953, when *The Times* had done one of its remarkable blanket jobs on the death of Stalin, the publisher apparently objected to a story in the paper's house organ, *Times Talk*, that detailed the way in which the coverage was assembled for publication.

"The account in Times Talk clearly said that the desk had prepared three pages of material in anticipation of the dictator's death," Ruth Adler [editor of *Times Talk*] wrote in a memo that betrayed some frustration, in response to a cavil by Arthur Hays Sulzberger. "I thought that passage indicated that the news department, in keeping with Times tradition, was completely ready when the death story broke. Then I used the service messages to show how the desk heads worked when the communications came up.

"To be told that the Stalin story is routine and that The Times handles all comparably big stories in routine manner is to strip Times Talk of any future coverage of major news events."

Even the staff understood that every extraordinary effort was more than routine, that doing the seemingly impossible was still noteworthy, if not newsworthy, in itself. Here is a memo from an assistant managing editor to the managing editor about how that morning's last edition was an extra prompted by the resignation of Georgi Malenkov as premier of the Soviet Union:

*From:* Theodore M. Bernstein

*To:* MR. CATLEDGE

### MEMORANDUM ON MALENKOV EXTRA, FEB. 8, 1955.

At 6 A.M., Joe Eisenberg of the Communications Department 'phoned me at home to tell me the news of Malenkov's resignation and wanted to know whether we could put out an "extra". I was a little dubious but he said he thought there were enough printers, pressmen and circulation people available. He said Dinsmore knew about it and I asked to speak to Dinsmore. He told me I would have to hang up and have Dinsmore call me, which he did. But, it developed that Dinsmore was already at home, having left the office apparently just a few moments before the bulletin came in at 5:41.

I hung up and got Eisenberg back on the 'phone and told him we would go ahead and try an "extra". I was about to tell him what to do with page one when he mentioned that Max Seigel of the Broadcast Desk had just arrived. I asked to speak to Seigel and asked did he have time to do the page one job. He said he had to get out a broadcast but would make time. So I told him to lift out the three-column picture that was on page one and substitute the A.P. story. I dictated the headline to him (a three-column R top) and also dictated an italic note to go at the end of the story. I concluded talking to Seigel at 6:20.

At 6:30 I telephoned Mike Egan of the Circulation Department to find out what the distribution prospects were. He told me he had rounded up sufficient mailers and deliverers. He apparently had been in touch with Nat Goldstein. I had him switch me to the Composing Room, where George Roche said that the headline was already set and the first take of copy was in type. At 6:35 Ed Nugent of Circulation 'phoned me at home to say he had got hold of two stereotypers and that everything else seemed to be okay. He said it might take some time to get the stereotypers into the plant but he was sure it would work out all right. At 6:40, in order to see what progress was being made, I again telephoned Roche in the Composing Room. He said the story was all set except the last take. I told him not necessarily to wait for the last take but to be sure the italic note at the end of the story was included. He said he, himself, had set the italic material so he was sure it would get in.

Apparently the page was ready to go within five minutes after that call, which would have been 6:45.

T. M. B.

February 8, 1955

For Americans, and particularly New Yorkers, many of whom are only one or two or three generations removed from their ancestral homelands, the foreign coverage by *The Times* has always been of prime importance. It has evoked cries of outrage from those who felt that the paper was not paying enough attention to those overseas places or was delinquent in giving a balanced picture of what was happening. Irish nationalists charged that *The Times* was too pro-English, Zionist Jews constantly thought that the paper slanted its news in keeping with its editorial stances, influenced, they said, by the personal attitudes of the publisher.

Still, the correspondents were always trying to interpret their part of the world to the public and, even more, to the editors on 43rd Street. Changing times, and increased expenses of shipping and keeping correspondents and their families abroad, dictated new approaches. The editors debated the question, whether to assign more people to more stations in a politically complex global situation or to have a reporter operate out of one base and cover a vaster amount of territory. There were arguments on both sides.

"Touring another area produces no miracles. . . . But it does do a lot for the correspondent's perspective, for East Africa is as different from West Africa as Scandinavia is from the Balkans," Lloyd Garrison, *Times* man in Lagos, Nigeria, wrote to foreign editor Seymour Topping in 1966. "In short, not all of Africa's peoples—or their problems and promise—are alike. Hence, whenever a correspondent has to generalize about this continent, he is treading shoaly water unless he has had at least a glimpse of other shores beyond his own swimming hole."

The foot that a *Times* correspondent placed on foreign soil produced a squeak or a thump back home. One particular thump was caused by a scoop written by Harrison E. Salisbury, considered by management to be one of its most brilliant reporters. Salisbury had gained entry to Hanoi in 1966 during the Vietnam War. He wrote graphic pieces that described the havoc wreaked by American bombing, stories that produced admiration and condemnation among *Times* readers. Clifton Daniel, managing editor, sent a note to executive editor Turner Catledge, analyzing Salisbury's journalism and some of the reaction.

The best foreign correspondents were not in awe of their own status. The best of them looked at themselves as good reporters and were not irrevocably wedded to a way of life channeled by visas and interpreters. Joseph Lelyveld, in 1966 a foreign correspondent awaiting assignment, gave evidence in a note to the editor in New York of what a good reportorial turn of mind required, and incidentally provides another key to learning how philosophies become policy at the paper:

*TC*

Mr. Catledge

1. The Publisher is perturbed about Harrison
Salisbury's pieces. He will undoubtedly want to talk
about them very soon after you get back. I will be
glad to give you a fill-in in detail. Meanwhile, my
summary conclusions are as follows:

Getting into Hanoi was a journalistic coup.
Harrison, as might be expected, very promptly dug up
some interesting facts that weren't known before. He
disclosed that there was considerably more damage to
civilian areas than Washington had ever intimated.
Washington was quick to acknowledge that this was so.

At the same time, he obviously gave comfort to North
Vietnam by affording an outlet for its propaganda and
point of view, and comfort to those who are opposed to
the bombing and opposed to the war. Our mail to date
shows more letters in favor of Harrison than against
him.

While Washington has sought to counteract the more
damaging allegations in Harrison's reporting, there has
been, so far as I know, no general denunciation of him or
of The Times from high quarters or any attempt to bring
pressure on the paper.

You will have seen Secretary Rusk's comments and
President Johnson's. In this connection, incidentally,
we forwarded to Harrison some questions suggested by
Secretary Rusk to be put to North Vietnamese officials.
We did not label them as coming from the Secretary of
State. We do not have any evidence as yet that Harrison
was able to ask these questions. They may not have
reached him in time for his interview with the Premier.

As you know, Harrison has complicated matters by
failing in his first dispatches to attribute casualty
statistics and other controversial information directly
to those from whom he received it. I asked him in a
telegram to do this, and he has subsequently complied.

The desk was instructed not to print anything without
attribution, or, if the attribution was obvious, as it was
in most cases, they should simply put it in. For example,
"147 were said to have been killed," or "This correspondent
was told,".

A note sent by managing editor Clifton Daniel to executive editor Turner
Catledge analyzing the reports from Hanoi by Harrison Salisbury.

"I'm sure that I will be just as happy in any post in which the main
story is social rather than diplomatic, if that distinction makes sense.
A friend of mine here told me that I'm not really interested in politics, and in a sense I think he was right. I would rather go to Harlem
than to the Senate to cover an important civil rights debate; similarly,

I would rather find myself working in Asia or Latin America than an important European capital. My ideal assignment would give me unlimited opportunities for feature stories and magaziners about people I can see and talk to, plus an occasional big news break."

This outline by a correspondent in the field would exemplify the new outlook on reporting when that reporter became executive editor of *The New York Times* nearly thirty years later. More than ever, *The Times* would be examining the way people live at home and abroad.

# CUBA TO VIETNAM:
# A TIDAL CHANGE

ARCHIVES are especially valuable in telling the story of measured decisions, of developments that involve forethought, detailed planning, and after the fact, long-range policy. *The Times* archives are less revealing when it comes to reconstructing the course of a "spot" news story that breaks suddenly, when it is only after the news has been written, printed, and circulated that editors and reporters have time to put down how they did it—what was actually happening—to the best of their recollection.

*The Times* coverage of the abortive Bay of Pigs invasion of Cuba reflects the questions prompted in the aftermath of a spot news story. The newspaper's coverage of the Pentagon Papers illustrates the well-documented thinking that goes into a story that is known to be coming. Each story represents as well a polar difference, one from the other, in the attitude of *The Times* toward official government policy.

In 1961, Cuban exiles made an abortive invasion of their homeland at a south-coast landing zone called the Bay of Pigs. Tad Szulc, the knowledgeable *Times* Latin American correspondent, had been writing stories for weeks about the preparations for an invasion. At the Foreign Desk in New York, these stories were toned down in the paper, in particular with reference to their description of the invasion as "imminent."

The restraint of *The Times* in exploiting fully its knowledge of what had been planned figured in a conversation in September 1962 at the White House. Soon after President John F. Kennedy had alerted the nation to the Cuban missile crisis, publisher Orvil Dryfoos had a wide-ranging interview with the president. Dryfoos later told his top *Times* executives that he had raised the issue of national security. Kennedy was surprised by the question, Dryfoos felt, and took "the offensive for the next 35 or 40 minutes." Dryfoos said that he himself did not like the idea of a "limited emergency with censorship and submission of material and the like, but I doubted that he wanted any emergency declared.

"I said the alternative is to continue to do as we are doing now, and when things happen that you know should not happen in the way of leaks of security matters, the thing to do is to call in the publishers and explain the matter to them," Dryfoos said.

The president cited a leak on a missile story that had been reported by Hanson W. Baldwin, *The Times*'s military columnist, and showed Dryfoos the original top-secret document from which the story had been obtained.

Dryfoos agreed that it was too bad that that story had appeared, but he reminded the president of stories *The Times* had not printed, including one about the U-2 overflights of Soviet territory and the Bay of Pigs invasion.

"I said, Mr. President, what would you have done? On another occasion we had a three-column head announcing the Cuban invasion in the office ten days or so before it took place. I said we had a problem with the Guatemala piece on January 10, 1960. What would you have done with them? What if we had run the Cuban story?

"He said, 'I wish you had run everything on Cuba.' I said if we had maybe I wouldn't be sitting here representing *The Times* either. He said, you have got to tell this story on Cuba; there is no question about it; I am just sorry you didn't tell it at the time."

In 1966, Clifton Daniel, then managing editor, involved himself in the Bay of Pigs fall-out, inspired by an account of *The Times*'s role written by Arthur M. Schlesinger, Jr., in his book about the Kennedy administration, *The Thousand Days*. In a speech, he attempted to set a fuzzy record straight.

Daniel, a conscientious newsman, recognized the slipperiness of events. In 1972, he wrote to Herbert L. Matthews, the *Times* foreign correspondent who early on reported on the Castro rebellion from its breeding place in the remote Sierra Maestre mountains (Matthews was himself a controversial figure, having been castigated by right-wingers for his reporting from Loyalist Spain during the Civil War there, and later for not having emphasized the Communist nature of Castro's uprising):

> Our exchange of letters shows how difficult it is to get the facts of history straight, and it reenforces the point I have so often made—that people who participate in great events

should keep some current record of what was said and done. That was not done in the case of the Bay of Pigs invasion, and my speech to the World Press Institute at Macalester College in 1966 was an effort to rectify that omission. As I said in that speech, "What actually happened is, at this date, somewhat difficult to say. . . ."

As you say, you and I do not disagree on the fundamentals of the Bay of Pigs story but I have, over the years, found it very irritating that the myth of our suppression of Tad Szulc's story persists in spite of all efforts to dispel it. I had hoped that my speech would serve that purpose but apparently it hasn't.

The Bay of Pigs incident prompted discord in the newsroom, and executives later conceded that *The Times* had not pursued the story leading up to the "invasion" with its expected diligence and had let down the readership by not airing the preparations with the detail they warranted.

Redemption and a turnabout by *The Times* in its vision of public responsibility erupted with the series of startling revelations contained in what became known as the Pentagon Papers. As the archivists record, on June 13, 1971, *The Times* published the first of a series of articles based on a secret government study of American participation in the Vietnam war. The copy of the forty-seven-volume study by analysts for the Department of Defense had been passed along to *The Times* outside official channels by Daniel Ellsberg, who had worked on the study. The report criticized American policies and found that the government had misrepresented its role to the public. The Justice Department, citing national security, obtained an order from a United States district court that enjoined *The Times* from publishing further articles on the report. The Supreme Court, in a ruling called historic, overturned that order and upheld the freedom of the press. *The Times* resumed publication of the study on July 1, 1971.

The enormous impact that publication of the Papers by *The Times* is evidenced by the fourteen cubic feet of readers' mail, news articles, litigation papers, notes, memoranda, pictures, reports, and the study itself in the archives.

That the story was not only a hot scoop but also a hot potato was evident from the first acquisition of the Papers. Traditionally, as we have seen, *The Times* had always been painstaking in its coverage of foreign affairs, including, of course, military matters, not to endanger what it saw as a public responsibility. Now, publisher Arthur Ochs Sulzberger and managing editor A. M. Rosenthal faced up to a most challenging issue, whether to publish a secret Pentagon study whose information was of a highly incendiary nature because it revealed the government's evasions and deceptions. The evolution of the story from conception to fact is told in the succession of archive memos.

On June 1, Abe Rosenthal in a lengthy memo to Punch Sulzberger, spelled out the plans and the rationale for the series.

---

CONFIDENTIAL
MEMORANDUM for:   Mr. Sulzberger         from A. M. ROSENTHAL
                  Mr. Reston

        I believe we are now in a position to give the
Publisher sufficient information on which to base a decision.

        I am submitting this material for two purposes:

        (1)  In case this story breaks elsewhere, we would
be in a position to publish the bulk of the story quickly.
What I am giving you is the guts of it.

        This would be our plan for publication in case the
story broke elsewhere:

        A piece by Rick Smith explaining the origins and
import of the Pentagon study.  Several pages will be inserted
in this story giving some of the highlights of the total
material.  This is in hand.

        This will be published on the first day.  Also to
be published on the first day is the first half of Neil
Sheehan's piece dealing with the most important aspects of
the material -- the events leading up to the Tonkin Gulf.

        The next day we would publish the second half of
the Tonkin Gulf story by Sheehan.  This whole story is in hand.

        The third day we would publish Sheehan's piece deal-
ing with the events leading to the bombing of North Vietnam
and continuing through the beginning of the land war in Asia.

        This piece is not yet in hand but should be available
early next week.  The Publisher will see this.

        It is important for us to publish the Sheehan material
early in the series because this is the material that we believe
is in the hands of McCloskey and others.  If we did it all
chronologically, we would not get to Sheehan until the fifth or
sixth day and by that time, the story might be busted by others.

        The fourth day we will start with the beginning
chronologically -- Fox Butterfield's piece on the Geneva Accords
and up through the early 1950's.  This is in hand.

        The fifth day we will publish Rick Smith's piece on
the Kennedy administration from 1961-1963.  This will be in
hand Thursday and the Publisher will see it.

The sixth day we will publish Rick Smith's piece on
the Diem coup. This is in hand.

Also in hand are pieces to be published subsequently
on Rostow by Kenworthy and another piece by Butterworth on the
roots of the insurgency.

Each day we will also publish textual documentation.

In hand to be submitted to the Publisher is the
documentation of all the stories listed above. Also to be
submitted to the Publisher is the textual documentation we
would publish with the total series.

(2) We are now in a position, I believe, where the
Publisher can make the decision not only in connection with
the possibility of the material being published elsewhere first
but in relation to the fundamental decision as to whether we
should publish if there is no substantive leak, when we have
the remaining few pieces in hand and the total series is ready
to go.

We all believe that the remaining few pieces will
not affect this basic decision, particularly since all the
documentation that we will print with them is now available
to the Publisher. If I believed that the few pieces not yet
in hand in any way could affect the basic decision on whether
or not to publish, I would not be submitting any. We have
the total documentation, to repeat, and most of the stories.
The remaining stories do not present any other legal, ethical
or journalistic problems that are not inherent in the material
now being submitted to the Publisher.

If we wait until all these pieces are in, we could
not submit them to the Publisher until after he returned from
Europe. I wish to make it clear that if we thought these
remaining pieces could substantively affect the crucial decision
on publication, I would wait.

If an affirmative decision is made on the basis of
this material, we will not only be in a position to publish
in case of an emergency but we will also be able to proceed
with printing the entire series as soon as possible even if
there is no leak.

I believe that even if the material is not exposed
elsewhere, we should print the series as soon as physically
possible.

As you will see, the whole series follows some rather
decided philosophical and journalistic ground rules.

What we are presenting is the Pentagon version of the
war and its origins. What our reporters have contributed is the
essential task of selecting the essence of 7,000 single-spaced
pages of Pentagon analysis and documentation and presented it
in a sequential and logical manner.

This is not The New York Times history, I emphasize,
but The New York Times's report on the Pentagon's history -- and
this is what makes it far different and far more significant,
in my opinion, than previously published material.

A. M. R.

The effect of the first story was enormous, both on the public and also on the government, which obtained a restraining order. Three weeks later, when the lower court's decision was reversed and *The Times* had a green light to continue, Rosenthal sent Sulzberger a confidential memo outlining future coverage.

Mr. Sulzberger

CONFIDENTIAL

As Scotty and I indicated the other day, I'm afraid we have to examine the question of how long the series will run in view of the enormous world impact and interest.

It revolves simply around the question of a couple of days more.

The decision was to print for seven days, although as you will recall the editors really felt we should run a longer series.

I would like to run nine days on the series. The reason is that we do have that many important stories to tell. The last one will be shorter.

I am attaching Jimmy's list of the stories we still have ahead.

I feel that there are no sound journalistic reasons at the moment for us to curtail the series.

I do feel that there are a great many sound journalistic reasons why we should tell the full story that we have to tell, particularly since it is simply a matter of a couple of days more and making it seven instead of nine, as I'm sure you will agree, is not a matter of principle. Journalistically, I think we would be hardput to explain why we killed a couple of good stories at a time when the whole world wanted information about the Pentagon papers. Our record has been spotless on this so far and I think it would be too bad if we laid ourselves open to criticism of not telling the whole story by taking a decision to lop off two days for no discernible journalistic principle.

Yours in brotherhood,

A. M. R.

P.S. The stories attached in Jimmy's list may not necessarily run in that order.

June 21, 1971

On that day, Rosenthal wired Seymour Topping, managing editor, who was visiting London:

LONDON

TOPPING INFORMATIVELY FEDERAL JUDGE GURFEIN RULED RESOUNDINGLY
SATURDAY IN FAVOR OF TIMES ON FREEDOM OF PRESS AND NATIONAL SECURITY
ISSUES AND REFUSED TO GRANT INJUNCTION. HOWEVER BAN ON PUBLICATION
IS CONTINUED THROUGH TUESDAY PENDING GOVERNMENT APPEAL BEFORE FULL
COURT OF APPEALS. LIKELIHOOD IS CASE WILL GO SWIFTLY TO UNITED
STATES SUPREME COURT. TIMES IS COVER STORY ON TIME AND NEWSWEEK
AND REACTION AROUND COUNTRY CONTINUES HEAVILY FAVORABLE. REGARDS
ROSENTHAL

6/21/71
11:45am
nc

*The Times* not only made the news but was swamped with reaction from its readers, as Kalman Seigel, who supervised the Letters to the Editor column on the editorial page, noted in a memo on that busy June 21: "This is a fine batch on an absolutely tremendous job. We're now passing our 1,654th letter on the Pentagon papers, and we're winning about five to one."

### Paying the Lawyers

Covering big stories with litigation complications does not come cheaply, as James C. Goodale, house counsel of *The Times,* indicated in a memo to Punch Sulzberger in late January 1972. Goodale summed up "the extent of legal activities for the News Department in 1971."

Total legal fees, he reported, amounted to $382,416, of which the Pentagon Papers cost $320,000, including $285,000 for outside fees and $17,000 for inside. Two other big cases accounted for another $55,000. "It was a busy year," Goodale concluded.

The flood of incoming kudos swamped the office. At the same time, a number of in-house congratulations had to be passed along to employees who had worked hard and secretly on a story that was as close to dynamite as any revelation that had appeared in newsprint.

The publisher responded favorably, but with several nervous cavils.

```
                                        from A. O. Sulzberger

MEMORANDUM for    MR. ROSENTHAL


Abe,

              I have reviewed once again the Vietnam story and
documents that would appear on Sunday, and I am prepared to authorize
their publication in substantially the form in which I saw them.

              However, I would make the following points:

              1.   In the unlikely event that the Federal Government
moves in court to force us to cease publication, we will honor any court
injunction.   Also, if the Government moves through any other process
to get us to surrender the documents, this is a decision I leave to Harding
Bancroft and my business and legal associates.

              2.   I ask that prior to publication either Harding or
Sydney be given ample time to read the material to ensure that we are
not taking any unnecessary risks and that no military secrets have slipped
in.

              3.   I urge you, once again, to do the tightest possible
editing job on all of this material, particularly in the light of the decision
to print the documents.   As I mentioned to you yesterday, I feel that
the stories I saw were still over-written and unnecessarily complicated.
I strongly recommend a very sharp blue pencil.

              Good luck.


                                        A. O. S.

June 10, 1971
cc: Mr. H. F. Bancroft
```

The extent to which this enormous *Times* scoop was nurtured by the large crew that inevitably had to work on it was underscored in a note on July 8, 1971, from Abe Rosenthal to Bertram A. Powers, head of the printers' union: "You should know that our composing room staff did a fine job in helping us complete our publication of the Pentagon papers. Nearly 60 of our I.T.U. people worked on this project at various times and not a single word of this confidential material was prematurely revealed."

About the same time, Rosenthal was commending the production staff that had created a composing and proof room and newsroom on the ninth floor, distant from prying eyes and news-calibrated noses, a "really inspirational feat," the managing editor wrote to Punch Sulzberger, who also passed along his thanks and greetings to the news staff and others who had landed *The Times* on page 1 of every major publication in the United States.

A year later, on the first anniversary of that first article, Abe Rosenthal wrote a piece entitled "What a Free Press Is All About." The article noted that the fallout continued, with the publication of books and the forthcoming trial of Daniel Ellsberg, the man who had been instrumental in giving the papers to *The Times*.

"So very much has been written about the decisions involved and yet, as all newspapermen know happens often, the essence has not been written," he observed. "The essence is this: Three times the reporters, editors, executives of The Times had placed before them, in one big bundle that simply would not go away, all those blood-and-bone issues that people spend lifetimes evading."

Further on, he wrote, "Some unpleasant 'things' happened, not because of the publication of the papers but because the Government rushed into battle against them. . . . By far the most important was that for the first time, a Government of the United States asked for and courts granted an injunction against newspapers—and prior restraint, death to a free press, had a precedent." It would be another two years until charges against Ellsberg would be dismissed and the government efforts to throttle leaks and publications gasped their last, at least in this case.

In a note to a friend, written in 1975, Abe Rosenthal confessed that he shared the terrors of being "taken" that nag at canny newspeople when big stories fall in their laps: "Listen, the greatest nightmare I had when I first saw the Pentagon Papers, was that they were written by a thousand SDS kids in some loft at Harvard. You know— one of them would say—I'll be McNamara and you be the Chairman of the Joint Chiefs. But believe me, they're real, they're real, they're real."

# 13

# STATE OF THE NATION

T HE "TELEGRAPH DESK" was the closest I came to big-time journalism when I showed up for my first night's work at *The New York Times* in 1946. It was only a few feet away from the copyboy's bench, at the north end of the newsroom horseshoe desk arrangement that began at the other end with what old-timers still called the Cable Desk. "Telegraph" and "cable" are extinct terms in the newsroom now, but they accurately described how each desk then received most of its news.

The Cable Desk got its name from the transoceanic cables that transmitted the foreign news. The Telegraph Desk was the conduit for national news that arrived by cross-country wires (the news agencies, such as the Associated Press, Reuters, and United Press International, are still known as "wire services"). In those days, there was a Western Union office that clicked away in *The Times*'s "wire room." Well into the twentieth century, cable and telegraph were the main conduits for telex—the teleprinters that carried long-distance communications. Telephones had come to *The Times* in 1890 (first *Times* phone number: Cortlandt 1470), and by midcentury reporters in the field could, as the communications arts developed, dictate stories over the telephone ("Get me rewrite, sweetheart," à la Hollywood) and painfully spell out names to a rewrite bank in the newsroom, or in a great leap forward at *The Times,* the recording room, where experienced operators placed the reporters' stories, as written, directly onto disks that they then copied out and sent to the appropriate desk.

The Telegraph Desk was peopled by a cadre of old-time newsmen, almost all of them, it seemed to me, given to cackling at each other in New England twangs. They were a well-read collection of men who were familiar with baseball and political lore, Emerson's essays and Caesar's *Gallic Wars* in the original (although that would have been a Foreign Desk story had it been so fortunate as to have broken out at a time when *The Times* could have covered it). The classics proved difficult criteria against which to match incoming deadline correspondence; you rarely heard kind words from these men about the copy they were charged with transforming into literate passages. There was a large helping of crustiness on that desk, but it was mostly outside, as befits crust, and many of them proved to be approachable and even helpful to the callow youths who mustered up sufficient nerve to approach them.

By 6:00 P.M. the copy came rolling in, accurately timed and in a flood tide. Stories came from wire room to a copy sorter's desk and then, marked with a T, delivered to what later became the National News Desk. The bulk of copy often seemed to originate in Washington, the work of Big Names like Arthur Krock and James Reston. For several hours the stories hurtled in piecemeal, pages from one account jumbled with copy from others, a mishmash of paper that had to be straightened out and put in correct sequence. This was done by a young clerk on the Telegraph Desk who passed the stories on to a stern-looking, gruff-spoken ramrod of an editor, Wilson L. Fairbanks,

---

### A Cause

*The Times* was purposely not a crusading paper from the moment it was bought by Adolph Ochs. But it could be investigative in its news columns and partisan in its editorials. One of the nearest flirtations with a crusade took place in 1914.

In that year Leo Frank, a Jewish New Yorker living in Atlanta, where he manufactured pencils, had been arrested in Georgia on charges of murdering a young woman employee. Ochs, a member of the American Jewish Committee, had been persuaded by the eminent lawyer and community leader Louis Marshall of Frank's innocence. *The Times* offered detailed coverage of the trial, and the case drew national attention. Frank wrote a personal letter to the publisher (reproduced on the next two pages). In this letter he expressed his faith in his vindication and his appreciation to *The Times* for its support. Frank, who was later convicted, sentenced to death, and his sentence commuted to life imprisonment, was lynched in 1915 by a band of vigilantes.

a Greek and Latin scholar. That clerk was Arthur Gelb, later to become the managing editor of *The New York Times*. Fairbanks, like many senior journalists in his time, was one of those editors who had taken the desk job years previously to end the wear and tear of chasing stories.

Although New York controlled of the flow of national news into the paper, the Washington Bureau retained until the 1960s a high de-

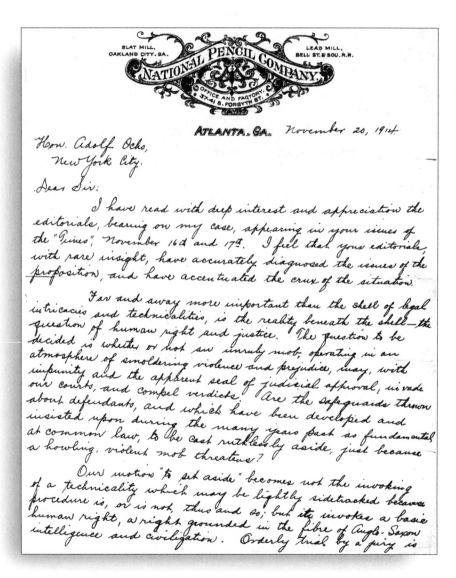

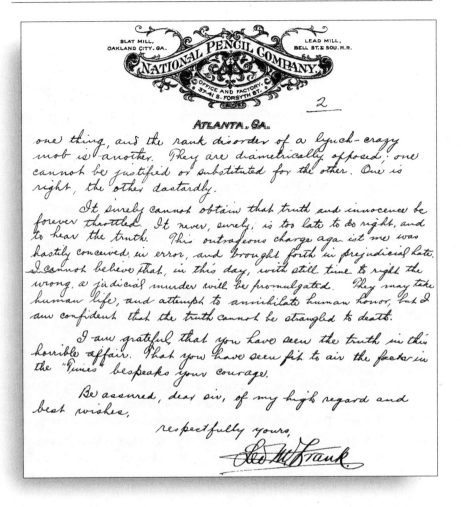

one thing, and the rank disorder of a lynch-crazy mob is another. They are diametrically opposed; one cannot be justified or substituted for the other. One is right, the other dastardly.

It surely cannot obtain that truth and innocence be forever throttled. It never, surely, is too late to do right, and to hear the truth. This outrageous charge against me was hastily conceived, in error, and brought forth in prejudicial hate. I cannot believe that, in this day, with still time to right the wrong, a judicial murder will be promulgated. They may take human life, and attempt to annihilate human honor, but I am confident that the truth cannot be strangled to death.

I am grateful that you have seen the truth in this horrible affair. That you have seen fit to air the facts in the "Times" bespeaks your courage.

Be assured, dear sir, of my high regard and best wishes,

respectfully yours,

Leo M. Frank

gree of independence. Under the leadership of two strong bureau chiefs, first Arthur Krock and later James Reston, the bureau often seemed to us in New York like a separate journalistic nation. I used to think that the Washington Bureau might any day, in a fit of pique, secede from *The Times* and publish its own newspaper. Its population appeared to be as different from us unpolished New York types as Yalies were from townies. The bureau men and women radiated charm, poise, neat haircuts, preppy rigging, and assurance when they flooded into 43rd Street usurping desks and chairs every four years for election night.

The National, or Telegraph, Desk spread its tentacles to every corner of the country. It boldly and superbly reported the spreading struggle for integration. It surveyed national education and was the desk through which the lunar-landing copy was channeled. But coverage of Washington was no less urgent than coverage of New York (sometimes more so, in the eyes of space-starved cityside staffers).

The archives feature many "Dear Arthur" letters between the two Arthurs, Krock and Sulzberger. Krock had succeeded to the chieftancy in Washington after the death of Richard V. Oulahan in 1931. It was not a job that he had set his cap for. AHS wrote to Ochs in February 1932, "As I wired you, Arthur Krock goes to Washington on Monday, February 14th to head the bureau. I felt more or less like an executioner in asking him to go, since it involves breaking up his family for the time being. . . . He has a lease on his apartment which, as I understand, runs through 1933, but he has made no reference to any living allowance in Washington and I have not raised the issue with him."

Five months later, Krock wrote to AHS, not yet "Dear Arthur" but "Dear Mr. Sulzberger," that he wanted to rejoin the New York staff when he had finished "having reorganized the Bureau." Krock went on to discuss the merits of candidates for bureau chief: "I believe there are only two staff men at Washington possibly competent to take over the position of Chief Correspondent. One is C.W.B. Hurd; the other is Turner Catledge. My personal opinion is that Mr. Catledge is the better qualified." Krock wrote that, should New York feel that Catledge was not sufficiently experienced, he himself would return to Washington for the next congressional session and prep Catledge for the job.

"As far as I am concerned, I should be best pleased with an arrangement by which I, with the title of Political Editor and headquarters in New York, could be given general supervisory scope over the Washington Bureau and make frequent visits there for the purpose of writing. I believe I could quickly demonstrate the value of this plan, which has the advantage of introducing a fresh viewpoint frequently in Washington. My objection to the fixed correspondent plan, based on a good deal of experience and observation, is that the capital as steady diet is demoralizing to good journalism."

Krock spent the rest of his long and productive working life in Washington, steering the bureau on an independent course that was

180 degrees away from those set by the home-office navigators in New York, the city he did not want to leave.

Although by virtue of his job he was one of the nation's best-known and most powerful Washington correspondents and despite the fact that he fostered the most promising talents in his bureau, Krock was sensitive about his prerogatives. A letter to AHS in 1946 complained about the play given to dispatches by James Reston, a distinguished young reporter for *The Times* who wrote out of the capital at the bureau and who had won the special esteem of the publisher and his family. At issue was the Q head, a box-type headline that announced to the reader that the piece below it spoke with inside authority that went beyond pure factual reporting, a sort of analytical article that was not quite an editorial opinion.

"I gather that the promotion of Mr. Reston to the Q head on Washington dispatches is by your order," Krock wrote. "Perhaps you will not be impressed . . . by the reasons for my objection, and see no reason why the matter should have been discussed with me in advance.

"When some years ago you told me you would like to substitute Mrs. [Anne O'Hare] McCormick's column for mine on Wednesday, the trend of the news offered sound basis for the change. I agreed, which should absolve me of any charge that I am petty about these things. I then began to contribute Wednesday pieces to the news columns, and the Q head was devised for display like Mr. [military editor Hanson W.) Baldwin's. I appreciated the compliment. I feel it is retracted when the head is used on other Washington dispatches. I think my service to The Times, in general and in particular, should impel you at all times to stand against any dilution of my position here.

"The latter observation, of course, is on the theory that the head of your Washington bureau continues to be responsible for what is published from this bureau. If that is no longer true, and Mr. Reston is at the head of an independent Washington bureau, then my point is a very different one. The Q head extension would then be only a part of a larger and more doubtful system."

Krock went on to express his support and admiration for Reston and declared, "I welcome the growing indications that he will head this Bureau one day. . . . But until you are ready to make him the Washington correspondent, or I am, I think he should not be given an equal status with me here in any particular."

AHS almost immediately acceded to Krock's demand and in a note to him said that he had asked Edwin L. James, the managing editor, to place background articles by Reston under other prominent two-column headlines. He observed that he did not agree with Krock and said, "You seem to overlook one fact entirely and that is that, regardless of what head is used over Mr. Reston's stories, he cannot sign them, 'by Arthur Krock.' "

The velvet-coated frictions persisted and the correspondence clues us in on the manner in which *The Times* did not manage so much as adumbrated its own delicate adjustments. In 1947, AHS was asked by James to clarify the Washington situation. AHS wrote to "Dear Scotty" Reston:

> When you first went down there, I talked the matter over with Mr. Krock and, at his suggestion, you were not attached to the Washington Bureau. In other words you were to act more or less independently with contact lines direct to New York. This has been working for some time now and, I think, not entirely satisfactorily.
>
> My suggestion, therefore, is that we change it and ask you to become a regular member of the Washington Bureau. In doing so, we will guarantee that you will not be given any picayune assignments. In fact, I think I am entirely safe in saying that you will be given the same degree of latitude as you now have. By merely making this change in the table of organization I think we will clear up some of the differences, expressed or unexpressed, that I know have been present.

A few months later, Krock indicated that he still had some reservations about Reston. In a letter to Turner Catledge, who had been his own original choice for bureau chief but left for a Chicago job and now was back with *The Times* in New York as assistant managing editor, Krock said: "Except for you I have never felt that anyone who has worked here with me completely meets the requirements of this exacting and dual job." Since Catledge had indicated that life in New York was not as pleasant as life in Washington had been, Krock had suggested that his "protégé" take over the bureau at year's end. Krock would continue to write pieces for the paper. Since Catledge was now going to remain in New York, Krock said he would not push his plans but would be trying to develop another prospect.

He wrote, "Reston may be able now, or when the time comes, to handle the executive end, but I feel very unsure of that. Also his eventual ambition seems to be toward another top job on the paper."

In 1953, twenty-one years after assuming leadership in Washington, Krock stepped aside to let Reston succeed him. His announcement to the staff followed a negotiation about where Reston would write a column for the daily, as Krock and Anne O'Hare McCormick were already doing on the editorial page, but not to appear on Saturday, the day that most journalists regarded as the readers' day off. The final agreement was embodied, like a high-level diplomatic document, in a "memorandum between me [AHS], Reston and Krock" and placed in the safe of an executive. Krock summed it up for the bureau:

"I planned this move for a much later time, but I made it when I did—a few weeks ago—because . . . Mr. Reston had received several very attractive offers to work elsewhere, some of them particularly tempting. I did not want The Times to lose his immensely valuable services, and I knew that I was in a position to offer him a strong inducement to stay with The Times for life. . . . In addition to taking over the Bureau Mr. Reston plans to do a column on the Sunday editorial page and frequent background articles in some fixed space on the news pages of the Daily."

On April 17 of that year, Krock sent a brief handwritten note to AHS, expressing gratitude for the publisher's graciousness in the affair, but even so, he injected a tart note.

"All may be as you say," he said, acknowledging the publisher's benevolent view of things, "though what I did was at least *intended* as a sacrifice. Now I am off for lunch with [Sunday editor Lester] Markel, who, I suspect, will try to drive me further underground."

The reference to Markel memorialized another source of in-house fighting, between the Sunday Department and the various divisions of the daily paper. An especially outspoken exchange erupted in 1948 when a bureau correspondent complained to Krock about a message Markel had sent to Cabell Phillips, his man in Washington, about a *Sunday Magazine* piece done by a freelance writer. The staffer said the message, which had been shown him by the freelance, said something like "Eureka! At last we have found someone in Washington besides Cabell Phillips who can write the way we want him to." The staffer called it a "gratuitous affront."

What followed was an exchange of "Dear Arthur–Dear Lester" correspondence. Markel wrote: "Arthur Sulzberger told me a month

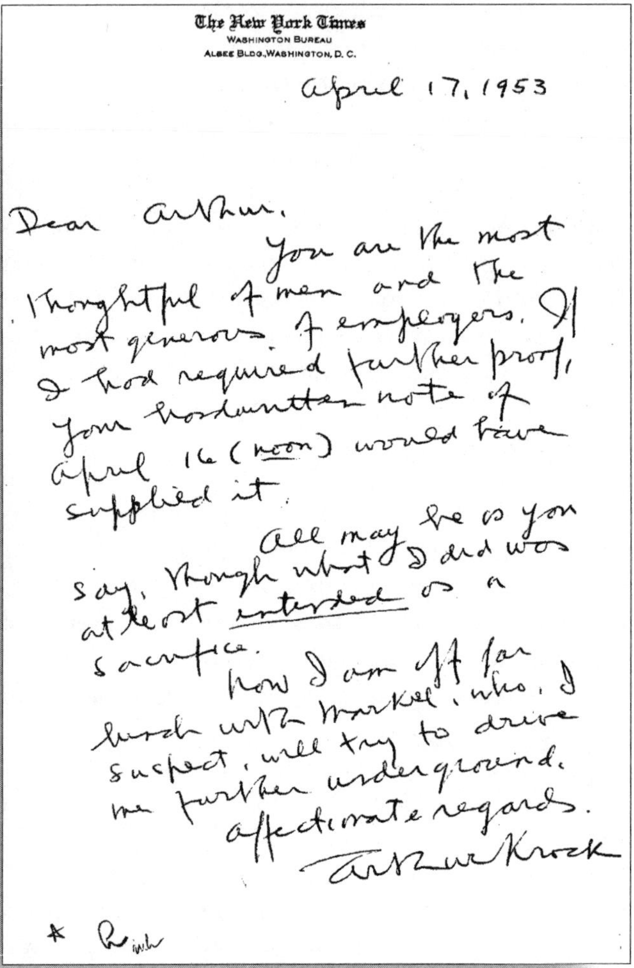

The New York Times
WASHINGTON BUREAU
ALBEE BLDG.,WASHINGTON, D. C.

April 17, 1953

Dear Arthur,

You are the most thoughtful of men and the most generous of employers. If I had required further proof, your handwritten note of April 16 (noon) would have supplied it.

All may be as you say, though what I did was at least intended as a sacrifice. Now I am off for lunch with Markel, who, I suspect, will try to drive me further underground.

affectionate regards.

Arthur Krock

* Reich

or so ago that he had had word from you that you wanted to be friendly with me. In the light of what has eventuated as a result of an innocent wire from me to Phillips, I wonder."

He said that his message had been sent "in a spirit of banter," expressing delight at finding a freelance for *Magazine* pieces "because, as you must be aware, we have had difficulty in getting Magazine articles in sufficient quantity out of Washington." No explanation was to the point, he insisted, because "I am reluctantly driven to the conclusion that you are intent on placing me in a difficult position, for what reason I cannot say."

In his reply, Krock gave as good as he got: "Finally, I did not report this disagreeable incident to the publisher and, since you are 'wondering' about some things, permit me to 'wonder' whether you would not have done so if the situation were reversed."

My own fondest recollection of the National News Desk, where my role, if any, was always a no-lines walk-on, revolves around election night, the quadrennial contest to choose a president. A special excitement enveloped the newsroom on those nights. By late afternoon, the Washington Bureau began to appear, appropriating desks from which their lesser New York colleagues had been ejected or sent off on assignments to polling places. A casting list was distributed, detailing who would be writing what stories and who would be assisting them. The efficient office managers and clerks had arranged "incoming" boxes at the desks of the appropriate reporters. One would do the national lead, another would write congressional results, and yet others would do the stories on local contests. It was a bewildering and complex maze in those years of handheld, handcrafted copy and it worked smoothly.

In addition to the Washington team, the focus of attention was on a sage and venerable political reporter, James O. Hagerty. Hagerty was lean and craggy. His paraphernalia consisted of a prodigious memory of who voted how and also of a fistful of cone-shaped charts that contained the voting history of pivotal districts.

The presence of so many well-known names who rarely came to New York, much less to the newsroom, the postprandial promenade by AHS, leading a contingent of distinguished visitors, the efficient hum of pros settling down to write history—all this spun a celebratory cocoon around the newsroom. The electric energy seemed to be shared downstairs and half a block away by the throngs that crowded Times Square to watch the results flash around the *Times* sign as it chugged around the one-building block where *The Times* had established itself early in the century.

The results clattered into the office, a whitewater surge of paper bulletins that threatened to overflow the in-boxes as well as the human computers whirring within the skulls of the reporters who were challenged to pick a winner that the statistics had yet to reveal. Putting out a newspaper was a ponderous proposition, no matter how speedy the workers. In those days, before television had preempted the election-return process and before computers could di-

The author, at right, monitoring election night returns in the newsroom in 1968, when Richard M. Nixon defeated Hubert H. Humphrey. (From R. Shepard's collection)

vulge the results in seconds after the polls closed, election night extras, off the press whenever a significant break in the count appeared (and often when it didn't) were expected. New leads had to be written, new heads created, new breaks in pages, new makeup, new plates brought to the presses, new schedules for the delivery trucks.

My first election assignment was to run copy, and a marathon night it turned out to be, the Truman–Dewey squeaker of 1948, when Hagerty, cannily and luckily, declined to declare a winner, as the *Chicago Tribune* did when it proclaimed Dewey's election. The very fact that a newspaper "claimed" or "conceded" an election before the votes were completely counted made as much news during election night as did the official results that arrived later. By 1952, the television screen had made its appearance in the newsroom and groups of reporters were chosen to monitor the networks. The impact on journalism was as great as the effect of the ascendancy of air travel had had on transatlantic-liner business.

The role that television plays in reporting the returns in short order was once played by newspapers. In New York, there was a hullabaloo of competition, not only in print but in the outdoor display of the vote count in the elaborate signs devised by papers for the huge election-night crowds that gathered in front of their offices. Ochs, displaying reportorial talent, described the scene to Effie in a letter, just before Election Day 1896.

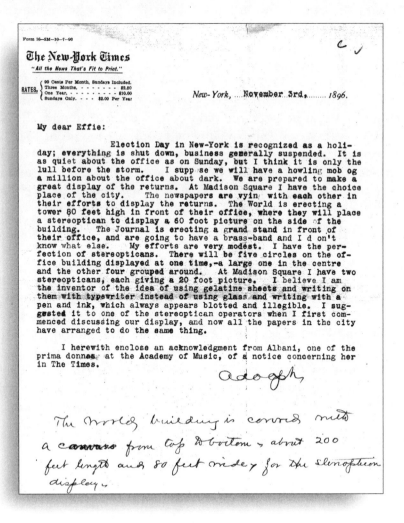

Form 16—8M—10—7—96

### The New-York Times
*"All the News That's Fit to Print."*

RATES: { 90 Cents Per Month, Sundays Included.
Three Months, · · · · · · · · $2.50
One Year, · · · · · · · · · $10.00
Sundays Only. · · · · $2.00 Per Year }

New-York, ...November 3rd,........1896.

My dear Effie:

Election Day in New-York is recognized as a holiday; everything is shut down, business generally suspended. It is as quiet about the office as on Sunday, but I think it is only the lull before the storm. I suppose we will have a howling mob og a million about the office about dark. We are prepared to make a great display of the returns. At Madison Square I have the choice place of the city. The newspapers are vying with each other in their efforts to display the returns. The World is erecting a tower 80 feet high in front of their office, where they will place a stereoptican to display a 60 foot picture on the side of the building. The Journal is erecting a grand stand in front of their office, and are going to have a brass-band and I don't know what else. My efforts are very modest. I have the perfection of stereopticans. There will be five circles on the office building displayed at one time,—a large one in the centre and the other four grouped around. At Madison Square I have two stereopticans, each giving a 20 foot picture. I believe I am the inventor of the idea of using gelatine sheets and writing on them with typewriter instead of using glass and writing with a pen and ink, which always appears blotted and illegible. I suggested it to one of the stereoptican operators when I first commenced discussing our display, and now all the papers in the city have arranged to do the same thing.

I herewith enclose an acknowledgment from Albani, one of the prima donnas at the Academy of Music, of a notice concerning her in The Times.

Adolph

*The World's building is covered with a canvas from top to bottom, about 200 feet length and 80 feet wide, for the stereoptican display.*

The morning after was a victory for Ochs, who had backed McKinley, and for *The Times,* which had drawn a crowd in Madison Square bigger than the one in City Hall Park. "The Times this morning compares most favorably with all the New-York newspapers," the new publisher wrote to his wife. "Everything worked nicely, and a few minutes ago told Mr. Trask that the greatest satisfaction I have out of it all is the knowledge I now have of the ability of my competitors and confidence in my own ability to compete with them."

Ochs jealously maintained the independence of his newspaper, especially in politics, that most treacherous of arenas into which so many publishers had tossed their hats and never retrieved them. In August 1900, the acting chairman of the New Jersey Republican State Committee offered to send 5,000 copies of the daily *Times* to readers he would choose. Ochs politely but firmly declined. "The New-York Times's advocacy of Mr. McKinley's election springs wholly from a sense of duty and responsibility we feel in the conduct of a widely circulated and influential newspaper, for the general welfare of our country. We cannot lend our aid in the free circulation of The New-York Times as a campaign document. People are too prone to believe that newspapers favor or oppose public policies for pay, and the free circulation at this time of copies of The New-York Times would in a manner justify such opinion." Finally, Ochs wrote, if he were to accept such a deal, the politician might then "for some reason infer" that *The Times* would not write anything unfavorable about the New Jersey Republicans.

This trepidation about incurring debts to interested politicians, an exemplary timidity, was challenged by the inevitable contact of publishers and editors with national leaders, as well as, of course, by the personal preferences of those connected with getting stories into the paper, whether reporter, headline writer, desk editor, or other. In 1982, Punch Sulzberger recognized the potential dangers if anyone besides the publisher plumped for candidates. In a note to the seven columnists regularly appearing on the Op-Ed page, he advised: "It is getting close to election time, so it seems appropriate to remind you once again to try and avoid going over the boundary or supporting individual candidates for office. This is a function that I should like to leave to the editorial page of The Times."

# HIGH-LEVEL
# INFLUENCE—ON US
# OR FROM US?

I notice in my mail a tendency to blame The Times for the overwhelming support by the whole press of the President in the last election," Scotty (a nickname derived from his birthland) Reston, referring to President Eisenhower, wrote to A. H. Sulzberger in January 1958. "This is no more than the usual tribute intelligent people paid to The Times for its preeminent position, but I think it increases our responsibility to be vigilant in reporting what is bad as well as what is good in the critical coming months."

Reston was replying to a mild AHS reprimand about a downbeat phrase the Washington columnist had employed; AHS stressed that it was necessary to avoid being negative. Reston did not disagree, but he added, "The problem is to find the delicate line between gnashing our teeth and misleading our readers."

One of *The Times*'s great advantages was its access to presidents and other policy makers. This easy entry, however, made it just as important for *Times*people not to be co-opted by those who understood the value of a friendly tone from the newspaper. And yet it was urgent that the opinion makers at *The Times,* which included columnists, correspondents, editors, and publishers, learn firsthand what was going on.

The relationship of *Times* executives to leaders of government has often been scrutinized. The question of who influences whom has various answers, all of them based more or less on mutual exploitation, the government to gain access to a most respected, often copied outlet and *The Times* to gain an exclusive edge on its competition. Under Ochs's administration, the paper was zealous about maintaining a patriotic posture, enhanced on the one hand by an awareness of its vulnerability as a Jewish-owned enterprise and on the other because of charges that it was excessively pro-British, because of an editorial position that had generally backed British positions on world issues.

Reaction to government wishes is evident in the Bay of Pigs story. Resistance to government wishes was never more emphatic than in the Pentagon Papers coverage. *The Times* has had much high-level contact with some presidents and almost none with others. Both Franklin D. Roosevelt and Richard Nixon, despite their contrasts in every other respect, remained shy of *The Times* and those in charge of its coverage.

The Ochs dynasty never entered the political arena in the way its journalistic forebear, Henry Raymond, did. Raymond, a founder of the Republican Party, was as much politician as pressman. Ochs, for all of his preferences and distastes, was essentially a newspaperman. He had ardently supported McKinley, but his politics was based less on personality than on principle, mostly conservatively Democratic.

It didn't seem to matter to presidents whether or not *The Times* had supported their campaigns. On June 18, 1920, for example, *The Times* ran a page 1 editorial on the nomination of Warren G. Harding for the presidency. Harding, it said, was a "very respectable Ohio

A note from William McKinley thanking Adolph Ochs for his support in the presidential campaign of 1900.

politician of the second class." He was never a leader of men. "We must go back to Franklin Pierce if we would seek a President who measured down to his political stature."

Yet, in November 1921, Julius Ochs Adler wrote enthusiastically about a visit to President Harding in the White House with his uncle, Adolph Ochs:

> He [Harding] at once recalled meeting Uncle Adolph many years ago in Chattanooga when he had planned to establish a paper there. . . . Uncle Adolph had told him that while there were a number of republicans in Chattanooga he did not believe a republican paper would prosper inasmuch as practically all republicans in the town were negroes and as he put it, negroes can't read. Mr. Harding claims this interview is responsible for his election to the Presidency, as without this advice he would probably have settled in Tennessee instead of Ohio.

Ochs went to Washington again in August 1923 to meet Calvin Coolidge, who had assumed the presidency upon Harding's death. Ochs wrote a confidential report summarizing his interview, during which the two discussed a broad range of domestic and foreign subjects. The president regretted "to witness departure of many churches and newspapers; when he went to church he liked to find them living up to their ideals instead of giving performances; liked to see the press measuring up to its real mission and ideals; too many comics and prize schemes."

Ochs described his visit more informally in a letter to his wife and his daughter. He was delighted to see that the president had a copy of *The New York Times* spread before him on his desk and to hear the president praise *The Times* as a newspaper that had become a national institution. Silent Cal, he wrote, was anything but taciturn, "the type of Vermont Yankee we picture."

Early in 1924, it was Arthur Hays Sulzberger's turn to meet presidents. "I had the rare opportunity today of talking to the only two living men who have been President of the United States [William Howard Taft was the other]—what is still more to the point we had lunch at the White House," he wrote to his parents. "The President had invited Mr. Ochs to be his guest while he was in Washington and Mr. Ochs, fearing to create the impression that The Times was sold bag and baggage to the Administration had declined—giving as an excuse that his daughter and son-in-law accompanied him. The result was that on arriving here this morning from Chattanooga, we found an invitation awaiting us to lunch at 1 P.M."

Mr. and Mrs. Coolidge gave a cordial greeting and "the President gave Iphigene his arm as they walked into the dining room." The "excellent" meal consisted of an appetizer of cold lobster, a chicken broth—spring lamb, potato patties, spinach, and stuffed apple cream puffs for dessert.

AHS good-humoredly noted that "Mr. Ochs kept up most of the conversation so that I am unable to say whether or not Mr. Coolidge is as taciturn as he is reported." When it came time to go, Iphigene received an "indefinite invitation to spend a week end at the White House."

Immediately after the election of Herbert Hoover in 1928, Ochs sent a congratulatory note: "Notwithstanding my high esteem and personal regard for you, in the free exercise of my honest opinion I preferred the election of your opponent New York's governor Alfred E. Smith." Hoover wrote back his appreciation for the fair campaign coverage in *The Times*. In the summer of 1930, Ochs was invited to visit Hoover at his camp on the Rapidan River, near Washington.

"The fact is, I was not looking forward to the trip [or] anticipating a pleasant time as I thought the party would rough it—fishing, horseback-riding, and things of that kind, and they weren't particularly my line."

The president singled out Ochs from the rest of the party to sit by him on the three-hour drive from the White House to the camp. In camp, "The time passed rapidly and very pleasantly. I was not called upon to do anything sporty, in fact nobody else did." Instead of fresh-air activity, Ochs and Hoover spent a good part of the day in conversation on a wide range of economic, political, and monetary matters.

On December 30, 1931, at the end of a gloomy year during which the Great Depression had deepened and seemed to offer no surcease from worry, Ochs made an after-dinner visit to the White House and spoke for more than two hours with Hoover.

"Of all the pessimistic views that have been presented to me, his was the most depressing I have heard," the publisher recorded in his notes on the meeting. "He is most deeply concerned; says we are on the brink of the most disastrous condition, and that it would be nothing short of miraculous if we escape what he fears may be the worst panic that has ever occurred in our history. He said there were at least five thousand financial institutions in the country that would be insolvent if forced to liquidate at present values. . . . He said, whether it is believed or not, that he never sought the presidency, and that he did not give a damn about being reelected; that he would gladly be relieved of the problems that are put up to him and get out of the hell in which he was living. . . . He asked my pardon for frankly saying he was disappointed in the attitude of The New York Times."

Ochs replied that *The Times* had not engaged in reckless criticism but indeed, had given Hoover "real support, even leaning backwards." Hoover referred to an editorial on his message and Ochs said

THE WHITE HOUSE
WASHINGTON

Warm Springs, Ga.,
November 26, 1934.

My dear Mr. Ochs:-

It is with regret that I find it necessary to write to you in regard to articles by a gentleman for whom I have high regard - Mr. Arthur Krock.

The particular occasion relates to Mr. Krock's article in the Times of November twenty first, which is in effect a personal attack on the Foreign Minister of Great Britain, Sir John Simon.

For your own information I may add that this article was carried in full by many British papers and coming from the New York Times was widely believed to be true. Also for your own information only may I add that Mr. Norman Davis and his colleagues were given great concern by this episode and feel that it has done much to hinder a friendly progress of negotiations in London.

One point I would make is that this article by Mr. Krock is so written as to make it appear that the statements of opinion are not his statements of opinion but are those of the State Department and my Administration as a whole. Frankly, I would not care if the opinions expressed were those of Mr. Krock but naturally I must object when the language implies that they are the opinions of the Government.

Presidents have almost always been sensitive to what appears in the *Times*. In his first term, Franklin D. Roosevelt was already disenchanted with Washington bureau chief Arthur Krock. In this letter of complaint he describes the importance of the paper as a disseminator of information.

he did not recall any criticism of the president's suggestions but that it did call for great leadership and "more vigorous action on the part of the President than he had displayed." Hoover said that he felt it was time for more support in matters that were nonpartisan. It was a wide-ranging conversation that touched upon all national and international issues, including Hoover's bitter criticism of liquid New York banks that would not help banks that were failing everywhere else. Almost every item would have made a first-page story in the paper but it is uncertain how much of it actually made its way into print.

The cordiality the publishers, politically Democratic for the most part, had enjoyed with the long string of Republican presidents did not extend to Franklin D. Roosevelt, who had been endorsed by *The*

> Finally, I must be frank in telling you that this is not the first occasion on which Mr. Krock has rendered a real disservice. I found it necessary to call his attention to a similar episode last year which seriously affected our national foreign policy. There have been a number of other incidents which I have passed over, and I shall not refer to them further.
>
> It is because the Times is so widely accepted because of the general fairness of its news stories that interpretive articles such as Mr. Krock writes are accepted as statements of news facts and it is only because of the splendid standing of the Times, not only in this country but abroad, that I am making this the first -- literally the first -- exception to my general rule of not writing to any Editor of any paper in regard to stories which their people send out from Washington.
>
> I know that you will appreciate the spirit in which I am sending this to you because you have often asked me to be quite frank with you and to call your attention to anything which I think is not wholly fair.
>
> With my warm regards,
>
> Faithfully yours,
>
> *Franklin D. Roosevelt*
>
> Adolph Ochs, Esq.,
> The New York Times,
> Times Square,
> New York, N. Y.

*Times* for all but one of his four terms. Roosevelt, according to correspondence in the archives, was leery of the paper, perhaps because of its power. Late in 1934, he wrote to Ochs, complaining about Arthur Krock, with whom the President early on had established a mutual distaste.

Ochs's reply, defending Krock and the article, also advised the president: "I should not for a moment tolerate what I thought to be mischievous, malicious or untrue writing in The New York Times. It is the fixed policy of The New York Times to aid the Government in every way possible and not willingly to embarrass it."

In 1940, Krock wrote to AHS with an anecdote told to him by Felix Belair of the Washington Bureau. At a press conference, FDR "took another occasion to gibe at The Times, the editorials, this time," the bureau chief reported. Belair then told the president that he had been about to ask a "political question" but decided not to. Krock wrote that the president said, "The Times wouldn't be interested, anyhow." "Why not?" "Oh, we take ourselves so seriously," said the president. "We carry the world on our shoulders. The Times can't be bothered about such things as you had in mind. How important The Times thinks itself," and so forth and so on. "I don't get the point of this and don't pretend to," Krock noted. "Maybe you can fathom something beyond his general grudge."

Krock himself apparently constituted a large part of the "general grudge." On Election Day 1944, with Roosevelt up for his fourth term, the correspondent wrote to AHS that it might be best, should FDR win, for Krock himself to be out of his office. "I am persona non grata at the White House, which the President has emphasized often by attentions to other Times executives and writers, and his election to a fourth term will mean that the 'non' in that phrase will assume capital letters. . . . Actually I have no fear that we shan't be able to get the news, as always in the past, and continue to be rated as the source of the most comprehensive and fairest news reports out of Washington, if arrangements continue as they are."

The fact that *The Times* can establish close personal contact with presidents does not, demonstrably, indicate cronyism. In 1979, Jimmy Carter wrote a very strong, not-for-publication letter "To the Publisher and Editors of *The New York Times*."

Punch's reply explained how news differs from editorials and columns. In a world that had changed so radically, it seemed that some things had not changed at all.

THE WHITE HOUSE

WASHINGTON

October 24, 1979

To the Publisher and Editors of The New York Times

Writing this letter is unpleasant for me because I believe that you have published one of the best newspapers in the country. However, I am increasingly concerned about the motivation and quality of The New York Times.

On too many occasions since I have been President you have published news articles and editorial columns which were seriously in error about matters with which I have been personally familiar. Some of them have involved public events and were damaging to our nation, while others have consisted of libelous statements about me and people close to me. You sponsor one columnist who is generally known to prevaricate and habitually to distort the truth. You could not fail to know these things.

It is impossible for a President or any other public official successfully to refute the inaccuracies which you print. This creates something of a dilemma for those of us who believe that the Times does care about accuracy, but who also realize that any corrective action must be predicated on a recognition of error and initiated by you.

As I am sure you know, the members of my family and my Administration have been exceptionally willing to answer any reasonable inquiry about themselves or their actions. Your more recent policy seems to be to print rumors or allegations first without regard to the confirmation of accuracy, and then to wait for some public denial to come from the people involved. This does not do justice to The New York Times I once knew nor to the readers like myself who have had confidence in you.

I have not written this letter for publication, but just as a friend of your newspaper who is concerned about its character and reputation and about the damage being caused by your news and editorial policy.

Sincerely,

Jimmy Carter

**The New York Times**
229 WEST 43 STREET
NEW YORK, N.Y. 10036

ARTHUR OCHS SULZBERGER
PUBLISHER

October 29, 1979

Dear Mr. President:

This will acknowledge your letter of October 24, addressed to me and the editors of The New York Times.

I find it difficult to respond to the broad accusation that we have published many news articles that have been "seriously in error" and "damaging to our nation."

Unquestionably, the pressures of time sometimes cause errors in our daily news report. When those errors are spotted, we notify our readers of the changed facts. After all, our stock in trade is the integrity of our report, and no one, least of all us, stands to gain by tampering with it.

I am well aware that the Presidential family is subjected to a strong spotlight, and am cognizant of the sensitive and personal nature of some of the stories we print. So, I assure you, are our editors. If we have been unfair or inaccurate, we would like to deal with your criticisms on a specific basis, for our only motive is to inform our readers accurately.

You will note that I have not commented on our editorial position or our individual columnists. These are articles of opinion and express either the view of the author or The Times. But, in either event, let me assure you that I seek both the same high standards of fairness and accuracy that is demanded in the news pages.

Believe me, when I say that we would like to deal with any specific problems, but, at the same time, please understand why I cannot accept the broad implications of your letter.

-2-

October 29, 1979

Let me add a personal note.   I have great
admiration for the way in which you have handled some of
the incredibly difficult questions facing our nation.    While
my colleagues and I may, and will,  differ with you in the
months ahead,  our goal is to do so in a constructive manner
and never damage our country.

As you have requested, we will, of course,
treat this correspondence on a "not for publication" basis.

With best wishes,

Sincerely,

*Punch*

President Jimmy Carter
The White House
Washington,  D.  C.   20500

bcc:  Mr. Frankel
        Mr. Gruson
        Mr. Rosenthal
        Mr. Wicker

There is no evidence in the archives that *The Times* has ever been
influential enough in modern times to swing a local, much less a national, election. For all that it may not sway masses, the paper demonstrably has influence with leaders. However, the influence is a polar
one, sometimes attracting, sometimes repelling the shapers of national destiny. For or against, *The Times* is a palpable element in
American national life.

# REPORTING:
# CITYSIDE
# AND OTHER

I T TOOK seven years from my copyboy start at *The Times* to get on staff or become a reporter, a period in which, I remarked, I might otherwise have become a brain surgeon. One of my proudest moments was when, with no ceremony at all, I was given "the shield," the press card issued by the New York City police that separates the elite of journalism from the support auxiliaries—clerical help, editors, printers, publishers, and others who do not get to go out of the office and bring in stories.

The press card has no magic properties in itself. It allows you to pass through police and fire lines, a dubious honor if someone is shooting or flamethrowing, but it has its own pasteboard charisma. It also identifies you as a person of some special influence. That fact opens doors barred to less documented citizens.

A press card has its liabilities, too. Meyer Liebowitz, a veteran *Times* photographer, was driving to an assignment with a reporter, a brash, overconfident type. Mike passed a red light and was stopped by a policeman. He gentled the cop with a bit of genial blarney and was about to drive off, ticketless, when the impatient reporter leaned across the front seat and imperiously snapped, "Officer, do you know who this is? This is Meyer Liebowitz, a *New York Times* photographer."

It was not the happiest moment to claim press priority. *The Times* had recently run stories on "cooping" cops, policemen who drowsed while on duty. The officer's placid countenance turned stormy. "So you're Meyer Liebowitz from *The New York Times* and you take pictures?" he asked rhetorically. Mike recalled, "The next thing I knew I had enough tickets to dress a battleship."

*The Times* always strictly warned staffers, and everyone else on its payroll, not to misuse the paper's authority. There was a young reporter, one of the well-bred, bright, Ivy League types, who stopped a train using the power of the press. He and his girlfriend had had a

The author, as he never looked in life, although reporters did wear fedoras and, on occasion, put their press shields in their hats. This photo was staged and taken by Phil Benjamin, an imaginative reporter who was counted among the best writers on staff.

late night out on the town and she had just missed the last train for Northampton, Massachusetts, where she went to school. The reporter drove her up to Inwood, where the train would cross the Harlem River bridge into the Bronx. He flagged down the train, but his press credentials were not sufficient excuse.

A clerk on the Night City Desk received the call from a voice at the police station that was shrieking, "You can't stop trains, even with a press card." The clerk, a seasoned deskman named Charles Krafft, handed the phone to Robert Garst, the editor. Garst turned red, then scarlet. The reporter was released—the power of the press, no doubt—but his reportorial career at *The Times* had been derailed.

*Times* reporters usually had more accessibility than others did, but they were also more certain of "upstairs" morning-after comment than others were. The definition of "upstairs" could be anywhere in the building. Upstairs would back its staff in public, and sacred cows were, it turned out, not sufficiently sacred for reporters to be fired because of probing stories.

Robert Moses was one of the most sacred of sacred cows at *The Times*. This imperious empire builder was an administrative poohbah in the city and state of New York, with all sorts of titles, from parks commissioner to chairman of the Triborough Bridge and Tunnel Authority. Mayors and governors rarely interfered with his projects, and Moses, an important figure in fashioning New York's parks, had established a friendship with AHS and Iphigene Sulzberger, who was one of the city's best friends when it came to parks. He was a hands-off figure for editors and reporters, and yet he was such a panjandrum that it was impossible to keep hands off. Hands-on meant conflict, because Moses rarely appreciated any questioning of anything within his vast province. He did not complain to the writers or even to their immediate bosses, but went right to the publisher.

In truth, the publisher did not intercede as much as it was generally believed he would. He bucked angry Moses epistles to his editors, who passed them on to the miscreant staffers. That was usually it. But letter-bucking has several meanings. It is always useful to complain to the head of any organization. If the Number 1 leader has no interest, the letter goes to a Number 2, who feels it may have significance because it came down from Number 1. By the time the letter finds its way down to Numbers 4, 5, or 6, its provenance has bestowed on it a special cachet and something may be done.

The archives contain reassuring evidence that the relationship between Moses and the publisher was often a mutual soft-soaping one. The Sulzbergers really admired Moses, but they also recognized that he was an ornery character. In a letter to AHS in 1951, Moses complained about an editorial that criticized him (he was then city planning commissioner) for behaving as "a sort of Obstruction Coordinator."

Moses sadly told "Dear Arthur" that "This is way below the belt and not the kind of thing you countenance." He reviewed his actions and concluded: "You have a right to your opinion, but not to attack and vilify your friends if their friendship means anything to you, not to speak of discouraging honest, alert public service at a time when it is generally at a very low ebb."

AHS passed the letter along to Charles Merz, in charge of editorials. "I must say I didn't like this piece when I saw it and I think Bob is correct. It isn't fair to call him an Obstruction Coordinator. What am I going to answer?"

Merz passed it along to William D. Ogdon, who had written the editorial. Ogdon wrote a long explanation that began, "In view of all the hard names that Robert Moses has called those who disagreed with him, through the years, and the nice things we have said about him on numerous occasions, I am somewhat surprised that he objects when we state our opinion sharply—which is what he always does." Merz composed a reply to Moses that recalled earlier tributes to him in the columns of *The Times*; he denied that there was any intention to "vilify" the builder and said that he didn't think the editorial had done so.

In June 1953, AHS sent a letter, STRICTLY PERSONAL AND CONFIDENTIAL, asking Moses if he would be embarrassed if *The Times* urged his candidacy for mayor. Moses declined with thanks.

Turner Catledge, the managing editor and later executive editor, found that Moses was heavy traffic on the news expressway. Every Moses story turned into a fender-bender at the very least. Here, dated December 1957, is a piece by Clayton Knowles that dented the administrator in the first paragraph: "Marshaling arguments in elaborate brochures is old hat for Robert Moses, chairman of the State Power Authority, but the one he released yesterday to quash opposition in a little upstate town, tops anything yet seen." The story went on to tell of an expensive forty-eight-page booklet designed to impress the 6,291 citizens of the town of their erring policy. The Moses letter, predictably, arrived the same day at the desk of Orvil Dryfoos—second-in-command to AHS—on Power Authority stationery.

The reply conceded that the lead in the story was "somewhat editorial" in its phrasing but defended the article as "a fair and objective piece of reporting." Knowles had no sinister purpose, Dryfoos assured Moses, and the piece was prompted because there had been comment on these brochures.

Two years later, in March 1959, Moses, on the letterhead of the Office of the Committee on Slum Clearance, was complaining about a letter from Charles Grutzner, another front-desk reporter, requesting an interview. Grutzner was looking into a Gramercy slum clearance project and had been told by Moses's office that written questions would have to be submitted before an interview would be

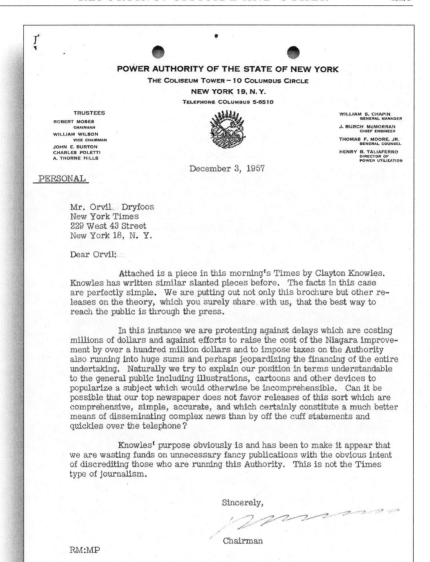

**POWER AUTHORITY OF THE STATE OF NEW YORK**
THE COLISEUM TOWER – 10 COLUMBUS CIRCLE
NEW YORK 19, N. Y.
TELEPHONE COLUMBUS 5-6510

December 3, 1957

PERSONAL

Mr. Orvil Dryfoos
New York Times
229 West 43 Street
New York 18, N. Y.

Dear Orvil:

   Attached is a piece in this morning's Times by Clayton Knowles. Knowles has written similar slanted pieces before. The facts in this case are perfectly simple. We are putting out not only this brochure but other re-leases on the theory, which you surely share with us, that the best way to reach the public is through the press.

   In this instance we are protesting against delays which are costing millions of dollars and against efforts to raise the cost of the Niagara improve-ment by over a hundred million dollars and to impose taxes on the Authority also running into huge sums and perhaps jeopardizing the financing of the entire undertaking. Naturally we try to explain our position in terms understandable to the general public including illustrations, cartoons and other devices to popularize a subject which would otherwise be incomprehensible. Can it be possible that our top newspaper does not favor releases of this sort which are comprehensive, simple, accurate, and which certainly constitute a much better means of disseminating complex news than by off the cuff statements and quickies over the telephone?

   Knowles' purpose obviously is and has been to make it appear that we are wasting funds on unnecessary fancy publications with the obvious intent of discrediting those who are running this Authority. This is not the Times type of journalism.

Sincerely,

Chairman

RM:MP

Sent by hand.

granted. Charlie, a top reporter, an unassuming man who smoked the cheapest White Owl cigars and, back from assignment, alternated between writing a page of copy and playing a hand of bridge, asked eight questions.

Moses did not answer him or the questions, but wrote to Dryfoos saying that the tone of Grutzner's queries showed that "Obviously it is not primarily directed at getting information. . . . What he wants from the manner in which these questions are phrased is material which would enable him to insinuate in his articles that the Committee has favored sponsors for its projects who get preferred and special treatment, that no legitimate bidder has a chance." Wounded, Moses said, "Mr. Grutzner's questions would indicate that our Committee is on trial and must defend itself against the implied charges in these questions in a tribunal established by The Times."

That spring and summer seemed to be especially clogged with Moses problems. On St. Patrick's Day, a curt note, hand-delivered to "Dear Orvil," begins, "I see that you continue the Grutzner 'news.' Your reporter and the copy editors who take their cue from him might have brought in the fact that . . ." Dryfoos passed the note to Catledge, who wearily acknowledged it and sent it back to the fourteenth floor with only the observation "He keeps it up, doesn't he?"

AHS had had enough. Moses had been invited to lunch at *The Times* to discuss his problems. He refused to come if reporters he did not like were invited. That did it. In what might be regarded as a modified Emancipation Act, AHS, on March 19, 1959, notified Dryfoos, "I'm not showing up for luncheon . . . I'm not going to have Bob Moses determine whom he's to meet at our luncheon table . . . and don't bring him back here when he comes."

Garst, in June, sent Orvil a list of *Times* reporters who were personae non gratae in the Moses camp. "His rule apparently is that we are in his good graces when we print something he likes and are in his bad graces when we do a thorough reporting job that covers all sides of the question. . . . Surely, so many good reporters cannot be wrong."

Things had gotten to the point that on June 23, AHS wrote a Moses-class reply to "Dear Bob," who had questioned whether the publisher believed his friend was up to benefiting "some crook." In the letter, AHS answered that he had not concluded that Moses was a crook "nor have I come to the conclusion, because of your treatment of The New York Times reporters as indicated by your unwillingness to see them, that you are a difficult man to get along with. I have known that for a long time. . . ."

Robert Moses was one of the most interesting examples of instances that brought *Times* executives, editors, and reporters into conflicting stances, but fortunately he was not typical of what most reporters dealt with most of the time. *Times* reporters were expected

to be ahead of the crowd and certainly more thorough than any
other newspaperperson would be on the morning after. The staff
represented a crazy quilt of personalities—journalism-school grads,
upgraded copyboys who had walked in off the street, friends and off-
spring of friends of well-placed *Times* officials, old-time reporters
whose work on other papers prompted management to make them
stars at *The Times*.

Reporting requires a keen mind, a quick eye, a sensitive ear, and
a nose for news. The metropolitan reporter is easily caught out by
readers the next morning. A foreign correspondent might misplace
an entire province to no great outcry, but let a local reporter misspell
a street and the mail piles up. There are few common threads that
link great reporters, no common bonds of temperament, vocabulary,
and lifestyle, not even a motivation greater than getting the story first
and most fully.

Homer Bigart and Peter Kihss were two great reporters at *The
Times*. Although they both came there, separately, from the *Herald
Tribune*, they could not have been more dissimilar.

Homer Bigart looked like everybody's idea of a Midwest bump-
kin. He had a round face, accentuated by Harold Lloyd eyeglasses
and a pudgy physique. His writing was the opposite of his looks. He
did not boggle at calling a diamond a spade. Homer's small-town
demeanor masked a high-tech sophistication that gave him an edge
when suave interviewees underestimated him. Homer won his
Pulitzers as a foreign correspondent, but his local reporting betrayed
the same curiosity and skepticism that brought him fame in places
like Zaire. During a riot on Wall Street by hard hats against anti–
Vietnam War protesters in the 1960s, Homer was the only reporter
who thought of speaking with the construction workers, who were
shunned by others.

I first heard of Peter Kihss when I was a young ship news reporter
assigned to go with my senior, Joseph Ryan, to cover an unusually
busy and newsy ship arrival. As we sailed out in the cutter to the liner,
Joe said to me, "We'll have to work today. There's Peter Kihss from
the Trib. He'll talk to everybody on the ship, from the cabin boy up."

Peter, in contrast to Bigart, was a tall, gangling man known to his
admirers as "the Vacuum Cleaner." Peter was the most scrupulous reporter I have ever met, a man whose goodness and dedication verged
on the naive. Yet his stories were marvels of detail, as though every trifle had been fed to him intravenously and become part of a meticu-

lously outlined account. Murray Schumach, one of the top *Times* reporters, told how Kihss would ask someone who had just made a self-
damning statement in a telephone interview if the other party *really*
wanted to say that, a reprieve Murray said he, Bigart, and most other
reporters would never have proffered.

Although he was one of the keenest, most thorough reporters,
Peter did not go for the jugular in his search for news. Once, when
he was gingerly discussing an exposé by another reporter on a story
he had originally been assigned to but had not come up with the req-
uisite newsy dirt on, he told me, "I always look into things and hope
the people we're talking to did not do what we thought they had."

Ship News was one of those beats that accompanied the rise of New
York as a great port and converted the city into a main channel of information from Europe. It lasted well into the age of air, which eventually carried not only more people but more messages more speedily
than water could. Ship News is now an extinct beat, having gone the
way of Arrival of Buyers and that much earlier casualty of time, the
hotel beat, where reporters made the rounds of leading New York
hostelries to see what news-making names might be in town.

The archives are not rich in ship news, but what I found there
prompted a rush of memory and stimulated the archives of my own
memory. In 1954 George Horne, the versatile editor of the department during my tenancy, asked Arthur Hays Sulzberger, a frequent
transatlantic voyager, to serve as informant, anonymously, on the situation at the passenger piers. Ship News was looking into the behavior of porters and others handling baggage who, it had been said,
were gouging passengers for larger-than-logical gratuities.

AHS's reply, which appears on the following page, made on the
same day that he received Horne's request, was as vehement and as
detailed as any he had given to any other question that had come
across his desk.

The nursing of publishers, editors, and assorted VIPs through
the raucous pandemonium attendant on a liner arrival was one of
the chores allotted to Ship News. Ship-line public relations was
alerted and customs was asked to issue an "expedite" that would get
the notable arrival through the hubbub with the least dislocation.
Sooner or later, it seemed, everyone in the office looked in at Ship
News for some sort of expedite or cruise discount. But that was a

*News Ideas*
*Transport News*

MR. GEORGE HORNE

I hope that I won't have a cerebral hemorrhage when I answer your memorandum.  The situation on the French Line dock at the time of the arrival of the Liberte was about as bad as anything I have ever witnessed, and I have been a traveler for a good many years!

There were porters standing around waiting for assignments, but because they did not wear French Line blouses and badges, I who was representing Mrs. Sulzberger and a lot of passengers stood for an interminable time waiting for a fellow in a blue smock who could handle the baggage.

Meanwhile, as I said, porters who were not as beautifully costumed were standing there idle.  The only thing that relieved me at all was that the man in front of me in line and the man behind me joined me in cursing the Line, the Union and the Port of New York.  I have to stop - I can feel the blood pressure rising!

When I finally did get a porter through the help of a Customs officer who was most courteous and attentive, I got hold of a great, big, pleasant fellow who got the luggage down very promptly after first putting on his blue smock, and I tipped him liberally.  He made no requests.

Many thanks, though, for all the help you gave me in advance of the arrival.

A.H.S.

November 1, 1954
mh

small part of the Ship News business, which played an important role in following the health of the port's major industry.

Ship News drifted out of business at *The New York Times* in the mid-1970s, becoming an aspect of Business News rather than its own creation. Its demise was a long time coming, ever since the 1950s, when airplanes began carrying more passengers across the western ocean than did the treadmill of transatlantic shipping that had been populating the Americas since the days of Columbus. There are not many surviving today who were members of what was called "the Ship News Fraternity," the reporters who sailed down the dawn-fringed harbor on Coast Guard cutters to scale, like a column of

The ship news reporters at work aboard a liner in New York Harbor.

ants, the ladders on the vast sides of the big liners as they slowed to
a halt off the Staten Island Quarantine Station on their way to the
North River piers.

   This is a vanished world. Battery Park City, Manhattan's newest
and most attractive extension into the harbor, sits on landfill that
buries the slip where United Fruit ships once disgorged city-sized
cargoes of bananas. A circumnavigation of Manhattan is a dismal
maritime review of piers that, once teeming with goods and people,
are now in senile decay, slipping into the murky river waters. This
was the liquid turf of the ship news reporter, a landsman living off
the sea.

   At West 14th Street are the remains of the Cunard pier, where
survivors of the *Titanic,* the maiden voyager that never made port,
finally reached New York. Upriver, in the West Twenties and Thirties, where the red-white-and-blue funnels of the United States Lines
freighter armada once created a forest of masts, only a residue of
small craft keep dockside ticking, feebly. The grand liner piers, from

West 44th to West 57th, were reception rooms for the finest ships afloat—the *Normandie,* the *Queen Mary* and *Queen Elizabeth,* the *Andrea Doria,* the *United States*—a panoply of floating luxury hotels the world will never again witness. Even though the seas today are filled with cruise ships, few of them can rival yesteryear's cross-ocean shipping for elegance. The liners were the icing on the maritime cake for Ship News, which covered the piers from Perth Amboy to Greenpoint, from the Erie Basin to Edgewater.

Covering ships meant that reporters wrote about regional economy, about waterfront crime, about industry and labor, about tugboat strikes that created heating-oil shortages in winter, about longshoremen's strikes that disrupted the national business, about fires and sinkings and murders and corruption. It was, in Ship News, as though one were reporting general news for a daily paper that confined its interest to the waterfront.

From the newspaper's general point of view, the "sexy" part of Ship News was the coverage of the liners, the interviews with the important, newsy passengers who were either coming to or going from New York. The reporters were expected to do their interviews as the ship lumbered up the harbor from Quarantine to her West Side berth. The shipping line usually supplied lists of the eminent aboard and brought the most illustrious to a makeshift pressroom, often stocked with liquor, as in the starboard Garden Lounge of the *Queen Mary.* Sometimes the interview might be held on deck, at the stern, so that the photographers would have a scenic skyline backdrop. A newsreel man named A. A.—"Double A," in speech—Brown was the moderator. "Stills first," he might ordain, allowing the newspaper photographers first shot at the victim. "Now, newsreels." "Okay, pencil press." In those prerecorder, pre-TV times, that meant the writing press.

One could get back to the newsroom with a half-dozen stories. There was the big-name interview, perhaps a judge back from the Nuremberg trials. Something for sports, a middleweight British pug coming to try his luck in America. Robert Oppenheimer, the atomic physicist returning from Europe, with a comment on the Rosenberg spy case. The president of a Swiss bank, a few paragraphs for the financial page. Samuel Goldwyn sternly eyeing me when I asked him about the "movie industry" in Europe, whence he was arriving: "Motion pictures are not an industry, they are an art." At *The Times,* we were often bogged down with presidents of banks or legalists and unable to join the cheesecake chase led by the *Women's Wear Daily* man, who had a rare talent for singling out women who might even fling their skirts north of the hips to get their pictures taken.

There might be a story about a mighty storm at sea, spun by the captain who wanted to explain the broken windows high up on the port side. And best of all, the ship might be bringing in a bird that came aboard in midocean. Bird stories were always fancied at the office, where they were translated almost automatically into features for the first page, second section, the second-front that was designed to offer surcease from the heavier news elsewhere in the paper.

All of this was usually finished by 9:00 A.M., when the passengers had already disembarked and, back on 43rd Street, nobody had yet come to work. This left leisure time for a morning-paper reporter, unlike the afternoon and wire-service reporters who had to telephone their findings right away. On the liners, this interval to noontime was generally filled by breakfast, a repast that was in reality a sumptuous feast rather than the usual morning victuals. Aboard the French Line, there were wines with each breakfast course, adding to the liquidity of the press, which had started with hard liquor—to conquer the harbor chill, of course—upon boarding. Drinking was part of the job and the reporter who could not hold his liquor might be carried down the gangway, but only after he, as true professional, had telephoned in his story.

Despite these luxurious perquisites, covering a ship as it ought to be covered—that is, thoroughly—involved a fair amount of footwork, a generalist's knowledge that might make questions for the specialists being interviewed, and a sharp nose for news. When AP's Joe Schroeder, one of the great New York reporters and a benevolent adviser to many younger staffers of all papers, was chatting with Edna Ferber on an inbound liner, the novelist mentioned how dirty New York streets would seem after a sojourn in Europe. Schroeder picked up on this casual remark and put the rest of us in the awkward position of having to use the AP copy when we returned from the ship to the office. It was the merest offhand comment, but it made news.

When I came to *The Times* they were still speaking about Skipper Williams, the ship news editor who had died a year or so earlier. T. Walter Williams was a character, which is not particularly newsworthy in a business that boasts many eccentrics. What was unusual was that his eccentric made-up stories made it into the pages of the "gray lady," with her reputation then for stodgy, just-the-facts-ma'am reporting. Skipper had created a cast of waterfront types who told tall tales sitting at pierside. I could not find them in *The Times* morgue, nor could I learn much in the archives. I was told that a reporter had appropriated the clippings with tales of Marmaduke Mizzle, the intrepid caraway-seed merchant of Mincing Lane, and others, but that they had then been lost. I did find a copy that had been made of one. A line or two is missing and it seems to have been published on a Thanksgiving Day. The story ran under a straight feature-piece head with no hint that it was a made-up yarn; in those days it was taken for granted that *Times* readers would be sufficiently sophisticated to recognize it for what it was. Here it is.

---

## Ben Fidd's Turkey-Eating Shark Rises as a Thanksgiving Ghos

### The Ancient Mariner Gazes Out to Sea and Comes Up With Tale of a Fish That Tried to Steal a Holiday Dinner

**By T. WALTER WILLIAMS**

Ben Fidd, the veteran watchman of the Chelsea piers and deep-sea sailor man, went to the Battery along the coast of Santa Helena and doing a good eleven knots on a bowline.

---

I arrived in Ship News in 1948, nearly three years after signing on at *The Times* as a copyboy. I was brought in through the intercession of John P. Shanley, a reporter in that department who persuaded the powers that my wartime experience as a radio operator in the Merchant Marine qualified me for the job. It was a pitch that Shanley employed with even stranger resonances eight years later to enlist me into the Radio-Television Department, where he had just been named editor. I entered this waterfront division with the title of news assistant, a newly created position one step ahead of a clerk and one step below a reporter.

George Horne presided over a staff of three reporters and two news assistants. The assistants' job was to prepare the large shipping and mails tables that anchored the Ship News page each day. It was an awesome task, involving calls to check arrival and departure times with the shipping lines twice a day. A wrong time printed in the paper might bring to a pier thousands of people who would lose little time in calling *The Times* to vent their rage. The tables also included a long roster of ship sailings and the destinations of the mail they were carrying. In addition, we printed a daily list of arrivals and departures of all ships in the harbor. It was information that came by ticker from the Ship News Reporters' Association in a building on lower Broadway, which, in turn, received the notices from the Ambrose Lightship and from the Coast Guard. Many stories came out of this, as names that were new to us brought in strange cargoes and stranger tales.

The biggest ship news broke before and after my sojourn in the department. The *Andrea Doria* sank when it collided with the Swedish liner *Stockholm* in 1956, about a year after I left the department. It was one of the proudest *Times* moments. A young reporter named Max Frankel, who would later become executive editor, was on night rewrite and pulled this story into a coherent whole from the fragments that filtered in on deadline at about 11:00 P.M. The nightly card game, in which reporters and editors whiled away the between-editions interval, provided a pool of talent that was dispatched to cover the agencies involved, to get to the scene of the drama as soon as possible, to start calling officials.

At first, there was joy in knowing that a *Times*man, Camille Cianfarra, was aboard the *Doria,* promising inside scoops. Tragically, Cianfarra was one of the casualties of the accident. One of the heroes of that first night was an ancient mariner, a former seagoing ship's radio operator, Bernard Murphy, who was in charge that evening at the radio station run by *The Times* to send the news by International Morse Code to the ships at sea. Barney Murphy was the first to pick up the distress traffic that alerted the world to the accident. The messages copied by Murphy filled a *Times* page and were "exclusive" to the newspaper—not because it had the inside track but because *The Times* had always made certain that it was prepared to cover anything.

The story of *The Times*'s coverage of the *Andrea Doria* sinking was in a long tradition of *Times* expertise in covering ship disasters. The paper was probably the first to go to press with the story of the *Titanic*. In 1987, the seventy-fifth anniversary of the *Titanic*'s fateful iceberg encounter was very much observed. The liner's sunken hulk had been discovered on the ocean floor. Groups of ship buffs and *Titanic* survivors had organized to memorialize the sinking in various meetings and exhibitions and by depositing a wreath in the Hudson River near where a rescue ship had landed survivors. I volunteered to write the story, recapping the sinking and summing up the various observances. I went to the morgue to check the clips on what had run before. There was a bulky envelope labeled "*Titanic.*" I unwrapped the cord that bundled the yellowed clippings.

The first clipping was a story on the fortieth anniversary of the sinking, and it was crisp, bright, and complete, with a lead that I could not better thirty-five years later. The author was Richard F. Shepard, then a news assistant in Ship News. Ship News had come and gone, the *Titanic* had disappeared and reappeared, and I was still working on the same story.

# BYLINES
# AND COLUMNS

*"Do you have a byline?"*

OUTSIDERS often ask that question when they meet someone from *The Times*. There are several answers: Everyone is born with a byline. Sometimes I have a byline, sometimes I don't. Who reads bylines, anyhow? Besides those written about, those who are overseers at *The Times,* and those who are critics not at *The Times*. And the writer's nearest and dearest.

Knowing all of this, the first byline in *The Times* is a proud moment. At least it was for me, even though I received it for a story that was guaranteed to be killed after the first edition. I wrote it for a long-gone department formally called Reserve News. It was informally called When Room in the office because it put together material that filled in empty spaces in the first edition, spaces that were being held open for late-arriving stories that would run in the later editions. The staff of two or three, headed by an elderly and erudite gentleman I knew as Commander Harding and assisted by an equally wise and knowledgeable and aged journalist, Harry Smith, spent their days making Ks, Ds, and Ms—the stories that went under headlines of those sizes and were the smallest that went into the paper—along with full-scale spreads. The material, from a wide range of obscure publications and otherwise overlooked wire-service filler, told of the record rainfall in Sumatra, of the population of Bora Bora, of the highest mountains east of the Mississippi. Come to think of it, When Room was a forerunner of the tabular material so highly esteemed in computer graphics in today's newspapers.

My piece was the first of several I did about what I called splinter minorities in New York—Assyrians in Yonkers, Waldensians and Basques and Maltese and Sephardic Jews from the old Turkish empire who had settled into the Lower East Side—groups that were tiny and often part of a larger minority. Since, paradoxically, much of the City Edition was shipped out of town, I didn't get much reaction.

My first byline in the main paper was bestowed while I was in Ship News. It was a story about the people who worked to keep rats from leaving ships in New York Harbor. Before the story appeared, an older reporter told me that it would not run because it was not a *New York Times* type of story; it was in bad taste, not appetizing to breakfast-time readers. No matter, it ran and on the sought-after front page of the second section, too, with a large photo, not of rats, but of inspectors.

In those days, around 1950, bylines were less common than they soon would be. A byline added cachet to a reporter's reputation and was specifically given because of the merits of what the writer had produced. At other papers, bylines were lavishly distributed; in the late 1800s, those who got bylines were strongly publicized in the pages of their journals. Until the late 1900s, *The Times* had strictures about bylines: only one to a writer in any day's paper; no double by-lines, where two people had worked on a story. Also no nicknames, like Mike and Bill and Chuck (all of which have, as a matter of fact, appeared in *The Times*) and no Abes and no Abrahams (thus, A. H. Weiler, A. H. Raskin, A. M. Rosenthal), because, it was said around the office, they sounded "too Jewish," although Meyer Berger and Emmanuel Perlmutter were frequent bylines.

The byline policy evolved just as new concepts of fairness and of personalizing the paper took hold. Abe Rosenthal, as executive editor, insisted that quality of story be considered before second bylines in one day's *Times* were awarded. "Reminder: the bylines over the Men in the News are to be given only when a special job has been performed," he wrote in a 1970 memo. "We once had no byline. Then we agreed that if special work were done, we would give the byline. Now we seem to be handing them out like crackerjacks. The purpose of this is not to kill bylines on Men in the News, but to make sure they have some meaning."

## COLUMNISTS

In *The Times* there are columnists and **Columnists.** The former are re-porters who are assigned to columns and at the whim of manage-ment may be taken off them and reassigned to covering candlelight processions or chasing fires. The boldfaced ones are the big guns, the men and women whose column is their permanent resting place in the paper. They appear on the Op-Ed page, in the *Sunday Maga-zine,* in other heavyweight venues. They do little other writing, although—rarely these days—one of them may write stories of page 1 grandeur; years ago, the Washington Bureau chiefs did both.

I have been a lower-case columnist, a relief pitcher, so to speak, for the regulars on the About New York column, and I had several stints as its sole writer, too. It was the best job I ever had on the paper and I could understand why so many newspeople set their caps for it. As columnist, you are more often than not in business for yourself. You need a fertile mind and open ears to select the material for that column, which may or may not be keyed to the day's news. Everyone who wrote that column—among them John Corry, Francis X. Clines, Anna Quindlen, Gay Talese, McCandlish Phillips, William Geist, Greg McGregor, Douglas Martin, Michael Kaufman, Tom Buckley—was a reporter who brought to it a different perception of the city he or she roamed. About New York differed from a feature story, which all of these handled so dexterously. It needed a certain personal spin, a touch of essay that was short of editorializing or preaching but made the writing as important as its subject. It took a knack, but it was a liberating experience for one harnessed to assignments.

About New York first appeared in October 1939, written by that quintessential New Yorker, the great reporter Meyer Berger. After a hiatus caused by World War II, the column was reinstated and written by Mike until his death in February 1959. The last column that month was written by Gay Talese, who had been the column's fill-in writer. AHS on February 9 urged Turner Catledge to omit the column "for the next few weeks as a notice of Mike's passing." Those "few weeks" lengthened into fourteen years while management, on and off, diddled with the idea of reviving it.

One of the most vigorous, if unavailing, arguments for its immediate restoration came from Ivan Veit, in charge of *Times* promotion. Veit acknowledged that *The Times* was a "solid, serious newspaper," but this solidity, he wrote to Orvil Dryfoos on February 24, 1959, "has given The Times an exaggerated reputation for ponderousness which is the greatest single obstacle to our growth." About New York manifested the sort of writing and warmth that encouraged new readership. The column was sorely needed, he argued, because "local New York news is a category in which we have not made our best impression." Fewer readers rated *The Times* best for local news than they did for foreign or Washington news and "it would not seem wise for us now to *subtract* from the attention we pay New York."

I was also for many years the columnist for the Going Out Guide feature, which I started in 1972 when the idea was initiated by Abe Rosenthal.

On October 27, 1960, after *The Times* announced its support for the candidacy of John F. Kennedy for president, "Scotty" Reston heard from his boss. AHS wrote:

Well, the secret is out and I know that it hasn't disappointed you—or surprised you.

I wish that you would reflect on this, however. It seems to me that you and Cy [C. S. Sulzberger] might have been a trifle less biased in what you wrote during the campaign. Actually, it has caused the paper some embarrassment. Since the two of you were so obviously pro-Kennedy, it made our readers suspicious of all the news stories that we published.

As you know, neither by word nor deed did I attempt to influence you, nor would I have wished to influence you in any other direction, if I had wished to do so at all. The only question that is in my mind is: Is it wise for a couple of chaps like you and Cy to tip your hands to the extent that you did? After all, I like to think of you as reporters, not pundits.

I imagine, though, that even the angels must once in a while tire of Heaven. So many of the columnists I have known, myself included, get a feeling that a column insulates them from "real" news work, that there is a monotony even in the most diverse of columns. Jack Gould, the radio-television critic who was my boss for eight years, once remarked that it would be a good idea to give a critic a sabbatical so that he could observe the greater world beyond the limits of his discipline. So it was with columnists. How to give an opinion without appearing to do so and how to do it without speaking for *The Times*? This called for experience, wisdom, patience, and an iron stomach.

# CULTURAL NEWS

THERE WAS panic in the back of the house. Well, if not panic, then worry. Big change was no longer in the wind; it was on the premises and promised to blow the fixed ways of a half-century out the third-floor window. The memo, on May 21, 1962, made it official. In one week the comfortable little virtually-self-governing satrapies that ruled over the coverage of art, theater, movies, radio and television, music, books, and dance would be merged into something with the highfalutin' title Cultural News.

In terms of documents, this notice—some saw it as a manifesto—is one of the archives' documents that most precisely pinpoint a moment of specific change in management at *The Times*. It was a declaration of independence for the arts, perhaps, but it threatened an established, independent way of life for those covering the beat.

As ominous as this uprooting seemed to us who worked the back of the room, which corresponded often enough to the back of the paper, we were nervous about the devils we didn't know who would supplant the ones we were long familiar with. Joe Herzberg, an old-timer and the newly named cultural news editor, had arrived at *The Times* not long before, bringing with him from the *Herald Tribune* the terrifying reputation of being one of the toughest city editors known to journalism. Beneath a shock of unruly gray hair, Joe's eyes peered out from a craggy face and gave a reporter a sense of guilt and instability that could only increase under his astute questioning.

Joe swept in like a stiff new broom. No more handout reporting—the days of rewriting press releases are over, he announced. Real news is what we want in the paper. Renaissance types, writers who could be expert on everything, would be the order of the day in the new order. The demarcations between the departments disappeared and secretaries were precipitated into a sort of steerage of desks, all facing the supreme desk of the cultural news editor.

May 21, 1962

To All Department Members:

Effective Monday, May 28, 1962, the procedure in the Drama, Music, Movies, Art and Radio-TV departments will be as follows:

Each department editor will report to me before noon on expected news stories, columns and reviews for the next day's paper. Those handling stories or columns will report to me between 3 and 4 P.M. for space allotments. If a story is in hand before that, report earlier.

The present system is too haphazard and has been tolerated because of the inconvenience during rebuilding. We are now represented at the 4:30 news conference and I wish to be informed of all stories. The bullpen likes to be alerted at the conference to all Page I and second-front possibilities.

All department editors should be in the office by 11 A.M. unless there is special reason for coming in later.

We are now one large department, with status equal to all other desks. I would like to see ideas flow from each department — ideas about people, about all aspects of the arts and entertainment fields. The space allotted must be used for superior copy. Space-filling is ended. The bullpen has been liberal in providing space and we should repay that generosity with good stories, crisply written.

Joseph G. Herzberg

cc: Mr. Daniel
    Mr. Garst
    Mr. Bernstein
    Mr. Jordan
    Mr. Crandall
    Mr. Burritt
    Mr. Radosta

One day early in his regime he summoned Abe Weiler, a fifty-year *Times*man and irrepressible wag who covered and reviewed movies. "Sorry, Joe, I'm busy painting a fresco," Weiler apologized in a pithy quip that encapsulated the tidal clash of cultures.

The system, until that time, had been for each department to be ruled by the critic and administered by an editor, who also served as reporter and/or columnist. Nominally, departments answered to the city editor, but except in cases of world-shattering cultural news—Jack Paar's walking out on the *Tonight* show or the quiz-show scandals—each department took care of itself.

In midweek, all hands turned to working on the Sunday pages in what was then called the Drama Section—later, the Arts and Leisure Section. Critic, editor, reporters all wrote headlines and captions and read proofs. The editors spent most of the press day up on the fourth floor kibitzing the compositors and cajoling the foreman into getting the corrections put through in time to make an early curtain, or a late dinner. All this while also filling the space for the morrow's daily paper.

This made for busy moments, but the tempo was familiar and so was the cast. Even people who disliked each other had learned how to work together without coming to blows. The staffs in the arts and letters sections were accustomed to hurling literate invective at their respective targets and even at each other but they had always been treated with a certain esteem at the paper. Reporters—and sometimes even editors—were well read, interested in theater and music; this was what made real New Yorkers out of a group that had an awfully high percentage of out-of-towners in it.

The big changes were that the distinct borders between the departments had blurred and that the reporters were now to report their stories to the cultural news editor rather than to the critic. The critic, whose position was as lofty as ever, found that his authority was not. He was no longer responsible for personnel (a welcome relief for many if not most of them) and for administration (also good news for people who wanted to write). But the critic had become a consultant rather than a decision maker.

The cultural news editor decided what stories should be covered, how long they should be, and how they would be laid out on the page. The critic would have his voice in what he wrote, but his voice would no longer necessarily be that of *The Times* in terms of overall coverage. This was important because it meant that other perceptions would determine the emphasis *The Times* would put on the arts. The newspeople would concentrate on prices of paintings and productions, the aesthetes feared, while the stress would be less than ever on quality of performance. Of course, there had never been such a clear distinction in the paper. When a big "news story" broke, it usually had been written for the City Desk, perhaps even by one of the front-desk general reporters rather than by a reporter in one of the backroom departments.

The decision to unify the department made good sense, a conclusion reached in retrospect when one could distinguish one's own interest in the old order from the objective benefit to the reader. The arts themselves were overlapping more than ever before. Lincoln Center could not be the preserve of any one department because it covered so many of the arts and it made sense that the paper should be a similar cover-all. In fact, many of the early scoops and "scandals" (also, in retrospect, pretty minor) hinged on Lincoln Center's early years, when a patrician management tried to dominate events as it had done in so many institutions and ran into a sans-culottes resistance that was to reshape the nature of orchestras, dance groups, opera, theater.

Joe Herzberg proved to be less of a monster than he might have wished to appear. He had a discerning ear and eye for news and he was demonstrably interested in the world he had been charged with covering. As cultural news editor, he was on a par with other senior editors, which meant that he went to the afternoon page 1 news conferences, made his own decisions, and reported only to the managing editor. He was, in his late years, a congenial spirit who loved a good story and could kibitz knowledgeably, as newspaper folk often do so well, on any topic, whether it was a subject he was expert on or not.

Although New York then had seven papers, *The Times* had become the arbiter of taste for many who supported the arts, most notably, theater. *The Times* could not move mass public taste, to be sure. *The Beverly Hillbillies* was a smash success no matter how much the series was derided by *Times* critics. But a serious show, such as *Playhouse 90* or a series televised more to satisfy the Federal Communications Commission, which decided on whether the public weal was sufficiently served to warrant a license renewal, could be destroyed by the cocked eyebrow of Jack Gould, the radio-TV critic (he didn't and it wasn't). Broadway producers and some directors and performers chafed at what they regarded as the hegemony of *The Times* in the drama. Yet as Clifton Daniel, then a top editor, once reminded them in a confrontational lunch with "the industry" at Sardi's, they themselves promoted the critic by quoting their favorable reviews in advertisements, even on theater marquees.

At a 1966 lunch of the Drama Desk—people who cover theater— Arthur Miller, the playwright, and one of the legion that chafed at the influence of the critics, proposed that, in light of the shrinking number of newspapers, *The Times* should have two critics review each play so that "they might cancel out each other's errors." Wouldn't work, Clifton Daniel, then managing editor, replied, accurately observing that only one of the two would be regarded as the critic of *The Times*. He read from a letter by Walter Kerr, who had just become the drama critic at *The Times* after a distinguished career in the same job at the *Herald Tribune*. Kerr, alarmed by the dearth of critical variety available to the public, suggested that *The Times* have two critics, one covering the theater as shows opened, in the daily paper, and the other writing on Sunday. This proposal became reality a year later, when Kerr stepped down from daily reviewing and for ten years wrote criticism for the Sunday Drama Section. Even then, although Kerr was never a less talented critic on Sunday, the Sunday spot placed him, and his successors, in a lesser role than that played by the daily starring critic.

The public's reliance on *Times* opinion arose directly from early policies of Adolph Ochs. Even before him *The Times* had covered the arts, but Ochs understood that the kind of paper he was creating would rely on a readership that appreciated a sober, dispassionate coverage of the news in general, a readership drawn from business and intellectual classes to whom the arts represented a necessary ingredient of gracious living.

He made the *Book Review* a centerpiece of *Times* coverage, a section that achieved preeminence in its field and also brought in revenue. It started as a Saturday section on October 10, 1896, almost immediately after he became publisher, and switched to Sundays on January 29, 1911. The Saturday *Review of Books* was a pioneering move that reflected Ochs's idea that it should be a literary newspaper unto itself, published as a tabloid-size section, as it is today. It has ever since been a leading literary organ of the United States, and, as the archives show, it overcame early distrust by the publishers to the point where it more than paid its way with advertising.

The pressure on the publisher, whoever it is, to make special waves on behalf of his friends and relatives, and even more remote acquaintances, has never diminished over the century. In 1901, for instance, Ochs received the letter on the following page from a friend and fledgling author whose living came from department stores back in Tennessee.

On the other hand, there are some things that are decidedly different. I have never been asked by an editor to take a special position, positive or other, on any book I have been given to review. Even

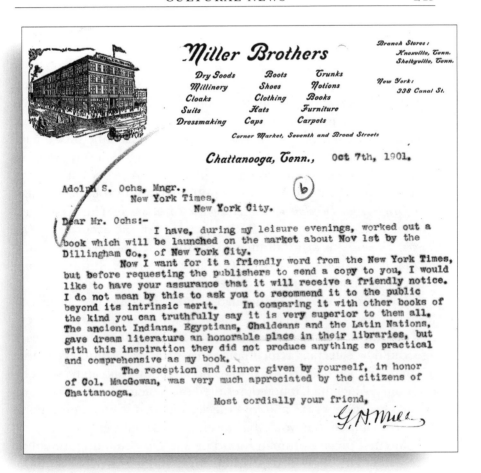

**Miller Brothers**

Dry Goods   Boots   Trunks
Millinery   Shoes   Notions
Cloaks   Clothing   Books
Suits   Hats   Furniture
Dressmaking   Caps   Carpets

Corner Market, Seventh and Broad Streets

Chattanooga, Tenn.,   Oct 7th, 1901.

Adolph S. Ochs, Mngr.,
  New York Times,
    New York City.

Dear Mr. Ochs:—
    I have, during my leisure evenings, worked out a book which will be launched on the market about Nov 1st by the Dillingham Co., of New York City.
    Now I want for it a friendly word from the New York Times, but before requesting the publishers to send a copy to you, I would like to have your assurance that it will receive a friendly notice. I do not mean by this to ask you to recommend it to the public beyond its intrinsic merit. In comparing it with other books of the kind you can truthfully say it is very superior to them all. The ancient Indians, Egyptians, Chaldeans and the Latin Nations, gave dream literature an honorable place in their libraries, but with this inspiration they did not produce anything so practical and comprehensive as my book.
    The reception and dinner given by yourself, in honor of Col. MacGowan, was very much appreciated by the citizens of Chattanooga.

        Most cordially your friend,

           G. N. Miller

though I understood that I was assigned the book because there was special interest in it (this does not apply to the regular book-critic staff, which makes its own choices), I was never challenged when I found the volume less than worthy. But I doubt that nowadays any editor would dare send a message soliciting a pan such as the one fired off in 1898 by the book editor to a prospective reviewer:

> Would you oblige The Times by writing for its Review of Books and Art an article on "Quo Vadis," as a bad book from the moral side, under some such title as
>
> YELLOW JOURNALISM IN LITERATURE
> "QUO VADIS" AND ITS HORRORS

I very much doubt if even the ablest exponent of Yellow Journalism would dare to print from the Tenderloin a story

such as Sienkiewicz has told in more than one chapter . . .
and the stronger you made it, the better.

The theater, reflecting its place in New York society, or in the various New York societies, from the robust popular fare of the Bowery theaters, to the more upscale productions of Broadway, had always been a *Times* centerpiece. *The Times* featured drama criticism from its very first days in print. The details of who these first critics were is no more than hazy deduction, prompted by those early years of unsigned stories. In 1970, Arno Press published a slim volume entitled *The Origin and Development of Dramatic Criticism in* The New York Times, *1851–1880,* by John Rothman, chief of the archives at *The Times.* The first to write "dramatic critiques" in *The Times* was either Fitz-James O'Brien or Charles C. Bailey Seymour, Rothman concluded—or maybe even someone else.

Raymond, Rothman found, had promised prospective readers of his new paper daily criticism of drama, painting, or any art that merited attention. The first issue of the paper announced that its coverage would be eclectic, "as inclination may prompt." Within a year and a half, *The Times* declared that it would abandon this catch-as-catch-can policy, which had, it noted, resulted in a system of plugs that were "mere advertisements," and told the readers that it would give more space to criticism that would be "careful, candid and impartial."

The first piece Rothman found in *The Times* that might qualify as a review, although its descriptive ingredients leave it in a limbo between news and criticism, was a piece about thirty lines long in the

> — The Bateman children made their first appearance since their return from Europe on Thursday evening. They were well received, but such tragedies as Richard III, are not calculated to display their talents to the best advantage. The most correct reading by two young children cannot dispel the feeling that the performance is a burlesque. They should have plays written for them, as in suitable characters they are unsurpassed. In the farce of the 'Young Couple,' they appear to better advantage, for their youth and size harmonize with the plot. Their acting here was surprising, and the audience seemed much better pleased than with their attempt at tragedy. At the close of the farce, they were 'called out,' and made the target for a broadside of bouquets. They gracefully acknowledged these compliments, and 'Charley' made a brief address. The audience was not so large as should have greeted the children, but when they become better known they cannot fail to have full houses.

paper of September 11, 1852. It was not what the authorities on Shubert Alley would call a "box-office review" but it was positive and encouraging.

The elusively amorphous roster of *Times* critics before 1884 has been succeeded by a dozen theater critics and then some in the more than a century behind us. The record holders among the incumbents were Edward A. Dithmar, from 1884 to 1918, and Brooks Atkinson, from 1925 to 1960, not counting his four years out during World War II, when he served, with distinction, as a war correspondent.

Atkinson perhaps came closest to the popular image of what a *Times* drama critic might be: a quiet, sandy-haired man, usually with a pipe in his mouth, who wore bow ties and wrote with a civility and grace that could demolish without anathematizing, He could charm without compromising his own stern litmus tests for what was worthy and what was trashy on his beat. His interests helped reshape American theater, what with his support for playwrights like Eugene O'Neill and his tireless journeys to garrets, apartments, and storefronts to "discover" the wave of theater after World War II that became known as Off Broadway.

I first met him when I was a copyboy, dispatched to his cubbyhole, a niche hollowed out in the morgue, where, late at night and just back from a noisy opening night, the critic sat and, by the bright light of a single lamp, wrote his review on a long yellow pad, in longhand. My job was to rush it out to the copy desk, where Mr. Atkinson's words, untouched except for hangers (marks that told the printers where to start new paragraphs), were relayed as written to the fourth-floor composing room. His copy usually went to a printer familiar with his neat handwriting and then, in metal, was passed along to a makeup man who specialized in inserting late reviews into the late city edition.

No sooner was the edition on the streets than the review was read to the breath-bated first-night-party crowd, usually at Sardi's, where the news was sent down from the advertising agency upstairs that would be engaged in excerpting critical comments to best advantage in the next day's ad. The hegemony of the critic in terms of judgment was total at *The New York Times*. Not everyone felt that way. A letter sent to Ochs in 1915 from William Hester, president of the *Brooklyn Eagle*, expressed another view.

Hester questioned whether it was right for a newspaper always to sustain "its representative in a fight with a theatrical manager." He was referring to a contretemps between *The Times* and the Shubert Enterprises, owners—then as today—of the lion's share of Broadway theaters. The Shuberts had barred a *Times* critic from attending the performance of a show and *The Times* had retaliated by refusing to run Shubert advertisements in the paper. This was an unprecedented abdication of profit because of a moral principle.

> [I] have come to the conclusion that there is no reason why the managers of a newspaper should allow an employee to build up a little empire of his own in the establishment. "Willy Winters" of the Tribune got so overbearing and inflated with his own importance that the managers could not get along with him and when the newspaper publisher tried to interfere he was met with the charge that the money-drawer was trying to influence the News Department, which meant that Mr. Winters must be allowed to browbeat the theatrical managers without restraint.

Hester's thoughts, which were not unique among publishers, were summed up by his reckoning that the question of theater involved three parties: the managers, the publisher, the critic. The manager, he said, was out to make money by attempting to please the public and was entitled to fair treatment. So was the publisher. The critic, he wrote, "is trying to build a name for himself completely indifferent to the interests of the paper." He continued:

> There is no need of severe criticism except to protect the public against obscene plays—and the police ought to take care of that. . . . The manager's opinion of a play ought to be as good or better than that of average theater-goers. . . . And there is no reason why any one man from a newspaper office should have the power of injuring another in the theatrical line any more than if he was conducting any other business in which he was trying to suit the public.

Ochs's reply eloquently, if courteously, summed up the stamp he had put on the paper. He agreed that much newspaper theater criticism was "unnecessary, and unimportant performances are treated too seriously." However, Hester's comments about critics and power did not apply at *The Times*.

We would not tolerate a critic who would traffic in the reputation of The Times or do his work otherwise than conscientiously in truth and fairness without a thought as to any personal benefit or advantage. . . .

With respect to the differences The New York Times has with the Messrs. Shubert, that has nothing to do so far as we are concerned with the character of the criticism. The Messrs. Shubert have for years terrorized the newspapers with their advertising patronage and when they shut their doors to a representative of The Times and excluded him from their theaters by no moral or legal right, our self-respect demanded that we not only contest their action in the courts but exclude their advertising from our columns and ignore their theaters. We may suffer some little money loss and our readers some little inconvenience, but we can both make the small sacrifice for honest and independent journalism.

A decade later, the debate between press and producer had not abated. Lee Shubert fired off a note to Ochs in 1927, complaining about an article in the Sunday Drama Section that had been written by a Russian theater critic on American styles in musical comedies and revues. Shubert observed that the piece, "Through Alien Eyes," must surely have been published without Ochs's knowledge because he could not believe that "readers of your valuable paper are more interested in the opinions of an alien than they are in what *your own dramatic critics think.*"

In his reply, Ochs confessed that he knew nothing about the writer and why he was given space in *The Times.* The author, he said, might have put things "more amiably," but he went on to chide Shubert.

I fear you are a bit supersensitive to dramatic criticisms. It is often unintelligent, harsh and unjust, but that is the penalty one must occasionally suffer when appealing for public favor and approval. If all criticism was favorable it would be valueless to the producer as well as to the public. Of course, criticism when adverse should be tempered with restraint and caution, and be constructive and not an attempt at phrase making and exhibition of the superior knowledge of the writer.

By the mid-1960s, a new front for dissension was opened when
*The Times* began to push for last-preview reviewing instead of the last-
minute deadline review that was the tradition. Stanley Kauffmann,
who came from *The New Republic* to serve as *The Times's* drama critic
from January to August 1966, began to attend preview performances. Kauffmann thought that "a play that took ten years to write
deserves more than a 50-minute review." This was a revolutionary
concept. The critic had always been expected to run back to the office before the final-curtain ovation started (even if the show had
been a turkey, there were always enthusiastic friends, relatives, in-
vestors filling first-night seats), to turn out a short-order literary assessment of a production.

The most dramatic show of resistance to this new one-jump-
ahead school of criticism came in 1964 from David Merrick, an iras-
cible producer whose high standards in presenting respectable
theater were not matched when it came to combating the press, particularly *The New York Times*. In 1985 William Honan, then cultural
editor of *The Times*, reviewed the reviewing situation in a long memo
that explained how theater and newspapers had changed.

"David Merrick sent Kauffmann his preview performance tickets
to Brian Friel's 'Philadelphia, Here I Come!' with a note which said
[with Merrick's characteristic mock-menace] 'At your peril.' Then
Merrick suddenly canceled the performance explaining that a rat
got in the generator; and blew out the theater's electrical system—all
of which [Sam] Zolotow reported in a front-page story."

At about that time, producers instituted a system of program previews in Broadway houses designed to eliminate the expensive out-of-
town tryouts. Ticket prices were theoretically, but not always, cheaper
than they were after the official opening-night date had been set.
Harold Prince, a prolific director, allowed critics in 1968 to choose
any one of four evening performances of *Cabaret*, which would be
regarded as openings, although their reviews could not appear before the final opening performance.

"We subscribe to the preview system, not just because we drifted
into it or because we are following anyone else's lead, but because we
have discovered good and sufficient reasons," Honan continued in
his memo. "First, our deadlines have been advanced in recent
years. . . . Second, even if we could cover opening nights and make
the second edition, we would certainly miss the National Edition
which closes at 9 p.m. Under the present system, theater reviews

## Cast of Characters

The Drama Department, in my time, ran to strong personalities. The strongest in print, Brooks Atkinson, was the mildest in person. Clara Rotter was the very soul of the department. A diminutive, scrawny woman, Clara was the house mother of the department and of all she came into contact with. She was utterly devoted to Atkinson. Once when he mentioned he would like to have back a letter he had mailed, Clara tracked down the New York postmaster general and arranged for its return (no, that may not have been according to the rules, but that's how strong Clara and *The Times* were). She attended to all the nuts and bolts of getting tickets for those who needed them, for arranging transportation, for giving holiday presents to kids of staffers. A question in the test for those wishing to join the press agents' union was "Who is Clara Rotter?" Sam Zolotow was a demon theater-news reporter, cigar smoker, and relentless pursuer of news. Almost nothing happened in show business that he did not soon know about. He once queried Arthur Miller about what he was up to. Writing a play, Miller said. What's its name? Mr. Z. asked. *Death of a Salesman,* Miller replied. What's it about? "Sam, it's about a salesman who dies," Miller said, disclosing all and nothing.

make all editions of the newspaper. . . . Third, we appreciate the concern of the small theaters about the prospect of facing a house full of dour-faced critics. In the old days, when openings were presented in huge Broadway houses, the critical establishment could be absorbed without creating a dampening effect. But since the early 1970s the majority of openings covered by The Times are not on Broadway, but in the institutional theaters that have blossomed. . . . Fourth, the present practice takes advantage of a change in the Broadway theater—the demise of the out-of-town tryout. . . . Indeed, it's because of Broadway's new preview system that the old-time opening nights can never be brought back."

Whether in Shubert Alley or in the office, the critic is a creature of controversy. Clifton Daniel, upon his accession to the high command of the News Department in the early 1960s, chided *The Times* critics collectively in a memo that attested to the ongoing preoccupation of the top editors with the cultural coverage of the newspaper: "Since I became managing editor of this newspaper, I have never spoken to any of the critics except to say good morning or good afternoon," the memorandum began. "But I am very conscious of the work you are doing, and I read it with great care and attention every day. I am sorry to say that it does not always satisfy me as a reader or please me as an editor."

Daniel did not mention names, but he listed their failings. First of all, he said, reviews frequently omitted factual details, such as where a performance was taking place. In addition to this "gross disregard for the simple fundamentals of journalism," the managing editor found that reviews too often ignored the "simple needs of the reader, namely, what the show was about, how it was performed and whether it was worth attending. Additional facts, information and comment are welcome, but a review is, first of all and fundamentally, a service to the reader," he wrote. "Aside from being a service to the reader, the review should be a pleasure to him."

Most reviews, he continued, were read by people who have not experienced the work under review and have no intention of buying the book or seeing the play. "People read reviews as part of their total cultural intake . . . they simply want to be entertained or enlightened by the review itself." Daniel relentlessly faulted poorly written, "incomprehensible" reviews by critics who show "an incredible lack of scholarship and simple journalistic competence.

"Finally, some of our criticism is entirely too smart-alecky and brash. A paper that has the standing and dignity of The New York Times should be persuasive, not abusive . . . I don't propose to tell critics what they should believe or what they should say. But as the managing editor of The New York Times, I have some right to advise critics how to say what they have to say. If our writing standards don't improve and we don't stop hearing so many complaints from the outside—not about our criticism, but about the way our criticism is presented, I am going to start looking around for some new critics."

On a subject about which there is absolutely no last word, one can report on the latest word, in archival time. This comes in a note from Arthur Gelb in 1989 responding to a memo from Punch Sulzberger. The publisher had just met with a topmost Shubert executive over a meal of warmed-over complaints similar to those discussed by their forebears.

"I guess I will never understand why, despite our abundant and caring coverage, producers and theater owners complain about us," Gelb wrote. "This has been the case ever since I can remember. Even the widely cherished Brooks Atkinson, when I was his assistant in the late '50s, was frequently and harshly attacked by a group of producers led by David Merrick. Brooks finally got fed up and told me this was one of the reasons he decided to give up the job. I suppose it's their way of trying to put us on the defensive and it can't be taken too seriously."

# READING, RHYTHM, REELING, AND OTHER ARTS

**F**IVE YEARS after that first memo creating a Cultural News Department was issued, there was even more panic in the back of the house. When cultural news staffers, secretaries, and clerks returned from lunch on Tuesday, July 11, 1967, they found a new pronunciamento on their desks. It announced that on the next day the department would be "restored to administrative control of the metropolitan desk."

Yet, the announcement noted, "The metropolitan editor, Arthur Gelb, is, of course, a former member of the cultural news department and is fully familiar with its affairs." Arthur might be new to us in that job but he was a familiar face.

Arthur Gelb was to be the central figure in cultural news coverage at *The Times* for more than twenty years, during both his tenure as metropolitan editor and his portfolio as managing editor of the paper for several years before he moved upstairs to be president of The New York Times Foundation. Arthur knew the field and loved it with an enthusiasm that, for those working in it, could be almost suffocating. But he always thrived in an atmosphere of excitement that communicated itself into the pages. Arthur, a tall, lanky fellow constantly simulating molecular motion, spilled over with the thrust of an uncapped oil well. Cultural News did not suffer for space or exposure during the Gelb years.

As a reporter, I felt the agitation of the condemned as Arthur hurtled down the aisle and stopped at my desk. Here's a great story, his patter ran, there's a lot of interest in it. More often than not, it *was* a great story, and one that had to be done with characteristic *Times* thoroughness in less than three hours. At other times, the great story was trumped during the day by an even greater story that elbowed aside the first great story of the day.

Although Arthur's personal stamp on *Times* cultural coverage was indelible, the transformation of that coverage in those years since the department was established mirrored the changes that had overtaken that aspect of human activity in a very short period of time. The attention given to arts other than theater was more emphasized than ever before, as multimedia became a popular word. Theater directors directed opera. Playwrights appeared as actors and they wrote for movies as well as for theater. Books became movies and movies became books. And over it all hovered the new Mr. Moneybags of the profitable arts, television, which created new definitions for art for the masses. The government and foundations funded the more rarefied (i.e., nonprofit) arts; and culture more than ever became a story immersed in politics.

Movies, dance, music, radio, and television produced more general-interest stories than they ever had before. Even the cultural decor had changed. In 1968, *The Times* retained a "contributor" to cover rock; a pay-as-you-write person, not a full staffer. Here is how Clifton Daniel alerted the fastidious ex-Marine publisher, Punch Sulzberger, about the newcomer's arrival.

> I want to warn you that while you were away, we took aboard (as a contributor, not as a staffer) another long-haired type.
>
> His name is Mike Jahn, and he is going to write pieces on folk/rock music.
>
> I don't want you to be startled if you see him in the office. In recommending Mr. Jahn, Arthur Gelb said in a memorandum, "I am afraid that as a folk/rock critic Mr. Jahn wears his hair in a somewhat bizarre style—in fact, he looks like a werewolf. But since his work will not require him to be in the office very much, I don't think he'll bite any of us."

*The Times* had a long history of leading in cultural coverage while, at the same time, not setting an avant-garde pace that would outstrip its readers. As in all fields, the paper's gingerly approach was sometimes more evident in its advertising acceptance than in its news columns. Always the elusive question of good taste was decided on the spot.

The question of what's fit to print and what is not constantly recurs. In 1920, Upton Sinclair, the popular muckraking author of *The Jungle,* an exposé of meatpacking practices, wrote *The Brass Check,* an exposé of journalism and advertising, a book that compared news-paper people to prostitutes whose bawdy-house tokens were brass checks. *The Times* refused to run an advertisement for the novel because, as the letter from the publisher's office phrased it, "Under its rules The New York Times declines your advertisement for the reason that the book in question is made up very largely of attacks upon character and credit, and contains statements, charges and insinuations that we know of our own knowledge to be false, slanderous and libelous."

In 1933 Arthur Hays Sulzberger responded to a complaint and an insinuation from a letter that was critical of a criticism:

> You ask whether or not it is the policy of The Times to accept money for an advertisement and in the same issue review the book unfavorably. The answer to that question is that the review appears without respect to the advertisement. There have been instances in the past where we have refused to profit by accepting the advertisement of a book, on the grounds that it was indecent, where we have felt obligated at the same time to review it from a news standpoint.
>
> The entire problem of review is difficult. If there is to be good criticism, there must of necessity be adverse criticism. I confess to the feeling that if the author of the review in question felt as irritated as apparently he was, he should have returned the book stating that he was not the proper person to do it justice. That, however, is a doctrine of perfection which one would not be apt to encounter.

In June of that same year, AHS actually stopped the presses to kill a review of a book called *The Investor Pays*. He saw the review, for the Sunday Book Section, on a Monday and immediately put a halt to the printing.

"I killed the article largely for the reason that in the end of the second paragraph, italics were used, put in by the reviewer," he wrote in a memo immediately after his action. "Because of the general nature of the review this to my mind indicated that the reviewer was far too much interested in putting across a point of view of his own, whether or not it was shared by the author of the book."

Realizing his own inexpertise on the subject, he referred the piece to his financial editor, who found even more things wrong with it. About 16,000 copies of the review had been printed, but they were withdrawn.

"I wish to emphasize that the review, in my conception, was thoroughly improper in that it was difficult to determine from it which thoughts were those of the author and which those of the reviewer. Because of the nature of the article and the time of its publication, this was particularly objectionable. If The Times desires to express itself with respect to the banking situation, it has ample opportunity to do so on its editorial page."

As a business organization, *The Times* does not plunge into new ventures recklessly. New ideas can have a long gestation period, as in the case of *The Times* Best Sellers list. In 1935, the idea was kicked around. A memo from Charles Merz to AHS recommended the weekly publication of such a list, while another from J. Donald Adams, successor to Brooks Atkinson as editor of the *Book Review*, argued against it, or if necessary, running it on a monthly rather than a weekly basis. It was not until August 9, 1942, seven years later, that the Best Sellers list made its debut in the *Book Review*.

One stimulant for its introduction was the poor showing the section was making on the company's accounts. A memo to AHS reported that, for the year ended in August 1940, the *New York Times Book Review* spent $752,170 and took in, from advertising and circulation (as a separate purchase, apart from the full newspaper), $601,400, adding up to a loss of $150,770. A penciled scrawl on the piece of paper advises: "Try shorter reviews & hold down the size of section."

As critics' critic, AHS was not to be easily shrugged off as a countinghouse Philistine who tried to impose his ignorance on the informed members of his staff. The problem for AHS—some on the other end might say that the problem *with* AHS—was that he was a well-read, literate man who was able to make a logical exposition of his views and to communicate with those he was in charge of. His opinions were not narrow, but they were strong and based on a viewpoint rather than on whim. Here is a note written to the *Book Review* editor in 1937, a missive that illustrates AHS's intuitive stance on the part a critic must play.

> The music critic has the hardest time, as he frequently deals with old compositions played for the twenty-seventh time by the same orchestra. His report of the proceedings, therefore,

must essentially be critical. The critic of the drama in most cases, or of books, however, has the opportunity of dwelling upon the news of that which is before him. A story has been issued for the first time, and it is his job to tell the public what the story is about. You and I have discussed this frequently, and have taken into consideration just how much critical analysis of a book should appear, as compared with its news treatment. Somewhere or other there is a line, yet it is a continually varying one.

AHS observed that the case that had prompted this note went "far over the line."

The reviewer is completely without warrant in saying, "But it is a childishly conceived story," as he has no method of judging how the author conceived it. And why anyone who spends a few hours on a piece of work which has probably taken a year or two in preparation should think it is necessary to say "There is probably more nonsense in it than any dozen of the month's novels" is more than I can understand.

AHS and Iphigene often went to the movies and he was not reluctant to differ with film critic Bosley Crowther. While few dare tell the emperor he has no clothes, no one, and that includes publishers, refrains from telling the critic that he has been caught with his pants down, even if that, too, is subject to interpretation. For all his chiding, however, AHS seemed to have a basic respect for his film critic and, in his notes, sometimes asked the managing editor not to show Crowther what he was commenting on.

A month later, AHS observed to the managing editor that "it seems to me that Crowther actually derives a sort of satisfaction when he is able to write that a picture is poor." The publisher commented, "Certainly he is too grudging, in my opinion in pointing out anything that's good. Now please understand that I think he's an excellent critic and I don't want you to think anything to the contrary. I just think he's soured on the job and ought to be put out to pasture. Have you any ideas?"

Edwin James's response, a few days later, cited a pan Crowther had just given a new film, *The Great Gatsby*. He had told the critic that the review was "somewhat less kind than [those of] most of the other

6 June, 1949.

Mr. Edwin L. James,
Managing Editor,
The New York Times,
229 West 43 Street,
New York City 18, N.Y.

Dear Jimmie,

I am getting more and more disturbed about Crowther's
work.  It seems to me that he needs a change of scene because
he is too damned sore.  Whenever he says a nice word about a
picture, he instantly writes several lines which take back all
what he said.  Now, I do not know if the pictures are good or
bad and I certainly would not want him to write anything which
he does not believe, but the constant continuous crabbing, must
be as annoying to our readers as it is to me.

Please do not show this letter to him.  In fact, I
would appreciate it if you would do nothing at all about it,
except reading his reviews about the next few weeks and then
talk it over with me when I get home.

Now that Churchill's next volume gets of course deep
into the war, what would you think of illustrating it occasionally
with headlines from The New York Times?

I am getting some loud bleats here with respect to
some of Hanson Baldwin's political stories.  I don't happen to
have seen them, but as you know, I have spoken to him several
times about sticking to the military, and at the same time, I
have recognized the difficulty of doing so.  However, when he
does stray a-field, he ought to be right, and I am told this is
not always the case.

Cheerio.


Yours,


AHS/ck.                                    Arthur Hays Sulzberger.

An example of how the publisher established his authority, by working
through the top editor rather than directly with the writers. Here he touches
upon the film critic, the makeup on a Churchill series, and misgivings about the
military affairs editor's columns.

critics." Crowther immediately responded with a strong point-by-
point defense of his writing. James told AHS, "I am not going to let
him get me tangled up in a lot of technical details with respect to
which he can out-talk me. But I am agreeing with you that he could
easily be a little less sour on a number of occasions."

Crowther was never put out to pasture before retirement, although AHS continued to differ and carp at the critic. In 1954, he

was "disturbed" by a reference to Susan Hayward as "beautiful and exciting as she inadequately is."

"I think the word 'inadequately' is plainly insulting," said AHS in a rocket to the third-floor editor. "He is not called upon to pass on the lady's beauty. I don't know the girl, so it's not a question of my judgment against his. I just think it's extremely bad taste."

In 1956, he took exception to the tag line of a review of *The Benny Goodman Story* in which Crowther said, "The picture, produced by Universal-International, is in color and looks pretty good, if you're still interested in looking after reading this review."

AHS memoed: "I was most unhappy today with Mr. Crowther's review. . . . I don't care whether he liked it or not, but I certainly dislike the last paragraph. . . . Mr. Crowther's job is to tell what he thinks of a picture, not to try to keep people away from the movies."

To the credit of publisher and editor, Crowther was still in business when both of those had already left the scene on 43rd Street.

The publishers, AHS and his son Punch, had strong feelings for art and about art. Both served on the board of the Metropolitan Museum of Art, and Punch became its chairman in 1987. While their intervention on the content of the news columns was usually no more than a note from an influential reader, there are in the instance of art coverage two examples, one of the publisher as hands-on boss and the other of the publisher as hands-off leader.

AHS detested modern art. His feelings generated an unwonted vehemence against a *Times* writer on art. Dore Ashton, an art critic who had long been reporting on art for *The Times*, was widely respected by connoisseurs of the genre, but not on the fourteenth floor, where AHS prevailed and railed against modern art and Ms. Ashton. It wasn't uncommon for publishers to send rockets to their editors about items that pained them, but the stream of art commentary from AHS during the 1950s seems to have been stronger and more constant than those dealing with other topics.

"Please look at that abomination of a picture and the story written by Dore Ashton," he advised managing editor Turner Catledge on April 23, 1958. "Please read it. I don't generally get this positive about things that I don't understand, but I think I am going to say now definitely that I don't want anything of this kind in The New York Times again."

The publisher was particularly nettled by Ms. Ashton's observation: "However playful, witty, or bitter the titles of Klee's drawings were, he nearly always achieved self-sufficient images to which the titles were apposite rather than essential."

He attached a clipping of Ms. Ashton's review (which today might be read as a rather considered and intelligently contemplative comment on the art of Paul Klee) and asserted, "This particularly non-descriptive piece of fantasy of course is called 'Head of a Man.' Is that playful? Is it witty? Is it bitter? Certainly it is self-sufficient, provided that you can guess that it is the head of a man."

A year later, on May 19, 1959, AHS was still at it: "Please refer to page 30. Read Dore Ashton's columns and then look at the picture and tell me who's nuts. I'm not, honestly! Somehow or other we ought to do something about this."

The campaign was unremitting in its barrage of sarcasm and scorn, not only against Ms. Ashton, but against articles by others on the subject of modern art in the Sunday and daily art sections, even on the editorial page. At one point, Catledge replied to a choleric memo: "Please! Please! Don't list me as a defender of modern art as art. I defend it only as news; the same way I defend crime."

Ms. Ashton left *The Times* in 1960, but that was not the end of the modern-art debate in the pages and by the critics of *The Times* and by the critics of the critics. Letters, articles, and advertisements continued the dispute over the years. Four years later, a letter to AHS dated May 8, 1964, signed by nine participants in a seminar on contemporary art at the University of Southern California, called for Ashton's reinstatement.

So much for the hands-on publisher. Arthur Gelb recalls how Punch Sulzberger refrained from interfering with the news when the Cultural News Department was pursuing the question of whether a Grecian urn acquired by the Metropolitan Museum had been bought from sellers who had illegally obtained it. Because *The Times* publisher/Metropolitan Museum board member did not interfere, there is no account of the business in the archives. Years later, when Gelb and Punch were no longer in those jobs, the former editor asked the former publisher about this welcome standoffishness. Punch replied that he did not think it advisable to interfere, not as long as the reporting was accurate and balanced.

In 1976, the hegemony of the third floor over all cultural affairs was achieved when, with Abe Rosenthal as executive editor for the whole paper (except the editorial page), the News Department, in charge of the daily paper, and the Sunday Department, which issued the Week in Review, the *Book Review*, the *Magazine*, and the Arts and Leisure Section, among other weekly features, were unified. Although the Arts and Leisure and the Cultural News sections remained operationally separate, their editors, William Honan and Seymour Peck, respectively, both reported to Arthur Gelb. This system essentially remained in place, although the competition that had once ruffled relations between the eighth and the third floors was now regulated (in fact, Arts and Leisure moved from the eighth to the third floor, where it existed, almost interchangeably, with the Cultural News Section).

The affinity of *The Times* for cultural news coverage has long been evident, but what it should consist of and how it should be approached are the subjects of continuing contemplation. In March 1969, Abe Rosenthal, in a note to the new executive editor, James Reston, outlined the conclusions of a "Cultural Committee" assigned to examine what course *The Times* should take in its coverage:

"Culture—by which we mean news, trends and ideas in the arts and entertainment—is an important part of life everywhere. Since The Times is devoted to holding up a mirror to life, cultural activity must be part of the reflection. Cultural news is, moreover, a particularly Times subject."

The memo went on to recognize the primacy of New York, and of *Times* readers, in establishing the prominence of the arts: "We provide for our readers the only consistent daily account of cultural news available. They can get, if they wish, business news from the Wall Street Journal and sports from The Post, but it is only in The Times that they can find regular cultural coverage."

The attention that the paper could lavish on major cultural events ranked with the care that it took to ensure full coverage of historic occasions in other fields. On the following pages, for example, is the game plan initially suggested by Arthur Gelb to Abe Rosenthal for *The Times*'s coverage of the opening of the John F. Kennedy Center for the Performing Arts in Washington, D.C., in 1971.

Abe was intensely interested in the arts and culture of his city. He attended theater, concerts, movie screenings, and he wandered about town in search of jazz, his special love. This led to his idea for "a strong program of service information in the field of entertainment." In a memo to the publisher and other executives in September 1971, he suggested a daily column "under the direction of a sophisticated from ARTHUR GELB

MEMORANDUM for:

MR. ROSENTHAL                          August 2, 1971

The opening of the John F. Kennedy Center for the Performing Arts in Washington on September 8th, will be the country's biggest cultural event since the opening of Lincoln Center. Following is an outline of the coverage for the day preceding the opening (the paper of September 8), and for the opening itself (for the paper of September 9).

September 8

1.  Overall lead -- Nan Robertson.  The piece will tell us about the preparations for the opening; people arriving in Washington; last minute decorations; rehearsals; pre-opening parties, etc. -- 2.00 columns.

2.  A piece by Howard Taubman on what the Center's upcoming schedule for the season calls for, what groups it will be presenting from elsewhere in the nation -- 1.50 columns.

3.  A piece about the Center itself; the buildings that are ready, and the buildings that have not yet been completed, and what the time schedule for completion is. This will be accompanied by a chart showing the layout of the Center.  John Phillips -- 1.00 column.

4.  Aerial photos of the Center, and other photos, boxes, etc.

September 9

1.  Overall lead plus second edition changes -- Nan Robertson -- 2.50 columns.

2.  Review of concert and acoustics (second edition). Harold Schonberg -- 1.75 columns.

3.  Review of dance and concert (second edition).  Clive Barnes -- 1.25 columns.

4.  Howard Taubman -- news analysis on the significance of the Center to American cultural life -- 1.50 columns.

5.  John Phillips -- vignettes -- 1.50 columns.

news department man" that would feature events otherwise unnoted in the pages of the *The Times*.

The proposal came to fruition as the Going Out Guide on Monday, February 28, 1972. The "sophisticated" operative was me. I had been cultural news editor for two years, but I missed the freedom of going out on stories and I did not have any particular affection for the haggling over space and commas that is the editor's lot. Now I was turned loose to cover anything that anybody in town who was out for diversion might look to. This included nightclubs, small theaters, musical undertakings that did not fit into any special slotting in the

Mr. Rosenthal                                    Page Two

    6.  Ada Louise Huxtable -- architecture -- 2 columns.

    7.  Grace Glueck -- man in the news on Edward D. Stone,
architect for the Center -- 1.00 column.

    8.  Society, fashions, styles, etc., -- Charlotte
Curtis -- 1.50 columns.

    9.  Text of Nixon's remarks.

    10. List of principal guests plus photos, boxes, etc.

The coverage for September 8th comes to a page, and for the
9th, two pages.

*A.G.*
A.G.

:km

---

paper, museum exhibitions, you name it. I did not write about places
that did not measure up to my own standards and the beauty of it all
was that I went about anonymously, without declaring myself a man
from *The Times* until I had decided I would write about it. I paid my
way, on an expense account, of course. I did not do criticism and I
did not criticize restaurants, although I could write about any come-
dian or musician who worked in one. And I did a lot of ambience. A
very pleasant assignment in every respect.

Sometimes there were reverses. There was the time I wrote
about an ant colony being raised for some forgettable reason at Au-
tomation House on the East Side. By the time the column ran, the
ants had died and the phone kept jingling to find out where they
had gone.

Where in the world does *The Times* find its critics? The question is put
often, with intonations that betoken disbelief, sarcasm, or plain curiosity. Since I have reviewed for the paper and have always stressed
that I am not a critic, the distinction is seen by outsiders as overweening modesty or unacceptable naïveté on my part. You saw it, you
said you liked it, or didn't you? So you're a *Times* critic.

But there is a difference between the critic and the rest of us fill-ins. Theater and movie people know it and, as the archives from as far back as seventy-five years ago or so indicate, were complaining about not having their presentations reviewed by the critic instead of what appeared to them to be a pickup team chosen because they were on tap.

There is no quick answer to the question of where the critic comes from. When *The Times* was looking for a replacement for Brooks Atkinson, there were conversations between executives and theater directors and producers, informal conversations designed to solicit names. In the event, the paper chose one of its own, Howard Taubman, who was music critic, to move into the drama spot. Again, when John Martin, the doyen of dance critics, talked of retirement in 1960, Clifton Daniel asked him for suggestions for a replacement. Martin offered a number of names, each a good one but each with some sort of a reservation attached. Harold C. Schonberg, then music critic, suggested some names and commented, "We could come up with very few names. Music critics, goodness knows, are hard to come by. Dance critics seem an impossibility. Dance in America is a relatively sporadic phenomenon, and in all America there are only two full-time dance critics—on the *Times* and *Herald Tribune.*"

After exhaustive research and inquiry inside and outside the newspaper, Daniel wrote Agnes de Mille, the choreographer, in May 1961, that Martin had put off retirement for a year. "Accordingly, we are going to take one of the younger men in our talented Music De-partment and launch him as a dance-critic-in-training under the su-pervision of Mr. Martin."

That December, Daniel, sensitive to a beginner's probable lack of confidence, wrote to Allen Hughes, who was filing from Europe, a sort of progress report. He complimented the young critic on a piece from Brussels and suggested that at the very start the newcomer "should begin by reporting and gradually ease into criticism as your knowledge and competence in the field increased."

He went on to write, "As you surmise, there was some feeling here that the London criticism was extraordinarily harsh in light of the fact that you were reviewing the Royal Ballet for the first time. But I hope you won't worry too much about this or about my sug-gestions to you—the ones made in the beginning or the ones that may be made as you go along."

This way of getting a new critic was not necessarily typical, because there was no typical formula. Some, maybe most, critics were homegrown, like theater's Atkinson (who came from the *Book Review*), music's Schonberg and Taubman (who had both been reporters), radio-TV's Gould (who came from the *Trib* and from covering nightclubs). Others were "imports" brought in as critics or as specialty reporters: art's John Canaday (from museum work) and Brian O'Doherty (from Ireland and medicine), movie's Vincent Canby (from *Variety*), theater's Frank Rich (from *Time* magazine). Critics are made (and unmade) at *The Times*, almost never born.

In any event, the choice of a new critic apparently has always drawn the attention that approaches the level of the talk surrounding the work the critic is chosen to appraise. In 1960, Brooks Atkinson put it in laughable perspective in a note to AHS, approving of the choice of a new critic.

> I am one Times reader who looks forward to a fresh point of view in the drama criticisms. Getting one drama critic out and a new one in seems to have assumed the proportions of National Survival Week. There was a dark period when I was afraid that American civilization would collapse. But now the country is on an even keel again, and I think we can proceed to the election of a new president with confidence.

The neighborhood of Cultural News on the third floor kept changing as the department moved from space to space during the constant building redesigns. Reporters, generally but unanimously, are squirrelers and squirreling was a major operation in the elbow-to-elbow environment of Cultural News, where specialty publications and files towered up on desks, slopped over onto the floor, and were often invaluable for deadline research.

This dumping ground of culture caused consternation among those who relish a tight ship. One of these happened to be the publisher, Punch Sulzberger, who in December 1986 sent a memo to Arthur Gelb, the cultural czar. "Now that the third floor is 'under new management' [Max Frankel had just become executive editor] why don't we try, once again, to clean the place up.

"Walking back through the cultural news area is enough to turn one's stomach. I would be glad to supply the cart to throw the junk into. Can we please, please, please do this for the new year."

# DOWN THE TUBES

THEN there was the time I missed the big story that broke while I was watching it at home for a review in next morning's paper. It was Edward R. Murrow's *Person to Person,* an innocuous show to which the great broadcast journalist had been relegated. The half hour on that evening was a visit to the home of Sylvester (Pat) Weaver, the creative genius who had, among other things, created the *Today* and *Tonight* shows at NBC. In those days before videotape, it, like most dramas and public affairs and news programs, was done live.

Murrow was following Mrs. Weaver through her residence and there was a momentary confusion, whose cause I did not catch on my ten-inch screen. I wrote the ritual few words noting the show's appearance, a review as bland as the performance had been, telephoned it to the recording room, where skilled operators copied it from small plastic disks and sent it out to the copy desk. I went to bed secure in the feeling that I had done my job and that the space would be adequately filled in next morning's paper.

It was. Until I went to work the next morning. The *New York Post* had pounced on that one indistinct moment and made it into a large up-front story based on the fact that Mrs. Weaver had been stripped of more than mere dignity when a mischievous microphone line had snagged her dress and torn it off her. That and the cover-up were accomplished in seconds, but enough to make copy for a reporter with sharp eyes and a screen clear enough to give body to the fleeting vignette.

Burdened as I was with a sense of shame at having missed a big story, the last man I wanted to meet on the third floor was Frank S. Adams, the city editor, nominally in charge of the Radio-Television Department, and an editor who could look at a miscreant with a hanging-jury glare. Adams eyed me with what I took for malevolence.

"I'm glad you didn't mention that incident with Mrs. Weaver last night," he said. "Bad taste."

Breathing heavily with the relief one might feel when the guillotine sticks in its track on its downward plummet toward one, I groveled gratefully as best I could in agreement.

But in truth, had I seen it, I would have written about it with great glee. Frank Adams represented—luckily for me at that moment—the more staid old days. Jack Gould, the critic, was a keen reporter who realized what the new medium promised to do and he devoted his years to helping guide it. He was a critic not only of television shows but, more so, a critic of television itself.

In 1951, *The Times* ran a seven-part series of articles written by Gould on the impact of the young medium on American life. To produce the 20,000 words that told the story, more than a hundred staffers and special correspondents sent in a total of 101,000 words, according to an account Frank Adams sent to the front office. It was one of many articles in which Gould reached out to learn not only what was sent out on the tube but how that was affecting the expanding body of viewers.

His constant clucking over television quality, virtues, peccadilloes, and sins, along with his repeated scoops from his boundless sources in the business, earned him the sobriquet "Conscience of the Industry." This laconic, carelessly dressed man, always a retiring presence in public, did not relish the title, which, indeed, did sound excessively holy for a newshawk whose biggest joy was in beating everyone else to a story.

Gould's finest moment arrived in 1956, when Israel, Great Britain, and France took the Suez Canal and when the Hungarians rose in revolt against the Soviets. Jack Gould wrote several pieces, the most notable of them castigating the networks for televising the usual dross, like *Queen for a Day,* rather than picking up the free feeds of the important debates then being distributed by United Nations Television. It caused screams of anguish, cries of indignation, and shouts of approval and suggestions that Jack Gould be nominated for a Pulitzer Prize (at that time, the Pulitzer Prize was not yet being awarded for critical excellence). In response, the networks picked up parts of the debates, even at the expense of their own daytime soaps.

That episode overshadowed the response to a Gould column a few years later that criticized the telecasting of programs by a faith healer; the article drew 700 angry letters from the healer's followers and a smaller number from influential religious and community figures supporting Gould's contentions.

In the late 1940s, newspapers around the country were jumping on the television bandwagon, acquiring stations and enjoying the profits. *The Times,* which already owned radio stations WQXR-AM and -FM, was leery about joining the trend. Jack Gould once told me that he had been asked to study the possibilities but that Arthur Hays Sulzberger didn't want to "give away" the news or promote a rival medium.

For all that, AHS was clearly attracted to television as a viewer. There are scores of notes in the archives in which he criticizes the critics, comments on the programs he likes or not (see his memo on the following page), and goes to great lengths studying the program listings in *The Times.* As he got closer to retirement, he watched television more and more. Gould probably received more notes on the publisher's reaction to programs than any other critic did. AHS's comments were intelligent and often helpful in changing things for the better. As his eyesight deteriorated, AHS wanted clearer, maybe larger type for the television listings and he was insistent that they tell readers which programs were reruns.

In the mid-1950s, life was changing more radically than people might think. Airplanes had begun to carry more passengers across the Atlantic than ships did, and radio was beset by its younger electronic relative, television. Several calls came from people who were blind and complained that their favorite shows were leaving audio for video.

In September 1953, Gould sent a memo that it was time to revamp the program listings entirely.

"I think we have to face the fact that radio listening has dropped off during the nighttime hours and I question in my own mind whether there is the interest in the week's schedules that there once was."

He detailed how radio space could be pared, saving three columns a week in the daily, maybe more "because we now have to pad out the TV schedules to square off with the daily."

The publisher, for all of his disgust at much of television, nevertheless kept up with it. In 1956, he told Turner Catledge and Lester Markel that he had just had a color TV set installed . He complained that the listings no longer noted which programs were in color, as they once had, and observed that a large, boldface **C** would help from A. H. S.

MEMORANDUM for: MR. GOULD

I don't look at Television very much but the night
before last I had some time on my hands and watched
WCBS starting with the Arthur Godfrey show which I
thought was awful.

I then saw a movie which was about as bad as anything
I have ever seen.

Then came the Ed Wynn show, which I thought was terrible.

Then followed a suspense picture which undoubtedly was
a live show, but the fact that it was living didn't make
it any better.

In between all of these were the commercials crowded one
on top of the other.

My reason for writing you is to ask whether this was a
typical night on television. If so, then I applaud the
one funny thing that Ed Wynn said when he appeared as
an organ grinder wirh a monkey -- "Business is good
because Television drives so many people into the streets."

A.H.S.

April 27, 1950

viewers like himself. He told Catledge that a telecast of a musical, *Rosalinda,* had been so pleasant that he dissented strongly from his critic's appraisal.

In another heroic example of editor-bites-publisher, Catledge replied that he agreed with the critic when he first read the review and that "another source in the office who is good at such things" felt the same way and that the *Herald Tribune*'s critic "was not too favorably impressed." He added that these judgments were subjective and signed off by saying that he did not think the critic could be charged with "being shopworn" on his job.

In 1958, Gould reported to Catledge that "there is a new approach to television reviewing which is being studied by some of the

MR. CATLEDGE

There is nothing worse than criticizing a critic. I know that we must have confidence in them and that they are the judges. But I would like to enter a very real dissent to what Mr. Shanley wrote last night in reviewing Rosalinda. Mrs. Sulzberger and I watched it in color. It was beautifully done and the voices were extraordinarily good. The two leading women were both most attractive to look at. The dancing was charming. Of course the thing was dated, but the buffoonery was clever and well done. In other words, I disagree with Mr. Shanley at practically every point. *(going Hawaian, eh?) ah ah ah*

Now I raise this question: It seems to me that we have a tendency, in both our movie and television reviews, to be too crisp and too tart, as though the people who are doing the work didn't like their jobs. I find it disturbing. If I weren't the Publisher of The New York Times I would write a letter to Channel 4 and tell them how much I disagree with what I read today on page 53 of that well known newspaper.

A. H. S.

July 24, 1956
A
bc: Mr. Dryfoos

With the advent of television, Arthur Hays Sulzberger became one of its most intense viewers, to judge from the memos in which he complains to his editors about, in this instance, a television review with which he disagreed. Managing editor Turner Catledge replied with a defense of the critic's stance, but even then AHS took exception.

sponsors of the more outstanding programs." This would make previews available for press and sponsors, informing readers what they might want to look at that day rather than telling them about what they saw last night. Television in the late 1950s and early '60s was a field in which the world looked over your shoulder; I could always forecast how my day would go when I went to the candy store in the morning to buy my paper and saw the owner looking at me sadly: "I didn't agree with you about that one last night, Mr. Shepard." He was a bellwether figure and I knew my bosses and the rest of humanity would share his review of my review. Nothing fatal, of course, but daunting nonetheless.

AHS must have been riveted to the home screen in those years, to judge by the abundance of short memos. We ought to list *The Price Is Right*: "I think it's excellent and much the best 'game' show I've seen on TV" (no argument, listing accomplished).

Again: "I watched 'Arch of Triumph' the other night on TV and was horrified at the way it was cut. Frankly, I could not make head or tail of it"; probably cut to make way for "those awful ads." "I don't think Alfred Hitchcock, 9:30 P.M. Sundays, is deserving of a star." *Perry Mason* and *Maverick* were missing on the weekend: "Was this in the news?"

And, in February 1959, AHS informed Gould that, with Mrs. S. out, he had supper looking at television. He particularly loathed the cigarette commercials. Lacking a cutoff device, "I had to listen to those damned singing commercials. It's outrageous—so stupid. . . . I'm glad to say I'm devoting much less time to TV than I was last year!"

Gould, as avid a nicotine addict as ever befogged a newsroom, diplomatically agreed and replied that he was heartened by the publisher's decision to cut down on his television viewing: "If you are not looking at TV as much as formerly, then The Times is in the best of possible hands."

Although AHS relied more on television as his eyesight progressively made it more difficult to concentrate on the paper, after retirement he continued to send suggestions to *The Times*. Television had become more and more influential, and Punch Sulzberger took up where his father left off. In 1972, he complained about conflicts in listing: highlights recommending, and another listing panning, the same show. He specifically ordered: "Let's: 1) only recommend programs we recommend in the listings: 2) bold face those programs that we do recommend (which can be in excess of the ones we list under the photograph), and 3) put a bullet in front of all those that we do recommend." He signed off, "Ever hopefully."

Readers who recognized these foibles in listing television may not have been aware of the effect of television on the newspaper—and all other print journalism. Politicians soon learned that TV more closely suited their needs and strategies by giving them direct access to the public in a way that, if they so chose, did not allow for on-the-spot confrontation and questioning that might indicate another side to the story.

Sunday mornings at *The Times* were hours for reporters to "cover" the news and public-service shows relegated to that low-rating time spot. The public figures who appeared before panels of newsmen, often including *Times* reporters, frequently made news for otherwise quiet Monday-morning page 1s. For a while, the orders were to contact personally the figures who had spoken on the air and get the story directly from them so as not to have to give the credit to the broadcast program alone. It was an exasperating competition and *The Times* drew up rules on the participation of its staffers in such programs.

In a reiteration of long-standing policy, Abe Rosenthal reminded his editors in 1983 that there were no exceptions to the rule:

> When a reporter participates in a television program, he or she will not write stories dealing with the news developed in the program. It does not matter whether he or she participates as a conversationalist or merely asks questions. No exceptions.
>
> If there is no one to cover the story when news develops, use wire services. If no wire services, the reporter participating can inform the desk that there is a story and the desk can assign somebody to get it from the station or whatever.

This went to the heart of decision-making at *The Times*. (As in other areas, this decision has since been unmade, revised, and reinterpreted.) How to ensure *The Times* retained its reputation—and circulation and advertising—by covering television without appearing to put it down, as Hollywood and movie houses had tried, with no success at all? How to view an all-pervasive competitor, whose widespread coverage of events that did not suit *The Times*'s fit-to-print definition but aroused the interest of readers who were also viewers?

Abe Rosenthal felt strongly about holding broadcast news to the same standards that he applied to printed news. When newspapers print wire-service news they make it clear where the story is coming from, he said in a long 1974 memo; television and radio, he declared, usually do not. This was significant because this was how people got their news. This, he contended, was the basis for a story:

> My point in all this is that we have an obligation, since we devote so much space to TV, to report on the quality of TV news, to inform the reader just what it is that he is getting and how the whole process really works. We have and should give credit to TV news when they do something terribly good. But if we are to set ourselves up, as we have, as reporting on the whole TV news scene, then we have to examine the fundamentals and practices of TV and radio journalism.

Those fundamentals and practices, of newspapers and broadcasting, have radically changed. I do not think there are many people who could get into the Radio-Television Department on the credentials I had when I joined it in 1955. I was told of my new assignment while I was covering Ship News and I was surprised by this sea change. Until Jack Shanley, my friend who had recently become editor in that department under Jack Gould, spilled the beans to me:

"I told them that you had been a ship's radio operator during the war," he said gleefully. "They thought that gave you a great background."

# SOCIETY WITH STYLE

20

LTHOUGH I have written for almost every section in *The New York Times,* even some I have worked in remain a mystery. None are greater enigmas for me than Society News and Family/Style. This is usually shrugged off as soft news, and in the context of a world menaced by war and noxious fumes and economies that refuse to be tamed, that is perhaps true. Yet both are connected with the way people live, and there is great interest in that by those who can't live that way or who are looking for help on how to live that way. Society and Family/Style may be the softest ware of journalism but without the income they produce, the hardware that constitutes so much of the rest of the paper would find less space.

For a section that nearly everyone puts down as a snob page, geared to separating Society from society, it was always one of the departments that everyone, but everyone, at *The Times* seemed destined to visit at least once. Reporters, editors, publishers, printers, they all passed along requests for a few lines announcing a wedding, an engagement, a benefit gala. I fobbed close friends off by telling them that they were not sufficiently up to social snuff to merit mention in pages designed to record the rituals of the plutocracy. Others I told that it was impossible, that I could not even get my own in when I got married (truth: I never tried). For business contacts and a few others, I did bring their announcements to the department we called SocNews and, without promoting or pleading, merely whispered that they should go purely on merit.

I'm not sure what "merit" is in a wedding announcement. Unless the wedding involves a headline personality, what is the "merit" of one announcement over another? These musings are not mine alone; the archives show that they have been shared by almost every publisher and top editor faced with the question of who gets in and who doesn't.

In 1949, AHS wrote to an executive at another paper who had asked whether *The Times* had ever run a picture of a "colored wedding." The publisher replied that he didn't know of any picture or story involving a "Negro couple" on the society page, although photographs and stories about blacks who were members of committees with so-called social lights had appeared elsewhere in the paper and that included one wedding.

"The society page is, in effect, snobbish," AHS said. "I remember that when Fred Birchall was managing editor we were looking for a new society editor and he said he was trying to find someone who could write in such a manner that he, Birchall, would be able to read it without feeling like a butler. Unfortunately, one has to admit that there is an intangible something which makes a story available for the society page and, when one analyzes it, that something is a form of snobbery. That's the frankest answer I can give you" (AHS to John Bassett, *Montreal Gazette*, September 20, 1949).

The matter of admissibles and inadmissibles to the society page was clearer in the first part of the twentieth century, when social class was more arbitrarily delineated. In 1950, managing editor Edwin L. James outlined the dilemma of the democratically minded but socially straitjacketed. He was explaining the treatment of the marriage of a socially elevated white woman to a black man that had featured the fact in the headline.

"I hoped you would not put me in the position of defending the snobbery of society news," he wrote to AHS. "I have tried a number of times to make my position clear on that. I do not like the principle back of society news—that is, the process of selection. But, I am very confident that so long as we run society news we must do it on the selective basis, and that basis would certainly bar weddings in which Negroes were involved."

In his reply AHS said that he knew the bride's father, who had been his battery commander during World War I: "I had a profound respect for him at that time and have even a greater one for him now. It was important news for me not that his daughter married, but that he stood by his daughter when she married in such a manner which would have caused many parents to cut their child adrift."

AHS went on to say that he objected to the word "Negro" in the headline, although it was essential to appear in the body of the story. (Those headlines could be bothersome. A quarter-century later,

Punch Sulzberger was apologizing to John A. Roosevelt, son of Franklin Delano Roosevelt, for the headline on his daughter's wedding story in September 1976, JOAN ROOSEVELT BECOMES BRIDE OF UNDERTAKER, saying that the head was stupid and that "the headline writer deserves to have his head examined.")

The exclusion of African-American people from the society pages was raised by letter writers, including one in 1956 who observed that no black people were visible in a Sunday section that found room for more than a hundred photos. Robert E. Garst, assistant managing editor, said that *The Times* had indeed published pictures and stories about African Americans and elaborated: "Our thinking on this subject has got away from the old standard of 'Social Register' judgment of the newsworthiness of engagements or weddings. What we now try to do, and are gradually doing, is to base our judgment on the standing of the person in the community and his usefulness to it. I think it is a fact that, because of their numbers in the population, fewer Negroes than whites meet this new standard. But if they do, we are very happy to print such notices about them."

Actually, the first picture of a black woman on the society page appeared in September 1954, Garst noted in answering a letter in 1962. Since that time "more than thirty photographs of Negro engaged girls, brides and charity aides had appeared," he said.

The strictures of caste and class kept not only people of color from the society page. In 1927, Adolph Ochs received a curious letter from a rabbi, who enclosed a check for $8.55 for an "at home" notice that ran as an advertisement although his wish was to have the notice appear as a news item on the page. The *Times*man had at first accepted the item but, later, when it had not yet appeared, he told the inquiring clergyman that *The Times* "did not publish items of that kind." At that point, the rabbi recalled in his letter, he had telephoned Ochs and the notice was printed—but as an ad, for which he had been billed.

But a study of the society columns revealed that *The Times* did indeed publish items of that kind. "We also discovered that among the many items published, there did not appear a single Jewish name nor any reference to any social happening in any Jewish family," the letter continued. "This certainly appeared to use a vulgar but expressive phrase, to smell after Anti-Semitism. . . . I am loath to believe that Anti-Jewish bigotry could have been the reason for the non-publication of an item concerning a social event in my family, or any other Jewish family, in the columns of a newspaper of which you, who are one of the most prominent of our co-religionists in the city and in whose columns an unusual amount of space is given to Jewish public movements and the activities of Jewish organizations, are the editor and proprietor."

What, the rabbi asked, were the principles that guided the social columns? Perhaps the rabbi was not of sufficient standing to qualify, but he had seen others mentioned, all non-Jewish, who were also equally "insignificant," while none of "our co-religionists, not even those of highest social standing were mentioned, except in connection with non-Jewish functions."

In his reply, Ochs said that he had ordered the check returned to the rabbi and declared, "I must ask you to excuse me from entering into any discussion with you about the matter. The Times, as it appears each day, is the only answer we have to make to such criticism. I am fully aware of the fact that The Times is not a perfect product, and I realize it would be almost impossible to make it so. I appreciate, also, that there are differences of opinion with respect to what should or should not appear in a newspaper, but we exercise our best judgment as to what is news, having to rely, of course, in many instances, upon the intelligence of the people entrusted with the conduct of the various departments of the paper."

By the raucous 1960s, the bastions of upper-case Society were being overrun, even in *The Times.* Charlotte Curtis, the dynamic reporter and later editor in charge of Family/Style, produced splendidly sophisticated, often biting, coverage of high society, the jet set, and other chosen classes. Her writing caused some consternation among the older Sulzbergers but she was given freedom to climb the barriers, if not to break them down.

The question of what to do about those prized announcements remained one that everyone talked about but no one did anything about. The question would not go away and it was slowly modified to include the many sectors of New York life, but Society News was still a section of selection, items more difficult to assess objectively than most other news. Still, everyone wanted to gain access to it. People who worked on the paper were always under pressure to shoehorn something in. Even Punch Sulzberger could become exasperated, as, in 1969, when he complained to his executive editor that an engagement notice he had submitted had run without a photo, although he had specifically ordered one. He was embarrassed.

"As I have said to you a dozen times, I have no desire to put things into the paper and would be perfectly willing to get myself out of this business if someone could give me a logical reason as to why we do use what is run on the society page. It seems to me to be just a matter of individual judgment. I should like to reserve the prerogative of using mine, also."

Later that year, the publisher had a further thought about getting out from under in society. The *Houston Post* and the *Chronicle* had replaced all wedding announcements with paid ads. Check it out, he ordered. Charlotte Curtis objected to the idea: certain weddings would still have to be covered as news; the rich could, if they wanted, buy large ads that would give undue prominence to a wedding. Managing editor Clifton Daniel felt that engagements and weddings were news and should not be influenced "in any degree" by the wishes of those who are in the news to pay for its publication. No objection to the ads, but they should not replace the news items any more than the obituary ads should replace the obit news items.

A year later, it was proposed to cut Society News back by a column from its daily budget, about two and a half columns. Managing editor Seymour Topping, in a report to executive editor Abe Rosenthal, suggested employing new criteria, and a selection of stories that would be of more general interest. "Our present selection of engagement and wedding news in the current, more egalitarian social climate has become outmoded," he wrote.

Rosenthal recommended to the publisher that the daily paper no longer carry any engagement announcements or pictures. All photos of benefits should be eliminated with a piece once or twice a week that would list the more important benefits. The saved space would be used for "more stories of interest to women or, when these are not available, for general news."

Punch agreed, but, in the case of benefits, "I think we must set some criterion on what listings we will accept but, generally speaking, I would have them on the loose side, so as not to argue with our readers."

In 1972, a Family/Style committee discussed, among other things, a stream of "must use" engagement and wedding announcements channeled through the managing editor and asked for the practice to stop. These were mostly from the publisher, who did not send them directly to the department. Obviously, it was appropriate for the publisher to make specific requests. "However, if they come in too frequently, they do create a lot of gossip and yak about double standards and so on," Abe Rosenthal told Punch Sulzberger. It would help if they were submitted more "sparingly."

"I thought that the understanding among the committee of Family/Style (whatever happened to the women's page?) was that the publisher could send in an endless stream of engagement and wedding announcements. Everyone else was going to be limited," the publisher replied to the memo, with the humor and directness that made his memos so different from those of his grandfather. He offered to send them in directly to Society News, to spare the editors the onus. "Anyway, look at it this way—you should be grateful we do not print divorce announcements. Even though this is the mating season, I seem to have more friends going the divorce route than the marriage route."

The Four Fs at *The Times* sold papers, maybe even more than a page 1 story might. They were in the category called Food, Fashions, Family, Furnishings, the section's title from 1955 until 1971 when it was replaced by the name Family/Style. Whatever it was, it was dedicated to that segment of the readership that turned to what had been called Women's News, a rich repository of specialized stories that turned on the kitchen trade; as the years passed, it became clear that men also were turning to those pages and the section assumed a more unisex complexion, although the balance was still tilted to the female side.

As the archives attest, the publishers followed it aesthetically as well as commercially. Iphigene Sulzberger was a particular influence here, usually voicing, gently but firmly, a concern for stories that would be affordable for middle-class and working-class readers rather than solely for the more affluent. Her personal taste, mirrored by her husband's, was more for the laid-back and traditional rather than the freakishly innovative. She tactfully did not intrude herself directly into office matters but channeled her sensitivities through AHS or, later, Punch Sulzberger.

In 1959, she wrote to AHS (she had added, for his eyes only): "I am wondering what the main object of The Times Decorating column really is—is it to tell what is newest and most expensive or is it to be helpful to the average buyer (I started to say like myself but I re-

alized that I am apt to spend a great deal more than most buyers).
The furniture which I saw at the shops [that] were recommended to
me by The Times seemed to me to be suitable for very expensive
pent-houses or for the gardens of Hollywood stars."

The philosophies and the markets for a "woman's page" have
changed radically. In 1935, AHS responded to a fashion consultant
who had suggested innovations in the paper's coverage. Fundamentally, he said, there were no essential differences between the interests of men and women, and "a good newspaper will appeal to both."
Also, *The Times* felt that the paper should be departmentalized as little as possible.

Writing from London in 1950, AHS informed Sunday editor
Lester Markel: "Iphigene has just been over the 'HOME' section and
voices her old complaint that not sufficient emphasis is placed on
conservative decoration but only on modern. I pointed out to her
that the news lies more with modern."

The purpose of these selections is not to portray the crabbiness
of publishers; indeed, there are many compliments from them to the
woman's page to be found in the archives. But these complaints indicate the attention they gave to the details of what they regarded as
an important part of their paper. For instance, in 1951, AHS complained about color sections in an upcoming fashion section: "I understand page 1 is a coat, then on page 21, we have another coat.
That makes two out of seven pictures devoted to coats. Three out of
the seven are devoted to suits and two to high-style evening gowns.
What happens to dresses? Is this a proper balance?" One photograph, he said, was bad—"the model herself looks pregnant. In fact,
she looks so pregnant she split the coat."

Again, in 1956: "I have just seen the fashion pictures in next Sunday's magazine as well as those in today's Times. Do women have to
pose like fools in order to look nice in the new clothes? If so, they're
not like the women I know!"

"Why is it that the Advertising Department of The New York
Times still admits that women have breasts and figures and that our
Editorial Department denies it? Surely somebody's out of step," he
queried of the woman's page editor in 1957.

One of the ongoing tensions that afflicted the section was the un-
derlying belief of the advertisers, especially the big advertisers, that
the coverage was legitimately tied to the advertising. The truth was
sometimes more difficult to underline than was the intention firmly

laid down by Adolph Ochs that the only way to make a newspaper successful—therefore, more valuable to the advertiser—was never, never to allow an advertiser, or anyone else, influence the content of the news sections.

The publisher-heirs hewed to this viewpoint, except that they informally asked their editors to try to be somewhat accommodating to store executives with whom they had had correspondence. But when the pressure came in threats to withhold advertising for lack of news coverage, the answer was unequivocal: In 1962, *Times* vice president and general manager Amory Bradford wrote to a society of interior designers: "The Times does not respond to pressure from advertisers concerning the editorial content of the newspaper. Therefore we are not willing to discuss this question in response to your telegram which approaches it from the point of view of advertising support. There may be some justification for your position, but this is no way to raise it."

In 1942, a Macy's executive was objecting to the credit line given to stores below fashion photographs or drawings they had supplied. Macy's had not been receiving its fair share of these credits, which he described as advertising worth at least three times the regular advertising rate and he urged the abolition of credit lines. In his report to AHS, Lester Markel rebutted the argument, insisting that news was news, not advertising, that the credit lines informed the reader where to find the item pictured. "We ought to publish the news of fashion creation," the work of the designers who set the general fashion tone. "We ought to publish the news of fashion acceptance," he advised, "That kind of news originates in stores which cater to the larger rather than the smaller groups of women."

It was a lingering problem, the relationship of the stores to the news columns of *The Times*. Elizabeth Howkins, editor of that section, outlined a situation to Mr. Sulzberger in 1963.

"This is the day on which Mainbocher, the only remaining American couturier (and therefore an important fashion story though not an advertiser as is true of all couturiers), is releasing the story and pictures of its autumn collection," she wrote. She had given the couturier that date six months earlier when he had called to ask.

"You can imagine my predicament, then, when I saw the 'must' positions for the advertising as sold for Macy's and for Stouffers for the 18th," she said. Macy's felt that it could not change the date to accommodate the Mainbocher story, although it had indicated flexibility when it had contracted for the every-Wednesday ad, particularly if it "conflicted with Macy editorial material, which meant a great deal to them." The dilemma was resolved when Macy's agreed to go on a facing page, but required "some intimation of Women's News" on that page to satisfy the advertiser.

Monroe Green, the adroit and creative head of the Advertising Department, a month later, noted, in a report to Punch Sulzberger: "There is one general situation that is immediately apparent when one reflects on ever increasing, bitter exchanges between advertisers and The Times. This relates to the degree of flexibility in our Women's News area, weekdays and Sundays, in interpretation and application of the Adolph Ochs doctrine to 'give the news, impartially without fear or favor, regardless of any party, sect or interest involved.' It is not enough to simply parrot, faithfully but unimaginatively, the sort of thing The Times was saying in 1910. . . . In 1963 are we ever threatened by 'advertiser pressure'?"

Green, who passionately and sincerely believed that advertising was also news, spoke of the high stakes involved: "We must get over the naive concept that whenever the News Department encounters an advertiser, the conflict of interest is always total, so that nothing can be good for him which is not bad for us and vice versa. Life is not that simple. . . . It would be useful and constructive to explore those areas where Times news interest and advertiser 'publicity' interest coincide."

It was a thought that editors at the helm did not countenance and, when push came to shove, was not generally invoked.

In 1973 Abe Rosenthal unburdened himself to the publisher on the endless problem of angry department-store advertisers who still linked their space-buying with a perceived entitlement to news coverage. He declared that he had discussed the situation with Charlotte Curtis and others and was convinced they were doing a fair and responsible job.

"That does not mean, of course, that every store will always be happy with their decisions," he wrote. "The same thing can be said of any field of reporting. They fully understand their obligations as reporters and editors to look at all stores. But they already have a feeling, which to some extent I think is justified, that they are subject to special pressures and that complaints from advertisers about the space they get or do not get receive considerably more attention than the complaints on similar problems from other sources and other advertisers. I think that to keep pressing when one show or exhibition is not covered would seriously shake their confidence in the meaning and purposes of The Times. These people in Family/Style cover subjects of special interest to retail advertisers and nobody is more aware of it than they. But they also consider themselves newspaper people within the traditions of The Times."

# 21 THE GOOD THAT REMAINS . . .

T HERE are reporters who only write on their specialty, there are reporters who will write on anything, and there may even be reporters who hate to write anything. But sooner or later, all reporters write obits. Obituaries are among the most important items in the paper, read with inordinate interest by the public, with motherly concern by the top editors, and, sometimes dismayingly, with personal passion by the publisher. Obituary-writing, which always makes for lugubrious jokes on the outside, is actually a writing of biography and the appearance of an obit, long or short, can provide some of the most stimulating and absorbing reading in the pages of *The Times.*

No American paper sets more store by the quality of its obituaries than does *The New York Times.* I have written obits during my decades of reporting at *The Times,* and in 1986 I became, for a year, obituary editor.

Executive editor Max Frankel and managing editor Arthur Gelb, in conferring this unwanted honor on me, explained that someone with a good general memory was needed to centralize the obit operation, which had years previously been the domain of an Obit Copy Desk (it also handled society page news, like birth and wedding announcements). This had been supplanted by a system that made each section, each department responsible for obits in its field, in the belief that it knew more about them than others did. But the system had frayed, particularly for the shorter, less familiar obits which depended upon what could be found in "the clips" (the clippings in the morgue) rather than on personal reminiscence. The younger editors knew more and were brighter, but in the age of electronic memory they did not clutter their minds, as we had had to, with stray wisps of history that were part of the lives of men and women whose obits were at hand.

As obits editor, I had a staff of three superb journalists doing the advance obits that were the crown jewels of *The Times* and also three or four other reporters who worked on daily obits, the ones that came in during the day and for which there had been no material prepared. Obit writers were reporters endowed with broad outlooks, sensitive perceptions, a thirst for details, and abundant style. Alden Whitman had garnered the reputation for being a *Times* obituary writer with the panache that made a visit from him, to do "research on a story," as mitigating a factor for the eminent as death could allow. Alben Krebs and Eric Pace wrote obits that would have been a credit to professional biographers, advance obits based on months of reading books, clippings, documents. For years after they retired, the obits by Krebs and by Peter Flint, whose specialty was cinematic personalities, still were the stuff of page 1.

There was a bank of closely guarded advance obits, nearly 2,000 on file, but many had to be updated, like those of presidents, major political, business, and cultural figures, domestic and foreign. Some, who were fortunate enough to outlive their celebrity, were downgraded to shorter mention because the world little remembered what they had done. We paid attention to those in the spotlight and we were prodded into thinking about them when the news pages announced that they had gone in for an operation or were otherwise indisposed.

For all that, I would have been grateful to have had my own advance obit written. An advance obit, primed to go, always seemed to guarantee extra years of life. Unlike most newspaper writing, advance obits do not offer instant gratification. I wrote Fred Astaire's obit in 1981, when he was reported to be ill, and he did not die until 1987. I wrote John Wayne's obit in a hurry when he went into a Boston hospital for an operation; thanks to my advance, he survived for several years and even made some newsy appearances in between.

"It occurred to me the other day, and I meant to speak to you about it earlier, that I've never checked on General Greenbaum's obit," Arthur Hays Sulzberger, in 1962, told Turner Catledge, in reference to AHS's oldest friend, Edward S. Greenbaum, a lawyer. "He is, I'm delighted to say, in the best of health, and to work up a good obit on him is the best way of assuring his longevity!"

The certainty of death and the uncertainty of its timing could cause frustration. Whitman's obits were not appearing lately—was he still working on them? an executive memo queried in 1975. "Sure," came the penciled reply of Peter Millones, metropolitan editor. "But I think the problem is that nobody's dying—maybe it's a trend story."

Obits are a delicate matter and, in my experience, cause as much morning-after uproar as anything that appears in *The Times*. Perhaps because it is a final pronouncement that cannot be adjusted in future stories. But, as editor, I approached my telephone with some trepidation each morning. A name had been misspelled—that was easy, a simple "Correction" entry. A woman complained that she was the real wife of the deceased, not the one we mentioned—a call to a lawyer straightened that one out. An indignant daughter complaining that her father had been *the* founder, not the co-founder, as stated, and she wanted credit given—more complicated and took a month of checking to lead to a soft correction that was not completely a disavowal. Even worse, a complaint from "upstairs," based on a lamentation from the deceased's nearest and dearest to our highest circles at the way *The Times* had treated a person who had been a friend of (1) the publisher, (2) the executive editor, (3) the managing editor, (4) the head of a bureau.

For example, in 1905, Julius Ochs Adler wrote, as part of a general report to his uncle Adolph Ochs, vigorously complaining about the obit of Mortimer Schiff, a member of the prominent family of financiers:

> The death of Mortimer Schiff was a shock to everyone and The New York Times was unfortunately responsible in still further aggravating the grief of the family. You will notice the last paragraph of the clipping enclosed giving Mr. Schiff's obituary refers most clumsily and unskillfully to the suit and countersuit with his discharged butler, an event that happened twenty-four years ago. The Times was the only newspaper in New York City, including even the tabloids, which referred in any way to this blackmail suit.

Adler said that a postmortem discussion among the executives revealed a "divided opinion." Managing editor Birchall agreed that the reference was regrettable and clumsily handled but said that the item was necessary "in anything that purported to be an obituary of Mr. Schiff." Another executive, however, "agreed with me that when a man is dead it can hardly be considered necessary, even with the high standards of The New York Times that all the news should be printed, to rake up a twenty-four-year-old scandal that cannot possibly do anyone any good and only shock and hurt the grieving family and sympathetic friends."

There were many rules on obits, some lasting, some impermanent. Memos were issued reminding editors that funeral parlors and burial dates were not to be mentioned in obits, except for the most widely known famous; such details were the province of the death notice advertisements. Suicides were not to be placed on the obituary page, nor were the victims of accident or other violent fates; those obits, which now appear among the others, would be reported in the regular news section. Advance obits were never, never to be shown to outsiders, certainly not to the subject, and not without authorization to most insiders; this is still the standard at *The Times*. The obit writer should always, as much as possible, learn the cause of death, and in any case cite the name of the person who reported the death; there are several occasions when *The Times* has had to publish, embarrassedly, "corrections" that restored to the living one who had been wrongly reported dead.

Arthur Hays Sulzberger, in particular, was eager to elevate the quality of obits from mere bills of lading detailing the dates and recorded accomplishments of a life to essays that would put flesh on the bones, compose a portrait of the deceased. "Both are adequate, neither is outstanding," he commented in 1955 on two advance obits he had asked to read. "We made such a hit with the obit that we had on Colonel McCormick where we were able to introduce some warmth and give something of the inner character of the man. Both of these obits lack that."

The new era of writing obits so that the summation of a person's life preceded the litany of a career (after a lead announcing the death, of course) began in earnest with the accession of Abe Rosenthal as metropolitan editor. I can date it to 1963, late in the afternoon, when Abe and Arthur Gelb, the assistant metropolitan editor, came flying to the back of the newsroom and deposited sheaves of paper on my desk. Jean Cocteau had died and they wanted a big, brand-new obit in place of the skeletal one that had been on file. They wanted to inaugurate the age of reformed obits at that moment. Now I knew that Cocteau had been a playwright, a poet, an all-around writer, but I did not know much more. I flew to reference books, to the wire copy, and made calls to people who knew about such people and things. I put it together without much realization of what I had done, gave it to the desk, and went home. The next day I was off, but Arthur Gelb telephoned to congratulate me on the job, which was displayed on the front page.

"If you have to die, it's better to die in The Times," Abe Rosenthal noted, in part, in reply to a letter congratulating the paper for a fine job on an obit. "You must realize, however, that the time of day is extremely important. I have advised all my friends to die Monday through Friday, as early in the day as possible, preferably between ten and noon."

# NEW HORIZONS, NEW SCOOPS

CHECKBOOK journalism flourished in the highly competitive newspaper world of the late 1800s and early 1900s. Those were years of intense exploration and newspapers helped underwrite expeditions in return for exclusive accounts by the explorers. Before the days of instantaneous communication, such arrangements were profitable. They made good business sense for circulation and advertising. Such projects were in line with *The Times*'s ambition to be preeminent in telling the readers everything about the world in which they lived, a policy that made it a leader in scientific coverage.

There are in the archives dossier, "Facts About *The New York Times:* A Guide," three entire pages devoted to summaries of index cards listing the expeditions that involved the paper. The polar expeditions of Richard Evelyn Byrd, the Navy flier who established a warm and lasting working friendship with the publishers, constitute the largest single subject listed on these cards. *The Times* also participated in the voyage of Roald Amundsen to the North Pole (1926–1927), Martin Johnson's East African explorations (1930–1931), Frank E. Nicholson's probing into Carlsbad Caverns (1930), and other proposed globe-trotting, like an airship exploration of Arabia's "Empty Quarter."

In 1909, Ochs was caught up in the fever of a scoop. He wrote to his wife that he had just arrived back in New York and found "the office in the greatest excitement about our marvelous and overwhelming good luck" in regard to Robert E. Peary's arrival at the North Pole:

We are the exclusive publishers of Peary's story and only through us can newspapers get rights to reprint it. Every newspaper in New York is in a panic about our *stupendous scoop* and they are moving heaven and earth and offering all kinds of money to us and to our employes to get hold of the

story. Nothing in American journalism equals this achievement. The N.Y.T. is now flooded with telegrams from newspapers all over the world asking to buy the stories. Our orders
already exceed ten thousand dollars, all of which we shall
give Peary.

A clipping from the *Syracuse Herald* in the archives reveals that
such a journalistic triumph did not go unchallenged, although it was
stock-in-trade for newspapers at that time. The article tells how Judge
Learned Hand of the United States Circuit Court had set aside an
injunction sought by *The Times* that prohibited the *Sun* and the *World*
from publishing any portion of Commander Peary's account of his
trip to the pole. The other papers had taken the position that Peary,
an active-duty naval officer on a scientific expedition, had no right to
sell exclusive rights on his account:

> It seems to The Syracuse Herald that The Times may lose the
> fruits of its enterprise, together with the $5,000 which it gen-
> erously gave to Commander Peary when it seemed probable
> that his expedition was to fail because of the lack of financial
> aid. If Peary had the right to the exclusive sale of the account
> of his trip to the North Pole to a newspaper, why could he
> not, with equal justice to the public and fidelity to his gov-
> ernment, sell to a newspaper an exclusive account of a naval
> battle in which he might be the leader?

*The Times* had extensive arrangements with explorers, particularly Admiral Byrd, whose flights it covered intensively and who felt
an affection for the family that went beyond purely business dealings.

"We have decided to name after you a beautiful glacier in the
mountain mass of Marie Byrd Land," the explorer reported to Ochs
in 1931. "It is the only one of the kind I have ever heard of. A high
perpendicular peak that divides it at its foot. It is a good sized glacier.
There is a mountain at the glacier four or five thousand feet high
which I have named Iphigene. I have not told her about it. Perhaps
you would like to tell her. I would like to name this peak I speak of
in the glacier after one of your grandchildren."

Clearly charmed by the offer, Ochs replied, "With respect to the
name of the grandchild for the glacier peak—I would not like to
make a distinction among them, so, may I suggest the name 'Maru-

jupu,' i.e., Ma from Marian; Ru from Ruth; Ju from Judy, and Pu from Punch. That takes them all in, and it's a word that sounds euphonious and mysterious and may be acceptable to you."

On January 22, 1973, Punch added a footnote to the family penchant for leaving its mark on otherwise nameless parts of the globe. He thanked his fellow publisher, Malcolm S. Forbes, president of *Forbes* magazine, for putting his name to a stretch of highway in a Forbes development in Fort Garland, Colorado. With typically wry humor, he wrote:

> I have lived substantially frustrated because my mother has a glacier in the Antarctic named after her; my father has a bay named for him in that same friendly part of the world, and my grandfather has a highway running up to Lookout Mountain in Tennessee named for him. So, it really is a warm feeling to know that one has finally made it. As soon as I get snow tires on my camper, I'll be out to see the new interstate highway that you have named for me.

The relationship that *The Times* established with Charles A. Lindbergh was an especially close and newsmaking one for more than a decade, starting with his epic solo flight from New York to Paris. On May 20, 1927, Julius Ochs Adler wrote to "Dear Uncle Adolph" in Paris:

> Long before this letter reaches you, you will have learned the result of the flight which started from Roosevelt Field at 7:52 this morning. We were successful in getting the exclusive story on this basis:
>   1. $1000 if he takes off.
>   2. If the flight is unsuccessful but his story is still available at The Times option he will receive an additional $2000.
>   3. If the flight is successful he will receive an additional $4000, over the original $1000.
>   Maximum cost to us $5,000.
>   We have already secured over $3,000 from newspapers throughout the country who have bought the story so the net investment is not a large one.

A week later he recounted what had happened after the Lone Eagle's renowned flight across the ocean. "We have been very busy the last 48 hours as a result of the new Lindbergh series of articles which The Times secured. The terms as you know are $25,000. for outside syndication plus a $10,000. payment for rights in New York. It was a considerable plunge but we have been very fortunate so far."

Adler went on to describe the deals concluded with other publications and continued:

> Your cable approving of our gift to Lindbergh of the net revenue from the syndication of his Transatlantic flight was a welcome message. I frankly think it helped in securing this second series of articles.
>
> Circulation has been magnificent and the daily has continued well over 400,000. Last Sunday when the story actually broke we had available 668,000 copies as the advance sections had already printed and the cylinders were being reburnished. As we cabled you the paper sold for as high as $1 a copy in certain outlying sections of the city and one ingenious gentleman devised the plan of renting The Times at 5¢ per half hour.

Ochs maintained a personal relationship with the aviator, congratulating him on his marriage to Anne Morrow in 1929, sending condolences when their little son was kidnapped and killed in 1932.

The latter incident, although personally painful to the publisher and his family, did nothing to hinder circulation when the story broke late in the day. A memo on May 13, 1932, from Circulation, said: "Mail Room output reported at 5.00 a.m., 532,007 copies. Estimate prior to break of Lindbergh baby story, 479,000. . . . Times press start 10.50 p.m. Herald-Tribune press start 10.40 p.m. Herald-Tribune beat us at Times Square and terminals but Times beat *it* up Broadway above 160th as much as half an hour.

"Lindbergh story now probably 'through,' as far as any great circulation increase is concerned. Shall try to pull up Sunday order with Seabury hearing developments on Mayor Walker."

In December 1935 the Lindberghs, exhausted and desolate after their ordeal, departed for the sanctuary of England. But before they left, Lindbergh called Lauren D. (Deak) Lyman, an old friend and *Times* aviation reporter, and said he wanted to give the story of their departure only to him, because he did not trust others to give a correct report. It was agreed to hold the story for twenty-four hours after

Charles A. Lindbergh as he looked in 1927.

their ship had sailed. Murray Schumach, a reporter, remembers seeing Edwin James, the managing editor, and Lyman huddled around the ticker in the Ship News Department that listed arrivals and departures in the port. He wondered, but soon learned, why they were so interested in this specialized device. The Lindbergh story was printed in a late edition, a clean scoop.

Other news organs scrambled to play catch-up. Managing editor James was hopping mad because, he said, the Associated Press broke the 9:30 A.M. release date on *The Times*'s copyrighted story by sending it to out-of-town papers at 3:30 A.M. He gave AHS two editions of the *Chicago American* with the A.P. story and commented, "They took all they wanted of our story and didn't give us any credit whatsoever."

That was all the minor irritation in a triumphal week.

"Numerous people have asked me how it happened, and my answer has been in each case, 'It took eight years,' " AHS wrote in his congratulatory note to Lyman. "During that time, confidence was established in a man who had many reasons, some good and some bad, for being distrustful of the press and its representatives. It was, as I see it, another triumph of character—character of the newspaper which Mr. Ochs had created, character of the man who in this instance represented it."

# 23

# GETTING THE NAME RIGHT

I N GENERAL, it took time for *The Times* to accept a term, particularly one with deep social overtones. Sex, gender, and ethnicity are potentially explosive areas when descriptions are involved. *The Times* did not look at itself as being retrograde in adopting words and certainly did not regard its wariness as playing catch-up. A word, its editors felt, had to become firmly woven into the fabric of communications before it became printable, and even then, profanities and obscenities were almost never printable in any case.

By the mid-1970s, with a new stylebook in preparation, there were broader questions than how to address individuals. Entire bodies of humanity had emerged with new claims to dignified recognition or to appellations of their own choosing. Not only were people of color and women and homosexuals asserting rights to nomenclature, they were reading *The Times* and making their opinions known. Not for nothing had publisher Punch Sulzberger queried whether women and blacks had read over pertinent sections of the new book. Yes, he was assured, relevant editors had indeed reviewed it and initiated suggestions.

At about the same time, the noun "gay," except when it was part of the name of an organization or in a quote, was still unacceptable in its columns. Today it seems as though it should not have been a problem at all. Consciousness in regard to homosexuality was making itself felt, but slowly. Assistant managing editor Theodore M. Bernstein told editors in 1969 that letters had complained about the use of "homosexuals" in groupings of undesirable characters. "We should not use the word itself to indicate that such people are undesirable characters. If it is linked to another word that characterizes the type we are talking about—'homosexual prostitutes'—or if we say 'male prostitutes,' that is all right."

For instance, in the early 1970s I wrote a longish feature for a Weekend Section on a walk-around in Greenwich Village. It was an article that tried to capture the color and excitement of this lively neighborhood. I described Christopher Street and its absorbing street style, mentioning only its different lifestyles and avoiding mention of the homosexual contribution to it. No sooner was it in print than a letter came, lamenting the omission of people who had had such a positive influence on maintaining the animation of a street. In retrospect, it is clear that the letter writer was quite correct. Then, however, it had not been long since exhibitionistic homosexual bars in the Village and on the Lower East Side had been flaunting themselves in hopes of tourist trade with all of the falseness that rubbernecks saw in Chinatown opium dens. Homosexuality was still a snickering business and I was afraid to approach it in writing.

The change in attitude was evident in a memo to the Foreign Desk in 1983, a note that alluded to a military case that involved a question of homosexuality. "The use of words like 'innocence' or 'guilt' or 'charge' implies that a sexual preference is in itself some sort of wrongdoing. Where some kind of infraction related to homosexuality is involved, that is a different thing. . . . Let's all think twice about language in these cases, just as we do in any area where it might be possible to offend."

Meanwhile, many Italian Americans worried about the word "Mafia," which was rapidly becoming common coinage for any sort of organized criminality, and they were particularly sensitive to the epidemic of crime stories that might link their community with crime as a whole.

"The Times has tried to make it clear that the Mafia (or Cosa Nostra) is a closely contained criminal conspiracy of about 4,000 men of Italian birth or descent—only a minuscule fraction of the 20 million honest, decent Italian-Americans in this country," a *Times* executive wrote in reply to a complaint from a letter writer in 1970. "The Times has never identified anyone as a Mafioso unless he has been so described by a law enforcement official or his name is on the Department of Justice list of alleged Mafia members."

*The Times* did stop using the term "Cosa Nostra," but the perceptions outside continued to conflict with those inside. In a letter to an official of the Italian-American Civil Rights League in 1970, Abe Rosenthal reiterated that the paper would continue to resist any group pressure that tried to "dictate" news or editorial policies. He reproved the group for a demonstration that disrupted delivery of the paper but added, "we all still feel that it is the obligation of The Times to inquire deeply into any complaint that is raised."

He acknowledged that there was a need for the paper to report more on the Italian-American community in New York, but argued that *The Times*'s use of the word "Mafia" was accurately employed in its columns. It was a question, he said, that he had studied intensively, with a regard to all sensitivities, but had concluded that it was an appropriate descriptor relating to certain types of criminal activity.

Meanwhile, he reminded editors that "when we refer to the various ethnic communities, we should not designate them as 'Italian' or 'Irish,' as we still sometimes do. They are Americans and if their ethnic background is important, they should be called Irish-Americans or Italian-Americans, or whatever."

### REFERRING TO BLACKS

The proper allusion to people of color has been elusive when it comes to giving completely inoffensive satisfaction. In my years at *The Times,* I have seen the term, as applied to Americans, go from "Negro" to "black" to "African American." Why uppercase for the N in Negro, and lowercase for the b in black? Assistant managing editor Allan M. Siegal explained to a letter writer: "In the days when 'Negro' was a widely used term, we of course, capitalized it. But at that time, 'white' was customarily lowercased, being more of an informal description than a racial identification. In any event, when the term 'black' came into wide use in place of 'Negro,' we and most other publications followed the analogy of the widely accepted practice for 'white' and lowercased both terms."

This business of identification was, of course, tied in to the question of coverage of the black communities in general. In 1968, Bernstein, who had gained renown as an authority on language use, sent a long memorandum to Clifton Daniel that discussed coverage of "Negro news," a topic he found to be "fairly urgent."

> Imagine yourself, for the moment, to be a Negro living in a segregated section of the city. You pick up a copy of The New York Times. You find that by far the largest number of news items concerning Negroes relates to antagonisms and clashes with whites, to Negroes protesting or talking back, to items in

general that are concerned with the black-white confrontational. There are, to be sure, some items that present the face
of reconciliation and concord but these are distinctly a minority. Would you not feel, as a Negro, that you were being excluded from the community in general in the reporting of the
news, and that your segregation was being accentuated?

What I propose to overcome this feeling is an intensified
effort to find and cover Negro news. There must be countless
stories about the Negro middle class—the entrepreneurs, the
entertainers, the teachers, the scientists, the clubs, the trade
organizations—that we are not reporting. I suggest that we
search out such news.

Bernstein continued with a suggestion, should such a search be
unfruitful, that *The Times* modify "its currently accepted news standards to produce items of interest to the Negro community." He acknowledged that there might be "an instant reflex of resistance" to
his idea but explained, "just as business is relaxing its standards to
hire what have hitherto been regarded as unemployables, a newspaper like The Times should relax its standards to put to work news
items that hitherto have been regarded as unemployable."

Items of this interest should not be grouped in one section or
page, he wrote, because that would "compound the idea of segregation" and they should not be written in "a condescending manner." He
urged that Society News publish an occasional engagement picture
and cover benefits from within the Negro community.

"I don't mean to imply criticism of what our editors are now
doing; they are following news standards that have persisted since the
beginning of American journalism," Bernstein concluded, commenting that "we would incidentally be serving our own interests
since we could confidently look forward to increased circulation in
an area where there is great potential but relatively little actuality."

Abe Rosenthal's reaction was that the memo contained much to
think about but he was not eager about touching the news standards of
*The Times* to appeal to a segment of readership. "Actually, however, I do
not think this is a great problem. It seems to me that what Ted is saying
is that we should keep our eyes opened for more stories that affect and
involve the Negro community. I have no quarrel with this whatsoever."

One of the more zealous figures in keeping *The Times* equitable in
its race coverage was publisher Punch Sulzberger. In 1970, he queried

his editors about the play given to a particular story: "I am curious: why is it that when the National Guard kills four white students we put in on page 1, and when the National Guard kills six black people we put it on page 32?" Quite right, was the reply, with an explanation that the story had been front-page news the previous day with a report on the slaying of four black people but the additional carnage was moved back in the next day's paper because of other breaking news, with a failure of intra-office communication on the revised makeup.

In that same year, Punch objected to a story in the paper about Chrysler Corporation's employment program:

> The attached story from yesterday's newspaper I think is highly misleading and unfair and the kind of reporting that opens us up to attacks of being interested in the bizarre and the destructive.
>
> Almost any luxury item has probably got black employees involved in producing it and so what? And the Chrysler Corporation has probably done as much (and certainly a lot more than The New York Times) to get meaningful jobs for ghetto blacks.
>
> This kind of journalism, it seems to me, is like reporting two bad incidents in a hospital and then translating this into saying this is typical of every American hospital or taking a sloppy error in The New York Times and saying this is an indication that every column is composed of sloppy errors.

In 1972, executive editor A. M. Rosenthal sternly reminded the deskmen to defer to the reporter's usage in a story. This followed the substitution of "black" for "Negro" by a copy editor. Rosenthal wrote: "Policy: The decision as to whether to use black or Negro should be made by the reporter writing the story. The reason is that there are many subtleties and the reporter is best qualified to decide which usage is the proper one given the context of the story and the people about whom he is writing."

Rosenthal, in his memos, manifested a keen interest in keeping up with news of developments in black society. He ordered, in 1978, a series on what he described as "one of the most important stories in the country," black unemployment, particularly among urban youth. He did not miss the fact that *Times* overall reportage should not regard black society as monolithic. In 1981, he suggested to Punch Sulzberger that the publisher invite a group of Harlem businessmen to *The Times*. He himself was going to expand coverage of that segment of black life, which had not gained much attention in *The Times*, certainly not as much as the paper had given to other Harlem communities such as teachers, civil rights activists, ministers, and social workers.

In 1984, Rosenthal, with his reporter's instincts, returned from a meeting of black journalists in Atlanta with a story idea. He had heard a speech by Andrew Young, who said, "If you don't understand the role of churches in Black life, you don't understand Blacks." Rosenthal thought that *The Times* should do more along those lines and observed in his memo, "If Black churches are so important to Black life, then not covering them in the city kind of sets up criteria which unwittingly exclude certain Black stories from consideration."

Race at *The Times* was not only an issue in print, it was a matter of personnel as well. I recall that there were few, if any, African-American employees other than elevator men and porters when I began work there. The first black reporter was George Streator, a newspaperman, a resident of Edgecomb Avenue, in Harlem's well-to-do Sugar Hill neighborhood, and a son-in-law of Brigadier General Benjamin O. Davis, the first African-American general officer in the United States Army.

On October 30, 1945, managing editor Edwin L. James wrote to publisher Arthur Hays Sulzberger: "We are still trying to get a Negro reporter who looks promising. Here is one whom Mr. Joseph asked to write him a letter. I would appreciate very much your reaction to the letter."

The letter that Streator wrote to David H. Joseph, city editor, was a vigorous statement. If he started work at $75 a week, he wrote, he would regard it as a job with a future, that he would not have to live at a "peon's" standard, condemned to such a condition because of race and color. He would not spend all his time bemoaning the "Negro problem."

Negroes, he continued, are not a happy people and have deep suspicions of white people at virtually every meeting. Whites, he wrote, seem to enjoy the relationship and relish intellectual harassment of blacks. Negroes know the score in life, but "we do not play a large part in governing it."

He had worked with white men and women elsewhere, he wrote, and did not anticipate any trouble in doing so at *The New York Times*. It was generally felt, he said, that he was a reserved person, not easily establishing friendships with others. Experience had shown that this was the best way of dealing with relationships at work. In short, he looked for no difficulties at *The Times* "if there is a clear head and honest heart at the top," a situation that he was confident existed.

Streator was hired in 1945. He was, contrary to his own feistily self-proclaimed reserve, a very outgoing man with a friendly, chatty personality that ignored lines of color and class and was appreciated by myself, a lowly copyboy toward whom he showed no hint of staff superiority. George Streator stayed at *The Times* for three years and eight months, until 1949, when he left after some stories he had written on black educational institutions had drawn criticism from their managements. He became editor of the National Maritime Union's weekly, *The Pilot*.

*The Times*'s deliberate program brought in ever-increasing numbers of black reporters and editors and workers in other departments. This was given impetus, oddly enough, by the replacement of operator-controlled elevators by automatic elevators. The operators, almost all of them African American, were reassigned to a wide variety of clerical, mechanical, and other in-house jobs on all floors.

### REFERRING TO JEWS

Broad sections of Jewish readership have always had a curious and passionate relationship with *The Times* since the early days of Ochs ownership. Adolph S. Ochs was very conscious and proud of being a Jew when he purchased *The New York Times* and he, with no apparent confessional hang-ups, mixed as freely in Jewish social circles as he did in the general society of New York. Before his arrival, *The Times*, like almost every other New York daily, was loose in its reporting on Jewish New York, particularly when it came to writing, often in the most derogatory fashion, on the poor immigrant Jews who were crowding into the Lower East Side, not far from Printing House Square, where the New York press was centered. This type of ethnic reporting in the New York press affected the Irish, the Italians, the blacks, and others considered too status-poor to warrant dignified notice except as individuals who had risen "above" their own people.

As the twentieth century unfolded, *The New York Times* became an essential read for Jewish leadership in all its different persuasions. For as many who swore by its objectivity and admired its breadth of coverage, it seemed that there was an equal number ready to pounce on what they considered slights, or worse. Rabbis who excoriated *The Times* for its reporting, or lack of reporting, of anti-Semitic iniquities or for grudging attention to the Zionist movement nevertheless read the paper daily with the zeal of one scanning holy—or the devil's, depending upon viewpoint—text. This relationship of community to paper has been one of the most curious of *Times* readership phenomena.

Ochs and his son-in-law and successor, AHS, were Jews who regarded Jewishness as a faith, a religion, with no ethnic or national overtones. They sympathized with the plight elsewhere of co-religionists but rejected political movements that believed Jews should have their own state. Their relationships to their backgrounds inevitably affected, or were perceived as affecting, the approach of *The New York Times* to Jewish issues. In some cases, this may have been true; in others it demonstrably was not.

While Ochs, as seen through items in the archives, participated in Jewish activities and retained a warm feeling for "Jewishness," and, in fact, used expressions typical of European-Jewish life, AHS, a Columbia University–educated intellectual of those early-twentieth-century years when "logic" and "objectivity" and "reason" were believed to be the answer to emotionalism, faith, and visceral reaction, wrote movingly about the conflict within himself.

"I am truly grateful that I was born a Jew because of the rich inheritance that I have received thereby," he wrote in longhand to Ochs, about 1920. "I feel that I have profited from the prejudice which I know exists around me, but which fortunately has not often touched me. I think it has tended to make me more aggressive—more alert—more broadminded and tolerant. And so I deem it a privilege to 'stand up and be counted' as a Jew. I have a Jewish feeling—a Jewish religion—must I take what for me is a step backwards in order to show it?"

Whatever their thoughts about Palestine and Israel, *The Times* publishers worried, like many other Jews, about anti-Semitism and conceptions of others about Jews in the United States. In 1913, Ochs, a member of the Anti-Defamation League's original executive board, issued his rules on the use of the word "Jew," as they appear on the following page.

Over a period of years, mostly in the 1920s, Ochs developed a friendship and a correspondence with Samuel Untermyer, a prominent New York lawyer and reformer. They agreed on New York City politics but were at odds with each other over Jewish matters. In a let-

## Adolph S. Ochs' 'RULES FOR GUIDANCE'

1. The words "Jew" and "Jewish" can never be objectionable when applied to the whole body of Israel or to whole classes within the body, as, for instance, "Jewish wives," "Jewish children," "Jewish young men," and the like.

2. There can be no objection to the use of the words "Jew" or "Jewish" when contrast is being made with other religions. "Jews observe Passover, and Christians Easter"; "Jews are less susceptible to tuberculosis than other races"; these are perfectly fair and proper subjects of public comment.

However:

3. The application of the word "Jew" or "Jewish" to any individual is. to be avoided unless from the context it is necessary to call attention to his religion; in other words, unless the facts have some relation to his being a Jew or to his Jewishness. This rule should apply equally whether the word is used in a scandalous or discreditable connection or when it is used in connection with some praiseworthy or honorable act or achievement. Thus if a Jew is convicted of a crime he should not be called a "Jewish criminal," and, on the other hand, if a Jew makes a great medical or other scientific discovery, he should not be called a great "Jewish physician" or an eminent "Jewish scientist." In neither case had the man's Jewishness any connection with his conduct or with the disgrace or honor which that conduct entailed. The same rule applies in the case of other religions; if a Roman Catholic or a Protestant is convicted of a crime, he is not alluded to as a "Catholic criminal" or a "Protestant criminal." In view of the mediaeval opprobrium still surviving in connection with the term "Jew," it is the more just and important, therefore, to avoid a similar unfairness in speaking of Jews.

4. The word "Jew" is a noun, and should never be used as an adjective or verb. To speak of "Jew boys," "Jew girls" or "Jew stores" is both objectionable and vulgar.

The word "Jew" is a noun; "Jewish" is the adjective. The use of the word "Jew" as a verb—"to Jew down"—is a slang survival of the mediaeval term of opprobrium alluded to above and should be avoided altogether.

5. The word "Hebrew" should not be used instead of "Jew." As a noun it connotes rather the Jewish people of the distant past, as the ancient "Hebrews." It is used also as an adjective—"the Hebrew language," "Hebrew literature," etc.—but as such it has a historical rather than a religious connotation; one cannot say "the Hebrew religion," but "the Jewish religion."

5

ter to Ochs in 1922, Untermyer wrote, "A number of our friends in the Palestine movement, apparently inspired by the men who are conducting the publicity end of the pending campaign, have been complaining for some time that they can get no news whatever into the 'Times,' which they foolishly attribute to your own position on Zionism and which I told them was simply absurd."

While absolving Ochs of personally excluding such news from *The Times,* Untermyer added that the newspaper, which "greatly to its credit gives so much attention to Jewish affairs that have news value, has given little or no space to this movement." The lawyer was not complaining, he said, but thought Ochs might be interested in knowing about it.

In 1932, as Hitler was coming to power in Germany, Ochs declined an invitation to a testimonial dinner for Untermyer, apparently in honor of his work for persecuted Jews. "I am not in agreement with Mr. Untermyer in the wisdom of an international organization of Jews to combat the uncivilized and inhuman German regime, for I fear a strictly Jewish crusade may do more harm than good. I believe the condemnation of Germany should be universal, embracing all creeds and races, who believe in 'liberty, equality and fraternity.' "

He would rather pay tribute to the lawyer when he finished his reform tasks, "to reorganize the financial affairs of the City of New York in order to save the city from bankruptcy, and chastening Tammany for its own good from the inside of its organization." Then, he said, would be the fitting moment for a tribute.

Those were years when some Jews, particularly "uptown Jews" of high social and financial standing and more culturally assimilated than the more strident immigrants downtown, were sensitive about being too obtrusive in public politics. Ochs, in a 1928 letter to Untermyer, betrayed some of this sentiment. "My dear Sam," he wrote, "I am a great admirer of Herbert Lehman, but would very much dislike to see him take the race for governor this year. Think it would be unwise to have a Catholic and a Jew on the same ticket. Believe it would be a political mistake, and a liability to [New York governor Alfred E.] Smith throughout the country, if not in New York State. Herbert Lehman would make an ideal governor. . . . I hope some time he may be a candidate when the chances would be in his favor."

In 1931, *The Times* received widespread criticism in the Jewish press for its failure to report in detail on an anti-Jewish outbreak in Berlin, an incident widely reported in the British press and elsewhere as a serious manifestation of Nazism. The reporter in question responded to a query from AHS by explaining his lapse from his own point of view. AHS, in a polite reply, said he was writing so that "you may see how carefully we are watched." In a rather surprising reference to the source of the complaint, he added, "The American Jewish Committee is a group to which, feeling as I do, I could never belong even if I were not associated with a newspaper. I do not feel the ties which cause the group of high-minded men who compose its executive committee to watch the interests of the Jew as they do. Perhaps I was too fortunately born. That, however, in no sense detracts from their weight. . . . Also, do not gather from this that I am suggesting any disproportionate 'Jewish news.' I am not."

Two years later, a radio broadcast about Hitler by *The Times* Berlin Bureau chief, Frederick T. Birchall (formerly acting managing editor), drew caustic criticism of himself and his newspaper from Jewish circles. *The Day*, a Yiddish New York daily, attacked the Ochs *Times* for being unvocal in support of Jewish causes generally and now, in particular, of whitewashing Hitler. AHS was upset by the broadcast and little assuaged by Birchall's explanation that he had wanted to get his broadcast piece past the German censor and also to butter up Hitler in hopes of getting an interview. "The fact is that this movement has got away from Hitler. Its mouthpiece is now Göring, not the new Chancellor and Hitler dare not drop him. He even has to play along with him as far as he can."

AHS did not appreciate this clouded-crystal-ball explanation. It was unwise to broadcast, he said, particularly without the knowledge of the publisher. He wrote, "By reason of the censorship, the talk had to be more temperate than the splendid articles you have been sending us. Your remarks, therefore, were susceptible of the interpretation that you were speaking in defense of what has been taking place in Germany."

In September 1941, AHS received a letter, shown on the next page, from former president Herbert Hoover, long a leading figure in American relief efforts in Eastern Europe and Russia. A news story based on the Polish Jewish banker's account appeared, in harrowing detail (but not on page 1) a few days later. It was one of the earliest stories to indicate the extent of the extermination undertaken by the German government.

Anti-Semitism was an issue on which AHS could take a stand—it clearly worried him. Early in 1944, Frank S. Adams, who had been assigned to survey anti-Semitism in New York City, reported to the publisher that it was on the increase. It was an extraordinary and thorough study that, apparently, was sent directly to Sulzberger and did not appear in the paper.

In 1947, when the partition of Palestine was voted by the United Nations, *The Times* was sufficiently anti-Zionist to arouse the resentment of many New Yorkers and there was word of a "Jewish boycott" of the paper by readers and advertisers. Clifton Daniel, then bureau chief in Jerusalem, wrote to Sulzberger that "two Palestine newspapers have published reports that Homer Bigart's pro-Zionist and anti-British dispatches have caused a considerable increase in the

The Waldorf-Astoria Towers
New York City
September 11, 1941

My dear Mr. Sulzberger:

        I am sending herewith a short
article prepared by Dr. Henry Szoszkies
as to the situation of the Jewish people
in Poland. The Doctor was the general
manager of the Central Cooperative Bank
in Poland until the outbreak of the war,
and he is well known in European circles
as a Jewish writer. He was an executive
member of the Jewish Community in Warsaw
during the siege of September, 1939, and
a few months after the occupation. He
has kept in intimate touch with his people
since he got out of Poland.

        I feel the article ought to be
published for the information it contains
as to the treatment which these people are
receiving, and the desperate plight in
which they are now living. I am sending
it to you, thinking perhaps you might publish it without attaching it in any way to
the propaganda that I carry on once in
awhile in connection with food for the
people in the small democracies. And I
would prefer the last paragraph be omitted.

        With kind regards,

           Sincerely yours,

Mr. Arthur Hays Sulzberger   *Herbert Hoover*
The New York Times
229 West 43rd Street
New York City

circulation of the Herald Tribune [where Bigart worked before join-ing *The Times*], partly at the expense of The Times and mostly among Jewish readers."

Daniel asked for circulation figures and Sulzberger's statistics showed that the *Trib* had actually fared much worse than *The Times* during the slump period. He attributed the heavy loss for both pa-pers, on Saturday circulation, to "the five-day week and the suspen-sion of war work. . . . This ought to answer your Zionist critics. Incidentally, the Zionists are so pleased with our present editorial po-sition that it gives me grave doubts we are right."

In 1959, AHS was still worrying about having a "Jewish specialist." "Why is Spiegel in Jerusalem? I protested a long time ago about hav-ing a so-called Jewish specialist and now he's not only going to be a

Jewish specialist but a specialist in Jewish politics. I think it's wrong and I also don't know why I wasn't asked in view of the fact that I had expressed interest in this particular man. I have no complaint with him; it's the assignments he gets."

Actually, Irving Spiegel—"Pat" to his countless friends—was made a Jewish "specialist" by definition when he was assigned to a new "Jewish beat," whose function in part was to cover the anti-Zionist organization of prominent and influential Jews to which AHS himself had become attached. Spiegel, one of the most colorful characters in the newsroom, had been an ace police reporter and he took to his new assignment with the same rough-and-ready reportorial style that he had applied to commissioners and politicians. Spiegel covered all rabbis, all Jewish news, and his neighbors on the third floor could hear him shouting at rabbis to send the text of their sermons over right away, never mind that the Sabbath is an hour away, or it would never make the edition. He held on to his assignment for a quarter of a century, recognized by Jewish groups the nation over, from the most aristocratic and the most Reform to the most working-class and the most Orthodox. It was never on the books as a "Jewish beat," however, and when he retired, so did the assignment and the specialty.

When I first went to work at *The Times* in 1946, someone gave me a copy of a little red (actually brownish-red) book labeled "Style Book of The New York Times—1943." Even then, as a mere copyboy, I could feel that a sort of Holy Writ was being presented to me, that it was all right to put things any which way in other documents but in the pages of *The New York Times* there was either a Right Way or, unthinkable, a Correction.

In the pages of this modest, 101-page densely packed volume, a deskman's bible, lay the standards of *The New York Times* that would look at a reader over the breakfast table. It did not extend to social policy, but laid down rules for quotation marks, hyphenation, spelling, headline sizes, and also headings and styles for book reviews, business news, and other sections.

The new element, announced on the first page, was a "New General Rule of Names, Titles." This would rectify, it said, a lack of uniformity among *Times* desks:

> Except in the cases of pre-eminent public figures, the full
> name of the official or other person must be given the first

time the name is mentioned. This applies chiefly to officials—Senators, Representatives, heads of boards and bureaus, Governors, Mayors and the like. For example, Secretary of the Interior Harold L. Ickes, Secretary of Agriculture Claude R. Wickard, Senator Burton K. Wheeler, Mayor Fiorello H. La Guardia, Police Commissioner Lewis J. Valentine.

Robert E. Garst, who edited the style book, obviously realized that this detailed pecking order might appear capricious and more than what was really called for to inform the average *Times* reader. He added:

One reason for more meticulous recording of full names is that many of the figures in the current news will pass from the pages of newspapers in a few years, but THE NEW YORK TIMES [that's the type with which the paper referred to itself

> **Foreign Equivalents of Mr. and Mrs.**
> (184) When names of citizens of foreign countries are mentioned, the following rules should be observed with regard to the insertion of titles corresponding to our own Mr. and Mrs., etc.:
>
> Mr. Mrs. and Miss are used for citizens of Great Britain.
> Mr., Mrs. and Miss for citizens of the following countries:
>
> | | | | |
> |---|---|---|---|
> | Bulgaria | Lithuania | Norway | Turkey |
> | China | Greece | Albania | Russia |
> | Egypt | Hungary | Denmark | Japan |
> | Estonia | Latvia | Siam (Thailand) | Switzerland |
> | Finland | Netherlands | Sweden | |
>
> M., Mme. and Mlle. are used for the following:
>
> | | | | |
> |---|---|---|---|
> | Rumania | France | Yugoslavia | Haiti |
> | Belgium | Czechoslovakia | Poland | |
>
> Signor, Signora and Signorina are used for citizens of Italy.
> Herr, Frau and Fraeulein are used in Germany and Austria.
> Senhor, Senhora, Senhorita are used in Brazil and Portugal.
>
> Señor, Señora and Señorita are used for citizens of the following countries:
>
> | | | | |
> |---|---|---|---|
> | Argentina | Panama | Bolivia | Dominican Republic |
> | Chile | Spain | Paraguay | Honduras |
> | Cuba | Mexico | Uruguay | Costa Rica |
> | Guatemala | Venezuela | El Salvador | Peru |
> | Ecuador | Nicaragua | Colombia | |
>
> **But** when a foreigner has taken up permanent residence here, United States usage should be followed.
> This rule applies to all departments of the paper, including news stories, feature matter, society material, Magazine, Book Review, financial matter, etc., but should not be construed too literally in every case. Where a person's nationality is doubtful or unimportant to the story, the American designation will suffice, but in cable stories, foreign feature matter and in society copy where lists of foreign guests are given, and in all other material where there is a definite indication of citizenship, the above rules should be scrupulously observed.
> The various desks should give special attention to this section, since the responsibility for initiating the proper title will rest mainly with those handling the copy—the principal duty of the proofroom being to check up on the proper usage in the matter of spelling, abbreviations, etc.

*Times* style on titles for foreign names in the news, as spelled out in the 1943 style book. Note that some countries are assigned English titles while others are in French.

in those days] remains as a permanent record which will be searched for its accounts of events long after the principals of those events have gone from memory. Another reason is that this method has long been a sound journalistic practice.

If one had the time for it, an editor on 43rd Street could easily have made a full-time career solely out of study of *Times* usage and what, if anything, should be done about it. The old 1943 book's prissiness about titles on first mention went out the window in 1972, when Siegal notified Foreign Desk editors: "The quickest way to scare off a reader is by printing a lead stuffed full of unfamiliar names. No name of a person or an organization should appear in the lead (except, of course, as a gimmick in a feature) unless it is a household word."

The newspaper has not ever been swept by fashion in language but has always waited, sometimes to the frustration of those to whom it is applied, for innovating expression to become established usage.

Of all the controversies on titles, few have generated as much debate, internally and externally, as the ones about "Mr." and "Ms." The former was traditionally limited to law-abiding American males older than their teens. Foreigners in the news were accorded special treatment.

In 1959, there was even a conference on the proper use in the paper of "Mr.," "Mrs.," and "Miss." The results can be seen on the following page.

The stricture was modified in 1967 when a memo went to the Foreign Desk to the effect that "Any man held, accused or even convicted (etc.) of a *political* crime retains the 'Mr.'—even though the political crime may have entailed killing people. Thus, Guevara, Debray, Philby, Theodorakis, etc., all are entitled to 'Mr.' "

Abe Rosenthal opted for a policy that, with the exception of obviously ludicrous cases, would give every male the honorific. "We have had contact with a considerable number of criminologists, sociologists, penologists, etc., etc., and almost universally they think that our present policy is outdated and essentially destructive," he wrote.

The current policy constituted a "quagmire," he said, and that "an attempt to draw up a list of non-Mr. offenses, when even judges refer to every convicted criminal as Mr., would get us even deeper into the quagmire." So, every adult male should receive a "Mr.," except in sports and in certain instances of major artistic figures, like Picasso.

*Style* ( *Foreign New Deal*

The results of a conference on the proper use of "Mr.", "Mrs." and "Miss" follow :

USE OF "MR." --

Our long-established custom is to use "Mr." before the surname of any reputable man.

For youths under 21 the nature of the story would be controlling and there is no reason why "Mr." should not be used in appropriate cases.

For persons convicted of crime or persons of generally unsavory reputations "Mr." is not used. But there are exceptions which should be referred to Desk Heads and by them to higher executives if necessary. For example, it was decided that "Tough Tony" Anastasia, the Brooklyn waterfront boss, should be called "Mr." since he has no criminal record himself. This decision was extended to James Hoffa on the same ground, despite his close connection with gangster elements. Another instance considered was that of Malcolm White, a manufacturer on trial at Newburgh for the murder of a union leader. We continue to use "Mr." White unless he is convicted, at which time we drop the "Mr."

It was agreed that "Mr." should not be used in sports page stories but if sports figures appear in general news stories, obits, etc., "Mr." should be used.

For persons of pre-eminence, especially in the arts, even during life but certainly after death, "Mr." is not used.

When the names of a reputable and a disreputable person appear in the same sentence or in close proximity, the copy should be edited to minimize the discrimination by using a pronoun or other identification for one man.

USE OF "MRS." AND "MISS" --

It was decided that "Mrs." and "Miss" could be used at will, since the designation shows marital status. In disreputable cases "the Smith girl" is also proper, but "the Smith woman" has an offensive sound and in most cases we should try to "write around" it.

### 

October 22, 1959

On November 20, 1973, a memo to the staff stated: "Starting with the issue of Monday, December 3, 1973, we are revising our style on the use of 'Mr.' We will use that honorific (or a title other than 'Mr.') in front of nearly every surname of an adult male on second and subsequent references, except in a handful of cases described below."

If "Mr." caused a crisis of conscience, the campaign for "Ms." was a very battle of honorifics. Some papers had always referred to people, after first mention, merely by their surname. That would not do at *The Times*. But with the growth of feminism during the 1960s, the neutral "Ms.," as neutral as "Mr.," began to spread in common usage.

I remember that this became a sticky business for the reporter caught between a desk that did not recognize new nomenclature and women who demanded it. When I was interviewing women, either on phone or in person, I would always save for last the question, "How do I refer to you, Mrs. or Miss?"

The woman's reply was, often as not, that she preferred "Ms." Sorry, can't use that, I replied. If she insisted, I would have to say that I could not use her name directly in any reference after the first mention and would resort to "she said." The interviewee usually relented, but I did not feel happy about it.

Yet, as a *Times* executive wrote to Gloria Steinem, he himself would, if they were less acquainted, address a letter to her with "Ms.," because he knew she preferred this. Why, then, he asked rhetorically, do we not do this in the paper itself?

"We don't want to do that because it really is not part of the language yet and because an awful lot of people would object," he answered his own query. He wrote that by allowing "Ms." in its pages, *The Times* would be pressured by others to be addressed by whatever honorific they chose: Comrade, Brother, Citizen. Or the paper could

---

### Mr. Ochs, Courtly but Conservative

Ochs did not set a policy about women reporters, but he reflected the prevailing male attitudes of his day. Early in 1897, he wrote to a Miss Elizabeth Fry, of Louisville, Kentucky:

My Dear Miss Fry:

Your very clever letter is at hand. I assure you that if I had any intention of sending a woman out on a mission to accomplish an almost impossible journalistic feat, my first thought would turn to you, but The New York Times is run along very conservative lines. It does not belong to the school of new journalism and consequently its representatives are not required to do deeds of daring or to seek sensations. If at any time I should find need in our editorial department of a capable lady, I will certainly remember you.

do away with honorifics altogether, a decision that would create a hodgepodge and would be a dereliction of responsibility.

By 1974, a division of opinion had memos flying back and forth, from daily to Sunday Department to publisher. Some argued that the time had come for "Ms." One missive from the eighth floor (Sunday) pointed out that the paper had long allowed people to be referred to as they wished; it cited female staffers who used "Miss" with their maiden names instead of "Mrs." with their married names. The memo urged free choice that included "Ms."

From the third floor, Abe Rosenthal sent a reply indicating that he was reluctant to plunge into "Ms." "The reasons are stylistic, journalistic and social," he wrote and went on to explain that "stylistically, The Times should use the best-accepted usage and not be in a position of coining usage or giving undue acceptability to usages of the moment by formalizing them in its style. If we did the latter, we would

---

### Gender Genre

Never mind Ms., but the use of "woman" or "women" as adjective had been discouraged in 1980 by "Winners & Sinners" (the sheet occasionally issued to staff by an editor; it singled out passages that had appeared in print and were either very bad in usage or were very laudable) "to promote equal treatment for men and women in the news."

However, months later, Allan M. Siegal told all desks, "The 'rule' is being followed mindlessly, and we often look silly. The silliest thing that happens is that 'woman' often gets changed automatically to 'female' in copy, as if we were writing about puppies."

Al Siegal put it clearly: "Here is the real rule: If a noun, unadorned, is neither male nor female, we don't modify it to show we are talking about women."

No more "female academics," which implied that academics were normally male. Preferred usage, when required, would be "women on campuses" or "faculty women" or "academic women." Test yourself, Siegal advised. Before using "female" as a modifier, mentally substitute "male." If "male" fits awkwardly or seems superfluous, so will "female."

lose our claim of being the guide to the best-accepted usage, a claim which we cherish and which is regarded highly by many readers, including teachers and other professionals."

Max Frankel, then head of the Sunday Department, argued that "Ms." was ripe for acceptance by *The Times*: "What makes this different from the discussion of any other honorific is that 'Miss' and 'Mrs.'—as perceived by a fair number of women—are not simply neutral titles that some no longer like. They define women entirely in terms of marital status, when that standard is not applied to men. . . . I fail to see why accepting that corrective and fashion is any more difficult for us than the manner in which we gradually shifted from 'Negro' to 'black,' allowing the two terms to coexist where desired."

A few weeks later that December, Punch Sulzberger weighed in with: "At the end of the year, like Solomon, I cast my vote 'NO' for Ms."

The Ms. question would not go away. When Geraldine Ferraro ran for vice president in 1984, *The Times* referred to Mrs. Ferraro, although her husband's name was Zaccaro and she used her own, her maiden name, in her own line of work. About a year later, Abe Rosenthal suggested to Punch Sulzberger that it might be time to see if they still felt as strongly about not permitting "Ms." as they had.

The turnabout erupted suddenly, on June 19, 1986, when Rosenthal posted a staff announcement announcing an Editors' Note for the next morning's paper, reproduced on the page opposite.

"Mr." and "Mrs." raised a ruckus, but "I" did not. Journalists did not use "I" in their writing, even if the editorial board went heavy on "we." "I" removed the illusion of impartiality, even of disembodied opinion, in columns that could otherwise be intensely personal, and those columns were by the critics and reviewers. We struggled to ferret grace out of sentences that spoke of visceral reactions to performance but had to be couched in clumsy passages that made individual passion appear shared by the world, or in cutesy makeshifts—"This corner felt that . . ."

One of the first (probably the first) to break the "I" level was John Canaday, who came out of the museum world, was not a newspaperman, but was a successful author of mystery novels. Canaday brought to art coverage an easy, bright style that, sprinkled with "I"s, left no doubt that the opinions expressed were his own. He used "I" sparingly, but that use opened the floodgates.

from A. M. ROSENTHAL

MEMORANDUM for:    THE STAFF

The following will appear in the paper tomorrow:

EDITORS' NOTE

Beginning today, The New York Times will use "Ms." as an honorific in its news columns.

Until now, "Ms." had not been used because of the belief that it had not passed sufficiently into the language to be accepted as common usage.

The Times believes now that "Ms." has become a part of the language, and is changing its policy.

The Times will continue to use "Miss," or "Mrs." when it knows the marital status of a woman in the news unless she prefers "Ms."

"Ms." will also be used when a woman's marital status is not known, or when a married woman wishes to use her maiden name professionally or in private life.

A. M. R.

June 19, 1986

---

AHS stepped on touchy ground just after Christmas 1958, when he queried the third floor about the proper ID of Jesus Christ. "I have no desire to start a religious war but . . ." he wrote, saying that Jesus of Nazareth became known as Jesus Christ, "meaning Jesus the Lord. When we call him 'Christ,' we are therefore calling him Lord. Why shouldn't our style be Jesus? I don't mean to rewrite the carols or to change quotes but I've noticed frequently during this season we ourselves said 'Christ' when we could have said 'Jesus.'"

A week later, what the editors said had already been general *Times* practice became official *Times* policy.

# 24 THE MORALS SQUAD

NOT LONG after I had joined the Ship News Department as a news assistant in the late 1940s, I was invited, with all the others in Ship News, to the Christmas party of the United States Lines at one of the clubs downtown. It was a lively, friendly affair where "the Ship News Fraternity" from all the newspapers and agencies sat around the festive board and drank, and ate and drank. As we left the lunch table to return to work, an official, perhaps a vice president of the company, shook hands with each of us. When my turn came, I felt not only a warm handshake but also the crisp rub of paper. When I looked at it out by the elevator, in an envelope was a $25 savings bond, purchased for $18.75.

The acceptance of gifts was at that time strictly forbidden by *The Times*, but the prohibition seemed honored in the breach during the holiday season by the specialized departments covering news—our department, business news, radio-television, real estate, movies, society, and others—that at other times and circumstances were known to have thrown favor-seekers bearing gifts out of the office with warnings not to come back. Yet before Christmas, the gifts—"the loot," one reporter called it—piled up in the third-floor reception room. The job of carrying it back to our cubicle often fell to me, the youngest in the department. I usually felt like an uncomfortable ink-stained Santa Claus bearing a pile of tinsel-bound packages through the newsroom, passing by general staff reporters whose virtue was intact, perhaps by conscience, but certainly for the lack of regular corporate contacts who routinely sent gifts to everyone they did business with.

"How do you keep honest, taking all that?" one reporter snapped at me while I was en route.

"Easy, we throw the cards away without looking at them," I replied.

314

A flip retort, and not an entirely honest one. Of course we looked as we took. But for all that there was no less integrity among those donees than there was among the nongifted staff. It was understood and often demonstrated that reporters could, the next day after lugging home their bottles of liquor or their embossed diaries or their electric blankets, go for the jugular of the corporate donor should the need arise. Reporters tend to be an ungrateful lot, professionally, and in defense of their honor relish demonstrating that they can't be bought even for a case of Scotch.

The problem, if any, in the departments was not gifts. It was one faced by anyone covering one area, gift-giving or not, whether in Washington or in a police shack. The sources that a reporter developed often led to close personal acquaintance, even friendship, and gave the source easier access to the paper (any paper) than others had.

Still, the idea of presents made many, including myself, moderately uncomfortable. The bond made me feel seedier, somehow, than if I had received even a more expensive book or bottle, or something else. A bond was too much like cash and it felt wrong. But I did not return it because I did not feel secure enough on the job to manifest such piety. The tide of gifts continued.

In 1953, AHS sent a note to the editor of Women's News. He said that the scandal of favor-taking by the presidential aide Sherman Adams "makes me wonder if any gifts are received by people who work on The New York Times from people who do business with The Times."

The editor replied that she had looked into it and was happy to report that the department was in the clear. But, she added, "Of course at Christmas time various gifts do arrive, but most of them are of a trifling nature, and this practice has been so firmly established for so long that I would not know how to eradicate it."

Jack Gould, the television critic, did know how to eradicate it. In the fall of 1959, when the press was having a field day over the quiz-show scandals, pontificating on the low moral estate of broadcasting, Gould wrote a column. He inveighed against the hypocrisy of print media, whose people accepted Christmas gifts and happily went on junkets paid for by the organizations they were supposed to be covering. It was a hard-hitting column that caused a stir at *The Times* and other papers and, naturally, in broadcasters' public relations offices in charge of junkets and gifts. Gould told me that the piece had been submitted for approval to Orvil Dryfoos, in the absence of AHS. Dryfoos let it go but commented that Gould was opening a can of worms because *The Times* was also a business organization that gave gifts to others *it* did business with (in Ship News, I accompanied another reporter every season to bring a case or two of liquor for the customs officers, who paved the way for easy entry for our VIPs, and for the Coast Guard, which delivered bundles of *The Times* to incoming liners).

Upon his return from Europe, AHS sent Gould a mildly reproving note:

### MR. GOULD

Dear Jack:

I was in Europe during the television unmasking and only returned on Tuesday, which accounts for the fact that I'm just catching up with your piece in that day's paper.

Frankly, I don't think you were fair to us. As you know, we have a totally different point of view about junkets from most newspapers, and it seemed to me that your piece could very well have excepted us specifically, even though you did say that not everybody fell for the junket idea.

On Christmas gifts, which I confess I don't like, it seems to me that there's a vast difference between that and the rigging of a show. It's as though our first page were made to be deceptive, whereas of course you know we try to print the news as honestly as we know how. A rule against accepting Christmas gifts would be impossible to enforce because, as you pointed out, they would just be sent to the home. I get some gifts myself. The man who buys our waste paper, for instance, sends me four or six initialled handkerchiefs every Christmas. As you know, that doesn't influence our contract for the sale of waste paper and to refuse the gift would, it seems to me, be more awkward than to accept it.

If you have any ideas about that, I'd be happy if you'd come up to see me some day and tell me about it. But as I said, I don't feel that we were quite fairly treated in what you wrote on Tuesday.

                                        A. H. S.

October 29, 1959
mh

In response, Gould wrote, "The worst thing, it seemed to me, was to adopt a sanctimonious position and then have the roof fall in." He explained that he was not sure that there was not "one black sheep" at *The Times* who did not comply with the anti-junket policy, one that even required sports reporters accompanying teams to pay their own carfare—at the paper's expense—when traveling with them. He cited several recent instances of misbehaving employees and added that he had been informed by "the business world that for a Times man you simply set up a junket to coincide with his vacation."

He admitted that he, too, did not know a solution for the Christmas-gift syndrome because presents could be sent to the home if not to the office. If it involved only small, inconsequential remembrances, that would be acceptable, but taking *The Times* as a whole, "we are actually talking about thousands and thousands of dollars." As for himself, he found that gifts could be minimized by telling the prospective givers that it was a problem for him, because, as a critic, his motives might be misconstrued. He had substantially cut down on gifts this year, would have the problem licked the next year, without involving *The Times* at all.

From that day on, Gould accepted not even the most trivial promotional tchotchke from a broadcaster. The gift ban became even more official than earlier. Annually, the season to be jolly was sobered by a reminder from above that *Times* people do not accept gifts, that letters had been posted to discourage prospective donors, that facilities were available for sending gifts back. Gifts for the rest of us were virtually eliminated and, to tell the truth, I don't believe we felt any the worse off, except that now we would have to buy liquor to give away as presents ourselves instead of drawing from Christmas stock.

There were other avenues of temptation that, like gift-giving, had become institutionalized. Lunches were small-fry problems; years ago impecunious newsmen did not pick up the tab when they dined with subjects. Nor did *The Times* offer to pay for such lunches for those below executive level. Perhaps that would smack of checkbook journalism. Once, on assignment to interview a shipping mogul at the swank Plaza Hotel, Bob Burns, ship news reporter from the *Herald Tribune,* and I enjoyed our lunch, asked our questions, and warily eyed the check when we were through. It just lay there until the shipping baron asked if it would indicate an attempt to buy coverage if he paid for the lunch. Since neither of us had more than subway fare in our pockets, we agreed it was the best solution to avoid one-upmanship by *The Times* or the *Trib.*

When I did the Going Out Guide column, *The Times* always paid for my evenings out and my days' sightseeing. I did not disclose who I was and what I was about until after I had paid. Sometimes the proprietor attempted to hand me the money I had just spent. Rather than preach, I handed it back to him, explained that I could take it but that I then could not write about his establishment and, in any event, I would be reimbursed by *The Times*. I never had any problem retaining my virtue.

The question of freebies, free tickets to the press, has always been a bedeviling one. Here, again, the probity of *Times* policy conflicted with the virtual but not virtuous reality of the relationship of the paper and the events it reported on.

"I have been informed that it is the policy of your newspaper not to accept 'free passes' to theaters or entertainments," the editor of the *Muncie* (Indiana) *Star* and *News* wrote to Adolph Ochs in 1901. "When the Morning Star was started, at my request, the same policy was adopted but now there is a disposition on the part of some of the parties interested to accept season tickets to the theater. Would you please be kind enough to briefly state your reasons why a newspaper should not accept 'free passes'?"

Ochs's answer, in a letter written October 26, 1901, was Solomonically shrewd. Why, he asked, are free tickets offered? If they are given in exchange for free advertising, who gets the best of the bargain? If an obligation is created, its value and influence must be taken into consideration. At *The New York Times,* he continued, it is found to be more advantageous to demand pay for advertising and for *The Times* to pay for what is needed for itself. Perhaps this did not apply in the writer's case, but it is best to view these matters as a business transaction: newspaper influence should never be a matter of barter.

During the hundred years of family ownership, *The Times* has constantly asserted and reasserted the principle that employees should buy tickets to the theater, to sports events, to any box-office diversion, unless their work is directly connected to the project. In more recent times, executives and editors have bought their tickets, even though they, like the cultural news editor, were legitimately involved in keeping up with what was showing. When I worked in Cultural News, however, I and others rarely hesitated to ask press agents for press tickets; the rationale, mostly valid, I believe, was that if we were to write about the cultural field it was better to know what was in it instead of interviewing others over the telephone when deadlines neared.

But, like so many things in life, the freebie situation expanded. The printer who made sure your page received its corrections in short order was certainly not out of line when he wanted a pair of tickets for his wedding anniversary. It was out of line when he wanted it for his cousin visiting from Des Moines, but no more so than when we asked for the same for other dear ones who did not work at the paper. The more sensitive among us never asked for tickets on weekends, when houses were more likely to be sold out, and never requested more than a pair for personal use while a show was in hit status, with no seats available. The house-seat situation was something else. A number of the highest-price tickets are set aside in theaters for last-minute purchase by important personages, press or not. The fact that they were bought mitigated the sense of obligation but often contrarily manifested a sense of press influence because house seats were not available to the general public, particularly for hot-ticket shows.

Like an ancient mine cut loose from its mooring, the subject of tickets surfaces continually and is just as continually under fire from management. *The Times,* with a staff much larger than any other newspaper or periodical, always is given a bulkier presence in articles or books that address the situation, and sooner or later, everyone in the business seems to have a go at it. Producers and others are quick, perhaps even eager, to disclose how many tickets go to the press, especially to *The Times.* This produces new strictures from on top and the problem disappears, for a while.

Punch Sulzberger was particularly nettled by the thorny ticket issue. In 1966, he told managing editor Clifton Daniel that he had been hearing complaints about the number of requests from *Times* people for free and paid-for tickets for opening nights.

Cultural news editor Joseph Herzberg told Daniel that the first-night free list "has obviously gotten out of hand . . . and puts us in the position of being under an obligation." The total list included five, among them the publisher, who bought their tickets, and seven, all in the Drama Department except the editor of the Sunday Arts and Leisure Section, who received free tickets. Another two dozen were executives and high-ranking editors who also bought tickets during the year.

Herzberg announced to his staff that only the critic would receive opening-night tickets to Broadway openings. The others in the Drama Department would go on a second-night list. An effort would be made to cut down on requests for house seats.

But four years later, Punch read a piece in *Playbill*, the Broadway theater program, about the influence of *The Times* when it came to securing free tickets. Who was getting freebies, he wanted to know, and who was paying for tickets through *The Times*? *Playbill* was out of date, he was assured by the third floor. Three free pairs were now taken by the daily critic, the Sunday critic, and the man in charge of Cultural News. Four pairs were given to people covering theater for the second-night performances.

In 1973, tickets for sports events were under scrutiny. For some events, as many as forty complimentary tickets were given to *The Times* Sports Department. This was traditional, but, said Abe Rosenthal, "under present conditions what was traditional is no longer acceptable." No free tickets at all were to be accepted or requested.

The flow of tickets had been clearly stanched. In 1964, Robert Garst, responding to a query about freebies from a journalism school, cited one unstanchable exception to the no-free-ticket rule: "There is one exception to this, the circus. For generations the Ringling management has distributed a limited number of passes to every newspaper in cities on its circuit. These are accepted without any thought of favoritism toward the circus, since only one or two reporters are involved in covering opening night and perhaps several subsequent feature stories."

P.S.—Those passes are tax tickets, so that the recipient still has to pay a dollar or so, proving that these days even the price of free has gone up.

Otherwise the ticket monster has been beheaded. Or has it? Fast forward to 1978. Punch Sulzberger:

*CULT NEWT*

from A. O. Sulzberger

MEMORANDUM for    MR. ROSENTHAL

Abe,

When I had my two tickets picked up for the opening of "Ballroom" which I had requested and <u>purchased</u>, I was offered two press tickets free of charge.

I thought we had very firmly established rules, whereby the two critics were the only ones who received free theater tickets.    Everyone else from the publisher on down must pay for any theater tickets requested.    This is true for sporting events and all kindred exhibitions.

Will you please put this rule into effect and make it clearly understood.

A. O. S.

December 12, 1978

# 25

# KEEPING THINGS CLEAR AND CORRECT

I N A newspaper, as with the Rockettes, style is everything. It is supposed to impose order while enhancing attractiveness. At *The Times,* the style book—that copy desk vade mecum, nemesis of loose-minded reporters—is a guide to shaping the appearance of the paper and to establishing a uniformity of usage. The writer, whether headline-creating editor or writing reporter, must work his or her genius within these bounds of *Times* practice—and also be aware of its constant amendment. Language is the vehicle with which a newspaper makes its living (no reflection on picture papers, where captions are almost everything, or even on television), and *The Times* has presided over its use with the reverence of a bishop interpreting Scripture.

Style involves technical definitions of grammar—the perennial and incurable confusion between "that" and "which"—and taste, the ineffable but recognizable aura that (certainly not which!) defines a civilized person's manners in words and tone. In this, the style book was supplemented by "Winners & Sinners," the one-sheet commentary on things that had recently appeared in the paper. First issued on September 19, 1951, from the "southeast corner of the newsroom" by Ted Bernstein, the *Times* guru of grammar and wizard of words, and continued by his successors, it complimented "bright passages" that had made their way into stories, cited inviting leads and rewarding headlines, "trophies of a head hunter." In these cases, it mentioned the names of the creators. It tactfully did not in the instances of bad leads, terrible heads, inept story structure, biased writing, and "itchy pencil," which meant monkeying by copy editors who inserted mistakes into otherwise accurate stories. When a new edition of "Winners & Sinners," written with humor and a wit that could be biting, hit the third floor, reporters and editors eagerly, but unostentatiously, scanned it to see whether they were represented for

better or for worse, whether it was safe to laugh at some other unfortunate's misdemeanor or to hold the laugh until one was sure one
was well out of it.


## CORRECTIONS

It was, doubtless, in the best interests of readers and of justice to stan-
dardize the placement of corrections at the bottom of the page 2
News Summary, but for reporters, it was a mixture of nuisance and
embarrassment. I, and other reporters, hated not only to make a mistake in print but to get caught out on it. It was true that the only one
who never made such errors was one who never reported. It was also
true, as they used to say, the doctors bury their mistakes, while ours
hang out for everyone to see. But still, a mistake indicated ineffi-
ciency, a laxity. In earlier times, when a complaint was made directly
to a reporter about an error, the writer could promise to make it
right in the next story on the same topic. If it could not hold, the reporter could write a very short correction and hope it would be
buried at the bottom of some riotous page under a tiny headline, "A
Correction."

As boss, Abe Rosenthal, who had gone through all of that as reporter, worried about corrections and the way they were played in the
paper. In 1970, he called attention to the fact that "corrections or denials or amplifications don't really catch up with the original because
they are not given proper display." Two years later, he told editors, "I
think that we are a little too stingy about printing corrections," that
they tend to get buried and are difficult to find. He suggested that a
new typographical format should be devised to handle corrections
and that they be anchored in the paper so that readers would know
where to find them.

On June 2, 1972, the establishment of a Correction niche for the
daily paper, beneath the News Summary and Index, became policy;
longer corrections would be noted in that space by a reference to
their position elsewhere in the paper. Publisher Punch Sulzberger
wondered, in a memo, "if we are not over-penalizing ourselves by always anchoring it in that spot," although he welcomed the idea in
general. However, the editor, giving assurance that he would not
stack up heaps of space-stealing corrections, prevailed.

Rosenthal was still intent on a corrections policy. He advised his
editors that, having established the Correction box, he was still both-

ered about the question of denials of stories that had been given a big play. He cited instances where, for instance, a story about a lowering of oil prices by Saudi Arabia ran on the front page, but a subsequent denial was given shorter shrift on an inside page. Without dictating formula solutions, he urged editors to accord denials the same importance that they gave the original story.

Corrections can be long or brief. One of the most prominent appeared at the top of page 1 on July 13, 1987. Under "A Correction," it was an article that corrected a misleading impression left by a pre-

vious day's article on congressional testimony by Lieutenant Colonel
Oliver North. Such front-page confessionals were not habit-forming;
the next one on that page, but beneath a two-column head on the
lower left, appeared seven years later, on October 15, 1994, to amend
an overstatement of funds released to deposed Haitian leaders.

At the other end of the correction scale were those dealing with
comparatively innocent errors that bore somewhat amusing overtones—such as the correction on November 10, 1974, that read:
"The recipe for purée of knob celery on Page 84 of today's Sunday
*Magazine* calls for one too many cups of milk. One cup of milk is sufficient."

My favorite correction was not one of mine—who would relish
one's own correction? It appeared on December 15, 1990, nearly two
months after the error was committed. It has an only–in–New York
flavor about it and also indicates that *The Times* is less than fully impervious to human presence.

## Corrections

•

An article in Weekend on Oct. 19
about the best restaurant dishes in
New York misstated an address and
a phone number for Trastevere,
recommended for linguine with clam
sauce. The restaurant is at 309 East
83d Street; its phone number is
(212) 734-6343.

The address and phone number
shown were for another restaurant,
then known as Trastevere 84, at 155
East 84th Street; (212) 744-0210.
(Trastevere 84 has since changed its
name to Tevere 84.) As a glatt kosher
restaurant, Tevere 84 does not serve
the clam dish. A letter from its owners, dated Nov. 14, reported the error
but went unnoticed because of the
restaurant writer's absence on medical leave.

One of the largest corrections was one, I am reluctant to say, that
I figured in. I was assistant on the Weekend Section when somehow
we got the huge map of booths in a Central Park fair confused, printing an earlier map instead of a later, revised one. This was not as hor-

rendous as a misprint on a bomber's chart, perhaps, but it meant that the souvlaki stand was placed where the African jewelry should be. Abe Rosenthal was appalled when he learned about the mix-up and ordered the true map to be printed as a correction the next morning, a Saturday, still in time for the event. "It'll be the biggest correction we ever printed," he commented in a tone that indicated he did not appreciate such new records.

For all of Rosenthal's scrupulous, even fanatic, concern for keeping the corrections policy of *The Times* fair, or fairer than any other in journalism, the problem would not go away. In 1980, Punch Sulzberger was complaining that even more effort was called for. He fired off a memo about a story in Science News that had made an error important to Bristol-Myers. He had suggested running the correction in the spot where the mistake had occurred, but instead it showed up in the Correction box.

He wrote: "I still think and I am not using any of the aforementioned as my reasoning that we are enormously reluctant to admit error. Surely, we will correct the age of a person or the date that a play will open, but when it comes to something of a more important nature, it is a very painful undertaking. And when we do it, we do not do it, generally speaking, very graciously. . . . I don't think we lose anything by admitting our errors. Rather, I think it strengthens our position."

On March 4, 1983, a much-talked-about Editors' Note made its debut, just below the Correction box. This departure did not address factual error but attempted to set right stories that had been printed but which were considered, after the fact, to have been "lapses of fairness, balance, or perspective." There had been inchoate editors' notes in the form of letters to the editor from the top editors themselves, as one in 1963 by Turner Catledge regretting that a page 1 eight-column headline had referred to Lee Harvey Oswald as Kennedy's "assassin," although he had never been tried for the crime. An even more vivid example occurred when Abe Rosenthal wrote a letter caustically critical of the obituary of a former Polish premier; the obit had been an obsequiously polite tribute to the man's life, and Rosenthal, who had covered Poland and been ejected from the country by the Polish government, was outraged that the man's iniquities had not been frankly and truthfully exposed in this wrap-up of his life. The Editors' Note, far more effectively than a letter to the editor, carried the weight of official policy.

The next month, Rosenthal was responding to criticism of the innovation he felt was breaking new journalistic ground. "It is true that no newspaper has ever criticized itself as we are," he wrote in a note to Punch Sulzberger. "I have often made similar criticism of overplaying a senseless derogatory story, but not in public. But what happened after we printed the Editors' Note was both bizarre and comical. Instead of taking it at its face value as an earnest effort to be candid, all kinds of conspiracy theories were spread about. . . . The truth is that we were trying to tell the truth about ourselves, and will continue to do so whenever we can."

## GOOD WRITING

*The Times* has, for more than half a century, been concerned about the quality of its writing, but often, like the weather, no one seemed able to do more than talk, or send memos, about it. The realization that action would make its words speak louder inspired managing editor Edwin L. James to send a memo to his second-in-command, Raymond McCaw, on May 18, 1933:

A new campaign has started. And it looks like a good one:
Namely, we want less complicated leads on stories and, generally speaking, more straight-away expression. . . . I know perfectly well that we are herein trying to correct the age-old tradition of writing leads on stories. Perhaps, a good formula would be that the head serve as a lead and that the body of the story should be straight-away from start to finish. And, it might be a good idea to limit the first sentence of the story to a maximum of 20 words.

No sooner had James issued his reform bill than he was wiring Arthur Krock in Washington to complain about a lengthy lead in a story from the bureau that went beyond the borders of brevity. Krock replied, "That sentence surprised this bureau also, and no one more than Catledge, the author of the story, who had written a short introductory sentence in accordance with requests. His sentence was clear, adequate and literate. The horror to which you call attention was the contribution of the copy desk. This happens very frequently but I have gotten too weary to complain."

Obviously, James's campaign languished. By 1946, the writing in the *Wall Street Journal,* particularly in its in-depth page 1 features gracefully written and thoughtfully deployed, aroused attention on 43rd Street. James told his desk heads, "Much is being said about the short sentences in the leads on the Wall Street Journal, which represents a studied effort on its part. I have been asked to suggest that you study them." He did not say who had asked him, but since the only person in a position to question the managing editor directly was the publisher, it was probably A. H. Sulzberger who had prompted him.

The next good-writing drive was organized in the early 1950s, at the instigation of Catledge, then a managing editor who still remembered his own twenty-year-old problems with short leads. The job of running the project, however, fell to assistant managing editor Robert E. Garst, he of style-book fame. Earlier efforts, he reported, had been unfruitful because directives went only to top editors and did not infiltrate the ranks. But in 1950, the staff was intimately linked to better writing when AHS instituted monthly writing prizes, $100 for major articles and photographs and $25 for eye-catching shorts, those pieces of fewer than a few hundred words that were bright and informative and, of course, pithy. The publisher was quoted as describing the point of the awards in this way: "As originally instituted by me, the prize was for the purpose of stimulating clear, concise, well-written English and good newspaper presentation. . . . I have the feeling that on some occasions it has been given for enterprise. . . . Certainly enterprise should be a very important factor; but it is a writing prize and I think that should be borne in mind."

This was not enough for Catledge, who became fixated on new writing styles that could meet the challenge of changing newspaper times just when television was starting to change reading habits. His good-writing effort went for new basic approaches. "There is something else we have to tell the reader these days," he told a meeting of newsmen. "We have to tell them what the news means. . . . We have to tell it to him quickly in a way that he understands . . . we have to tell it to him interestingly . . . we have to tell it to him accurately. Now this business of explaining the news is rapidly becoming one of the most important phases of journalism."

As for better writing, he didn't want to lay down rules, such as regulating the length of sentences. He was interested in "brevity, simplicity and clarity" and suggested that the reporter "approach your story as if you were writing a letter to an individual reader who knows nothing about the subject with which you are dealing." Catledge's policy of "depth in reporting" had by 1955 become "a matter of course to give in any news story the background required to understand it," Garst wrote in his report. Separate background and explanatory stories were used as needed.

Garst concluded: "The appearance of The Times these days is far different and much more attractive than it was a decade, or even three or four years ago. Among these improvements is the use of more and larger pictures, more carefully taken, selected and processed. Others are a moderate unfreezing of the make-up pattern and a greater use of multi-column headlines."

Catledge brought Abe Rosenthal back from Tokyo to serve as metropolitan editor in hopes that his own brilliance in covering foreign arenas would spur the sort of reporting that *The Times* now needed. He also gave recognition to a new style of feature writing best exemplified by Gay Talese, a young and gifted reporter whose use of language and attention to otherwise unobtrusive aspects of life—a piece about the hands seen all day by a subway change-maker, for example—made for stimulating reading. It was different in tone and expression but not different from the intense interest in the lives of people that had been exemplified by Meyer Berger.

All of these changes did not go unchallenged. Old-timers objected to the new emphasis on color in writing because, they felt, it impinged on the just-the-facts-ma'am reporting that had made *The Times* the reference work for the whole world of journalism. The resistance was illustrated amusingly by a veteran rewrite man who was assigned to write a D head, a very short item, on the appointment of a new president of a Brooklyn bank. He turned in his hundred-plus words but a subeditor called him back to the desk and said, "You know, we're trying to humanize people, get some color in, see what you can do." The rewrite man smiled, said not a word, went back to his desk, made a telephone call, put his original one page of copy into his typewriter, and wrote the color as the last line: "He also likes cats."

The 1943 style book, more or less a technical manual, makes no reference at all to obscenity. But thirty years later, the revised style book has an extended reference to "obscenity, vulgarity, profanity." It effectively laid down the guidelines that apply today. The "Obscenity" entry starts with the statement by Adolph Ochs when he assumed ownership of the paper that *The New York Times* would use "language that is parliamentary in good society."

This policy remains unchanged, the style book said, although "profanity in its milder forms can on some occasions be justified." Some "notable exceptions" are cited, those that help shed light on the news, such as words that appeared in the 1974 transcripts of the Watergate tapes.

And then there was the "sons of bitches" brouhaha that had *The Times* apologizing to President Kennedy for an accurate quotation. In a wrap-up of a dramatic story detailing how the president had gotten the steel companies to back off from a price increase in 1962, the account had the chief executive saying bitterly, "My father always told me that all business men were sons of bitches, but I never believed it till now!"

The appearance of such an expletive in the pages of *The Times* occasioned as much comment as the fact that the president had used it. The White House press secretary said that his boss had been misquoted. Publisher Orvil Dryfoos sent Kennedy a handwritten note apologizing for *The Times*'s use of a quote without his permission. The president, with his usual charm, accepted Dryfoos's "sorry about that" with a note of his own, shown on the next page.

The Associated Press Log, a weekly analysis of its own coverage, reported that others had not used the expression in their stories. *The Times*'s use of the quote was picked up by other papers and, the Log noted, "may become as familiar as anything else said in 1962."

The style book reflected the view of Abe Rosenthal, who held very strongly that vulgar language should find its way into print only under the most exceptional circumstances. "I think we should use hell, damn, etc. very sparingly and only when necessary," he wrote a financial columnist who quoted someone's saying, "How the hell . . ." Rosenthal went on to say, "They should not be used casually or simply because the person being interviewed uses them. If we do, we will fill the paper with them and change its tone."

In a letter to an editor of another paper, he wrote, "We have been known to use a number of hell's and damn's and even a couple of bitch's. But we use even those sparingly and only when they are important to the context of the story or of the quote." He said that there were those in the office who favored printing an obscenity if somebody in the story used it because it gave a fuller understanding of character and situation. There was, he conceded, some validity to that argument.

"But a newspaper has a certain taste and tone, set by its editors and by its readers," he wrote, saying that it was not an ethical issue but one

THE WHITE HOUSE
WASHINGTON

*Original letter*
*for OCD Scrapbook*

May 4, 1962

Dear Orvil:

I very much appreciated your letter of April 25th concerning the quote in the New York TIMES. As you may
know, the quote from the paper has been used constantly by the extreme right-wing press.

It was unfortunate that an Assistant Managing Editor
of the TIMES should have sent a wire to Mr. William
Loeb contradicting the denial made by my Press Secretary, Mr. Salinger, as we had, on a number of occasions, told representatives of the New York TIMES
that the quote was inaccurate.

I realize, however, that these things can happen in
the best run newspapers, as well as governments.

With very best wishes,

*Sincerely,*

*Jack Kennedy*

Mr. Orvil Dryfoos
Publisher
New York TIMES
New York, New York

*Copies sent to lunch Group. AHS
AHB, HFB, AOS, D.Schwarz, W.Ogdon, C.C.Daniel, C.Merz*

of taste. The fact that someone said it did not validate its use automatically because reporters are not stenographers and they are selective in choosing quotes. "But more importantly, to my mind, is the fact
that obscenities have become so common these days that if we began
using them we would have them sprinkled throughout the paper and
it would give a different feel and tone to the paper. Most newspapers
in this country do not use 'Mr.' but we do. A matter of taste."

Punch Sulzberger was in full agreement. In 1974, he telephoned
the night shift to delete the last two words of a Washington story that
had a Nixon administration official saying someone had done a

"crappy job." "Won't you pass the word, once again, that just because the people in the Nixon Administration have filthy mouths and just because they were recorded on tape, it is not a license for our reporters to use those words. Indeed, it is not necessary to quote them when the President of the United States says something dirty. If it is an important part of the story, I can understand our having to use it," he wrote, saying that its use in this instance was inexcusable.

Punch was as close a reader of *The Times* as any outsider, and he was no more reluctant to voice an opinion than any outsider was. It was as a reader that he proved to be a vigilant overseer of *Times* style. In 1970, he told the third floor: "That was an excellent piece by Eileen [Shanahan, a Washington Bureau reporter] this morning, but she had an unprecedented unprecedent—two to be exact. Professor Catledge had a great rule about that word, which was that practically nothing is unprecedented. I agree with him." Ten years later, he was remarking on a Sunday book review, enclosing a marked passage that baffled him: "Every once in awhile I get absolutely fascinated at the incredible gobbledegook that finds its way into the pages of The New York Times. . . . I can only assume that the editor was awed by the selection of her words and felt stupid if he didn't know what on earth she was talking about."

# 26

# CHANGING
# FACES

FOR A newspaper that has always been jealously esteemed by its readers for its resistance to trendiness, *The Times* has never ceased modifying itself, sometimes so gradually and so minutely that no one besides the comma-chasers has ever noticed, sometimes in a manner considered so revolutionary as to provoke letters to the editor from devoted readers. After a while, those changes themselves have become enshrined as part of the old *Times* and zealously guarded by a newer generation of preservationists.

In 1924, Julius Ochs Adler reported to Ochs about one respected but unavailing reader's reaction to change: "In conversation with Senator Nathan Straus, he expressed a feeling on his part as well as a number of his friends and associates of marked departure in policy of The New York Times, with specific reference to the vast amount of feature stuff that is running through its news columns. He pointed to such items as the Amundsen expedition, the Byrd expedition, Oratorical contest, Current Events contest, etc." The senator felt that *The Times* was "getting away from the sound policy on which it has been built over many years of hard struggle, of a complete NEWSpaper, with emphasis on the 'news.' "

For readers and *Times* management the perennial question has been: How much of a good thing can you stand? This had to do with the size of the paper, which generally ranged from middleweight to obese: in World War II, spy trainees were taught how to disable an opponent by belting him with a copy of the Sunday *Times*. In 1924, Arthur Hays Sulzberger, then learning the business, sent a handwritten note to publisher Adolph Ochs. "There has been quite some discussion recently relating to reducing the size of the Times in order to meet the criticism that the paper is too large," he wrote.

The intelligent critic, he continued, can also "complain with justice" about the length of our news stories. "Here again however he

must be discerning. So much of the value of the Times lies in the fact
that its reports are the most complete that we cannot lightly curtail
them. To do anything more than to read copy and edit more carefully, which can of course always be done to advantage, would require
a complete reorganization of our reportorial staff and the basis of
their pay which I would not advocate, even though or because we
stand alone in our present method."

By 1949, costs had mounted so alarmingly that AHS suggested
that eight columns be cut from the news space. In 1955, managing
editor Turner Catledge was explaining to Orvil Dryfoos why the News
Department had consumed more than its space quota allowed.

"Remember, we had eighteen columns on Einstein's death one
day; we had the Bandung Conference, at which we had three men
and gave it a better play than any American newspaper—and possibly
any paper in the world; we also had quite a number of vaccine stories, most of them with large pictures. All of these items were not in
the ordinary run of the news. It was hardly possible for us to cut back
the regular news content of the paper to bring our consumption
back to the quota, unless we were going to strip it to the bone."

The archival guidebook, "Facts About *The New York Times*," which exists only in a loose-leaf binder and is a compilation of photocopies
of the invaluable catalog cards, is a treasure store of *Times*iana.

For example, opposite are two cards that, in a nutshell, describe
the history of *The Times* logotype, or first-page name-bearing heading.

More often than not, the lead story on page 1 is under a one-
column headline in the upper right-hand corner. This is the best-
known *Times* head, one that informs the reader that all may not be
well with the world but that there is no particular need to panic this
morning. For many decades, this was the rather numbing standard
head over most stories, including the account of Abraham Lincoln's
assassination.

Back in the 1950s, copy editors, honing their craft during
between-editions lulls, doodled classic *Times* heads of major events.
One, I recall, was "Moses, On Mount, Hands Down 10-Point Plan."
However, it takes no particular astuteness to note that nowadays,
even on one-column mornings, *The Times* spreads itself in a luxury
of multi-column heads and photographs.

Banner headlines, those that streamed all the way across the page,
were rare in the 1800s, according to the archivists, but appeared more

```
                                                FACTS
Logotype   cont.                                Card 2

At the inception of The Times the logotype
was "New-York Daily Times" and there was a
separate logotype "New-York Evening Times."
for the afternoon edition. Note the hyphen,
the period, and the absence of "The."
  On Sept. 14, 1857, the logotype was changed
to "The New-York Times." (adding "The" and
dropping "Daily").
  On Dec. 1, 1896, the hyphen between "New"
and "York" was dropped.
  On Feb. 21, 1967, the type was changed and
the period was dropped.
                                                cont.
```

Capsule history fills index cards in the archives. Here, on two cards from "Facts About *The New York Times:* A Guide," the evolution of the newspaper's title is outlined, describing when a hyphen had been used in "New-York" and a period appeared at the end of its masthead. Raymond had instituted the period in imitation of *The Times* of London. It lasted until 1967, when it was dropped after a team from New York University reported that the cost of ink to print the period amounted to $45 a year.

```
Logotype                                        FACTS
                                                Card 3

In March 1971 a separate logotype - a "piano
keys" design with the letters NYT - was
adopted to distinguish between the company
and the newspapers. It was used for the
first time on April 12, 1971; and appears
on the annual report, corporate documents,
in letterheads, on business cards, etc.
Both logotypes appear on the editorial page,
respectively in the newspaper's and the
company's mastheads.
About the period: Henry J. Raymond adopted it
                                                cont'd
```

The edition announcing Lincoln's assassination. The black column rules emphasized the state of mourning.

often, starting with World War I. One of the largest-size banner heads consisted of only five words on one line, on July 22, 1969. In 96-point letters, capitals more than an inch high, photographic enlargements of 60-point letters, it proclaimed: MEN WALK ON MOON.

The subject of headlines, page 1 and other, eight columns and shorter, has always been on the minds of top executives who come across in the archives as surrogates for the readers. Punch Sulzberger, in 1973, questioned whether "we are going overboard in using the large head," a page-wide streamer to announce the resignation of Vice President Nelson Rockefeller when, as the publisher noted, it was known for days that the resignation was coming. "Don't you think we should hold down on these big heads and save them for more momentous news? . . . I feel we are going overboard in using the large head."

In the mid-1970s *The Times* began large-scale face-lifting. On April 30, 1976, the paper began regular publication of a four-section daily

# The New York Times

LATE CITY EDITION
Weather: Rain, warm today; clear tonight. Sunny, pleasant tomorrow. Temp. range: today 80-68; Sunday 71-68. Temp.-Hum. Index yesterday 69. Complete U.S. report on P. 33.

VOL. CXVIII...No. 40,721                    NEW YORK, MONDAY, JULY 21, 1969                    10 CENTS

# MEN WALK ON MOON

## ASTRONAUTS LAND ON PLAIN; COLLECT ROCKS, PLANT FLAG

### Voice From Moon: 'Eagle Has Landed'

EAGLE (the lunar module): Houston, Tranquility Base here. The Eagle has landed.

HOUSTON: Roger, Tranquility, we copy you on the ground. You've got a bunch of guys about to turn blue. We're breathing again. Thanks a lot.

TRANQUILITY BASE: Thank you.

HOUSTON: You're looking good here.

TRANQUILITY BASE: A very smooth touchdown.

HOUSTON: Eagle, you are stay for T1. [The first step in the lunar operation.] Over.

TRANQUILITY BASE: Roger. Stay for T1.

HOUSTON: Roger and we see you venting the ox.

TRANQUILITY BASE: Roger.

COLUMBIA (the command and service module): How do you read me?

HOUSTON: Columbia, he has landed Tranquility Base. Eagle is at Tranquility. I read you five by. Over.

COLUMBIA: Yes, I heard the whole thing.

HOUSTON: Well, it's a good show.

COLUMBIA: Fantastic.

TRANQUILITY BASE: I'll second that.

APOLLO CONTROL: The next major stay-no stay will be for the T2 event. That is at 21 minutes 26 seconds after initiation of power descent.

COLUMBIA: Up telemetry command reset to reacquire on high gain.

HOUSTON: Copy. Out.

APOLLO CONTROL: We have an unofficial time for that touchdown of 102 hours, 45 minutes, 42 seconds and we will update that.

HOUSTON: Eagle, you loaded R2 wrong. We want 10254.

TRANQUILITY BASE: Roger. Do you want the horizontal 55 15.2?

HOUSTON: That's affirmative.

APOLLO CONTROL: We're now less than four minutes from our next stay-no stay. It will be for one complete revolution of the command module.

One of the first things that Armstrong and Aldrin will do after getting their next stay-no stay will be to remove their helmets and gloves.

HOUSTON: Eagle, you are stay for T2. Over.

Continued on Page 4, Col. 1

### VOYAGE TO THE MOON

By ARCHIBALD MacLEISH

Presence among us,
                    wanderer in our skies,
dazzle of silver in our leaves and on our
    waters silver,

O
    silver evasion in our farthest thought—
"the visiting moon" . . . "the glimpses of the moon" . . .

and we have touched you!

                    From the first of time,
before the first of time, before the
    first men tasted time, we thought of you.
You were a wonder to us, unattainable,
    a longing past the reach of longing,
a light beyond our light, our lives—perhaps
    a meaning to us . . .

                    Now
our hands have touched you in your depth of night.

Three days and three nights we journeyed,
    steered by farthest stars, climbed outward,
crossed the invisible tide-rip where the floating dust
    falls one way or the other in the vast between,
followed that other down, encountered
    cold, faced death—unfathomable emptiness . . .

Then, the fourth day evening, we descended,
    made fast, set foot at dawn upon your beaches,
sifted between our fingers your cold sand.

We stood here in the dusk, the cold, the silence . . .

and here, as at the first of time, we lift our heads.
Over us, more beautiful than the moon, a
    moon, a wonder to us, unattainable,
a longing past the reach of longing,
a light beyond our light, our lives—perhaps
    a meaning to us . . .

                    O, a meaning!

over us on these silent beaches the bright
    earth,
                    presence among us

Neil A. Armstrong moves away from the leg of the landing craft after taking the first step on the surface of the moon

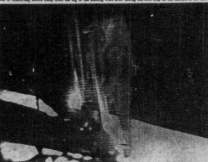

Col. Edwin E. Aldrin Jr. climbing down the ladder. The television camera was attached to a side of the lunar module.

Mr. Armstrong, right, and Colonel Aldrin raise the U.S. flag. A metal rod at right angles to the mast keeps flag unfurled.

### A Powdery Surface Is Closely Explored

By JOHN NOBLE WILFORD
Special to The New York Times

HOUSTON, Monday, July 21—Men have landed and walked on the moon.

Two Americans, astronauts of Apollo 11, steered their fragile four-legged lunar module safely and smoothly to the historic landing yesterday at 4:17:40 P.M., Eastern daylight time.

Neil A. Armstrong, the 38-year-old civilian commander, radioed to earth and the mission control room here:

"Houston, Tranquility Base here. The Eagle has landed."

The first men to reach the moon—Mr. Armstrong and his co-pilot, Col. Edwin E. Aldrin Jr. of the Air Force—brought their ship to rest on a level, rock-strewn plain near the southwestern shore of the arid Sea of Tranquility.

About six and a half hours later, Mr. Armstrong opened the landing craft's hatch, stepped slowly down the ladder and declared as he planted the first human footprint on the lunar crust:

"That's one small step for man, one giant leap for mankind."

His first step on the moon came at 10:56:20 P.M., as a television camera outside the craft transmitted his every move to an awed and excited audience of hundreds of millions of people on earth.

**Tentative Steps Test Soil**

Mr. Armstrong's initial steps were tentative tests of the lunar soil's firmness and of his ability to move about easily in his bulky white spacesuit and backpacks and under the influence of lunar gravity, which is one-sixth that of the earth.

"The surface is fine and powdery," the astronaut reported. "I can pick it up loosely with my toe. It does adhere in fine layers like powdered charcoal to the sole and sides of my boots. I only go in a small fraction of an inch, maybe an eighth of an inch. But I can see the footprints of my boots in the treads in the fine sandy particles."

After 19 minutes of Mr. Armstrong's testing, Colonel Aldrin joined him outside the craft.

The two men got busy setting up another television camera out from the lunar module, planting an American flag onto the ground, scooping up soil and rock samples, deploying scientific experiments and hopping and loping about in a demonstration of their lunar agility.

They found walking and working on the moon less taxing than had been forecast. Mr. Armstrong once reported he was "very comfortable."

And people back on earth found the black-and-white television pictures of the bug-shaped lunar module and the men tramping about it so sharp and clear as to seem unreal, more like a toy and toy-like figures than human beings on the most daring and far-reaching expedition thus far undertaken.

**Nixon Telephones Congratulations**

During one break in the astronauts' work, President Nixon congratulated them from the White House in what, he said, "certainly has to be the most historic telephone call ever made."

"Because of what you have done," the President told the astronauts, "the heavens have become a part of man's world. And as you talk to us from the Sea of Tranquility it requires us to redouble our efforts to bring peace and tranquility to earth.

"For one priceless moment in the whole history of man all the people on this earth are truly one—one in their pride in what you have done and one in our prayers that you will return safely to earth."

Mr. Armstrong replied:

"Thank you Mr. President. It's a great honor and privilege for us to be here representing not only the United States but men of peace of all nations, men with interests and a curiosity and men with a vision for the future."

Mr. Armstrong and Colonel Aldrin returned to their landing craft and closed the hatch at 1:12 A.M., 2 hours 21 minutes after opening the hatch on the moon. While the third member of the crew, Lieut. Col. Michael Collins of the Air Force, kept his solitary vigil in the command ship, the two moon explorers settled down to sleep.

Outside their vehicle the astronauts had found a bleak

Continued on Page 2, Col. 1

### Today's 4-Part Issue of The Times

This morning's issue of The New York Times is divided into four parts. The first part is devoted to news of Apollo 11 and includes Editorials and letters to the Editor (Page 18).

Photos on the landing on the moon appear on Page 17.

General news begins on the first page of the second part. The News Summary and Index is on the first page of the third part, which includes sports news, obituaries (Page 51) and transportation news and weather reports (Pages 32 and 42).

paper, which was to become a standard Monday-through-Friday feature. Friday became the first of the four-section days, with the appearance on that day of the new Weekend Section, and a business-financial rounding out the quartet, supplementing the usually first and second sections.

As usual, this was not an approach that *The Times* had rushed into. As far back as 1924, Julius Ochs Adler had suggested to Adolph Ochs that "supplemental additions to the daily Times" consist of sixteen-page tabloid rotogravure sections.

Adler disputed the theory that the Sunday paper should be "unusually large" in contrast to the daily because people had more leisure time to read on Sundays. Wrong on two counts, he argued. Most *Times* readers, he wrote, are "people who are able to indulge their love of the out-doors on this one day of rest in the week, and one finds scores of thousands of Times readers dotting the golf courses, tennis courts, bridle paths, motoring, skating, hiking, etc., frequently arising as early on Sundays as any other day and not even having the time usually devoted to reading the paper on their way to business, allotted for this purpose." In the second place, other readers "arise late, dress leisurely, go to church, then Sunday dinner, calling or receiving calls in the afternoon and so the day goes without any more time for newspaper reading than on a week day."

In October 1968, a news committee of editors met at Tarrytown House, an upstream think tank, to deliberate on the merits of a four-part *Times*. At that time, the presses were not equipped to print anything larger than a two-section ninety-six-page daily paper; anything larger demanded a four-section edition. I, unwittingly, was caught up in this and didn't learn until long after what had happened.

I was in charge of the Cultural News Department when Arthur Gelb, our boss, came in under a full head of steam from the Tarrytown conference and told me, that afternoon, to indent the main culture stories, fit them into a four-column hole in the page, and get some large pictures at the top. When? Right now, at 3:00 P.M. for tomorrow's paper. What? Unheard of! How are we going to get the composing room to do that? I protested, but Arthur insisted. He wanted to show the people at the conference how it could be done with no fuss. It was done (with some fuss) and looked not bad the next morning.

Now, the background. Gelb, shortly after having become metropolitan editor, was given control of the Second Front, the first page of the second section, which had been a page devoted to news of the city and the state, mostly with shots of people's heads attached to stories that, no matter how readable, were not allowed to jump onto another page (one story was given clearance to jump, but others were severely cut). In conferring jurisdiction, managing editor Clifton Daniel told Gelb that he could use worthy stories from Cultural News (which Gelb already supervised) and even from the National Desk.

Gelb, with picture editor John Morris, worked out a horizontal makeup, two stories at the top of the page, illustrated with lively photographs. The new formula was a success, and when Gelb attended the Tarrytown meeting, he spoke to general manager Walter E. Mattson and secured his okay to do cosmetic surgery on the cultural news pages. Gelb, as was his way, rushed back to New York, cleared the change with Max Ginsburg, then in charge of theatrical advertising, and descended upon me that Monday afternoon. In those days, as Arthur recalls, there were things that could be consummated without enduring long engagements.

The publisher was eager to move *The Times* into more attractive formats but he was cautious about having his editors rush into stultifying makeup in their effort to please. He sounded the alarm in a memo to his editors on June 11, 1974. "I have been somewhat unhappy over the last few months with a number of changes in our format that seemed to occur without any particular thought as to the ultimate package that we deliver to the reader."

Sulzberger observed that each section had its own specific guidelines. The chief of design, "the key man," he wrote, was Louis Silverstein, the visionary corporate art director charged with creating a *Times* profile that would be anything but stodgy or gray. Designer pages in the daily paper was a new concept, although the Sunday sections had long been subject to the ministrations of the Corporate Art Department. Before this new arrangement, which had Silverstein's name in an unprecedented niche on the masthead, makeup editors, each assigned to a page in the daily, drew lines according to the needs of the story schedule.

Silverstein's revolution, inspired at the top to the dismay of some of those lower down who were more comfortable with long-standing practice, had transformed the look of the Op-Ed page, opposite the very traditional editorial page, and had given smashing new looks to the new suburban Sunday sections that were launched in that great year of change, 1976. Punch did not want changes instituted without input from Silverstein and final approval from the publisher. It was Silverstein who gave each part of the paper its distinctive look, so that one glance from a reader would tell him where he was.

At about that time, John D. Pomfret, then assistant to the publisher and coordinator of planning, was deep into the concept of a four-part paper that would be more than a mere elaboration of the two-section *Times*. Each of the papers should feature a special section. Pomfret elaborated on his thinking in January 1976:

"Our major business problem is the weakness of the daily circulation," he wrote to his boss, general manager Walter E. Mattson. "Our penetration of the segment of the market we consider our target audience is thin in the city and worse in the suburbs. Some of our most loyal readers are sinking their roots deeper in the suburbs as they find their jobs as well as their homes are there."

He suggested a Friday Weekend entertainment section and made tentative suggestions for other days.

All this became reality with the Weekend Section that April, whose novel editorial departure was planned by Arthur Gelb and his weekend section editor, Marvin Siegel. It was an instant success and those of us who worked on it were especially proud of two issues early that summer. One was the Bicentennial Op Sail edition, which thousands of New Yorkers carried with them that July 4 as the best guide to the bewildering parade of tall ships and the eruption of events and spectacles that marked the day. The other, only weeks later, was the section that welcomed to the city the Democratic National Convention in Madison Square Garden, a section that proved to be a marvelously good guide to the city, not only for visitors but for natives.

"The front page of The Times is perhaps its most important single journalistic asset and trademark," Abe Rosenthal wrote in a memo in the early 1970s. "The front page presents to the readers not only the most important stories, but the judgment of the editors as to their relative importance. It is thus not only the news but the news plus The Times. It has, as you know, a considerable impact on other newspapers and on television. It also has an impact on the news itself. Therefore, the placement of news on the front page is a matter of some moment. Very often what The Times considers front page news becomes front page news because of that very fact."

At a time when newspapers were changing as a result of other technical changes in the world, one question was: What should be on the front page of *The New York Times*? Russell Baker, then based in Washington, D.C., addressed the subject in a short note, Baker-style, in August 1969:

Dear Abe:

Important Thought: The dead branch of American journalism is the Front Page. In a morning paper most of its stories have been known to TV-radio listeners for 8 to 24 hours. The Front Page exists largely for the benefit of librarians and researchers. In most papers, including ours, the news begins on Page 2. People on top of the news—except newspapermen and politicians—are losing the habit of reading Page One because they assume (rightly) that they've already heard all that. To save the best display page in the paper, we have to go back to filling it with news.

End of Important Thought.

Rosenthal answered that Baker had expressed a "damn Important Thought" that had also been nagging him for a long time. He himself had been advising his editors to treat page 1 with loving care. For instance, he urged that a story should tell the reader what it's about before "the jump," or the continuation from the first page; sometimes long-delayed anecdotal leads forced the reader to turn to the jump to learn what was being written about.

Changes had been made continually on the page 1 look for years, Rosenthal observed, and its appearance had been spruced up with broader headlines and more photographs. In 1984, he was still exhorting department heads to "better planning and more thought" in this area, not so much about changes in appearance or judgment but in terms of adding interest and imagination.

Four parts, six columns, *The Times* was obviously caught up in the spirit of '76. But one innovation, not entirely visible to the reader, also descended on the paper that year. It was the advent of the computer, the electronic newsroom, and a radical change in the technology that put news in print.

I had always resisted even the electric typewriter because I did not appreciate any device that would write faster than I could think. One afternoon, as I was pounding out a short item on my trusty typewriter, Howard Angione, czar of computing in the newsroom,

*Electronic Newsroom*

**Mr. Sulzberger**

**Eureka!  Moment in history!**

**Last night the first pieces of copy were actually transmitted from news room through the CRTs to the composing room and turned into stories for the paper.**

**A. M. R.**

**August 17, 1976**

**cc:  Mr. Mattson**

Abe Rosenthal's memo to Punch Sulzberger, announcing the first transmission of stories by computer from the newsroom directly to the composing room on August 17, 1976.

plucked me out of my seat and brought me over to one of the new machines and said, "Write your story here." I could handle the keyboard but I had difficulty in realizing that the machine automatically went to a new line and my hand kept trying to sweep the nonexistent return bar. That was my complete instruction and initiation to the device that I so feared at first and was so smitten with later that I ran out to buy one for myself.

# 27

# OVERSEAS AND OTHER SPECIAL EDITIONS

U NLIKE the Ten Commandments, the words of *The New York Times* are not set in unchangeable stone. The paper has delivered itself in numerous versions and languages other than the one it brings to New York newsstands every morning.

A century before Miami newspapers conceived of bilingual editions, *The Times* had already printed, at three separate intervals, special Spanish-language compilations to serve a Latin American market. These short-lived supplements appeared first on March 25, 1878, then, in eight pages, in April 1885 (according to the archives, there was another in between those dates but nobody seems to know when). None of them lasted long but they demonstrated that even then *The Times* viewed itself as more of an international institution than as merely just another New York daily.

The Spanish-language edition of 1885.

But even earlier, *The Times* took note of New York's precipitately expanding immigrant population. In 1871, the paper, responding to a demand from one community for more accessible information on its great scoop that exposed the criminal machinations of Boss William Marcy Tweed's Ring, *The Times* came out with an issue in German, a one-shot publication for a politically aware body of newcomers.

As befits a newspaper that is global in scope, *The Times* to this day maintains its interest in non-English-speakers. From April 1992 until February 1994, with the establishment of open doors in the regions that were successors to the Soviet Union, *The Times* published a weekly Russian-language edition available in Moscow.

In addition to these international forays, *The Times* has constantly immersed itself in publishing ventures related to its own big daily paper. Horace Greeley, over at the *Tribune,* might have been busy echoing the cry to young men to go West, but in 1852 *The Times for California* was following the young men to that other coast. The paper was printed by *The Times* in New York and sent West by mailboat. *The Times*'s fascination with California has been a constantly nagging one.

In October 1962, the first issue of a new Western Edition, printed in Los Angeles with teletypeset copy sent from New York, appeared on the Pacific Rim. It was not a box-office success and folded in January 1964. Ex–New Yorkers in Los Angeles felt that it was a limp replica of the swollen paper they missed from back home, an anemic wraith lacking those ads that added bulk and filled out the picture of what was going on in New York. Ironically, the West Coast edition kept *The Times*'s record for continuity intact, in a way, when the hefty East Coast paper was shut down by a strike in 1962–1963. The Western Edition concept was expanded into one that envisioned a National Edition printed at many sites around the country. The first of these was printed in Chicago, with satellite-borne New York copy, on August 18, 1980.

This was not the first century in which *The Times* tinkered with the urge to speak to Europe through its own pages. The archives refer to a special edition, *The Times for Europe,* sold there in 1856 and 1857. For a paper with the largest staff of foreign correspondents in the world, the idea of getting *The New York Times* to readers abroad seemed obvious, particularly in the days after World War II when Americans, beneficiaries of a strong dollar, were ferried at first by cheap ocean passage and later by airliner, in numbers that often ap-

From April 1992 until February 1994 the *Times* published a Moscow edition. The slogan "All the news that's fit to print" retains its familiar position, even in Russian.

*The Times for California,* published in 1852.

peared to be a reverse summertime migration. More than that, it would be attractive, it was felt, to business and political figures on the Continent who already respected *The Times*'s mystique.

During World War II, publisher AHS proposed *The New York Times Overseas Weekly* for Americans serving abroad. The first issue, made from plastic plates prepared on 43rd Street, were flown to Iran for printing on August 22, 1943. The edition lasted until 1949 and, at its peak, was printed in a score of overseas locations.

In December 1948, *The Times* finally reached Europe on a regular basis with an International Air Edition, printed in New York and flown to Paris for distribution. Six months later, the process was shortened by flying the mats—the matrices that were rolled off when pressed by the metal type in which the page was set—to Paris to be printed. The paper moved to Amsterdam in 1952 and soon began calling itself the International Edition, with printing also being done in Lima, Peru, for

The first issue of *The New York Times Overseas Weekly* for Americans serving abroad made from plates from New York and flown to Teheran for printing, from 1943 to 1949.

South American distribution (this latter lasted only from 1955 to 1957). In 1960, transatlantic teletypesetting eliminated the air transport and *The Times* began coming out in Europe on the same day as it did in New York. Four years later, *The Times* was a true Paris clone of the New York

edition, with its own copy desk and composition in Paris, with teletype-
setters harnessed only for stock-market tables.

For all that, *The Times* met tough competition with the long-
entrenched, if still unprofitable, *Paris Herald Tribune,* and in 1967
Punch Sulzberger announced that the paper would join with the *New
York Herald Tribune* (which had stopped publication in New York a
year earlier, but whose owner, Whitney Communications, wanted to
keep its overseas paper alive) and the *Washington Post* in Paris to publish the *International Herald Tribune* in Paris. That paper would reach
seventy-two countries with the "largest circulation of any American
newspaper ever printed abroad." Today, it is published by *The Times*
and the *Washington Post,* with other editions in Asia.

In 1967, *The Times* published a paper that never was. In May, a hy-
brid newspaper, the *World Journal Tribune,* which incorporated the remains of three other papers, died, and New York was left with only
one afternoon daily, the *New York Post.* The possibility that there was
an afternoon vacuum waiting to be filled inspired ideas of competition at the two morning dailies, *The New York Times* and the *New York
News.* With the tentative caution of an elephant stepping onto a frail
bridge, *The Times* launched the project headed by A. M. Rosenthal,
then assistant managing editor. Walter E. Mattson, then production
manager, notified other executives that a feasibility study would be
made and said, "You should not feel inhibited by the conventional
wisdom at The Times."

Exhaustive analyses were submitted while, on the editorial side,
Rosenthal began to invent an entirely new paper, one that would adhere to *Times* journalistic verities but would be quite different from
its sober sire. In June, managing editor Clifton Daniel outlined to
Rosenthal the features that the publisher wanted in the new journal.
It is an interesting memo because it pointed in a direction that *The
Times* itself would be following within a very short time, combining its
traditional thrust with a new one matched to the changing desires
of the reading public:

> Fixed paging—32–48 pages. A front page in which news is
> played in relative terms according to the news judgment of
> the editors. A paper in which the desk, and not the writers
> in the field will control the content. Complete stock tables.
> A women's page centered on news of fashion, which is one

# NEW YORK TODAY

FINAL

FRIDAY, JULY 7, 1967

Vol. 1, No. 1 © The New York Times Company 00¢

## Letter From Italy

### Florence Calls It A Miracle

By PETER CARVELL

KNIGHTED: Queen Elizabeth II dubs Sir Francis Chichester a knight at the Royal Naval College today.

## McNamara Gets Plea for Troops

SAIGON, South Vietnam—Defense Secretary Robert S. McNamara, arriving in Vietnam today for his ninth visit, heard a request for more United States troops from his military commander, Gen. William C. Westmoreland.

### Costs of War As Visit Begins

**11,534 Dead**

**600 Planes Lost**

**Over $25-Billion in '67**

**Forces at 466,000**

*(From AP, UPI and Staff.)*

### VIEWPOINT

## The Lessons of Vietnam

*George Ball Deplores 'Creeping Involvement'*

By GEORGE W. BALL
Former Under Secretary of State
for Kennedy and Johnson

## Bullet Kills Girl Driver

A bullet killed a 17-year-old girl as she drove along the Belt Parkway in Brooklyn in rush-hour traffic this morning.

Nancy McEwan of Garden City, L. I., was alone in her car driving to a summer secretarial job, when the bullet struck her in the head at about 8:30 A.M.

STRIKE INCIDENT: A caseworker, entering the Melrose Welfare Center in the Bronx this morning, spits at pickets. Mayor Lindsay today thanked caseworkers who have stayed on the job (Story on Page 4).

### Of Our Time

## Is the Hippy an Updated Flapper?

*The Psychiatrist Delve, and Thornton Wilder Compares*

By ALEXANDER PATERSON | By T. H. GARDINER

WEATHER: Sunny, mild today; fair tonight; partly cloudy tomorrow. Temp. range: today 77-58, Sat. 76-69. Temp.-Hum. Index 72, Sat. 70.

## Rossetti Named Tammany Chief

By SCOTT WILLIAMS

Old-line Manhattan Democratic leaders kept their firm grip on the New York County organization today when they easily elected Assemblyman Frank L. Rossetti as county leader.

Frank G. Rossetti

In 1967, the *Times,* scouting possibilities for an afternoon paper following the demise of one of the two surviving afternoon dailies, experimented with this concept. It never hit the stands.

of the biggest industries in New York. . . . At least a page of service information on entertainment and the arts. A theater critic, and perhaps critics in other areas, but the critics to devote most of their time to evaluating performances for the service page. (We should feel no obligation to review every movie, art show and music performance in town.) TV previews on the service page.

In brief, the Publisher describes his venture as a service newspaper also carrying the latest news. He seems to oppose a large number of staff correspondents, but offers no objection to the fire-brigade sort of coverage.

By mid-July, a pilot issue of *New York Today* had been run off, amid great secrecy, protected by a security force and with each of the 200 copies registered for delivery to select executives. Turner Catledge, executive editor of *The Times,* reviewed it for Punch Sulzberger. He commended the editors for their boldness and organizational skill.

Catledge generally admired the makeup and the innovative six-column page as well as the quality of its features. On the other hand, he wrote in his critique, "As attractive as the paper turned out to be it is not as attractive and distinctive as I think a product of The New York Times should be; and as for content it is not as newsy as I would expect of a Times product." Catledge evinced all of the caution that an executive wedded to *The Times*'s way of doing things might suffer from when urged to veer 180 degrees from the course.

On September 1, a second pilot issue, this time called *The New York Forum,* was run off. It featured many variations of the first and also innovations that made it, as Rosenthal explained in an interview with *Editor and Publisher,* a trade magazine, "a package that in total concept is different from any other U.S. newspaper, but it's still a newspaper not a magazine."

*The Times* had invested money, work, and talent in this venture, but on October 1, Punch Sulzberger told the staff in a memo:

For almost five months, one question has dominated all of us here at The Times. Would the answer be "yes" or would the answer be "no"?

This memorandum is to let you know that the decision we have finally reached is "no." The New York Times will not publish an evening newspaper.

The publisher reviewed the project and detailed the care that went into its study, the need to avoid snap judgments and how it all added up to a conclusion that "an evening edition did not come out as an acceptable, longtime bet."

"There was another persuasive aspect to the problem," he wrote. "We were determined from the start that we would take no step that threatened to diminish the quality or slow the progress of The New York Times itself. . . . If we wanted a newspaper of New York Times quality we would have to use a lot of The New York Times people to achieve the result. I can tell you that this added a great deal to the unattractiveness of the whole proposal. We are not going to take on any activity that detracts in any way from our main job on The Times."

Finally, he observed that the paper had learned from its experimentation and that "valuable ideas were born which will find a home in The Times itself." This was prophetic. Within a decade Abe Rosenthal would be in charge of the news at *The Times* and would be presiding over the changes that would revolutionize the look and the tone of *The New York Times* in a new era.

Eventually, a large-type edition for the visually impaired, a *Times* issued in fax editions, and a *Times* on-line in computers, all testify to a mammoth outreach governed by technical dexterity.

# FORECASTS
# AND PHOTOS

WINTER, Christmas Night 1947. A quiet night, with many people off and the newsroom in an unwonted languor that bespeaks a slow news night, so quiet that you could hear a snowflake fall. Here am I, at *The Times* less than two years, still a copyboy but filling in as a city desk clerk, at the nerve center of the newsroom. And I have been on page 1 every day this week, although I have never yet written a story for the paper. And although the world, except for the family and friends I have been bragging to, is unaware of it, I have even been appearing above the lead story on the upper right-hand side, and I know I have been read by more people than get to many stories on inside pages. My spot is the weather ear, the little box that contains the forecast and various temperatures, just to the right of the logo that announces *The New York Times*. The weather report has just arrived by messenger from the Weather Bureau downtown, near Battery Park, and I am working out the wording for the next day's forecast, trying to translate it accurately into the fewer words that the weather box can hold—the weather report on an inside page is infinitely more detailed. The forecast on this night is for snow the next day and the problem for me is to figure out whether the box will say "snow ending during the afternoon" or "snow ending in the afternoon," a delicate choice with subtle overtones that, at this great remove, elude me.

I nervously weighed the pros and cons and showed the result to the senior city desk clerk, who okayed it. The weather ear proved to be a memorable one because it was way off the mark. It snowed all the next day, December 26, and into the night, and piled up a paralyzing 25.8 inches on the city. People were skiing on Madison Avenue. That night when I walked home to the West Side with several copies of the next day's *Times* for my family and neighbors, people offered me, in vain, a dollar for one copy. Well, it was a memorable page 1 appearance for me and one that did not even warrant a correction, although it had misstated the future.

Of all the topics addressed in *The Times,* the weather is not only one of the most talked about but one that *The Times* is most constantly exhorted to do something about. Readers are agitated about social and political issues but these come and go. But concern about the weather coverage seems perennial and it cuts across lines that divide strong opinions into eloquent camps on the Op-Ed page. Among those readers most perturbed about the look of the weather in *The Times* are the publishers. The memos in the archives from Arthur Hays Sulzberger and his son, Arthur Ochs Sulzberger, tell a story of continuing restlessness about the weather within their newspaper and their support for ever more news about it.

In 1934, AHS approved the introduction of a weather map. He thought that most interest in weather came during the summer months and that the map should run from early spring to late fall. "If we start this it must be well done. I should think that a reporter might be found with the ability to draw a neat map. . . . In addition to being a student of the weather and knowing what it means, the reporter should have the ability to write the picturesque weather stories which both summer and winter demand." On August 4, 1934, a three-column weather map, accompanied by a story, made its debut. AHS took a keen personal interest.

Weather got to everyone, high and low, and the influentials wrote their comments directly to the publisher, who passed them along. A personal friend, a lawyer named Henry S. Hendricks, asked AHS in late December 1941 whether the paper could restore the times of sunset and sundown that had been removed with other shipping and weather information after Pearl Harbor. The times were restored, because they were of no help to the enemy, and a grateful Hendricks wrote a warmly appreciative letter and explained his interest: "My primary use of this information is the observance of the Sabbath which, as you no doubt know, in accordance with the custom of our ancestors, runs in reference to sundown."

AHS passed the word to managing editor Edwin L. James: "Just to show that you never can tell! This is what the rising and setting of the sun means to a man who happens to be a fairly orthodox Jew."

This business of weather involved highest levels who were also deciding how World War II and the subsequent cold war, as well as various other earthly upheavals, should be covered. They took weather

August 7, 1934

Mr. McCaw:

Would you be good enough to make the point that Mr. Kieran or whoever wrote today's weather story that the purpose of running the chart is to let the people understand how weather is judged or how a weather forecast is made. Therefore, our story which accompanies the chart should be in that vein. For example, we say "the high pressure area and its surrounding zones of established barometric pressure indicated fair and warmer weather today, followed tomorrow by unsettled weather and probable showers". I think that what we should have said would have been something like this:

The high pressure area which has been giving New York the exceptionally fine weather which it has had for the last three days is now moving out to sea with the result that the winds rotating about the high are now drawn from the South. The indication is, therefore, for warmer weather. The clear skies are apt to give way to clouds as the low now hanging over northern Ontario moves toward this vicinity.

Do I make the point clear? We should interpret the map, not merely give a weather statement.

A. H. S.

A memo from Arthur Hays Sulzberger to managing editor Raymond H. McCaw in August 1934, urging greater clarity in weather stories that should better match the weather charts, along with an idea of how the publisher would have done it.

seriously. One of the longer correspondences began in 1947 when the Birmingham, Alabama, Chamber of Commerce lamented the omission of their city from the weather map and claimed that it hurt them in their quest for prestige that would lure more business their way. The correspondence went to AHS, who passed it along to

Turner Catledge, who raised objections. It could be put on the map should the publisher wish, but he and James had agreed that the American South (their own native heath) was already well represented and cited other states that were not on the chart because the Weather Bureau map represented areas rather than particular spots.

Birmingham kept up the battle, apparently, because four years later, in 1951, responding to a request, the Weather Bureau included Birmingham on the weather map. Catledge had resisted during that time, in part because "the Birmingham people later attempted to bring into consideration the fact that they had some advertising business to place and rather implied that they expected a quid pro quo from The New York Times by including that city in the map. I told the Advertising Department I did not think we should consider it at the time, especially under the pressure implied."

However, he surrendered with characteristic grace, writing tersely to AHS: "Hurrah for Birmingham!"

AHS kept an eye on the weather. In 1959, he found that the map misplaced San Juan, Puerto Rico, and wondered why the reports from Cuba and Haiti were not mapped. He fussed about the bureau's newly introduced Discomfort Index, later called the Temperature-Humidity Index, and wondered whether to run it in the weather ear and broadcast it on WQXR, *The Times* radio station, whose news was prepared by *Times* staffers in the newsroom: "I still question its worthwhileness. After all, it merely tells you whether you had any reason to be uncomfortable the day before. It doesn't predict." (A year later, he relented, saying he had disliked the term "discomfort" and now appreciated its objectivity.)

By 1963, Punch Sulzberger, as publisher, was making weather waves. He notified Catledge that "last weekend when I was out at the Hamptons I practically froze to death because I was misled by our weatherman who as you will remember predicted hot and humid weather." He suggested that there might be a story in the forecasts put out by private forecasters, which, to him, seemed more accurate.

In 1966, another VIP weighed in on the weather. Alfred A. Knopf, the book publisher, wrote to Punch that *The Times,* among other papers, had been mistaken over the years "in ignoring the great interest that a daily story about the weather would have for any number of readers." Knopf said that such a story would enlighten the public on the reasons why the forecasts so often proved wrong. In supplying information for a reply, Clifton Daniel told Turner Catledge, "I know the Publisher's feeling about weather forecasting, but I don't think we should commit ourselves to a daily story on the weather as proposed by Alfred Knopf. . . . We should report extremes of weather, but perfectly normal weather is not news, and variations from the temperatures predicted by the weather forecasters are not either."

"I am still not particularly satisfied with the content of the page," Punch told Abe Rosenthal in February 1970, speaking of the transportation page, where the weather news then appeared. "I instigated a revision of the weather map and, as you know, this has been undertaken by our Corporate Art Department. . . . It seems to me that there is only one final decision to be made and that is are we listing the correct cities on the map (for instance, Chattanooga was listed at my father's request years ago because he wanted to know if his relatives and friends were having good weather)."

Rosenthal, who boldly had told the publisher that he and others felt the weather map chewed up space with material easily found in the tables, resolutely defended the weather report when a journalistic acquaintance wanted to be told about tides in the Hamptons and Connecticut and wouldn't mind sacrificing other nitty-gritty on the page, such as the time Venus would rise and how the weather was in Saigon.

"I regret deeply that Venus has no importance in your life," he replied, with typical humor. "Let me assure you that if we were to leave out the rise of Venus for just one day, our weather and planet buffs would rise themselves in outrage." And, anyhow, he added, the tide table did appear every day—in the Sports Section.

I enjoyed having a photographer accompany me on assignment. The *Times*'s photographers were usually a chatty, vocal, and professional bunch who often, in covering a general street assignment, lent authority to the reporter by virtue of their official-looking cameras, much more convincing than a mere pencil and notebook. Photographers have to be nimble and alert because rarely can they recapture a certain instant of time and they can never do it later by telephone. As a writer, I always said that a thousand words were worth one picture, but the truth is that a good photograph boosted the visibility of a story.

*The Times* was not generally acclaimed as a "picture paper," but by all accounts it was a pioneer in photography. Its first photographs appeared in its *Illustrated Sunday Magazine,* launched in September

1896, soon after the Ochs takeover. On July 4, a year later, it scooped the New York press with the publication of sixteen photographs made in June at the procession celebrating Queen Victoria's sixtieth year on the throne; the operation, which used finer-quality paper than ordinary newsprint, cost $5,000, an 1897 fortune, but well worth it. In 1914, *The Times* initiated its rotogravure section, the first American newspaper to do so on a regular basis. The rotogravure lasted until 1942.

Ochs, it was said, had formulated the principle that no picture should be published in *The Times* that a reader at the breakfast table might find unappetizing. AHS, although encouraging the use of more photography in the news columns, maintained a sense of delicacy. In August 1948, a Russian leaped from a third-floor window of the Soviet consulate on the Upper East Side, where she had been held captive. She survived and was immured once again by the consulate staff. *The Times,* it was said, had received a photo of the plunge in time for the next day's paper, but felt that it was too grim to be viewed at the breakfast table.

In 1954, the photograph of the newlywed Joe DiMaggio and Marilyn Monroe kissing openmouthed was published and cost the picture editor his job. (He became the field and stream columnist.) AHS remained sensitive to the look of photos on grounds other than morals and ugliness. He demanded journalistic integrity at the same time that he forbade any "free advertising" by displaying brand names that showed up in pictures. For instance, in July 1959, he questioned why the brand names SOS and Dash were blacked out on boxes in the American kitchen exhibit in a photograph depicting a Moscow visit by then–Vice President Nixon with Nikita Khrushchev, the Soviet premier. The names had remained in the photo of the same event that was printed in the Week in Review a day later.

"Did we do this deliberately and if so why?" he asked the third floor.

"Yes, we did this deliberately," Catledge answered. He explained that the Art Department insisted that there was a rule that required the elimination of brand names and other commercial identification from pictures. He said that the Art Department had been disabused of this notion and that it should never again cut anything unless so marked by the newsroom picture desk.

The publisher may have changed at *The Times* but the publisher's eye remained as wide open and as inquisitive about photography as

ever. Punch Sulzberger manifested an even greater knowledge of—
and impatience with—it than his father or grandfather had. He was
zealous in his detestation of photographs that were not clear and that
were distorted images of what the camera had in front of it.

"The photographs in today's paper are at an all-time low, both
in numbers of pictures and subject matter," he communicated to his
managing editor in 1970, offering a critique of those he liked and
those he didn't. He also allotted more money to get more equipment
and asked "Can't we get some action out on page 1?"

His caustic criticism, interspersed with praise for photos he admired, continued with memos such as one in 1971: "If an amateur
had been cropping Mr. Nixon's face on page 1, he succeeded," he
noted and continued: "I think we have used that same photograph of
the anti-war demonstrators about 50 million times. Why didn't we
just single one out and bring up his head, since there was no action
in the picture anyway. We ran, or could have run, a good picture of
the President on page 1. Why repeat it on page 16? Take a look at the
News and see if you don't think their front page picture of [New York
mayor John] Lindsay at the Chamber of Commerce isn't better than
ours, or, indeed, the one on the split page which shows all of the old
pictures that dominate that room."

# The Last Word

THIS IS THE END of this book, in midstory. It has not been a complete, play-by-play account, any more than other accounts have been. But all who have written about *The New York Times* have hewed off different slices of the subject because to tell the full story would be much too much of a mouthful, consisting of testimonies from everyone who ever worked there.

The vaunted journalistic objectivity of the paper is, in its history, severely dented by the countless personal perceptions of those who have participated in putting *The Times* together. *The Times* is this, *The Times* is that—and each version is as right or as wrong as the next. My own account has been colored by my own experiences and any similarity between it and any other is highly coincidental and unlikely.

What conclusions can be drawn from this miscellany? One is that publishers do influence what goes into their paper. Another is that while they may come on caustically and nitpicking, they are cautious in approaching the great changes that will carry *The Times* through any stage in that constant cliff-hanger called the newspaper business. Ochs left AHS advice, and AHS passed along wisdom to Dryfoos and Punch.

We do not yet know what, if any, strictures were laid down by Punch for young Arthur Ochs Sulzberger, Jr.—these are tomorrow's archives, not yet laid to rest. Each generation accepted the generalities of its elders but when it came down to specifics, each went its own way. Dramatic changes in reading habits and technology are at hand, but on the eve of the twenty-first century, the house of Ochs still tops the cast list on the masthead of the paper and there is every reason to believe that the stamp of the family will remain *The Times*'s hallmark for years to come.

In a note direct from the publisher to you, the reader (bypassing the archives), Arthur Ochs (Punch) Sulzberger expresses, if not his vision, at least his hope for the best of *Times* to come. Punch retains the offices that he occupied as publisher from 1963 to 1991* on the hallowed fourteenth floor. On the walls there are portraits of his grandfather Adolph and pictures of the various homes inhabited by *The Times* on its long trek uptown.

At the wall behind him are two machines, one a computer, the other a typewriter. In the briefest possible sense, they sum up the eras Punch has brought together. He was born into *The Times,* so to speak, but he didn't work for it until 1954, after World War II and Korean War duty in the Marine Corps and a stint as a reporter at the *Milwaukee Journal.*

"I was a sort of third man in a one-man bureau in Rome," he recalled with the infectious laugh of a man who views the world in modest perspective. "They brought me back and put me into the business side. The thing that struck me was that we had all of our eggs in one basket. The only diversification we had in the company was our ownership of [radio station] WQXR—if it made a nickel that was good— and our half-ownership in Spruce Falls [Power and Paper Company, at Kapuskasing, Ontario, an enterprise engaged in making newsprint]. Those were our sole outside sources of revenue, and so if and when we had industrial relations problems, we had no staying power."

When he became publisher, upon the death of Orvil Dryfoos at the end of a four-month strike in 1962–1963, the realization of vulnerability went with him. He acquired a series of magazines, including *Family Circle,* as well as three small newspapers and *The Times*'s first television station.

"And that started us off on the diversification route, and [on April 27, 1967] the company went public, so we had a stocked trade.

"That was the first thing I wanted to do. The second thing I wanted to do was to bring the Sunday and the News Departments together. Turner Catledge became executive editor. But the guy who really pulled it [the big changes in the content and approach] all together at *The New York Times* was Abe [Rosenthal]."

Punch recalled how, as publisher, he established the principle of working on a budget, particularly in a newsroom where such a planned existence had never been considered.

"If the News Department was spending too much money, my father would go down and say to Mr. James: 'Stop spending so much

---

* Mr. Sulzberger became board chairman of the company in 1973, but he still held the title of publisher.

money.' Jimmy [Edwin L.'s nickname] James never saw the numbers."

Punch considered the changes in the company whose very business is reporting on change:

"The generational gap is most evident to me when they came and brought me this thing behind me." He gestured at the sleek computer and then pointed affectionately at the typewriter. "*That's* what I like. When I want to write something important, that's what I use, not this. But there's no doubt in my mind that the computer is here to stay. And that *The New York Times* will have to adapt to the age of the computer. Just how that's all going to happen I don't know.

"I am utterly convinced that the newspaper as we know it, written on a piece of paper and delivered to your door, is going to be around for a long, long time because there's nothing more useful and nothing more practical than producing it this way. At the same time we're going to be taking great advantage of the computer. Where I see *The Times* and the computer tied together, for instance, is when the president makes a speech. We will cover the speech in our own way. And then we will put on the bottom of the story—it's being done with other papers—'For the full text of the president's speech, call up so-and-so on your computer.' You can tie into all sorts of things the president is speaking about.

"But the tradition of *The New York Times* is still going to be there. We're here to stay."

Punch spoke of the various explorations being made by *The Times* along the electronic superhighway and then returned to the important thread that runs through the history of the paper.

"There's no shortage of news in the world today. What *The New York Times* sells is not news. What we sell is judgment. We look at the news for you, the nonprofessional, and use our judgment, and every morning we tell you what we think is the most important story. Now if you don't want our judgment, you can do it yourself, but that's a full-time task. I'd rather go fishing and let somebody else do that.

"But, in the end, you're back to basics. I don't care what it is you run, a magazine, a television station. If you have high quality, you do well. Quality pays. That's been proven over and over again at *The New York Times*."

# Index

## ABOUT THE AUTHOR

RICHARD F. SHEPARD joined *The New York Times* as a copy-boy in 1946, served as reporter, editor, columnist of About New York and the Going Out Guide, and retired in 1991. He was born in the Bronx in 1922, attended Townsend Harris High School and City College, and lives in Queens. He is the author of three books, *Going Out in New York, Live and Be Well: A Celebration of Yiddish Culture in America,* and *Broadway: From the Battery to the Bronx.*